The Medieval Mind

Old Western Culture Reader

Volume 11

THE MEDIEVAL MIND

OLD WESTERN CULTURE READER

VOLUME 11

Companion to *Christendom: The Medieval Mind*,
a great books curriculum by Roman Roads Press

ROMAN ROADS PRESS
MOSCOW, IDAHO

The Medieval Mind: Old Western Culture Reader, Volume 11

Published by Roman Roads Press
Moscow, Idaho
romanroadspress.com

Series Editor: Daniel Foucachon
Cover Design: Valerie Anne Bost, Daniel Foucachon, and Rachel Rosales
Interior Layout: Carissa Hale

Printed in the United States of America

The Medieval Mind: Old Western Culture Reader, Volume 11
Roman Roads Media, LLC
ISBN: 978-1-944482-19-0 (paperback)

Version 1.2.0 November 2021

This is a companion reader for the Old Western Culture curriculum by Roman Roads Press. To find out more about this course, visit www.romanroadspress.com.

OLD WESTERN CULTURE

Great Books Reader Series

THE GREEKS

VOLUME 1	*The Epics*
VOLUME 2	*Drama & Lyric*
VOLUME 3	*The Histories*
VOLUME 4	*The Philosophies*

THE ROMANS

VOLUME 5	*The Aeneid*
VOLUME 6	*The Historians*
VOLUME 7	*Early Christianity*
VOLUME 8	*Nicene Christianity*

CHRISTENDOM

VOLUME 9	*Early Medievals*
VOLUME 10	*Defense of the Faith*
VOLUME 11	*The Medieval Mind*
VOLUME 12	*The Reformation*

EARLY MODERNS

VOLUME 13	*Rise of England*
VOLUME 14	*Politics and Poetry*
VOLUME 15	*The Enlightenment*
VOLUME 16	*The Novels*

Contents

Compendium

Thomas Aquinas

Translated by Cyril Vollert S.J.

Chapter 1:
Scope of the Present Work

To restore man, who had been laid low by sin, to the heights of divine glory, the Word of the eternal Father, though containing all things within His immensity, willed to become small. This He did, not by putting aside His greatness, but by taking to Himself our littleness. No one can say that he is unable to grasp the teaching of heavenly wisdom; what the Word taught at great length, although clearly, throughout the various volumes of Sacred Scripture for those who have leisure to study, He has reduced to brief compass for the sake of those whose time is taken up with the cares of daily life. Man's salvation consists in knowing the truth, so that the human mind may not be confused by divers errors; in making for the right goal, so that man may not fall away from true happiness by pursuing wrong ends; and in carrying out the law of justice, so that he may not besmirch himself with a multitude of vices.

Knowledge of the truth necessary for man's salvation is comprised within a few brief articles of faith. The Apostle says in Romans 9:2-8: "A short word shall the Lord make upon the earth"; and later he adds: "This is the word of faith, which we preach" (Rom. 15:8). In a short prayer Christ clearly marked out man's right course; and in teaching us to say this prayer, He showed us the goal of our striving and our hope. In a single precept of charity He summed up that human justice which consists in observing the law: "Love therefore is the fulfilling of the law" (Rom. 13:15). Hence the Apostle, in 1 Corinthians 13:13, taught that the whole perfection of this present life consists in faith, hope, and charity, as in certain brief headings outlining our salvation: "Now there remain faith, hope, and charity." These are the three virtues, as St. Augustine says, by which God is worshiped. [*De doctrina christiana*, I, 35 (*PL*, XXXIV]

Wherefore, my dearest son Reginald, receive from my hands this compendious treatise on Christian teaching to keep continually before your eyes. My whole endeavor in the present work is taken up with these three virtues. I shall treat first of faith, then of hope, and lastly of charity. This is the Apostle's arrangement which, for that matter, right reason imposes. Love cannot be rightly ordered unless the proper goal of our hope is established; nor can there be any hope if knowledge of the truth is lacking. Therefore the first thing necessary is faith, by which you may come to a knowledge of the truth. Secondly, hope is necessary, that your intention may be fixed on the right end. Thirdly, love is necessary, that your affections may be perfectly put in order.

Chapter 2: Arrangement of Our Topics Concerning Faith

Faith is a certain foretaste of that knowledge which is to make us happy in the life to come. The Apostle says, in Hebrews 11:1, that faith is "the substance of things to be hoped for," as though implying that faith is already, in some preliminary way, inaugurating in us the things that are to be hoped for, that is, future beatitude. Our Lord has taught us that this beatific knowledge has to do with two truths, namely, the divinity of the Blessed Trinity and the humanity of Christ. That is why, addressing the Father, He says: "This is eternal life: that they may know You, the only true God, and Jesus Christ, whom You sent" (John 17:3). All the knowledge imparted by faith turns about these two points, the divinity of the Trinity and the humanity of Christ. This should cause us no surprise: the humanity of Christ is the way by which we come to the divinity. Therefore, while we are still wayfarers, we ought to know the road leading to our goal. In the heavenly fatherland adequate thanks would not be rendered to God if men had no knowledge of the way by which they are saved. This is the meaning of our Lord's words to His disciples: "And where I go you know, and the way you know" (John 14:4).

Three truths must be known about the divinity: first the unity of the divine essence, secondly the Trinity of persons, and thirdly the effects wrought by the divinity.

Chapter 3: The Existence of God

Regarding the unity of the divine essence, we must first believe that God exists. This is a truth clearly known by reason. We observe that all things that move are moved by other things, the lower by the higher. The elements are moved by heavenly bodies; and among the elements themselves, the stronger moves the weaker; and even among the heavenly bodies, the lower are set in motion by the higher. This process cannot be traced back into infinity. For everything that is moved by another is a sort of instrument of the first mover. Therefore, if a first mover is lacking, all things that move will be instruments. But if the series of movers and things moved is infinite, there can be no first mover. In such a case, these infinitely many movers and things moved will all be instruments. But even the unlearned perceive how ridiculous it is to suppose that instruments are moved, unless they are set in motion by some principal agent. This would be like fancying that, when a chest or a bed is being built, the saw or the hatchet performs its functions without the carpenter. Accordingly there must be a first mover that is above all the rest; and this being we call God.

Chapter 4: The Immobility of God

We clearly infer from this that God, who moves all things, must Himself be immovable. If He, being the first mover, were Himself moved, He would have to be moved either by Himself or by another. He cannot be moved by another, for then there would have to be some mover prior to Him, which is against the very idea of a first mover. If He is moved by Himself, this can be conceived in two ways: either that He is mover and moved according to the same respect, or that He is a mover according to one aspect of Him and is moved according to another aspect. The first of these alternatives is ruled out. For everything that is moved is, to that extent, in potency, and whatever moves is in act. Therefore if God is both mover and moved according to the same respect, He has to be in potency and in act according to the same respect, which is impossible. The second alternative is likewise out of the question. If one part were moving and another were moved, there would be no first mover Himself as such, but only by reason of that part of Him which moves. But what is *per se* is prior to that which is not *per se*. Hence there cannot be a first mover at all, if this perfection is attributed to a being by reason of a part of that being. Accordingly the first mover must be altogether immovable.

Among things that are moved and that also move, the following may also be considered. All motion is observed to proceed from something immobile, that is, from something that is not moved according to the particular species of motion in question. Thus we see that alterations and generations and corruptions occurring in lower bodies are reduced, as to their first mover, to a heavenly body that is not moved according to this species of motion, since it is incapable of being generated, and is incorruptible and unalterable. Therefore the first principle of all motion must be absolutely immobile.

Chapter 5: The Eternity of God

The further conclusion is evident that God is eternal. For everything that begins to be or that ceases to be, is affected in this way through motion or change. But we have just shown that God is absolutely immobile. Consequently He is eternal.

Chapter 6: Necessity of God's Existence

The same line of reasoning clearly shows that God necessarily exists. For everything that has the possibility of being and of not being, is mutable. But God is absolutely immutable, as has been demonstrated. Therefore it is impossible for God to be and not to be. But anything that exists in such a way that it is impossible for it not to exist, is necessarily Being itself, *ipsum esse*. Necessary existence, and impossibility of nonexistence, mean one and the same thing. Therefore God must necessarily exist.

Moreover, everything that has a possibility of being and of not being, needs something else to make it be, for, as far as it itself is concerned, it is indifferent with regard to either alternative. But that which causes another thing to be, is prior to that thing. Hence something exists prior to that which has the possibility of being and of not being. However, nothing is prior to God. Therefore it is impossible for Him to be and not to be; of necessity, He must be. And since there are some necessary things that have a cause of their necessity, a cause that must be prior to them, God, who is the first of all, has no cause of His own necessity. Therefore it is necessary for God to be through Himself.

Chapter 7: The Everlasting Existence of God

From all this it is evident that God exists always. For whatever necessarily exists, always exists; it is impossible for a thing that has no possibility of not being, not to be. Hence such a thing is never without existence. But it is necessary for God to be, as has been shown. Therefore God exists always.

Again, nothing begins to be or ceases to be except through motion or change. But God is absolutely immutable, as has been proved. Therefore it is impossible for Him ever to have begun to be or to cease to be.

Likewise, if anything that has not always existed begins to be, it needs some cause for its existence. Nothing brings itself forth from potency to act or from non-being to being. But God can have no cause of His being, since He is the first Being; a cause is prior to what is caused. Of necessity, therefore, God must always have existed.

Furthermore, whatever pertains to anyone in some other way than by reason of an external cause, pertains to him of himself. But existence does not come to God from any external cause, since such a cause would have to be prior to Him. Therefore God has existence of Himself, *per se ipsum.* But what exists *per se* exists always and necessarily. Therefore God exists always.

Chapter 8:
Absence of Succession in God

Clearly, therefore, no succession occurs in God. His entire existence is simultaneous. Succession is not found except in things that are in some way subject to motion; for prior and posterior in motion cause the succession of time. God, however, is in no sense subject to motion, as has been shown. Accordingly there is no succession in God. His existence is simultaneously whole.

Again, if a being's existence is not simultaneously whole, something can be lost to it and something can accrue to it. That which passes is lost, and what is expected in the future can be acquired. But nothing is lost to God or accrues to Him, since He is immutable. Therefore His existence is simultaneously whole.

From these two observations the proper meaning of eternity emerges. That is properly eternal which always exists, in such a way that its existence is simultaneously whole. This agrees with the definition proposed by Boethius: "Eternity is the simultaneously whole and perfect possession of endless life."

Chapter 9:
Simplicty of God

A similar course of reasoning clearly shows that the first mover must be simple. For any composite being must contain two factors that are related to each other as potency to act. But in the first mover, which is altogether immobile, all combination of potency and act is impossible, because whatever is in potency is, by that very fact, movable. Accordingly the first mover cannot be composite.

Moreover, something has to exist prior to any composite, since composing elements are by their very nature antecedent to a composite. Hence the first of all beings cannot be composite. Even within the order of composite beings we observe that the simpler things have priority. Thus elements are naturally prior to mixed bodies. Likewise, among the elements themselves, the first is fire, which is the simplest of all. Prior to all elements is the heavenly body, which has a simpler construction, since it is free from all contrariety. Hence the truth remains that the first of beings must be absolutely simple.

Chapter 10: Identity of God with His Essence

The further conclusion follows that God is His own essence. The essence of anything is that which its definition signifies. This is identical with the thing of which it is the definition, unless *per accidens* something is added to the thing defined over and above its definition. Thus whiteness is added to man, over and above the fact that he is a rational and mortal animal. Hence rational and mortal animal is the same as man; but whiteness, so far as it is white, is not the same as man. In any being, therefore, in which there are not found two factors whereof one is *per se* and the other *per accidens*, its essence must be altogether identical with it. In God, however, since He is simple, as has been shown, there are not found two factors whereof one is *per se* and the other *per accidens*. Therefore His essence must be absolutely the same as He Himself.

Moreover, whenever an essence is not absolutely identical with the thing of which it is the essence, something is discerned in that thing that has the function of potency, and something else that has the function of act. For an essence is formally related to the thing of which it is the essence as humanity is related to man. In God, however, no potency and act can be discerned: He is pure act. Accordingly He is His essence.

Chapter 11: Identity of Essence and Existence in God

God's essence cannot be other than His existence. In any being whose essence is distinct from its existence, *what* it is must be distinct from that *whereby* it is. For in virtue of a thing's existence we say that it is, and in virtue of its essence we say what it is. This is why a definition that signifies an essence manifests what a thing is. In God, however, there is no distinction between what He is and that whereby He is, since there is no composition in Him, as has been shown. Therefore God's essence is nothing else than His existence.

Likewise, we have proved that God is pure act without any admixture of potentiality. Accordingly His essence must be the ultimate act in Him; for any act that has a bearing on the ultimate act, is in potency to that ultimate act. But the ultimate act is existence itself, *ipsum esse.* For, since all motion is an issuing forth from potency to act, the ultimate act must be that toward which all motion tends; and since natural motion tends to what is naturally desired, the ultimate act must be that which all desire. This is existence. Consequently the divine essence, which is pure and ultimate act, must be existence itself, *ipsum esse.*

Chapter 12: God Not Contained Under Any Genus

We infer from the above that God is not contained as a species within any genus. Species is constituted by specific difference added to genus. Hence the essence of any species possesses something over and above its genus. But existence itself, *ipsum esse,* which is God's essence, does not comprise within itself any factor that is added to some other factor. Accordingly God is not a species of any genus.

Furthermore, since genus potentially contains specific differences, in every being composed of genus and differences, act is commingled with potency. But we have shown that God is pure act without any commingling of potency. (Cf. chap. 9) Therefore His essence is not composed of genus and differences; and so He is not in any genus.

Chapter 13: God is Not a Genus

We go on to show that God cannot be a genus. *What* a thing is, but not *that* it is, comes from its genus; the thing is established in its proper existence by specific differences. But that which God is, is very existence itself. Therefore He cannot be a genus.

Moreover, every genus is divided by some differences. But no differences can be apprehended in very existence itself. For differences do not share in genus except indirectly, so far as the species that are constituted by differences share in a genus. But there cannot be any difference that does not share in existence, since non-being is not the specific difference of anything. Accordingly God cannot be a genus predicated of a number of species.

Chapter 14:
God Not a Species Predicated by Individuals

God cannot be, as it were, a single species predicated of many individuals. Various individuals that come together in one essence of a species are distinguished by certain notes that lie outside the essence of the species. For example, men are alike in their common humanity but differ from one another in virtue of something that is outside the concept of humanity. This cannot occur in God, for God Himself is His essence, as has been shown. Therefore God cannot be a species that is predicated of several individuals.

Again, a number of individuals comprised under one species differ in their existence, and yet are alike in their one essence. Accordingly, whenever a number of individuals are under one species, their existence must be different from the essence of the species. But in God existence and essence are identical, as has been demonstrated. Therefore God cannot be a sort of species predicated of many individuals.

Chapter 15:
The Unicity of God

The conclusion is evident that there can be but one God. If there were many gods, they would be called by this name either equivocally or univocally. If they are called gods equivocally, further discussion is fruitless; there is nothing to prevent other peoples from applying the name "god" to what we call a stone. If they are called gods univocally, they must agree either in genus or in species. But we have just shown that God can be neither a genus nor a species comprising many individuals under Himself. Accordingly a multiplicity of gods is impossible.

Again, that whereby a common essence is individuated cannot pertain to many. Although there can be many men, it is impossible for this particular man to be more than one only. So if an essence is individuated by itself, and not by something else, it cannot pertain to many. But the divine essence is individuated by itself, since God's essence is not distinct from His existence; for we have shown that God is His essence. Hence God cannot be more than one only.

Another consideration is the following. A form can be multiplied in two ways: first, by specific differences, as in the case of a generic form; in this way color is differentiated into the various species of color; secondly, by the subjects in which it inheres, for example, whiteness. Therefore any form incapable of being multiplied by specific differences cannot be multiplied at all, if it is a form that does not exist in a subject. Thus whiteness, if it were to subsist without a subject, would not be more than one. But the divine essence is very existence, *ipsum esse*, which does not admit of specific differences, as we have shown. Since, therefore, the divine existence is a quasi-form subsisting by itself, seeing that God is His existence, the divine essence cannot be more than one. Accordingly a plurality of gods is impossible.

Chapter 72: The Cause of Diversity

If the unity and multiplicity of things are governed by their being, and if the entire being of things depends on God, as has been shown to be the case, the cause of plurality in things must be sought in God. How this comes about, must now be examined.

Any active cause must produce its like, so far as this is possible. The things produced by God could not be endowed with a likeness of the divine goodness in the simplicity in which that goodness is found in God. Hence what is one and simple in God had to be represented in the produced things in a variety of dissimilar ways. There had to be diversity in the things produced by God, in order that the divine perfection might in some fashion be imitated in the variety found in things.

Furthermore, whatever is caused is finite, since only God's essence is infinite, as was demonstrated above. The finite is rendered more perfect by the addition of other elements. Hence it was better to have diversity in created things, and thus to have good objects in greater number, than to have but a single kind of beings produced by God. For the best cause appropriately produces the best effects. Therefore it was fitting for God to produce variety in things.

Chapter 73: Diversity in Things According to Degree and Order

Diversity among things was rightly established according to a definite order, so that some things might be more excellent than others. For this pertains to the lavishness of the divine goodness, that God should communicate a likeness of His goodness to created things, so far as possible. God is not only good in Himself, but exceeds other beings in goodness, and guides them toward goodness. Consequently, that the likeness which created beings bear to God might be heightened, it was necessary for some things to be made better than others, and for some to act upon others, thus leading them toward perfection.

The basic diversity among things consists chiefly in diversity of forms. Formal diversity is achieved by way of contrariety; for genus is divided into various species by contrary differences. But order is necessarily found in contrariety, for among contraries one is always better than the other. Therefore diversity among things had to be established by God according to a definite order, in such a way that some beings might be more excellent than others.

Chapter 74: Incorporeal Substances Requisite for the Perfection of the Universe

A being is noble and perfect in the measure that it approaches likeness to God, who is pure act without any admixture of potency. Therefore beings that are supreme among entities must be more in act and must have less of potency, whereas inferior beings must be more in potency. How this is to be understood, we must now examine.

Since God is eternal and immutable in His being, those things are lowest in the scale of being, as possessing less likeness to God, which are subject to generation and corruption. Such beings exist for a time, and then cease to be. And, since existence follows the form of a thing, beings of this kind exist while they have their form, but cease to exist when deprived of their form. Hence there must be something in them that can retain a form for a time, and can then be deprived of the form. This is what we call matter. Therefore such beings, which are lowest in degree among things, must be composed of matter and form. But beings that are supreme among created entities approach most closely to likeness with God. They have no potency with regard to existence and non-existence; they have received everlasting existence from God through creation. Since matter, by the very fact that it is what it is, is a potency for that existence which is imparted through form, those beings which have no potency for existence and non-existence, are not composed of matter and form, but are forms only, subsisting in their being which they have received from God. Such incorporeal substances must be incorruptible. For all corruptible beings have a potency for non-existence; but incorporeal beings have no such potency, as we said. Hence they are incorruptible.

Furthermore, nothing is corrupted unless its form is separated from it, for existence always follows form. Since the substances in question are subsisting forms, they cannot be separated from their forms, and so cannot lose existence. Therefore they are incorruptible.

Between the extremes mentioned, there are certain intermediate beings which have no potency for existence and nonexistence, but which have a potency for *ubi*, or presence in place. Such are the heavenly bodies, which are not subject to generation and corruption, since contrarieties are not found in them. However, they are changeable according to local presence. Thus in some beings there is found matter as well as motion. For motion is the act of a being in potency. Accordingly such bodies have matter that is not subject to generation and corruption, but is subject only to change of place.

Chapter 75: Intellectual Substances

The substances mentioned above, which are called immaterial, must also be intellectual. A being is intellectual for the reason that it is free from matter. This can be perceived from the very way it understands. The intelligible in act and the intellect in act are the same thing. But it is clear that a thing is intelligible in act because it is separated from matter; we cannot have intellectual knowledge of material things except by abstracting from matter. Accordingly we must pronounce the same judgment regarding the intellect; that is, whatever is immaterial, is intellectual.

Furthermore, immaterial substances hold the first place and are supreme among beings; for act naturally has precedence over potency. But the intellect is clearly superior to all other beings; for the intellect uses corporeal things as instruments. Therefore immaterial substances must be intellectual.

Moreover, the higher a thing is in the scale of being, the closer it draws to likeness with God. Thus we observe that some things, those pertaining to the lowest degree, such as lifeless beings, share in the divine likeness with respect to existence only; others, for example, plants, share in the divine likeness with respect to existence and life; yet others, such as animals, with respect to sense perception. But the highest degree, and that which makes us most like to God, is conferred by the intellect. Consequently the most excellent creatures are intellectual. Indeed, they are said to be fashioned in God's image for the very reason that among all creatures they approach most closely to likeness with God.

Chapter 76: Freedom of Choice in Intellectual Substances

This fact shows that such beings have freedom of choice. The intellect does not act or desire without forming a judgment, as lifeless beings do, nor is the judgment of the intellect the product of natural impulse, as in brutes, but results from a true apprehension of the object. For the intellect perceives the end, the means leading to the end, and the bearing of one on the other. Hence the intellect can be the cause of its own judgment, whereby it desires a good and performs an action for the sake of an end. But what is a cause unto itself, is precisely what we call free. Accordingly the intellect desires and acts in virtue of a free judgment, which is the same as having freedom of choice. Therefore the highest substances enjoy freedom of choice.

Furthermore, that is free which is not tied down to any one definite course. But the appetite of an intellectual substance is not under compulsion to pursue any one definite good, for it follows intellectual apprehension, which embraces good universally. Therefore the appetite of an intelligent substance is free, since it tends toward all good in general.

Chapter 77: Order and Degree Among Intellectual Beings

Intellectual substances are superior to other substances in the scale of perfection. These same substances must also differ from one another in degree. They cannot differ from one another by material differentiation, since they lack matter; if any plurality is found among them, it must be caused by formal distinction, which establishes diversity of species. In beings that exhibit diversity of species, the degree and order existing in them must be taken into consideration. The reason is that, just as addition or subtraction of a unit causes variation of species in numbers, so natural entities are found to vary in species by the addition or subtraction of differences. For instance, what is merely alive, differs from what is both alive and endowed with sense perception; and the latter differs from what is alive, endowed with sense, and rational. Therefore the immaterial substances under discussion must be distinct according to various degrees and orders.

Chapter 78: Order and Degree in Intellectual Operation

Since the nature of a being's activity is in keeping with its substance, the higher intellectual substances must understand in a more perfect way, inasmuch as they have intelligible species and powers that are more universal and are more unified. On the other hand, intellectual substances that are less perfect must be weaker in intelligence, and must have species that are more numerous and less universal.

Chapter 79: Inferiority of Man's Intellectual Nature

Infinite progression is impossible in any series. Among intellectual substances, one must ultimately be found to be supreme, namely, the one which approaches most closely to God. Likewise, one must be found to be the lowest, and this will be the most intimately associated with corporeal matter.

This can be explained in the following way. Understanding is proper to man beyond all the other animals. Evidently, man alone comprehends universals, and the relations between things, and immaterial objects, which are perceptible only to the intelligence. Understanding cannot be an act performed by a bodily organ, in the way that vision is exercised by the eye. No faculty endowed with cognitive power can belong to the genus of things that is known through its agency. Thus the pupil of the eye lacks color by its very nature. Colors are recognized to the extent that the species of colors are received into the pupil; but a recipient must be lacking in that which is received. The intellect is capable of knowing all sensible natures. Therefore, if it knew through the medium of a bodily organ, that organ would have to be entirely lacking in sensible nature; but this is impossible.

Moreover, any cognitive faculty exercises its power of knowing in accord with the way the species of the object known is in it, for this is its principle of knowing. But the intellect knows things in an immaterial fashion, even those things that are by nature material; it abstracts a universal form from its individuating material conditions. Therefore the species of the object known cannot exist in the intellect materially; and so it is not received into a bodily organ, seeing that every bodily organ is material.

The same is clear from the fact that a sense is weakened and injured by sensible objects of extreme intensity. Thus the ear is impaired by excessively loud sounds, and the eye by excessively bright lights. This occurs because the harmony within the organ is shattered. The intellect, on the contrary, is perfected in proportion to the excellence of intelligible objects; he who understands the higher objects of intelligence is able to understand other objects more perfectly rather than less perfectly. Consequently, if man is found to be intelligent, and if man's understanding is not effected through the medium of a bodily organ, we are forced to acknowledge the existence of some incorporeal substance whereby man exercises the act of understanding. For the substance of a being that can perform an action by itself, without the aid of a body, is not dependent on a body. But all powers and forms that are unable to subsist by themselves without a body, cannot exercise any activity without a body. Thus heat does not by itself cause warmth; rather a body causes warmth by the heat that is in it. Accordingly this incorporeal substance whereby man understands, occupies the lowest place in the genus of intellectual substances, and is the closest to matter.

Chapter 80: Different Kinds of Intellect and Ways of Understanding

Since intellectual being is superior to sentient being, just as intellect is superior to sense, and since lower beings imitate higher beings as best they may, just as bodies subject to generation and corruption imitate in some fashion the circulatory motion of heavenly bodies, it follows that sensible beings resemble, in their own way, intellectual beings. Thus from the resemblance of sense to intellect we can mount to some knowledge of intellectual beings.

In sensible beings a certain factor is found to be the highest; this is act, that is, form. Another factor is found to be the lowest, for it is pure potency; this is matter. Midway between the two is the composite of matter and form.

We expect to find something similar in the intellectual world. The supreme intellectual being, God, is pure act. Other intellectual substances have something of act and of potency, but in a way that befits intellectual being. And the lowest among intellectual substances, that whereby man understands, has, so to speak, intellectual being only in potency. This is borne out by the fact that man is at first found to be only potentially intelligent, and this potency is gradually reduced to act in the course of time. And this is why the faculty whereby man understands is called the possible intellect.

Chapter 81: Reception of Intelligible Forms in the Possible Intellect

As was stated above, the higher an intellectual substance is in perfection, the more universal are the intelligible forms it possesses. Of all the intellectual substances, consequently, the human intellect, which we have called possible, has forms of the least universality. This is the reason it receives its intelligible forms from sensible things.

This can be made clear from another point of view. A form must have some proportion to the potency which receives it. Therefore, since of all intellectual substances man's possible intellect is found to be the closest to corporeal matter, its intelligible forms must, likewise, be most closely allied to material things.

Chapter 82: Man's Need of Sense Faculties for Understanding

However, we must realize that forms in corporeal things are particular, and have a material existence. But in the intellect they are universal and immaterial. Our manner of understanding brings this out. That is, we apprehend things universally and immaterially. This way of understanding must conform to the intelligible species whereby we understand. Consequently, since it is impossible to pass from one extreme to another without traversing what lies between, forms reaching the intellect from corporeal objects must pass through certain media.

These are the sense faculties, which receive the forms of material things without their matter; what lodges in the eye is the species of the stone, but not its matter. However, the forms of things received into the sense faculties are particular; for we know only particular objects with our sense faculties. Hence man must be endowed with senses as a prerequisite to understanding. A proof of this is the fact that if a man is lacking in one of the senses, he has no knowledge of sensible objects that are apprehended by that sense. Thus a person born blind can have no knowledge of colors.

Chapter 83: Necessity of the Agent Intellect

This discussion brings out the truth that knowledge of things in our intellect is not caused by any participation or influence of forms that are intelligible in act and that subsist by themselves, as was taught by the Platonists and certain other philosophers who followed them in this doctrine. No, the intellect acquires such knowledge from sensible objects, through the intermediacy of the senses. However, since the forms of objects in the sense faculties are particular, as we just said, they are intelligible not in act, but only in potency. For the intellect understands nothing but universals. But what is in potency is not reduced to act except by some agent. Hence there must be some agent that causes the species existing in the sense faculties to be intelligible in act. The possible intellect cannot perform this service, for it is in potency with respect to intelligible objects rather than active in rendering them intelligible. Therefore we must assume some other intellect, which will cause species that are intelligible in potency to become intelligible in act, just as light causes colors that are potentially visible to be actually visible. This faculty we call the agent intellect, which we would not have to postulate if the forms of things were intelligible in act, as the Platonists held.

To understand, therefore, we have need, first, of the possible intellect which receives intelligible species, and secondly, of the agent intellect which renders things intelligible in act. Once the possible intellect has been perfected by the intelligible species, it is called the habitual intellect (*intellectus in habitu*), for then it possesses intelligible species in such a way that it can use them at will; in other words, it possesses them in a fashion that is midway between pure potency and complete act. But when it has these species in full actuality, it is called the intellect in act. That is, the intellect actually understands a thing when the species of the thing is made the form of the possible intellect. This is why we say that the intellect in act is the object actually understood.

Chapter 103: The Divine Goodness as the End of All Action and Movement in Creatures

The divine goodness is not only the end of the creation of things; it must also be the end of every operation and movement of any creature whatever. The action of every being corresponds to its nature; for example, what is hot, causes heat. But every created thing has, in keeping with its form, some participated likeness to the divine goodness, as we have pointed out. Therefore, too, all actions and movements of every creature are directed to the divine goodness as their end.

Besides, all movements and operations of every being are seen to tend to what is perfect. Perfect signifies what is good, since the perfection of anything is its goodness. Hence every movement and action of anything whatever tend toward good. But all good is a certain imitation of the supreme Good, just as all being is an imitation of the first Being. Therefore the movement and action of all things tend toward assimilation with the divine goodness.

Moreover, if there are many agents arranged in order, the actions and movements of all the agents must be directed to the good of the first agent as to their ultimate end. For lower agents are moved by the higher agent, and every mover moves in the direction of his own end. Consequently the actions and movements of lower agents must tend toward the end of the first agent. Thus in an army the actions of all the subordinate units are directed, in the last instance, to victory, which is the end intended by the commander-in-chief. But we showed above that the first mover and agent is God, and that His end is nothing else than His goodness. Therefore all the actions and movements of all creatures exist on account of the divine goodness, not, of course, in the sense that they are to cause or increase it, but in the sense that they are to acquire it in their own way, by sharing to some extent in a likeness of it.

Created things attain to the divine likeness by their operations in different ways, as they also represent it in different ways conformably to their being. For each of them acts in a manner corresponding to its being. Therefore, as all creatures in common represent the divine goodness to the extent that they exist, so by their actions they all in common attain to the divine likeness in the conservation of their being and in the communication of their being to others. For every creature endeavors, by its activity, first of all to keep itself in perfect being, so far as this is possible. In such endeavor it tends, in its own way, to an imitation of the divine permanence. Secondly, every creature strives, by its activity, to communicate its own perfect being, in its own fashion, to another; and in this it tends toward an imitation of the divine causality.

The rational creature tends, by its activity, toward the divine likeness in a special way that exceeds the capacities of all other creatures, as it also has a nobler existence as compared with other creatures. The existence of other creatures is finite, since it is hemmed in by matter, and so lacks infinity both in act and in potency. But every rational nature has infinity either in act or in potency, according to the way its intellect contains intelligibles. Thus our intellectual nature, considered in its first state, is in potency to its intelligibles; since these are infinite, they have a certain potential infinity. Hence the intellect is the species of species, because it has a species that is not determined to one thing alone, as is the case with a stone, but that has a capacity for all species. But the intellectual nature of God is infinite in act, for prior to every consideration it has within itself the perfection of all being, as was shown above. Accordingly intellectual creatures occupy a middle position between potency and act. By its activity, therefore, the intellectual creature tends toward the divine likeness, not only in the sense that it preserves itself in existence, or that it multiplies its existence, in a way, by communicating it; it also has as its end the possession in act of what by nature it possesses in potency. Consequently the end of the intellectual creature, to be achieved by its activity, is the complete actuation of its intellect by all the intelligibles for which it has a potency. In this respect it will become most like to God.

Chapter 104: The End of the Intellectual Creature

A thing may be in potency in two ways: either naturally, that is, with respect to perfections that can be reduced to act by a natural agent; or else with respect to perfections that cannot be reduced to act by a natural agent but require some other agent. This is seen to take place even in corporeal beings. The boy grows up to be a man; the spermatozoon develops into an animal. This is within the power of nature. But that lumber becomes a bench or that a blind man receives sight, is not within the power of nature.

The same is the case with our minds. Our intellect has a natural potency with regard to certain intelligible objects, namely, those that can be reduced to act by the agent intellect. We possess this faculty as an innate principle that enables us to understand in actuality. However, we cannot attain our ultimate end by the actuation of our intellect through the instrumentality of the agent intellect. For the function of the agent intellect consists in rendering actually intelligible the phantasms that of themselves are only potentially intelligible. This was explained above. These phantasms are derived from the senses. Hence the efficacy of the agent intellect in reducing our intellect to act is restricted to intelligible objects of which we can gain knowledge by way of sense perception. Man's last end cannot consist in such cognition.

The reason is that, once the ultimate end has been reached, natural desire ceases. But no matter how much we may advance in this kind of understanding, whereby we derive knowledge from the senses, there still remains a natural desire to know other objects. For many things are quite beyond the reach of the senses. We can have but a slight knowledge of such things through information based on sense experience. We may get to know that they exist, but we cannot know what they are, for the natures of immaterial substances belong to a different genus from the natures of sensible things and excel them, we may say, beyond all proportion.

Moreover, as regards objects that fall under sense experience, there are many whose nature we cannot know with any certainty. Some of them, indeed, elude our knowledge altogether; others we can know but vaguely. Hence our natural desire for more perfect knowledge ever remains. But a natural desire cannot be in vain.

Accordingly we reach our last end when our intellect is actualized by some higher agent than an agent connatural to us, that is, by an agent capable of gratifying our natural, inborn craving for knowledge. So great is the desire for knowledge within us that, once we apprehend an effect, we wish to know its cause. Moreover, after we have gained some knowledge of the circumstances investing a thing, our desire is not satisfied until we penetrate to its essence. Therefore our natural desire for knowledge cannot come to rest within us until we know the first cause, and that not in any way, but in its very essence. This first cause is God. Consequently the ultimate end of an intellectual creature is the vision of God in His essence.

Chapter 105: Knowledge of the Divine Essence by the Created Intellect

The possibility of such knowledge must be investigated. Manifestly, since our intellect knows nothing except through an intelligible species of the thing known, the species of one thing cannot disclose the essence of another thing.

In proportion as the species, whereby the mind knows, is remote from the thing known, the less perfect is the knowledge our intellect has of that thing's essence. For example, if we should know an ox by the species of an ass, we would have an imperfect knowledge of the essence of the ox, for our concept would be limited to its genus. Our knowledge would be still more defective if we were to know the ox through the medium of a stone, because then we would know it by a more remote genus. And if our knowledge were gained through the species of a thing that did not agree with the ox in any genus, we could not know the essence of the ox at all.

Previous discussion has brought out the fact that no creature is associated with God in genus. Hence the essence of God cannot be known through any created species whatever, whether sensible or intelligible. Accordingly, if God is to be known as He is, in His essence, God Himself must become the form of the intellect knowing Him and must be joined to that intellect, not indeed so as to constitute a single nature with it, but in the way an intelligible species is joined to the intelligence. For God, who is His own being, is also His own truth, and truth is the form of the intellect.

Whatever receives a form, must first acquire the disposition requisite to the reception of that form. Our intellect is not equipped by its nature with the ultimate disposition looking to that form which is truth; otherwise it would be in possession of truth from the beginning. Consequently, when it does finally attain to truth, it must be elevated by some disposition newly conferred on it. And this we call the light of glory, whereby our intellect is perfected by God, who alone by His very nature has this form properly as His own. In somewhat the same way the disposition which heat has for the form of fire can come from fire alone. This is the light that is spoken of in Psalm 35:10: "In Your light we shall see light."

Chapter 106: Fruition of Natural Desire in the Beatific Vision

Once this end is reached, natural desire must find its full fruition. The divine essence thus united to the intellect of the one who sees God, is the adequate principle for knowing everything, and is the source of all good, so that nothing can remain to be desired. This, too, is the most perfect way of attaining likeness with God: to know God in the way He knows Himself, by His own essence.

Of course, we shall never comprehend Him as He comprehends Himself. This does not mean that we shall be unaware of some part of Him, for He has no parts. It means that we shall not know Him as perfectly as He can be known, since the capacity of our intellect for knowing cannot equal His truth, and so cannot exhaust His knowability. God's knowability or truth is infinite, whereas our intellect is finite. But His intellect is infinite, just as His truth is; and so He alone knows Himself to the full extent that He is knowable; just as a person comprehends a demonstrable conclusion if he knows it through demonstration, but not if he knows it only in an imperfect way, on merely probable grounds.

This ultimate end of man we call beatitude. For a man's happiness or beatitude consists in the vision whereby he sees God in His essence. Of course, man is far below God in the perfection of his beatitude. For God has this beatitude by His very nature, whereas man attains beatitude by being admitted to a share in the divine light, as we said in the previous chapter.

Chapter 107: Beatitude Essentially in the Act of the Intellect

We should note that, since advance from potency to act is motion, or at least is similar to motion, the process of arriving at beatitude has points of resemblance with natural motion or change. In natural motion we may consider, first, a certain property whereby the mobile object has a proportion to such and such an end, or is inclined in its direction. We observe this, for instance, in the earth's gravity with respect to whatever is borne downward. No object would move naturally toward a definite end unless it had a proportion to that end. We may consider, secondly, the motion itself toward its end; thirdly, the form or place toward which there is motion; and fourthly, the repose in the form educed or in the place reached.

Similarly, with regard to intellectual movement toward an end, there is, first, the love inclining toward the end; secondly, the desire which is a sort of motion toward the end, and the actions issuing from such desire; thirdly, the form which the intellect receives; and fourthly, the resulting delight, which is nothing else than the repose of the will in the end as reached.

In the same way, the end of natural generation is a form and the end of local motion is a place. However, repose in a form or a place is not the end, but follows upon the attainment of the end; and much less does the end consist in motion or in proportion to the end. Likewise the ultimate end of an intellectual creature is the direct vision of God, but not delight in God. Such delight accompanies attainment of the end and, as it were, perfects it. Much less can desire or love be the ultimate end, because they are present even before the end is reached.

Chapter 114: The Meaning of Good and Evil in Things

A question worthy of consideration arises at this point. As the term "good" signifies perfect being, so the term "evil" signifies nothing else than privation of perfect being. In its proper acceptation, privation is predicated of that which is fitted by its nature to be possessed, and to be possessed at a certain time and in a certain manner. Evidently, therefore, a thing is called evil if it lacks a perfection it ought to have. Thus if a man lacks the sense of sight, this is an evil for him. But the same lack is not an evil for a stone, for the stone is not equipped by nature to have the faculty of sight.

Chapter 115: Impossibility of an Evil Nature

Evil cannot be a nature. Every nature is either act or potency or a composite of the two. Whatever is act, is a perfection and is good in its very concept. And what is in potency has a natural appetite for the reception of act; but what all beings desire is good. Therefore, too, what is composed of act and potency participates in goodness to the extent that it participates in act. And potency possesses goodness inasmuch as it is ordained to act; an indication of this is the fact that potency is esteemed in proportion to its capacity for act and perfection. Consequently no nature is of itself an evil.

Likewise, every being achieves its fulfillment according as it is realized in act, for act is the perfection of a thing. However, neither of a pair of opposites achieves fulfillment by being mixed with the other, but is rather destroyed or weakened thereby. Therefore evil does not realize its full capacity by sharing in good. But every nature realizes its full capacity by having existence in act; and so, since to be good is the object of every being's natural tendency, a nature achieves fulfillment by participating in good. Accordingly no nature is an evil.

Moreover, any nature whatever desires the preservation of its being, and shuns destruction to the full extent of its power. Consequently, since good is that which all desire, and evil, on the contrary, is that which all shun, we must conclude that for any nature existence is in itself good, and non-existence is evil. To be evil, however, is not good; in fact, not to be evil is included in the notion of good. Therefore no nature is an evil.

Chapter 116: Good and Evil as Specific Differences and as Contraries

We have next to inquire how good and evil may be regarded as contraries and genera of contraries and differences constituting species of a sort, namely, moral habits. Each member of a pair of contraries is some kind of nature. For non-being can be neither genus nor specific difference, since genus is predicated of a thing according to *what* it is (*in eo quod quid*) and difference according to *what sort* of thing it is (*in eo quod quale quid*).

We must note that, as physical entities receive their species from their form, so moral entities receive their species from the end which is the object of the will and on which all morality depends. In physical entities, moreover, the presence of one form entails the privation of another, as, for instance, the form of fire entails the privation of the form of air. In moral entities, similarly, one end involves the privation of another end. Since the privation of a due perfection is an evil in physical entities, the reception of a form which implies the privation of the form that ought to be possessed, is an evil; not, indeed, because of the form itself, but because of the privation its presence involves. In this sense, to be on fire is an evil for a log of wood. In the field of morality, likewise, the pursuit of an end that entails the privation of the right end is an evil, not on account of the end itself, but because of the privation necessarily implied. It is in this way that two moral actions, directed to contrary ends, differ as good and evil. Consequently the corresponding contrary habits differ in good and evil as by specific differences, and as being contrary to each other. This is so, not on account of the privation from which evil receives its designation, but on account of the end which involves the privation.

This is the sense in which some philosophers understand Aristotle's assertion, that good and evil are genera of contraries [*Categories*, XI, 14a 25], namely, of moral contraries. But if we examine the matter closely, we shall find that in the sphere of morals, good and evil are differences rather than species. Hence it seems better to say that good and evil are called genera according to the opinion of Pythagoras, who reduced everything to good and evil as to supreme genera. This position does, indeed, contain some truth, in the sense that in all contraries one member is perfect, whereas the other is deficient. This is clear in the case of white and black, sweet and bitter, and so on. But invariably, what is perfect, pertains to good, and what is deficient, pertains to evil.

Chapter 117: Impossibility of Essential or Supreme Evil

Knowing that evil is the privation of a due perfection, we can easily understand how evil corrupts good; this it does to the extent that it is the privation of good. Thus blindness is said to corrupt sight because it is the privation of sight. However, evil does not completely corrupt good, because, as we remarked above, not only form, but also potency to form, is good; and potency is the subject of privation as well as of form. Therefore the subject of evil must be good, not in the sense that it is opposed to evil, but in the sense that it is a potency for the reception of evil. This brings out the fact that not every good can be the subject of evil, but only such a good as is in potency with respect to some perfection of which it can be deprived. Hence in beings which are exclusively act, or in which act cannot be separated from potency, there can, to this extent, be no evil.

As a result, nothing can be essentially evil, since evil must always have as its foundation some subject, distinct from it, that is good. And so there cannot be a being that is supremely evil, in the way that there is a being that is supremely good because it is essentially good.

Further, we see clearly that evil cannot be the object of desire, and that it cannot act except in virtue of the good connected with it. For only perfection and end are desirable; and the principle of action is form. However, since a particular perfection or form involves the privation of some other perfection or form, it can happen incidentally that privation or evil may be desired and may be the principle of some action; not precisely because of the evil, but because of the good connected with it. An example of what I here mean by "incidentally" is the musician who constructs a house, not in his capacity of musician, but in the capacity of being also a builder.

From this we may also infer that evil cannot be a first principle, for a principle *per accidens* is subsequent to a principle that is such *per se*.

Chapter 127: Control of Lower Bodies, but Not of the Human Intellect, by Higher Bodies

Among intellectual substances, therefore, some are divinely governed by others, that is, the lower by the higher. Similarly lower bodies are controlled, in God's plan, by higher bodies. Hence every movement of lower bodies is caused by the movements of heavenly bodies. Lower bodies acquire forms and species from the influence thus exercised by heavenly bodies, just as the intelligible exemplars of things descend to lower spirits through higher spirits.

However, since an intellectual substance is superior to all bodies in the hierarchy of beings, the order of providence has suitably disposed matters in such a way that no intellectual substance is ruled by God through a corporeal substance. Accordingly, since the human soul is an intellectual substance, it cannot, so far as it is endowed with intelligence and will, be subject to the movements of heavenly bodies. Heavenly bodies cannot directly act upon or influence either the human intellect or the human will.

Again, no body acts except by movement. Hence whatever is acted upon by a body, is moved by it. But the human soul, regarded as intellectual, according as it is the principle of the will, cannot be moved by bodily movement, since the intellect is not the act of any bodily organ. Therefore the human soul cannot be subject, in its intellect or will, to any influence emanating from heavenly bodies.

Furthermore, impressions left in lower bodies from the impact of heavenly bodies are natural. Therefore, if the operations of the intellect and will resulted from the impression made by heavenly bodies, they would proceed from natural instinct. And so man would not differ in his activity from other animals, which are moved to their actions by natural instinct. And thus free will and deliberation and choice and all perfections of this sort, which distinguish man from other animals, would perish.

Chapter 128:
Indirect Influence of Heavenly Bodies on the Human Intellect Through the Senses

Nevertheless we should not lose sight of the fact that the human intellect is indebted to the sense powers for the origin of its knowledge. This is why intellectual knowledge is thrown into confusion when the soul's faculties of phantasm, imagination, or memory are impaired. On the other hand, when these powers are in good order, intellectual apprehension becomes more efficient. Likewise, a modification in the sensitive appetite tends to bring about a change in the will, which is a rational appetite, as we know from the fact that the object of the will is the good as apprehended. According as we are variously disposed in the matter of concupiscence, anger, fear and other passions, a thing will at different times appear to us as good or evil.

On the other hand, all the powers of the sensitive part of our soul, whether they are apprehensive or appetitive, are the acts of certain bodily organs. If these undergo modification, the faculties themselves must, indirectly, undergo some change. Therefore, since change in lower bodies is influenced by the movement of the heavens, the operations of the sensitive faculties are also subject to such movement, although only *per accidens*. And thus heavenly movement has some indirect influence on the activity of the human intellect and will, so far as the will may be inclined this way or that by the passions.

Nevertheless, since the will is not subject to the passions in such a way as necessarily to follow their enticement, but on the contrary has it in its power to repress passion by the judgment of reason, the human will is not subject to impressions emanating from heavenly bodies. It retains free judgment either to follow or to resist their attractions, as may seem to it expedient. Only the wise act thus; the masses follow the lead of bodily passions and urgings. For they are wanting in wisdom and virtue.

Chapter 129: Movement of Man's Will by God

Everything that is changeable and multiform is traced back, as to its cause, to some first principle that is immobile and is one. Since man's intellect and will are clearly changeable and multiform, they must be reduced to some higher cause that is immobile and uniform. The heavenly bodies are not the cause to which they are reduced, as we have shown; therefore they must be reduced to yet higher causes.

In this matter the case of the intellect differs from that of the will. The act of the intellect is brought about by the presence of the things understood in the intellect; but the act of the will is accounted for by the inclination of the will toward the things willed. Thus the intellect is adapted by its nature to be perfected by something external that is related to it as act to potency. Hence man can be aided to elicit an act of the intellect by anything external that is more perfect in intelligible being: not only by God but also by an angel or even by a man who is better informed; but differently in each instance. A man is helped to understand by a man when one of them proposes to the other an intelligible object not previously contemplated; but not in such a way that the light of the intellect of one man is perfected by the other, because each of these natural lights is in one and the same species.

But the natural light of an angel is by nature of a higher excellence than the natural light of man, and so an angel can aid a man to understand, not only on the part of the object proposed to him by the angel, but also on the part of the light that is strengthened by the angel's light. However, man's natural light does not come from an angel, for the nature of the rational soul, which receives existence through creation, is produced by God alone.

God helps man to understand, not only on the part of the object proposed by God to man, or by an increase of light, but also by the very fact that man's natural light, which is what makes him intellectual, is from God. Moreover, God Himself is the first truth from which all other truth has its certitude, just as secondary propositions in demonstrative sciences derive their certitude from primary propositions. For this reason nothing can become certain for the intellect except through God's influence, just as conclusions do not achieve certitude in science except in virtue of primary principles.

With regard to the will, its act is a certain impulse flowing from the interior to the exterior, and has much in common with natural tendencies. Accordingly, as natural tendencies are placed in natural things exclusively by the cause of their nature, the act of the will is from God alone, for He alone is the cause of a rational nature endowed with will. Therefore, if God moves man's will, this is evidently not opposed to freedom of choice, just as God's activity in natural things is not contrary to their nature. Both the natural inclination and the voluntary inclination are from God; each of them issues in action according to the condition of the thing to which it pertains. God moves things in a way that is consonant with their nature.

This exposition brings out the fact that heavenly bodies can exert an influence on the human body and its bodily powers, as they can in the case of other bodies. But they cannot do the same with regard to the intellect, although an intellectual creature can. And God alone can touch the will.

Chapter 130: Government of the World by God

Second causes do not act except through the power of the first cause; thus instruments operate under the direction of art. Consequently all the agents through which God carries out the order of His government, can act only through the power of God Himself. The action of any of them is caused by God, just as the movement of a mobile object is caused by the motion of the mover. In such event the mover and the movement must be simultaneous. Hence God must be inwardly present to any agent as acting therein whenever He moves the agent to act.

Another point: not only the action of secondary agents but their very existence is caused by God, as was shown above. However, we are not to suppose that the existence of things is caused by God in the same way as the existence of a house is caused by its builder. When the builder departs, the house still remains standing. For the builder causes the existence of the house only in the sense that he works for the existence of the house as a house. Such activity is, indeed, the constructing of the house, and thus the builder is directly the cause of the becoming of the house, a process that ceases when he desists from his labors. But God is directly, by Himself, the cause of very existence, and communicates existence to all things just as the sun communicates light to the air and to whatever else is illuminated by the sun. The continuous shining of the sun is required for the preservation of light in the air; similarly God must unceasingly confer existence on things if they are to persevere in existence. Thus all things are related to God as an object made is to its maker, and this not only so far as they begin to exist, but so far as they continue to exist. But a maker and the object made must be simultaneous, just as in the case of a mover and the object moved. Hence God is necessarily present to all things to the extent that they have existence. But existence is that which is the most intimately present in all things. Therefore God must be in all things.

Moreover, whoever, through the agency of intermediate causes, carries out the order he has foreseen, must know and arrange the effects of these intermediate causes. Otherwise the effects would occur outside the order he has foreseen. The prearranged plan of a governor is more perfect in proportion as his knowledge and design descend to details. For if any detail escapes the advertence of the governor, the disposition of that detail will elude his foresight. We showed above that all things are necessarily subject to divine providence; and divine providence must evidently be most perfect, because whatever is predicated of God must befit Him in the highest possible degree. Consequently the ordinations of His providence must extend to the most minute effects.

Chapter 142: God's Goodness and the Permission of Evil

God's permission of evil in the things governed by Him is not inconsistent with the divine goodness. For, in the first place, the function of providence is not to destroy but to save the nature of the beings governed. The perfection of the universe requires the existence of some beings that are not subject to evil, and of other beings that can suffer the defect of evil in keeping with their nature. If evil were completely eliminated from things, they would not be governed by divine providence in accord with their nature; and this would be a greater defect than the particular defects eradicated.

Secondly, the good of one cannot be realized without the suffering of evil by another. For instance, we find that the generation of one being does not take place without the corruption of another being, and that the nourishment of a lion is impossible without the destruction of some other animal, and that the patient endurance of the just involves persecution by the unjust. If evil were completely excluded from things, much good would be rendered impossible. Consequently it is the concern of divine providence, not to safeguard all beings from evil, but to see to it that the evil which arises is ordained to some good.

Thirdly, good is rendered more estimable when compared with particular evils. For example, the brilliance of white is brought out more clearly when set off by the dinginess of black. And so, by permitting the existence of evil in the world, the divine goodness is more emphatically asserted in the good, just as is the divine wisdom when it forces evil to promote good.

Chapter 143: God's Special Providence Over Man by Grace

Accordingly, divine providence governs individual beings in keeping with their nature. Since rational creatures, because of the gift of free will, enjoy dominion over their actions in a way impossible to other creatures, a special providence must be exercised over them in two respects. First, with regard to the aids God gives to rational creatures in their activity, secondly, with regard to the recompense allotted for their works. God gives to irrational creatures only those aids by which they are naturally moved to act. But to rational creatures are issued instructions and commands regulating their lives. A precept is not fittingly given except to a being that is master of his actions, although in an analogous sense God is said to give commands to irrational creatures also, as is intimated in Psalm 148:6: "He made a decree, and it shall not pass away." But this sort of decree is nothing else than the dispensation of divine providence moving natural things to their proper actions.

The deeds of rational creatures are imputed to them in blame or in praise, because they have dominion over their acts. The actions of men are ascribed to them not only by a man who is placed over them, but also by God. Thus any praiseworthy or blameworthy action that a man performs is imputed to him by the person to whose rule he is subject. Since good actions merit a reward and sin calls for punishment, as was said above, rational creatures are punished for the evil they do and are rewarded for the good they do, according to the measure of justice fixed by divine providence. But there is no place for reward or punishment in dealing with irrational creatures, just as there is none for praise or blame.

Since the last end of rational creatures exceeds the capacity of their nature and since whatever conduces to the end must be proportionate to the end according to the right order of providence, rational creatures are given divine aids that are not merely proportionate to nature but that transcend the capacity of nature. God infuses into man, over and above the natural faculty of reason, the light of grace whereby he is internally perfected for the exercise of virtue, both as regards knowledge, inasmuch as man's mind is elevated by this light to the knowledge of truths surpassing reason, and as regards action and affection, inasmuch as man's affective power is raised by this light above all created things to the love of God, to hope in Him, and to the performance of acts that such love imposes.

These gifts or aids supernaturally given to man are called graces for two reasons. First, because they are given by God gratis. Nothing is discoverable in man that would constitute a right to aids of this sort, for they exceed the capacity of nature. Secondly, because in a very special way man is made *gratus*, or pleasing to God, by such gifts. Since God's love is the cause of goodness in things and is not called forth by any pre-existing goodness, as our love is, a special intensity of divine love must be discerned in those whom He showers with such extraordinary effects of His goodness. Therefore God is said chiefly and simply to love those whom He endows with these effects of His love by which they are enabled to reach their last end, which is He Himself, the fountainhead of all goodness.

Chapter 144: Remission of Sin by the Gifts of Grace

Sins arise when actions deflect from the right course leading to the end. Since man is conducted to his end not only by natural aids, but by the aids of grace, the sins men commit must be counteracted not by natural aids alone, but also by the helps which grace confers. Contraries exclude each other; therefore, as the aids of grace are taken from man by sin, so sins are forgiven by the gifts of grace. Otherwise man's malice in committing sin would be more powerful in banishing divine grace than the divine goodness is in expelling sin by the gifts of grace.

Furthermore, God's providence over things is in harmony with their mode of being. Changeable things are so constituted that contraries can succeed each other in them; examples are generation and corruption in corporeal matter, and white and black in a colored object. Man is changeable in will as long as he lives his earthly life. Hence man receives from God the gifts of grace in such a way that he is able to forfeit them by sin; and the sins man commits are such that they can be remitted by the gifts of grace.

Besides, in supernatural acts, possible and impossible are regarded from the standpoint of divine power, not from the standpoint of natural power. The fact that a blind man can be made to see or that a dead man can rise, is owing not to natural power but to divine power. But the gifts of grace are supernatural. Therefore a person's capacity to receive them depends on divine power. To say that, once a person has sinned, he cannot receive the gifts of grace, is derogatory to the power of God. Of course, grace cannot co-exist with sin; for by grace man is rightly ordered to his end, from which he is turned away by sin. But the contention that sin is irremissible, impugns the power of God.

Chapter 145:
No Sin Unforgivable

The suggestion might be put forward that sins are unforgivable, not through any lack of power on God's part, but because divine justice has decided that anyone who falls from grace shall never more be restored to it. But such a position is clearly erroneous. There is no provision in the order of divine justice to the effect that, while a person is on the road, he should have assigned to him what belongs to the end of the journey. But unyielding adherence to good or to evil pertains to the end of life's course; immobility and cessation from activity are the terminus of movement. On the other hand, the whole of our present life is a time of wayfaring, as is shown by man's changeableness both in body and in soul. Accordingly divine justice does not determine that after sinning a man must remain immovably in the state of sin.

Moreover, divine benefits do not expose man to danger, particularly in affairs of supreme moment. But it would be dangerous for man, while leading a life subject to change, to accept grace if, after receiving grace, he could sin but could not again be restored to grace. This is so especially in view of the fact that sins preceding grace are remitted by the infusion of grace; and at times such sins are more grievous than those man commits after receiving grace. Therefore we may not hold that man's sins are unforgivable either before or after they are committed.

Chapter 146:
Remission of Sin by God Alone

God alone can forgive sin. For only the one against whom an offense is directed can forgive the offense. Sin is imputed to man as an offense not only by another man, but also by God, as we said above. However, we are now considering sin as imputed to man by God. Accordingly, God alone can forgive sin.

Again, since by sin man is deflected from his last end, sins cannot be forgiven unless man is again rightly ordered to his end. This is accomplished through the gifts of grace which come from God alone, since they transcend the power of nature. Therefore only God can remit sin.

Further, sin is imputed to man as an offense because it is voluntary. But only God can effect a change in the will. Consequently He alone can truly forgive sins.

Chapter 147: Some Articles of Faith on the Effects of Divine Government

This, then, is the second of God's effects, namely, the government of things, and especially of rational creatures, to whom God gives grace and whose sins He forgives. This effect is touched on in the Creed. When we profess that the Holy Spirit is God, we imply that all things are ordained to the end of divine goodness, since it belongs to God to order His subjects to their end. And the words of the Creed which express our belief that the Holy Spirit is "the Life-giver," suggest that God moves all things. For, as the movement flowing from the soul to the body is the life of the body, so the movement, whereby the universe is moved by God is, so to speak, a certain life of the universe.

Further, since the entire process of divine government is derived from the divine goodness, which is appropriated to the Holy Spirit, who proceeds as love, the effects of divine providence are fittingly thought of in connection with the person of the Holy Spirit.

As regards the effect of supernatural knowledge, which God produces in men through faith, the Creed proclaims: "I believe in... the Holy, Catholic Church"; for the Church is the congregation of the faithful. Concerning the grace which God communicates to men the Creed states: "I believe in... the communion of saints." And with respect to the remission of sin it says: "I believe in... the forgiveness of sins."

Chapter 148: All Creation for Man

All things are directed to the divine goodness as to their end, as we have shown. Among things ordained to this end, some are closer to the end than others, and so participate in the divine goodness more abundantly. Therefore lesser creatures, which have a smaller share in the divine goodness, are in some way subordinated to higher beings as to their ends. In any hierarchy of ends, beings that are closer to the ultimate end are also ends with respect to beings that are more remote. For instance, a dose of medicine is administered to procure a purge, the purge is designed to promote slimness, and slimness is desirable for health; and thus slimness is, in a sense, the purpose of the purging, as the purging is the purpose of the medicine. And such subordination is reasonable. As in the order of efficient causes, the power of the first agent reaches the ultimate effects through intermediate causes, so in the order of ends, whatever is farther removed from the end attains to the ultimate end through the intermediacy of beings that are closer to the end. Thus, in our example, the medicine has no relation to health except through purging. Similarly, in the order of the universe, lower beings realize their last end chiefly by their subordination to higher beings.

The same conclusion is manifest if we turn our attention to the order of things in itself. Things that come into being by a natural process, act as they are equipped by nature to act. As we observe, however, imperfect beings serve the needs of more noble beings; plants draw their nutriment from the earth, animals feed on plants, and these in turn serve man's use. We conclude, then, that lifeless beings exist for living beings, plants for animals, and the latter for men. And since, as we have seen, intellectual nature is superior to material nature, the whole of material nature is subordinate to intellectual nature. But among intellectual natures, that which has the closest ties with the body is the rational soul, which is the form of man. In a certain sense, therefore, we may say that the whole of corporeal nature exists for man, inasmuch as he is a rational animal. And so the consummation of the whole of corporeal nature depends, to some extent, on man's consummation.

Chapter 149: The Ultimate End of Man

Man's consummation consists in the attainment of his last end, which is perfect beatitude or happiness, and this consists in the vision of God, as was demonstrated above. The beatific vision entails immutability in the intellect and will. As regards the intellect, its questing ceases when at last it comes to the first cause, in which all truth can be known. The will's variability ceases, too; for, when it reaches its last end, in which is contained the fullness of all goodness, it finds nothing further to be desired. The will is subject to change because it craves what it does not possess. Clearly, therefore, the final consummation of man consists in perfect repose or unchangeableness as regards both intellect and will.

Chapter 150: Consummation of Man in Eternity

We showed in an earlier chapter that the idea of eternity involves immutability. As motion causes time, in which priority and posteriority are discerned, so the cessation of motion puts a stop to priority and posteriority; and so nothing remains but eternity, which is simultaneously whole. Therefore in his final consummation man attains eternal life, not only in the sense that he lives an immortal life in his soul, for this is a property of the rational soul by its very nature, as was shown above, but also in the sense that he is brought to the perfection of immobility.

Chapter 151: Reunion with the Body Requisite for the Soul's Perfect Happiness

We should note that the disquiet of the will cannot be wholly overcome unless natural desire is completely satisfied. Elements that are by nature destined for union, naturally desire to be united to each other; for any being seeks what is suited to it by nature. Since, therefore, the natural condition of the human soul is to be united to the body, as was pointed out above, it has a natural desire for union with the body. Hence the will cannot be perfectly at rest until the soul is again joined to the body. When this takes place, man rises from the dead.

Besides, final perfection requires possession of a being's original perfection. But the first perfection of anything requires that it be perfect in its nature, and final perfection consists in attainment of the last end. In order, therefore, that the human soul may be brought to complete perfection with regard to its end, it must be perfect in its nature. This is impossible unless the soul is united to the body. For by nature the soul is a part of man as his form. But no part is perfect in its nature unless it exists in its whole. Therefore man's final happiness requires the soul to be again united to the body.

Moreover, the accidental and all that is contrary to nature cannot be everlasting. But a state wherein the soul is separated from the body is surely *per accidens* and contrary to nature, if naturally and *per se* the soul has a longing for union with the body. Therefore the soul will not be forever separated from the body. Accordingly, since the soul's substance is incorruptible, as was shown above, we conclude that the soul is to be reunited to the body.

Chapter 152: Separation of the Body and Soul Both Natural and Contrary to Nature

We may have a suspicion that separation of the soul from the body is not *per accidens* but is in accord with nature. For man's body is made up of contrary elements. Everything of this sort is naturally corruptible. Therefore the human body is naturally corruptible. But when the body corrupts the soul must survive as a separate entity if the soul is immortal, as in fact it is. Apparently, then, separation of the soul from the body is in accord with nature.

In view of these considerations, we must take up the question, how this separation is according to nature, and how it is opposed to nature. We showed above that the rational soul exceeds the capacity of all corporeal matter in a measure impossible to other forms. This is demonstrated by its intellectual activity, which it exercises without the body. To the end that corporeal matter might be fittingly adapted to the soul, there had to be added to the body some disposition that would make it suitable matter for such a form. And in the same way that this form itself receives existence from God alone through creation, that disposition, transcending as it does corporeal nature, was conferred on the human body by God alone, for the purpose of preserving the body itself in a state of incorruption, so that it might match the soul's perpetual existence. This disposition remained in man's body as long as man's soul cleaved to God.

But when man's soul turned from God by sin, the human body deservedly lost that supernatural disposition whereby it was unrebelliously subservient to the soul. And hence man incurred the necessity of dying.

Accordingly, if we regard the nature of the body, death is natural. But if we regard the nature of the soul and the disposition with which the human body was supernaturally endowed in the beginning for the sake of the soul, death is *per accidens* and contrary to nature, inasmuch as union with the body is natural for the soul.

Chapter 153: The Soul's Resumption of the Same Body

Since the soul is united to the body as its form, and since each form has the right matter corresponding to it, the body to which the soul will be reunited must be of the same nature and species as was the body laid down by the soul at death. At the resurrection the soul will not resume a celestial or ethereal body, or the body of some animal, as certain people fancifully prattle [Origen,

Peri Archon, III, 6]. No, it will resume a human body made up of flesh and bones, and equipped with the same organs it now possesses.

Furthermore, just as the same specific form ought to have the same specific matter, so the same numerical form ought to have the same numerical matter. The soul of an ox cannot be the soul of a horse's body, nor can the soul of this ox be the soul of any other ox. Therefore, since the rational soul that survives remains numerically the same, at the resurrection it must be reunited to numerically the same body.

Chapter 154: Miraculous Nature of the Resurrection

When substances corrupt, the survival of the species, but not the restoration of the individual, is effected by the action of nature. The cloud from which rain is produced and the cloud which is again formed by evaporation from the fallen rain water, are not numerically the same. Accordingly, since the human body substantially dissolves in death, it cannot be restored to numerical identity by the action of nature. But the concept of resurrection requires such identity, as we have just shown. Consequently the resurrection of man will not be brought about by the action of nature, as some philosophers [Empedocles] have held in their theory that, when all bodies return to the position formerly occupied after untold cycles of years, then also men will return to life in the same numerical identity. No, the restoration of all who rise will be effected solely by divine power.

Moreover, it is clear that senses once destroyed, and anything possessed as a result of generation, cannot be restored by the activity of nature, for the simple reason that the same numerical being cannot be generated several times. If any such perfection is restored to anyone, for example, an eye that has been torn out or a hand that has been cut off, it will be through divine power which operates beyond the order of nature, as we said above. Therefore, since all the senses and all the members of man corrupt in death, a dead man cannot be brought back to life except by divine action.

The fact that, as we hold, the resurrection will be effected by divine power, enables us to perceive readily how the same numerical body will be revived. Since all things, even the very least, are included under divine providence, as we showed above, the matter composing this human body of ours, whatever form it may take after man's death, evidently does not elude the power or the knowledge of God. Such matter remains numerically the same, in the sense that it exists under quantitative dimensions, by reason of which it can be said to be this particular matter, and is the principle of individuation. If then, this matter remains the same, and if the human body is again fashioned from it by divine power, and if also the rational soul which remains the same in its incorruptibility is united to the same body, the result is that identically the same man is restored to life.

Numerical identity cannot be impeded, as some object, by the consideration that the humanity is not numerically the same as before. In the view of some philosophers, humanity, which is said to be the form of the whole, is nothing else than the form of a part, namely, the soul, and they admit that humanity is the form of the body also, in the sense that it confers species on the whole. If this is true, evidently the humanity remains numerically the same, since the rational soul remains numerically the same.

Humanity, however, is that which is signified by the definition of man, as the essence of anything whatever is that which is signified by its definition. But the definition of man signifies not form alone but also matter, since matter must be comprised in the definition of material things. Hence we shall do better to say, with others, that both soul and body are included in the notion of humanity, although otherwise than in the definition of man. The notion of humanity embraces only the essential principles of man, prescinding from all other factors. For, since humanity is understood to be that whereby man is man, whatever cannot truly be said to constitute man as man, is evidently cut off from the notion of humanity. But when we speak of man, who has humanity, the fact that he has humanity does not exclude the possession of other attributes, for instance, whiteness, and the like. The term "man" signifies man's essential principles, but not to the exclusion of other factors, even though these other factors are not actually, but only potentially, contained in the notion of man. Hence "man" signifies as a whole, *per modum totius*, whereas "humanity" signifies as a part, *per modum partis*, and is not predicated of man. In Socrates, then, or in Plato, this determinate matter and this particular form are included. Just as the notion of man implies composition of matter and form, so if Socrates were to be defined, the notion of him would imply that he is composed of this flesh and these bones and this soul. Consequently, since humanity is not some third form in addition to soul and body, but is composed of both, we see clearly that, if the same body is restored and if the same soul remains, the humanity will be numerically the same.

The numerical identity in question is not frustrated on the ground that the corporeity recovered is not numerically the same, for the reason that it corrupts when the body corrupts. If by corporeity is meant the substantial form by which a thing is classified in the genus of corporeal substance, such corporeity is nothing else than the soul, seeing that there is but one substantial form for each thing. In virtue of this particular soul, this animal is not only animal, but is animated body, and body, and also this thing existing in the genus of substance. Otherwise the soul would come to a body already existing in act, and so would be an accidental form. The subject of a substantial form is something existing only in potency, not in act. When it receives the substantial form it is not said to be generated merely in this or that respect, as is the case with accidental forms, but is said to be generated simply, as simply receiving existence. And therefore the corporeity that is received remains numerically the same, since the same rational soul continues to exist.

If, however, the word "corporeity" is taken to mean a form designating body (*corpus*), which is placed in the genus of quantity, such a form is accidental, since it signifies nothing else than three-dimensional existence. Even though the same numerical form, thus understood, is not recovered, the identity of the subject is not thereby impeded, for unity of the essential principles suffices for this. The same reasoning holds for all the accidents, the diversity among which does not destroy numerical identity. Consequently, since union is a kind of relation, and therefore an accident, its numerical diversity does not prevent the numerical identity of the subject; nor, for that matter, does numerical diversity among the powers of the sensitive and vegetative soul, if they are supposed to have corrupted. For the natural powers existing in the human composite are in the genus of accident; and what we call "sensible" is derived, not from the senses according as sense is the specific difference constituting animal, but from the very substance of the sensitive soul, which in man is essentially identical with the rational soul.

Chapter 155: Resurrection to New Life

Although men will rise as the same individuals, they will not have the same kind of life as before. Now their life is corruptible; then it will be incorruptible. If nature aims at perpetual existence in the generation of man, much more so does God in the restoration of man. Nature's tendency toward never-ending existence comes from an impulse implanted by God. The perpetual existence of the species is not in question in the restoration of risen man, for this could be procured by repeated generation. Therefore what is intended is the perpetual existence of the individual. Accordingly risen men will live forever.

Besides, if men once risen were to die, the souls separated from their bodies would not remain forever deprived of the body, for this would be against the nature of the soul, as we said above. Therefore they would have to rise again; and the same thing would happen if they were to die again after the second resurrection. Thus death and life would revolve around each man in cycles of infinite succession; which seems futile. Surely a halt is better called at the initial stage, so that men might rise to immortal life at the first resurrection.

However, the conquest of mortality will not induce any diversity either in species or in number. The idea of mortality contains nothing that could make it a specific difference of man, since it signifies no more than a passion. It is used to serve as a specific difference of man in the sense that the nature of man is designated by calling him mortal, to bring out the fact that he is composed of contrary elements, just as his proper form is designated by the predicate "rational"; material things cannot be defined without including matter. However, mortality is not overcome by taking away man's proper matter. For the soul will not resume a celestial or ethereal body, as was mentioned above; it will resume a human body made up of contrary elements. Incorruptibility will come as an effect of divine power, whereby the soul will gain dominion over the body to the point that the body cannot corrupt. For a thing continues in being as long as form has dominion over matter.

Chapter 156: Cessation of Nutrition and Reproduction After the Resurrection

When an end is removed, the means leading to that end must also be removed. Therefore, after mortality is done away with in those who have risen, the means serving the condition of mortal life must cease to have any function. Such are food and drink, which are necessary for the sustenance of mortal life, during which what is dissolved by natural heat has to be restored by food. Consequently there will be no consumption of food or drink after the resurrection.

Nor will there be any need of clothing. Clothes are necessary for man so that the body may not suffer harm from heat or cold, which beset him from outside. Likewise, exercise of the reproductive functions, which is designed for the generation of animals, must cease. Generation serves the ends of mortal life, so that what cannot be preserved in the individual may be preserved at least in the species. Since the same individual men will continue in eternal existence, generation will have no place among them; nor, consequently, will the exercise of reproductive power.

Again, since semen is the superfluous part of nourishment, cessation of the use of food necessarily entails cessation of the exercise of the reproductive functions. On the other hand, we cannot maintain with propriety that the use of food, drink, and the reproductive powers will remain solely for the sake of pleasure. Nothing inordinate will occur in that final state, because then all things will receive their perfect consummation, each in its own way. But deordination is opposed to perfection. Also, since the restoration of man through resurrection will be effected directly by God, no deordination will be able to find its way into that state; whatever is from God is well ordered. But desire for the use of food and the exercise of the reproductive powers for pleasure alone, would be inordinate; indeed, even during our present life people regard such conduct as vicious. Among the risen, consequently, the use of food, drink, and the reproductive functions for mere pleasure, can have no place.

Chapter 157: Resurrection of All the Bodily Members

Although risen men will not occupy themselves with activities of this sort, they will not lack the organs requisite for such functions. Without the organs in question the risen body would not be complete. But it is fitting that nature should be completely restored at the renovation of risen man, for such renovation will be accomplished directly by God, whose works are perfect. Therefore all the members of the body will have their place in the risen, for the preservation of nature in its entirety rather than for the exercise of their normal functions.

Moreover, as we shall bring out later, men will receive punishment or reward in that future state for the acts they perform now. This being the case, it is no more than right that men should keep the organs with which they served the reign of sin or of justice during the present life, so that they may be punished or rewarded in the members they employed for sin or for merit.

Chapter 172: Man's Reward or Misery According to His Works

This leads to our next point. If there is a definite way of reaching a fixed end, they who travel along a road leading in the opposite direction or who turn aside from the right road, will never reach the goal. A sick man is not cured by using the wrong medicines, forbidden by the doctor, except, perhaps, quite by accident.

There is such a definite way of arriving at happiness, namely, the practice of virtue. Nothing will reach its end unless it performs well the operations proper to it. A plant will not bear fruit if the procedure natural to it is not followed. A runner will not win a trophy or a soldier a citation, unless each of them carries out his proper functions. To say that a man discharges his proper office is equivalent to saying that he acts virtuously; for the virtue of any being is that which makes its possessor good and also makes his work good, as is stated in the second book of the *Ethics* [Aristotle, II, 6]. Accordingly, since the ultimate end of man is eternal life, of which we spoke previously, not all attain it, but only those who act as virtue requires.

Besides, as we said above, not natural things alone, but also human affairs, are contained under divine providence, and this not only in general but in particular. But He who has care of individual men has disposal of the rewards to be assigned for virtue and of the punishments to be inflicted for sin. For punishment has a medicinal value with regard to sin and restores right order when violated by sin, as we stated above; and the reward of virtue is happiness, to be granted to man by God's goodness. Therefore God will not grant happiness to those who act against virtue, but will assign as punishment the opposite of happiness, namely, extreme wretchedness.

Chapter 173: Reward and Misery Postponed to the Next World

In this matter we should note that contrary causes beget contrary effects. Thus action that proceeds from malice is contrary to action that proceeds from virtue. Accordingly wretchedness, in which evil action issues, is the opposite of happiness, which virtuous action merits. Furthermore, contraries pertain to the same genus. Therefore, since final happiness, which is reached by virtuous action, is a good that belongs not to this life but to the next life, as is clear from an earlier discussion, final wretchedness, also, to which vice leads, must be an evil belonging to the next world.

Besides, all goods and ills of this life are found to serve some purpose. External goods, and also bodily goods, are organically connected with virtue, which is the way leading directly to beatitude, for those who use such goods well. But for those who use these goods ill, they are instruments of vice, which ends up in misery. Similarly the ills opposed to such goods, as sickness, poverty, and the like, are an occasion of progress in virtue for some but aggravate the viciousness of others, according as men react differently to such conditions. But what is ordained to something else cannot be the final end, because it is not the ultimate in reward or punishment. Therefore neither ultimate happiness nor ultimate misery consists in the goods or ills of this life.

Chapter 174: Wretchedness Flowing from the Punishment of Loss

Since the wretchedness to which vice leads is opposed to the happiness to which virtue leads, whatever pertains to wretchedness must be understood as being the opposite of all we have said about happiness. We pointed out above that man's ultimate happiness, as regards his intellect, consists in the unobstructed vision of God. And as regards man's affective life, happiness consists in the immovable repose of his will in the first Good. Therefore man's extreme unhappiness will consist in the fact that his intellect is completely shut off from the divine light, and that his affections are stubbornly turned against God's goodness. And this is the chief suffering of the damned. It is known as the punishment of loss.

However, as should be clear from what we said on a previous occasion, evil cannot wholly exclude good, since every evil has its basis in some good. Consequently, although suffering is opposed to happiness, which will be free from all evil, it must be rooted in a good of nature. The good of an intellectual nature consists in the contemplation of truth by the intellect, and in the inclination to good on the part of the will. But all truth and all goodness are derived from the first and supreme good, which is God. Therefore the intellect of a man situated in the extreme misery of hell must have some knowledge of God and some love of God, but only so far as He is the principle of natural perfections. This is natural love. But the soul in hell cannot know and love God as He is in Himself, nor so far as He is the principle of virtue or of grace and the other goods through which intellectual nature is brought to perfection by Him; for this is the perfection of virtue and glory.

Nevertheless men buried in the misery of hell are not deprived of free choice, even though their will is immovably attached to evil. In the same way the blessed retain the power of free choice, although their will is fixed on the Good. Freedom of choice, properly speaking, has to do with election. But election is concerned with the means leading to an end. The last end is naturally desired by every being. Hence all men, by the very fact that they are intellectual, naturally desire happiness as their last end, and they do so with such immovable fixity of purpose that no one can wish to be unhappy. But this is not incompatible with free will, which extends only to means leading to the end. The fact that one man places his happiness in this particular good while another places it in that good, is not characteristic of either of these men so far as he is a man, since in such estimates and desires men exhibit great differences. This variety is explained by each man's condition. By this I mean each man's acquired passions and habits; and so if a man's condition were to undergo change, some other good would appeal to him as most desirable.

This appears most clearly in men who are led by passion to crave some good as the best. When the passion, whether of anger or lust, dies down, they no longer have the same estimate of that good as they had before.

Habits are more permanent, and so men persevere more obstinately in seeking goods to which habit impels them. Yet, so long as habit is capable of change, man's desire and his judgment as to what constitutes the last end are subject to change. This possibility is open to men only during the present life, in which their state is changeable. After this life the soul is not subject to alteration. No change can affect it except indirectly, in consequence of some change undergone by the body.

However, when the body is resumed, the soul will not be governed by changes occurring in the body. Rather, the contrary will take place. During our present life the soul is infused into a body that has been generated of seed, and therefore, as we should expect, is affected by changes experienced in the body. But in the next world the body will be united to a pre-existing soul, and so will be completely governed by the latter's conditions. Accordingly the soul will remain perpetually in whatever last end it is found to have set for itself at the time of death, desiring that state as the most suitable, whether it is good or evil. This is the meaning of Ecclesiastes 11:3: "If the tree fall to the south or to the north, in what place soever it shall fall, there shall it be." After this life, therefore, those who are found good at the instant of death will have their wills forever fixed in good. But those who are found evil at that moment will be forever obstinate in evil.

Chapter 175: Forgiveness of Sin in the Next World

This enables us to perceive that mortal sins are not forgiven in the next world. But venial sins are forgiven. Mortal sins are committed by turning away from our last end, in which man is irrevocably settled after death, as we have just said. Venial sins, however, do not regard our last end, but rather the road leading to that end.

If the will of evil men is obstinately fettered to evil after death, they forever continue to desire what they previously desired, in the conviction that this is the best. Therefore they are not sorry they have sinned; for no one is sorry he has achieved what he judges to be the best.

But we should understand that those who are condemned to final misery cannot have after death what they craved as the best. Libertines in hell will have no opportunity to gratify their passions; the wrathful and the envious will have no victims to offend or obstruct; and so of all the vices in turn. But the condemned will be aware that men who have lived a virtuous life in conformity with the precepts of virtue obtain what they desired as best. Therefore the wicked regret the sins they have committed, not because sin displeases them, for even in hell they would rather commit those same sins, if they had the chance, than possess God; but because they cannot have what they have chosen, and can have only what they have detested. Hence their will must remain forever obstinate in evil, and at the same time they will grieve most agonizingly for the sins they have committed and the glory they have lost. This anguish is called remorse of conscience, and in Scripture is referred to metaphorically as a worm, as we read in Isaiah 66:24: "Their worm shall not die."

Chapter 176:
Properties of the Bodies of the Damned

As we said above, in speaking of the saints, the beatitude of the soul will in some manner flow over to the body. In the same way the suffering of lost souls will flow over to their bodies. Yet we must observe that suffering does not exclude the good of nature from the body, any more than it does from the soul. Therefore the bodies of the damned will be complete in their kind, although they will not have those qualities that go with the glory of the blessed. That is, they will not be subtle and impassible; instead, they will remain in their grossness and capacity for suffering, and, indeed, these defects will be heightened in them. Nor will they be agile, but will be so sluggish as scarcely to be maneuverable by the soul. Lastly, they will not be radiant but will be ugly in their swarthiness, so that the blackness of the soul may be mirrored in the body, as is intimated in Isaiah 13:8: "Their countenances shall be as faces burnt."

Chapter 177:
Suffering Compatible with Incorruptibility in the Bodies of the Damned

Although the bodies of the damned will be capable of suffering, they will not be subject to corruption. This is a fact we have to admit, even though it may seem to disagree with present experience, according to which heightened suffering tends to deteriorate substance. In spite of this, there are two reasons why suffering that lasts forever will not corrupt the bodies undergoing it.

First, when the movement of the heavens ceases, as we said above, all transformation of nature must come to a stop. Nothing will be capable of alteration in its nature; only the soul will be able to admit some alteration. In speaking of an alteration of nature, I mean, for instance, a change from hot to cold in a thing, or any other such variation in the line of natural qualities. And by alteration of the soul, I mean the modification that takes place when a thing receives a quality, not according to the quality's natural mode of being, but according to its own spiritual mode of being; for example, the pupil of the eye receives the form of a color, not that it may be colored itself, but that it may perceive color. In this way the bodies of the damned will suffer from fire or from some other material agent, not that they may be transformed into the likeness or quality of fire, but that they may experience the effects characteristic of its qualities. And this experience will be painful, because the effects produced by the action of fire are opposed to the harmony in which the pleasure of sense consists. Yet the action of hell-fire will not cause corruption, because spiritual reception of forms does not modify bodily nature, except, it may be, indirectly.

The second reason is drawn from a consideration of the soul, in whose perpetual duration the body will be forced, by divine power, to share. The condemned person's soul, so far as it is the form and nature of such a body, will confer never-ending existence on the latter. But because of its imperfection, the soul will not be able to bestow on the body immunity from suffering. Consequently the bodies of the damned will suffer forever, but will not undergo dissolution.

Chapter 178: Punishment of the Damned Prior to the Resurrection

This discussion makes it clear that both happiness and wretchedness are experienced chiefly in the soul. They affect the body secondarily and by a certain derivation. Hence the happiness or misery of the soul will not depend on the well-being or suffering of the body; rather, the reverse is true. Souls remain in existence after death and prior to the resumption of the body, some adorned with the merit of beatitude, others disfigured by deserved wretchedness. Therefore we can see that even before the resurrection the souls of some men enjoy the happiness of heaven, as the Apostle indicates in 2 Corinthians 5:1: "For we know, if our earthly house of this habitation is dissolved, that we have a building of God, a house not made with hands, eternal in heaven." A little below, in verse 8, he adds: "But we are confident and have a good will to be absent rather from the body and to be present with the Lord." But the souls of some will live in torment, as is intimated in Luke 16:22: "The rich man also died, and he was buried in hell."

Chapter 179: Spiritual and Corporal Punishment of the Damned

We should realize that the happiness enjoyed by the souls of the saints will consist exclusively in spiritual goods. On the other hand, the punishment inflicted on the souls of the damned, even before the resurrection, will not consist solely in spiritual evils, as some have thought; lost souls will also undergo corporal punishment.

The reason for this difference is as follows. When the souls of the saints were united to their bodies here in this world, they observed right order, not subjecting themselves to material things but serving God alone. And so their whole happiness consists in the enjoyment of Him, not in any material goods. But the souls of the wicked, in violation of the order of nature, set their affections on material things, scorning divine and spiritual goods. In consequence, they are punished not only by being deprived of spiritual goods, but by being subjected to the tyranny of material things. Accordingly, if Sacred Scripture is found to promise a reward of material goods to the souls of the saints, such passages are to be interpreted in a mystical sense; for spiritual things are often described in Scripture in terms of their likeness to material things. But texts that portend the corporal punishments of the souls of the damned, specifying that they will be tormented by the fires of hell, are to be understood literally.

Chapter 180: The Soul and Corporeal Fire

The assertion that a soul separated from its body can be tortured by corporeal fire should not seem nonsensical when we reflect that it is not contrary to the nature of a spiritual substance to be confined to a body. This happens in the ordinary course of nature, as we see in the union of the soul with the body. The same effect is sometimes produced by the arts of black magic, by which a spirit is imprisoned in images or amulets or other such objects. The power of God can undoubtedly bring it about that spiritual substances, which are raised above the material world by their nature, may nevertheless be tied down to certain bodies, such as hell-fire; not in the sense that they animate the body in question, but that they are in some way fettered to it. And this very fact, brought home to the consciousness of a spiritual substance, namely, that it is thus subjected to the dominion of a lowly creature, is grievous to it.

Inasmuch as this awareness is distressing to the spiritual substance, the contention that the soul "burns by the very fact that it perceives itself to be in fire" [St. Gregory the Great, *Dialogi*, IV, 29], is substantiated. Thus understood, the fire is plainly spiritual, for what directly causes the distress is the fire apprehended as imprisoning. But inasmuch as the fire in which the spirit is incarcerated is corporeal fire, the further statement made by Gregory is borne out, namely, that "the soul is in agony not only because its perceives, but also because it experiences, the fire."

Furthermore, since this fire has the power of imprisoning the spiritual substance, not of its own nature, but by the might of God, the view is fittingly expressed by some that the fire acts on the soul as an instrument of God's vindictive justice. This does not mean that the fire acts on the spiritual substance as it acts on bodies, by heating, parching, and consuming; its action is restrictive, as we said. And since that which directly afflicts the spiritual substance is the awareness that the fire incarcerates it for its punishment, we can reasonably suppose that the suffering does not cease even if, by God's dispensation, the spiritual substance should happen for a time to be released from the fire. In the same way a criminal who has been sentenced to perpetual irons feels no dimunition of his unremitting pain even though the chains should be struck off for an hour.

Chapter 181: Punishments of Purgatory for Unexpiated Mortal Sins

Although some souls may be admitted to eternal beatitude as soon as they are released from their bodies, others may be held back from this happiness for a time. For it sometimes happens that during their lives people have not done full penance for the sins they have committed, but for which they have been sorry in the end. Since the order of divine justice demands that punishment be undergone for sins, we must hold that souls pay after this life the penalty they have not paid while on earth. This does not mean that they are banished to the ultimate misery of the damned, since by their repentance they have been brought back to the state of charity, whereby they cleave to God as their last end, so that they have merited eternal life. Hence we conclude that there are certain purgatorial punishments after this life, by which the debt of penalty not previously paid is discharged.

Chapter 182: Punishment in Purgatory for Venial Sins

It also happens that some men depart this life free from mortal sin but nevertheless stained with venial sin. The commission of such sins does not, indeed, turn them from their last end; but by committing them they have erred with regard to the means leading to the end, out of undue attachment to those means. In the case of some perfect men sins of this kind are expiated by the fervor of their love. But in others these sins must be atoned for by punishment of some sort; no one is admitted to the possession of eternal life unless he is free from all sin and imperfection. Therefore we must acknowledge the existence of purgatorial punishment after this life.

Such punishments derive their cleansing power from the condition of those who suffer them. For the souls in purgatory are adorned with charity, by which their wills are conformed to the divine will; it is owing to this charity that the punishments they suffer avail them for cleansing.

This is why punishment has no cleansing force in those who lack charity, such as the damned. The defilement of their sin remains forever, and so their punishment endures forever.

Chapter 183: Eternal Punishment for Momentary Sin Not Incompatible with Divine Justice

The suffering of eternal punishment is in no way opposed to divine justice. Even in the laws men make, punishment need not correspond to the offense in point of time. For the crime of adultery or murder, either of which may be committed in a brief span of time, human law may prescribe lifelong exile or even death, by both of which the criminal is banned forever from the society of the state. Exile, it is true, does not last forever, but this is purely accidental, owing to the fact that man's life is not everlasting; but the intention of the judge, we may assume, is to sentence the criminal to perpetual punishment, so far as he can. In the same way it is not unjust for God to inflict eternal punishment for a sin committed in a moment of time.

We should also take into consideration the fact that eternal punishment is inflicted on a sinner who does not repent of his sin, and so he continues in his sin up to his death. And since he is in sin for eternity, he is reasonably punished by God for all eternity. Furthermore, any sin committed against God has a certain infinity when regarded from the side of God, against whom it is committed. For, clearly, the greater the person who is offended, the more grievous is the offense. He who strikes a soldier is held more gravely accountable than if he struck a peasant; and his offense is much more serious if he strikes a prince or a king. Accordingly, since God is infinitely great, an offense committed against Him is in a certain respect infinite; and so a punishment that is in a certain respect infinite is duly attached to it. Such a punishment cannot be infinite in intensity, for nothing created can be infinite in this way. Consequently a punishment that is infinite in duration is rightly inflicted for mortal sin.

Moreover, while a person is still capable of correction, temporal punishment is imposed for his emendation or cleansing. But if a sinner is incorrigible, so that his will is obstinately fixed in sin, as we said above is the case with the damned, his punishment ought never to come to an end.

Chapter 184: The Eternal Lot of Other Spiritual Substances Comparable with That of Souls

In his intellectual nature man resembles the angels, who are capable of sin, as also man is. We spoke of this above. Hence all that has been set forth about the punishment or glory of souls should be understood also of the glory of good angels and the punishment of bad angels. Men and angels exhibit only one point of difference in this regard: the wills of human souls receive confirmation in good or obstinacy in evil when they are separated from their bodies, as was said above; whereas angels were immediately made blessed or eternally wretched as soon as, with full deliberation of will, they fixed upon God or some created good as their end. The variability found in human souls can be accounted for, not only by the liberty of their wills, but also by the modifications their bodies undergo; but in the angels such variability comes from the freedom of will alone. And so angels achieve immutability at the very first choice they make; but souls are not rendered immutable until they leave their bodies.

To express the reward of the good, we say in the Creed: "I believe... in life everlasting." This life is to be understood as eternal not because of its duration alone, but much more because it is the fruition of eternity. Since in this connection there are proposed for our belief many other truths that concern the punishments of the damned and the final state of the world, the Creed of the Fathers sums up the whole doctrine in this proposition: "I look for... the life of the world to come." This phrase, "the world to come," takes in all these points.

Chapter 241: Christ as Judge

We clearly gather from all this, that by the passion and death of Christ and by the glory of His resurrection and ascension, we are freed from sin and death, and have received justice and the glory of immortality, the former in actual fact, the latter in hope. All these events we have mentioned (the passion, the death, the resurrection, and also the ascension) were accomplished in Christ according to His human nature. Therefore we must conclude that Christ has rescued us from spiritual and bodily evils, and has put us in the way of spiritual and eternal goods, by what He suffered or did in His human nature.

He who acquires goods for people also, in consequence, distributes the same to them. But the distribution of goods among many requires judgment, so that each may receive what corresponds to his degree. Therefore Christ, in the human nature in which He has accomplished the mysteries of man's salvation, is fittingly appointed by God to be judge over the men He has saved. We are told that this is so, in John 5:27: "He [the Father] hath given Him [the Son] power to do judgment, because He is the Son of man." There is also another reason. Those who are to be judged ought to see the judge. But the sight of God, in whom the judicial authority resides, in His own proper nature, is the reward that is meted out in the judgment. Hence the men to be judged, the good as well as the wicked, ought to see God as judge, not in His proper nature, but in His assumed nature. If the wicked saw God in His divine nature, they would be receiving the very reward of which they had made themselves unworthy.

Furthermore, the office of judge is a suitable recompense by way of exaltation, corresponding to the humiliation of Christ, who was willing to be humiliated to the point of being unjustly judged by a human judge. To give expression to our belief in this humiliation, we say explicitly in the Creed, that He suffered under Pontius Pilate. Therefore this exalted reward of being appointed by God to judge all men, the living and the dead, in His human nature, was due to Christ, according to Job 36:17: "Your cause hath been judged as that of the wicked. Cause and judgment You shall recover."

Moreover, since this judicial power pertains to Christ's exaltation, as does the glory of His resurrection, Christ will appear at the judgment, not in humility, which belonged to the time of merit, but in the glorious form that is indicative of His reward. We are assured in the Gospel that "they shall see the Son of man coming in a cloud with great power and majesty" (Luke 21:27). And the sight of His glory will be a joy to the elect who have loved Him; to these is made the promise, in Isaiah 33:17, that they "shall see the King in His beauty." But to the wicked this sight will mean confusion and lamentation, for the glory and power of the judge will bring grief and dread to those who fear damnation. We read of this in Isaiah 26:11: "Let the envious see and be confounded, and let fire devour your enemies."

Although Christ will show Himself in His glorious form, the marks of the Passion will appear in Him, not with disfigurement, but with beauty and splendor, so that at the sight of them the elect, who will perceive that they have been saved through the sufferings of Christ, will be filled with joy; but sinners, who have scorned so great a benefit, will be filled with dismay. Thus we read in the Apocalypse 1:7: "Every eye shall see Him, they also who pierced Him. And all the tribes of the earth shall mourn because of Him."

Chapter 242:
All Judgement Given to the Son

Since the Father "has given all judgment to the Son," as is said in John 5:22, and since human life even at present is regulated by the just judgment of God—for it is He who judges all flesh, as Abraham declared in Genesis 18:25—we cannot doubt that this judgment, by which men are governed in the world, pertains likewise to the judicial power of Christ. To Him are directed the words of the Father reported in Psalm 109:1: "Sit Thou at My right hand, until I make Thy enemies Thy footstool." He sits at the right hand of God according to His human nature, inasmuch as He receives His judicial power from the Father. And this power He exercises even now before all His enemies are clearly seen to lie prostrate at His feet. He Himself bore witness to this fact shortly after His resurrection, in Matthew 28:18: "All power is given to Me in heaven and on earth."

There is another judgment of God whereby, at the moment of death, everyone receives, as regards his soul, the recompense he has deserved. The just who have been dissolved in death remain with Christ, as Paul desired for himself; but sinners who have died are buried in hell. We may not suppose that this division takes place without God's judgment, or that this judgment does not pertain to the judicial power of Christ, especially as He Himself tells His disciples in John 14:3: "If I shall go and prepare a place for you, I will come again and will take you to Myself, that where I am, you also may be." To be taken in this way means nothing else than to be dissolved in death, so that we may be with Christ; for "while we are in the body we are absent from the Lord," as is said in 2 Corinthians 5:6.

However, since man's recompense is not confined to goods of the soul, but embraces goods of the body which is again to be resumed by the soul at the resurrection, and since every recompense requires judgment, there has to be another judgment by which men are rewarded for what they have done in the body as well as for what they have done in the soul. This judgment, too, belongs rightfully to Christ, in order that, as He rose and ascended into heaven in glory after dying for us, He may also by His own power cause the bodies of our lowliness to rise again in the likeness of His glorified body, and may transport them up to heaven where He has preceded us by His ascension, thus opening the way before us, as had been foretold by Micah. This resurrection of all men will take place simultaneously at the end of the world, as we have already indicated. Therefore this judgment will be a general and final judgment, and we believe that Christ will come a second time, in glory, to preside at it.

In Psalm 35:7 we read: "Thy judgments are a great deep"; and in Romans 11:33 the Apostle exclaims: "How incomprehensible are His judgments!" Each of the judgments mentioned contains something profound and incomprehensible to human knowledge. In the first of God's judgments, by which the present life of mankind is regulated, the time of the judgment is, indeed, manifest to men, but the reason for the recompenses is concealed, especially as evils for the most part are the lot of the good in this world, while good things come to the wicked. In the other two judgments of God the reason for the requitals will be clearly known, but the time remains hidden, because man does not know the hour of his death, as is noted in Ecclesiastes 9:12: "Man does not know his own end"; and no one can know the end of this world. For we do not foreknow future events, except those whose causes we understand. But the cause of the end of the world is the will of God, which is unknown to us. Therefore the end of the world can be foreseen by no creature, but only by God, according to Matthew 24:36: "Of that day and hour no one knows, not even the angels of heaven, but the Father alone."

In this connection, some have found an occasion for going astray in the added words, "nor the Son," which are read in Mark 13:32. They contend that the Son is inferior to the Father, on the score that He is ignorant of matters which the Father knows. The difficulty could be avoided by replying that the Son is ignorant of this event in His assumed human nature, but not in His divine nature, in which He has one and the same wisdom as the Father or, to speak with greater propriety, He is wisdom itself intellectually conceived. But the Son could hardly be unaware of the divine judgment even in His assumed nature, since His soul, as the Evangelist attests, is full of God's grace and truth, as was pointed out above. Nor does it seem reasonable that Christ, who has received the power to judge "because He is the Son of man" (John 5:27), should be ignorant in His human nature of the time appointed for Him to judge. The Father would not really have given all judgment to Him, if the judgment of determining the time of His coming were withheld from Him.

Accordingly this text is to be interpreted in the light of the usual style of speech found in the Scriptures, in which God is said to know a thing when He imparts knowledge of that thing, as when He said to Abraham, in Genesis 22:12: "Now I know that you fear God." The meaning is not that He who knows all things from eternity began to know at that moment, but that He made known Abraham's devotedness by that declaration. In a similar way the Son is said to be ignorant of the day of judgment, because He did not impart that knowledge to the disciples, but replied to them in Acts 1:7: "It is not for you to know the times or moments which the Father hath put in His own power." But the Father is not ignorant in this way, since in any case He gave knowledge of the matter to the Son through the eternal generation. Some authors extricate themselves from the difficulty in fewer words, saying that Mark's expression is to be understood of an adopted son.

However that may be, the Lord wished the time of the future judgment to remain hidden, that men might watch with care so as not to be found unprepared at the hour of judgment. For the same reason He also wished the hour of each one's death to be unknown. For each man will appear at the judgment in the state in which he departs from this world by death. Therefore the Lord admonishes us in Matthew 24:42: "Watch ye therefore, because you know not what hour your Lord will come."

Chapter 243:
Universality of the Judgement

According to the doctrine thus set forth, Christ clearly has judicial power over the living and the dead. He exercises judgment both over those who are living in the world at present and over those who pass from this world by death. At the Last Judgment, however, He will judge the living and the dead together. In this expression the living may be taken to mean the just who live by grace, and the dead may be taken to mean sinners who have fallen from grace. Or else by the living may be meant those who will be found still alive at the Lord's coming, and by the dead those who have died in previous ages.

We are not to understand by this that certain of the living will be judged without ever having undergone death of the body, as some have argued. For the Apostle says clearly, in 1 Corinthinans 15:51: "We shall all indeed rise again." Another reading has: "We shall indeed sleep," that is, we shall die; or, according to some books, "We shall not indeed all sleep," as Jerome notes in his letter to Minervius on the resurrection of the body. But this variant does not destroy the force of the doctrine under discussion. For a little previously the Apostle had written: "As in Adam all die, so also in Christ all shall be made alive" (1 Cor. 15:22). Hence the text which reads: "We shall not all sleep," cannot refer to death of the body, which has come down to all through the sin of our first parent, as is stated in Romans 5:12, but must be interpreted as referring to the sleep of sin, concerning which we are exhorted in Ephesians 5:14: "Rise, you who sleep, and arise from the dead: and Christ shall enlighten you."

Accordingly those who are found alive at the Lord's coming will be marked off from those who have died before, not for the reason that they will never die, but because in the very act by which they are taken up "in the clouds to meet Christ, into the air" (1 Thessalonians 4:16), they will die and immediately rise again, as Augustine teaches.

In discussing this matter, we must take cognizance of the three phases which, apparently, constitute a judicial process. First, someone is haled into court; secondly, his cause is examined; and thirdly, he receives sentence.

As to the first phase, all men, good and evil, from the first man down to the very last, will be subject to Christ's judgment, for, as we are told in 2 Corinthians 5:10, "We must all be manifested before the judgment seat of Christ." Not even those who have died in infancy, whether they were baptized or not, are exempt from this universal law, as the Glossary on this text explains.

With regard to the second phase, namely, the examination of the case, not all, either of the good or of the wicked, will be judged. A judicial investigation is not necessary unless good and evil actions are intermingled. When good is present without admixture of evil, or evil without admixture of good, discussion is out of place. Among the good there are some who have wholeheartedly despised temporal possessions, and have dedicated themselves to God alone and to the things that are of God. Accordingly, since sin is committed by cleaving to changeable goods in contempt of the changeless Good, such souls exhibit no mingling of good and evil. This is not to imply that they live without sin, for in their person is asserted what we read in 1 John 1:8: "If we say that we have no sin, we deceive ourselves." Although certain lesser sins are found in them, these are, so to speak, consumed by the fire of charity, and so seem to be nothing. At the judgment, therefore, such souls will not be judged by an investigation of their deeds.

On the other hand, those who lead an earthly life and in their preoccupation with things of this world use them, not indeed against God, but with excessive attachment to them, have a notable amount of evil mixed up with the good of faith and charity, so that the element predominating in them cannot easily be perceived. Such souls will undergo judgment by an examination of their merits.

Similarly, with reference to the wicked, we should recall that the principle of approach to God is faith, according to Hebrews 11:6: "He that cometh to God must believe." Therefore in him who lacks faith there is found nothing of good which, mixed with evil, might render his damnation doubtful. And so such a one will be condemned without any inquiry into merits. Again, he who has faith but has no charity and, consequently, no good works, possesses, indeed, some point of contact with God. Hence an examination of his case is necessary, so that the element predominating in him, whether good or evil, may clearly emerge. Such a person will be condemned only after an investigation of his case. In the same way an earthly king condemns a criminal citizen after hearing him, but punishes an enemy without any hearing.

Lastly, with regard to the third phase of a judgment, that is, the pronouncement of the sentence, all will be judged, for all will receive glory or punishment in accord with the sentence. The reason is given in 2 Corinthians 5:10: "That every one may receive the proper things of the body, according as he hath done, whether it be good or evil."

Chapter 244: Procedure and Place of the Judgement

We are not to suppose that judicial examination will be required in order that the judge may receive information, as is the case in human courts; for "all things are naked and open to His eyes," as we are told in Hebrews 4:13. The examination is necessary for the purpose of making known to each person, concerning himself and others, the reasons why each is worthy of punishment or of glory, so that the good may joyfully acknowledge God's justice in all things and the wicked may be roused to anger against themselves.

Nor should we imagine that this examination is to be conducted by oral discussion. Endless time would be required to recount the thoughts, words, and deeds, good or evil, of each person. Therefore Lactantius was deceived when he suggested that the day of judgment would last a thousand years. Even this time would scarcely be enough, as several days would be required to complete the judicial process for a single man in the manner proposed. Accordingly the divine power will bring it about that in an instant everyone will be apprised of all the good or evil he has ever done, for which he is to be rewarded or punished. And all this will be made known to each person, not only about himself, but also about the rest. Hence, wherever the good is so much in excess that the evil seems to be of no consequence or vice versa, there will seem, to human estimation, to be no conflict between the good and the evil. This is what we meant when we said that such persons will be rewarded or punished without examination.

Although all men will appear before Christ at that judgment, the good will not only be set apart from the wicked by reason of meritorious cause, but will be separated from them in locality. The wicked, who have withdrawn from Christ in their love of earthly things, will remain on earth; but the good, who have clung to Christ, will be raised up into the air when they go to meet Christ, that they may be made like Christ, not only by being conformed to the splendor of His glory, but by being associated with Him in the place He occupies. This is indicated in Matthew 24:28: "Wheresoever the body shall be, there shall the eagles also (by which the saints are signified) be gathered together." According to Jerome [*In Evangelium Matthaei*, IV], instead of "body" the Hebrew has the significant word "joatham," which means corpse, to commemorate Christ's passion, whereby Christ merited the power to judge, and men who have been conformed to His passion are admitted into the company of His glory, as we are told by the Apostle in 2 Timothy 2:12: "If we suffer, we shall also reign with Him."

This is the ground for our belief that Christ will come down to judge somewhere near the place of His passion, as is intimated in Joel 3:2: "I will gather together all nations and will bring them down into the valley of Josaphat; and I will plead with them there." This valley lies at the foot of Mount Olivet, from which Christ ascended into heaven. For the same reason, when Christ comes for the judgment, the sign of the cross and other signs of the Passion will be displayed, as is said in Matthew 24:30: "And then shall appear the sign of the Son of man in heaven," so that the wicked, looking upon Him whom they have pierced, will be distressed and tormented, and those who have been redeemed will exult in the glory of their Redeemer. And as Christ is said to sit at God's right hand according to His human nature, inasmuch as He has been lifted up to share in the most excellent goods of the Father, so at the judgment the just are said to stand at Christ's right, as being entitled to the most honorable place near Him.

Chapter 245:
Role of the Saints in the Judgement

Christ will not be the only one to judge on that day; others will be associated with Him. Of these, some will judge only in the sense of serving as a basis for comparison. In this way the good will judge the less good, or the wicked will judge the more wicked, according to Matthew 12:41: "The men of Nineveh shall rise in judgment with this generation and shall condemn it." And some will judge by giving their approval to the sentence; in this way all the just shall judge, according to Wisdom 3:7 ff: "The just... shall judge nations." But some will judge with a certain judicial power delegated to them by Christ, having "two-edged swords in their hands," as is indicated in Psalm 149:6.

This last kind of judicial power the Lord promised to the apostles, in Matthew 19:28, when He said: "You who have followed Me, in the regeneration, when the Son of man shall sit on the seat of His majesty you also shall sit on twelve seats, judging the twelve tribes of Israel." We are not to conclude from this that only the Jews who belong to the twelve tribes of Israel will be judged by the apostles, for by the twelve tribes of Israel are understood all the faithful who have been admitted to the faith of the patriarchs. As for infidels, they will not be judged, but have already been judged.

Similarly, the twelve apostles who walked with Christ during His earthly life are not the only ones who will judge. Judas assuredly will not judge, and Paul, on the other hand, who labored more than the rest, will not lack judicial power, especially as he himself says, 1 Corinthians 6:3: "Know you not that we shall judge angels?" This dignity pertains properly to those who have left all to follow Christ, for such was the promise made to Peter in answer to his question in Matthew 19:27: "Behold, we have left all things and have followed Thee; what therefore shall we have?" The same thought occurs in Job 36:6: "He gives judgment to the poor."

And this is reasonable, because, as we said, the investigation will deal with the actions of men who have used earthly things well or ill. Correctness of judgment requires that the mind of the judge should be unswayed by those matters about which he has to judge; and so the fact that some have their minds completely detached from earthly things gives them a title to judicial authority.

The announcing of the divine commandments also contributes to the meriting of this dignity. In Matthew 25:31 we read that Christ will come to judge accompanied by angels, that is, by preachers, as Augustine suggests in a work on penance [Sermo 351, *De utilitate agendae poenitentiae*]. For they who have made known the precepts of life ought to have a part in examining the actions of men regarding the observance of the divine precepts.

The persons mentioned will judge by cooperating in the task of revealing to each individual the cause of the salvation or damnation both of himself and of others, in the way that higher angels are said to illuminate the lower angels and also men.

We profess that this judicial power belongs to Christ when we say, in the Apostles' Creed: "From thence He shall come to judge the living and the dead."

Chapter 246: The Foregoing Teachings Comprised in Articles of Faith

Having reviewed the doctrines pertaining to the truth of the Christian faith, we should advert to the fact that all the teachings thus set forth are reduced to certain articles: twelve in number, as some think, or fourteen, according to others.

Faith has to do with truths that surpass the comprehension of reason. Hence, whenever a new truth incomprehensible to reason is proposed, a new article is required. One article pertains to the divine unity. For, even though we prove by reason that God is one, the fact that He governs all things directly or that He wishes to be worshiped in some particular way, is a matter relating to faith. Three articles are reserved for the three divine persons. Three other articles are formulated about the effects produced by God: creation, which pertains to nature; justification, which pertains to grace; and reward, which pertains to glory. Thus seven articles altogether are devoted to the divinity.

Concerning the humanity of Christ, seven more are proposed. The first is on the incarnation and conception of Christ. The second deals with the nativity, which involves a special difficulty because of our Lord's coming forth from the closed womb of the Virgin. The third article is on the death, passion, and burial; the fourth on the descent into hell; the fifth on the resurrection; the sixth on the ascension; and the seventh treats of Christ's coming for the judgment. And so there are fourteen articles in all.

Other authorities, reasonably enough, include faith in the three persons under one article, on the ground that we cannot believe in the Father without believing in the Son and also in the Holy Spirit, the bond of love uniting the first two persons. However, they distinguish the article on the resurrection from the article on eternal reward. Accordingly, there are two articles about God, one on the unity, the other on the Trinity. Four articles deal with God's effects: one with creation, the second with justification, the third with the general resurrection, and the fourth with reward. Similarly, as regards belief in the humanity of Christ, these authors comprise the conception and the nativity under one article, and they also include the passion and death under one article. According to this way of reckoning, therefore, we have twelve articles in all.

And this should be enough on faith.

Dante's Cosmology

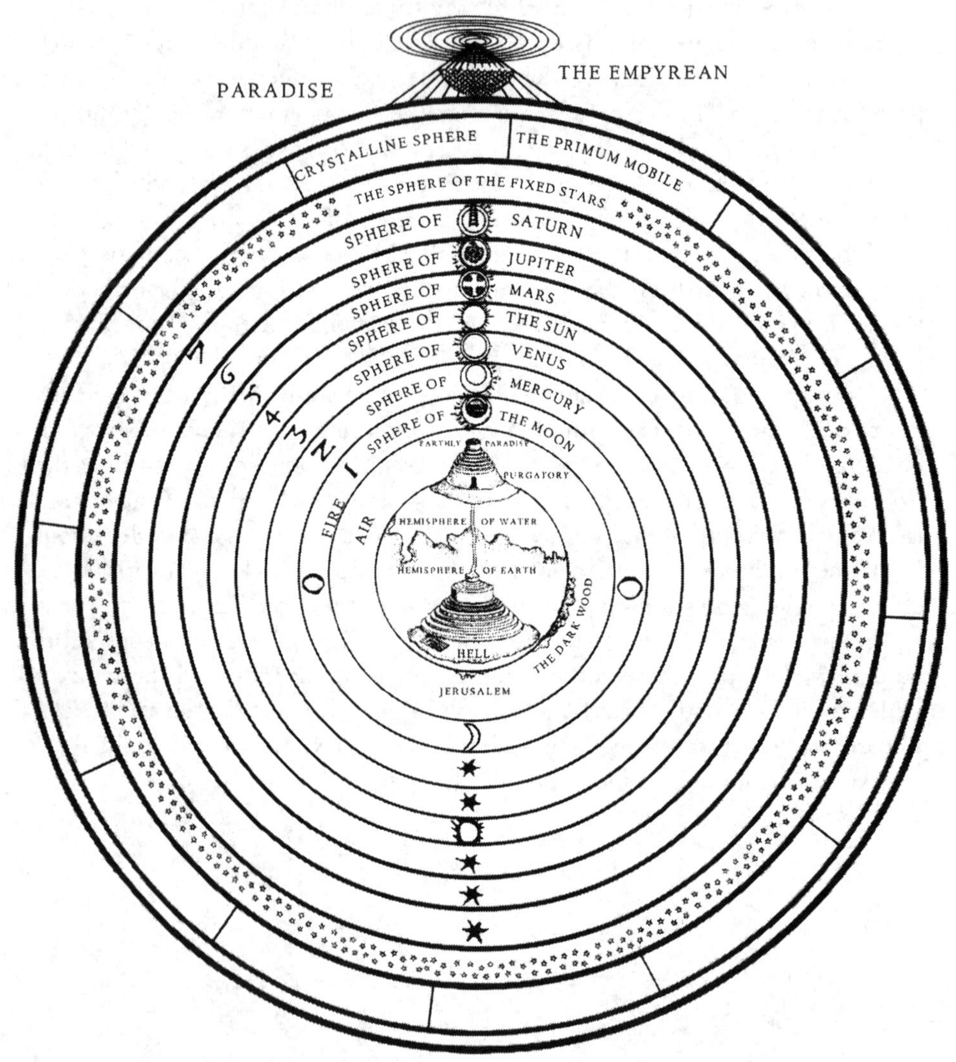

The Divine Comedy

Dante Alighieri

Translated by Henry Wadsworth Longfellow

MIDWAY upon the journey of our life
I found myself within a forest dark.

Gustave Doré

Inferno

Canto I

MIDWAY upon the journey of our life
I found myself within a forest dark,
For the straightforward pathway had been lost.

4 Ah me! how hard a thing it is to say
What was this forest savage, rough, and stern,
Which in the very thought renews the fear.

7 So bitter is it, death is little more;
But of the good to treat, which there I found,
Speak will I of the other things I saw there.

10 I cannot well repeat how there I entered,
So full was I of slumber at the moment
In which I had abandoned the true way.

13 But after I had reached a mountain's foot,
At that point where the valley terminated,
Which had with consternation pierced my heart,

16 Upward I looked, and I beheld its shoulders
Vested already with that planet's rays
Which leadeth others right by every road.

19 Then was the fear a little quieted
That in my heart's lake had endured throughout
The night, which I had passed so piteously

22 And even as he, who, with distressful breath,
Forth issued from the sea upon the shore,
Turns to the water perilous and gazes;

25 So did my soul, that still was fleeing onward,
Turn itself back to re-behold the pass
Which never yet a living person left.

28 After my weary body I had rested,
The way resumed I on the desert slope,
So that the firm foot ever was the lower.

31 And lo! almost where the ascent began,
A panther light and swift exceedingly,
Which with a spotted skin was covered o'er!

34 And never moved she from before my face,
Nay, rather did impede so much my way,
That many times I to return had turned.

37 The time was the beginning of the morning,
And up the sun was mounting with those stars
That with him were, what time the Love Divine

40 At first in motion set those beauteous things;
So were to me occasion of good hope,
The variegated skin of that wild beast,

43 The hour of time, and the delicious season;
But not so much, that did not give me fear
A lion's aspect which appeared to me.

46 He seemed as if against me he were coming
With head uplifted, and with ravenous hunger,
So that it seemed the air was afraid of him;

49 And a she-wolf, that with all hungerings
Seemed to be laden in her meagreness,
And many folk has caused to live forlorn!

52 She brought upon me so much heaviness,
With the affright that from her aspect came,
That I the hope relinquished of the height.

55 And as he is who willingly acquires,
And the time comes that causes him to lose,
Who weeps in all his thoughts and is despondent,

58 E'en such made me that beast withouten peace,
Which, coming on against me by degrees
Thrust me back thither where the sun is silent

61 While I was rushing downward to the lowland,
Before mine eyes did one present himself,

Who seemed from long-continued silence hoarse.

64 When I beheld him in the desert vast,
"Have pity on me," unto him I cried,
"Whiche'er thou art, or shade or real man!"

67 He answered me: "Not man; man once I was,
And both my parents were of Lombardy,
And Mantuans by country both of them.

70 Sub Julio was I born, though it was late,
And lived at Rome under the good Augustus,
During the time of false and lying gods.

73 A poet was I, and I sang that just
Son of Anchises, who came forth from Troy,
After that Ilion the superb was burned

76 But thou, why goest thou back to such annoyance?
Why climb'st thou not the Mount Delectable
Which is the source and cause of every joy?"

79 "Now, art thou that Virgilius and that fountain
Which spreads abroad so wide a river of speech?"
I made response to him with bashful forehead.

82 "O, of the other poets honour and light,
Avail me the long study and great love
That have impelled me to explore thy volume!

85 Thou art my master, and my author thou,
Thou art alone the one from whom I took
The beautiful style that has done honour to me.

88 Behold the beast, for which I have turned back;
Do thou protect me from her, famous Sage,
For she doth make my veins and pulses tremble."

91 "Thee it behoves to take another road,"
Responded he, when he beheld me weeping,
"If from this savage place thou wouldst escape;

94 Because this beast, at which thou criest out,
Suffers not any one to pass her way,
But so doth harass him, that she destroys him;

97 And has a nature so malign and ruthless,

That never doth she glut her greedy will,
And after food is hungrier than before.

100 Many the animals with whom she weds,
And more they shall be still, until the Greyhound
Comes, who shall make her perish in her pain.

103 He shall not feed on either earth or pelf,
But upon wisdom, and on love and virtue;
'Twixt Feltro and Feltro shall his nation be;

106 Of that low Italy shall he be the saviour,
On whose account the maid Camilla died,
Euryalus, Turnus, Nisus, of their wounds;

109 Through every city shall he hunt her down,
Until he shall have driven her back to Hell,
There from whence envy first did let her loose.

112 Therefore I think and judge it for thy best
Thou follow me, and I will be thy guide,
And lead thee hence through the eternal place,

115 Where thou shalt hear the desperate lamentations,
Shalt see the ancient spirits disconsolate,
Who cry out each one for the second death;

118 And thou shalt see those who contented are
Within the fire, because they hope to come,
Whene'er it may be, to the blessed people;

121 To whom, then, if thou wishest to ascend,
A soul shall be for that than I more worthy;
With her at my departure I will leave thee;

124 Because that Emperor, who reigns above,
In that I was rebellious to his law,
Wills that through me none come into his city.

127 He governs evervwhere and there he reigns:
There is his city and his lofty throne;
O happy he whom thereto he elects!"

130 And I to him: "Poet, I thee entreat,
By that same God whom thou didst never know,
So that I may escape this woe and worse,

133 Thou wouldst conduct me there where thou hast said,
That I may see the portal of Saint Peter,
And those thou makest so disconsolate."

136 Then he moved on, and I behind him followed.

Then he moved on, and I behind him followed.

Gustave Doré

Canto II

DAY was departing, and the embrowned air
Released the animals that are on earth
From their fatigues; and I the only one

Made myself ready to sustain the war,
Both of the way and likewise of the woe,
Which memory that errs not shall retrace.

O Muses, O high genius, now assist me!
O memory, that didst write down what I saw,
Here thy nobility shall be manifest!

And I began: "Poet, who guidest me,
Regard my manhood, if it be sufficient.
Ere to the arduous pass thou dost confide me.

Thou sayest, that of Silvius the parent,
While yet corruptible, unto the world
Immortal went, and was there bodily.

But if the adversary of all evil
Was courteous, thinking of the high effect
That issue would from him, and who, and what,

To men of intellect unmeet it seems not;
For he was of great Rome, and of her empire
In the empyreal heaven as father chosen;

The which and what, wishing to speak the truth,
Were stablished as the holy place, wherein
Sits the successor of the greatest Peter.

Upon this journey, whence thou givest him vaunt,
Things did he hear, which the occasion were
Both of his victory and the papal mantle.

Thither went afterwards the Chosen Vessel,
To bring back comfort thence unto that Faith,
Which of salvation's way is the beginning.

But I, why thither come, or who concedes it?
I not Aeneas am, I am not Paul,
Nor I, nor others, think me worthy of it.

34 Therefore, if I resign myself to come,
I fear the coming may be ill-advised;
Thou'rt wise, and knowest better than I speak."

37 And as he is, who unwills what he willed,
And by new thoughts doth his intention change,
So that from his design he quite withdraws,

40 Such I became, upon that dark hillside,
Because, in thinking, I consumed the emprise,
Which was so very prompt in the beginning.

43 "If I have well thy language understood,"
Replied that shade of the Magnanimous,
"Thy soul attainted is with cowardice,

46 Which many times a man encumbers so,
It turns him back from honoured enterprise,
As false sight doth a beast, when he is shy.

49 That thou mayst free thee from this apprehension,
I'll tell thee why I came, and what I heard
At the first moment when I grieved for thee.

52 Among those was I who are in suspense,
And a fair, saintly Lady called to me
In such wise, I besought her to command me.

55 Her eyes where shining brighter than the Star;
And she began to say, gentle and low,
With voice angelical, in her own language

58 'O spirit courteous of Mantua,
Of whom the fame still in the world endures,
And shall endure, long-lasting as the world;

61 A friend of mine, and not the friend of fortune,
Upon the desert slope is so impeded
Upon his way, that he has turned through terror,

64 And may, I fear, already be so lost,
That I too late have risen to his succour,
From that which I have heard of him in Heaven.

67 Bestir thee now, and with thy speech ornate,

And with what needful is for his release,
Assist him so, that I may be consoled.

Beatrice am I, who do bid thee go;
I come from there, where I would fain return;
Love moved me, which compelleth me to speak.

When I shall be in presence of my Lord,
Full often will I praise thee unto him.'
Then paused she, and thereafter I began:

'O Lady of virtue, thou alone through whom
The human race exceedeth all contained
Within the heaven that has the lesser circles,

So grateful unto me is thy commandment,
To obey, if 'twere already done, were late;
No farther need'st thou ope to me thy wish.

But the cause tell me why thou dost not shun
The here descending down into this centre,
From the vast place thou burnest to return to.'

'Since thou wouldst fain so inwardly discern,
Briefly will I relate,' she answered me,
'Why I am not afraid to enter here.

Of those things only should one be afraid
Which have the power of doing others harm;
Of the rest, no; because they are not fearful.

God in his mercy such created me
That misery of yours attains me not,
Nor any flame assails me of this burning

A gentle Lady is in Heaven, who grieves
At this impediment, to which I send thee,
So that stern judgment there above is broken.

In her entreaty she besought Lucia,
And said, "Thy faithful one now stands in need
Of thee, and unto thee I recommend him."

Lucia, a foe of all that cruel is,
Hastened away, and came unto the place
Where I was sitting with the ancient Rachel.

Beatrice am I, who do bid thee go.

Gustave Doré

103 “Beatrice” said she, “the true praise of God,
Why succourest thou not him, who loved thee so,
For thee he issued from the vulgar herd?

106 Dost thou not hear the pity of his plaint?
Dost thou not see the death that combats him
Beside that flood, where ocean has no vaunt?”

109 Never were persons in the world so swift
To work their weal and to escape their woe,
As I, after such words as these were uttered,

112 Came hither downward from my blessed seat
Confiding in thy dignified discourse,
Which honours thee, and those who’ve listened to it.’

115 After she thus had spoken unto me,
Weeping, her shining eyes she turned away;
Whereby she made me swifter in my coming;

118 And unto thee I came, as she desired;
I have delivered thee from that wild beast,
Which barred the beautiful mountain’s short ascent.

121 What is it, then? Why, why dost thou delay?
Why is such baseness bedded in thy heart?
Daring and hardihood why hast thou not,

124 Seeing that three such Ladies benedight
Are caring for thee in the court of Heaven,
And so much good my speech doth promise thee?”

127 Even as the flowerets, by nocturnal chill,
Bowed down and closed, when the sun whitens them,
Uplift themselves all open on their stems;

130 Such I became with my exhausted strength,
And such good courage to my heart there coursed,
That I began, like an intrepid person:

133 “O she compassionate, who succoured me,
And courteous thou, who hast obeyed so soon
The words of truth which she addressed to thee!

136 Thou hast my heart so with desire disposed

To the adventure, with these words of thine,
That to my first intent I have returned.

139 Now go, for one sole will is in us both,
Thou Leader, and thou Lord, and Master thou."
Thus said I to him; and when he had moved,

142 I entered on the deep and savage way.

Canto III

"THROUGH me the way is to the city dolent;
Through me the way is to eternal dole;
Through me the way among the people lost.

4 Justice incited my sublime Creator;
Created me divine Omnipotence,
The highest Wisdom and the primal Love.

7 Before me there were no created things,
Only eterne, and I eternal last.
All hope abandon, ye who enter in!"

10 These words in sombre colour I beheld
Written upon the summit of a gate;
Whence I: "Their sense is, Master, hard to me!"

13 And he to me, as one experienced:
"Here all suspicion needs must be abandoned,
All cowardice must needs be here extinct.

16 We to the place have come, where I have told thee
Thou shalt behold the people dolorous
Who have foregone the good of intellect."

19 And after he had laid his hand on mine
With joyful mien, whence I was comforted,
He led me in among the secret things.

22 There sighs, complaints, and ululations loud
Resounded through the air without a star,
Whence I, at the beginning, wept thereat.

25 Languages diverse, horrible dialects,
Accents of anger, words of agony,
And voices high and hoarse, with sound of hands,

28 Made up a tumult that goes whirling on
For ever in that air for ever black,
Even as the sand doth, when the whirlwind breathes.

31 And I, who had my head with horror bound,
Said: "Master, what is this which now I hear?
What folk is this, which seems by pain so vanquished?"

34 And he to me: "This miserable mode
Maintain the melancholy souls of those
Who lived withouten infamy or praise.

37 Commingled are they with that caitiff choir
Of Angels, who have not rebellious been,
Nor faithful were to God, but were for self.

40 The heavens expelled them, not to be less fair;
Nor them the nethermore abyss receives,
For glory none the damned would have from them."

43 And I: "O Master, what so grievous is
To these, that maketh them lament so sore?"
He answered: "I will tell thee very briefly.

46 These have no longer any hope of death;
And this blind life of theirs is so debased,
They envious are of every other fate.

49 No fame of them the world permits to be;
Misericord and Justice both disdain them.
Let us not speak of them, but look, and pass."

52 And I, who looked again, beheld a banner,
Which, whirling round, ran on so rapidly,
That of all pause it seemed to me indignant;

55 And after it there came so long a train
Of people, that I ne'er would have believed
That ever Death so many had undone.

58 When some among them I had recognised.
I looked, and I beheld the shade of him

Who made through cowardice the great refusal.

61 Forthwith I comprehended, and was certain,
That this the sect was of the caitiff wretches
Hateful to God and to his enemies.

64 These miscreants, who never were alive,
Were naked, and were stung exceedingly
By gadflies and by hornets that were there.

67 These did their faces irrigate with blood,
Which, with their tears commingled, at their feet
By the disgusting worms was gathered up.

70 And when to gazing farther I betook me,
People I saw on a great river's bank;
Whence said I: "Master, now vouchsafe to me,

73 That I may know who these are, and what law
Makes them appear so ready to pass over,
As I discern athwart the dusky light."

76 And he to me: "These things shall all be known
To thee, as soon as we our footsteps stay
Upon the dismal shore of Acheron."

79 Then with mine eyes ashamed and downward cast,
Fearing my words might irksome be to him,
From speech refrained I till we reached the river.

82 And lo! towards us coming in a boat
An old man, hoary with the hair of eld,
Crying: "Woe unto you, ye souls depraved

85 Hope nevermore to look upon the heavens;
I come to lead you to the other shore,
To the eternal shades in heat and frost.

88 And thou, that yonder standest, living soul,
Withdraw thee from these people, who are dead!"
But when he saw that I did not withdraw,

91 He said: "By other ways, by other ports
Thou to the shore shalt come, not here, for passage;
A lighter vessel needs must carry thee."

And lo! towards us coming in a boat
An old man, hoary with the hair of eld,
Crying: Woe unto you, ye souls depraved

Gustave Doré

94 And unto him the Guide: "Vex thee not, Charon;
It is so willed there where is power to do
That which is willed; and farther question not."

97 Thereat were quieted the fleecy cheeks
Of him the ferryman of the livid fen,
Who round about his eyes had wheels of flame.

100 But all those souls who weary were and naked
Their colour changed and gnashed their teeth together,
As soon as they had heard those cruel words.

103 God they blasphemed and their progenitors,
The human race, the place, the time, the seed
Of their engendering and of their birth!

106 Thereafter all together they drew back,
Bitterly weeping, to the accursed shore,
Which waiteth every man who fears not God.

109 Charon the demon, with the eyes of glede,
Beckoning to them, collects them all together,
Beats with his oar whoever lags behind.

112 As in the autumn-time the leaves fall off,
First one and then another, till the branch
Unto the earth surrenders all its spoils;

115 In similar wise the evil seed of Adam
Throw themselves from that margin one by one,
At signals, as a bird unto its lure.

118 So they depart across the dusky wave,
And ere upon the other side they land,
Again on this side a new troop assembles.

121 "My son," the courteous Master said to me,
"All those who perish in the wrath of God
Here meet together out of every land;

124 And ready are they to pass o'er the river,
Because celestial Justice spurs them on,
So that their fear is turned into desire.

127 This way there never passes a good soul;

And hence if Charon doth complain of thee
Well mayst thou know now what his speech imports."

130 This being finished, all the dusk champaign
Trembled so violently, that of that terror
The recollection bathes me still with sweat.

133 The land of tears gave forth a blast of wind,
And fulminated a vermilion light,
Which overmastered in me every sense,

136 And as a man whom sleep hath seized I fell.

Canto IV

BROKE the deep lethargy within my head
A heavy thunder, so that I upstarted,
Like to a person who by force is wakened;

4 And round about I moved my rested eyes,
Uprisen erect, and steadfastly I gazed,
To recognise the place wherein I was.

7 True is it, that upon the verge I found me
Of the abysmal valley dolorous,
That gathers thunder of infinite ululations.

10 Obscure, profound it was, and nebulous,
So that by fixing on its depths my sight
Nothing whatever I discerned therein.

13 "Let us descend now into the blind world,"
Began the Poet, pallid utterly;
"I will be first, and thou shalt second be."

16 And I, who of his colour was aware,
Said: "How shall I come, if thou art afraid,
Who'rt wont to be a comfort to my fears?"

19 And he to me: "The anguish of the people
Who are below here in my face depicts

That pity which for terror thou hast taken.

Let us go on, for the long way impels us."
Thus he went in, and thus he made me enter
The foremost circle that surrounds the abyss.

There, as it seemed to me from listening,
Were lamentations none, but only sighs,
That tremble made the everlasting air.

And this arose from sorrow without torment,
Which the crowds had, that many were and great
Of infants and of women and of men.

To me the Master good: "Thou dost not ask
What spirits these, which thou beholdest, are?
Now will I have thee know, ere thou go farther,

That they sinned not; and if they merit had,
T'is not enough, because they had not baptism
Which is the portal of the Faith thou holdest;

And if they were before Christianity,
In the right manner they adored not God;
And among such as these am I myself

For such defects, and not for other guilt,
Lost are we and are only so far punished,
That without hope we live on in desire."

Great grief seized on my heart when this I heard,
Because some people of much worthiness
I knew, who in that Limbo were suspended.

"Tell me, my Master, tell me, thou my Lord,"
Began I, with desire of being certain
Of that Faith which o'ercometh every error,

"Came any one by his own merit hence,
Or by another's, who was blessed thereafter?"
And he, who understood my covert speech,

Replied: "I was a novice in this state,
When I saw hither come a Mighty One,
With sign of victory incoronate.

55 Hence he drew forth the shade of the First Parent,
And that of his son Abel, and of Noah,
Of Moses the lawgiver, and the obedient

58 Abraham, patriarch, and David, king,
Israel with his father and his children,
And Rachel, for whose sake he did so much,

61 And others many, and he made them blessed;
And thou must know, that earlier than these
Never were any human spirits saved."

64 We ceased not to advance because he spake,
But still were passing onward through the forest
The forest, say I, of thick-crowded ghosts.

67 Not very far as yet our way had gone
This side the summit, when I saw a fire
That overcame a hemisphere of darkness.

70 We were a little distant from it still,
But not so far that I in part discerned not
That honourable people held that place.

73 "O thou who honourest every art and science,
Who may these be, which such great honour have,
That from the fashion of the rest it parts them?"

76 And he to me: "The honourable name,
That sounds of them above there in thy life,
Wins grace in Heaven, that so advances them."

79 In the mean time a voice was heard by me:
"All honour be to the pre-eminent Poet;
His shade returns again, that was departed."

82 After the voice had ceased and quiet was,
Four mighty shades I saw approaching us;
Semblance had they nor sorrowful nor glad.

85 To say to me began my gracious Master:
"Him with that falchion in his hand behold,
Who comes before the three, even as their lord.

88 That one is Homer, Poet sovereign;

He who comes next is Horace, the satirist;
The third is Ovid, and the last is Lucan.

91 Because to each of these with me applies
The name that solitary voice proclaimed,
They do me honour, and in that do well."

94 Thus I beheld assembled the fair school
Of that lord of the song pre-eminent,
Who o'er the others like an eagle soars.

97 When they together had discoursed somewhat,
They turned to me with signs of salutation,
And on beholding this, my Master smiled;

100 And more of honour still, much more, they did me,
In that they made me one of their own band
So that the sixth was I, 'mid so much wit.

103 Thus we went on as far as to the light,
Things saying 'tis becoming to keep silent,
As was the saying of them where I was.

106 We came unto a noble castle's foot,
Seven times encompassed with lofty walls,
Defended round by a fair rivulet;

109 This we passed over even as firm ground;
Through portals seven I entered with these sages;
We came into a meadow of fresh verdure.

112 People were there with solemn eyes and slow,
Of great authority in their countenance;
They spake but seldom, and with gentle voices.

115 Thus we withdrew ourselves upon one side
Into an opening luminous and lofty,
So that they all of them were visible.

118 There opposite, upon the green enamel,
Were pointed out to me the mighty spirits,
Whom to have seen I feel myself exalted.

121 I saw Electra with companions many,
'Mongst whom I knew both Hector and Aeneas,

Caesar in armour with falcon eyes;

I saw Camilla and Penthesilea
On the other side, and saw the King Latinus,
Who with Lavinia his daughter sat;

I saw that Brutus who drove Tarquin forth,
Lucretia, Julia, Marcia, and Cornelia,
And saw alone, apart, the Saladin.

When I had lifted up my brows a little,
The Master I beheld of those who know,
Sit with his philosophic family.

All gaze upon him, and all do him honour.
There I beheld both Socrates and Plato,
Who nearer him before the others stand;

Democritus, who puts the world on chance,
Diogenes, Anaxagoros, and Thales,
Zeno, Empedocles, and Heraclitus;

Of qualities I saw the good collector,
I mean Dioscorides; and Orpheus saw I,
Tully and Livy, and moral Seneca,

Euclid, geometrician, and Ptolemy,
Galen, Hippocrates, and Avicenna,
Averroes, who the great Comment made.

I cannot all of them portray in full,
Because so drives me onward the long theme,
That many times the word comes short of fact.

The sixfold company in two divides;
Another way my sapient Guide conducts me
Forth from the quiet to the air that trembles;

And to a place I come where nothing shines.

Canto V

THUS I descended out of the first circle
Down to the second, that less space begirds,
And so much greater dole, that goads to wailing.

4 There standeth Minos horribly, and snarls;
Examines the transgressions at the entrance;
Judges, and sends according as he girds him.

7 I say, that when the spirit evil-born
Cometh before him, wholly it confesses;
And this discriminator of transgressions

10 Seeth what place in Hell is meet for it;
Girds himself with his tail as many times
As grades he wishes it should be thrust down.

13 Always before him many of them stand;
They go by turns each one unto the judgment;
They speak, and hear, and then are downward hurled.

16 "O thou, that to this dolorous hostelry
Comest," said Minos to me, when he saw me,
Leaving the practice of so great an office,

19 "Look how thou enterest, and in whom thou trustest;
Let not the portal's amplitude deceive thee."
And unto him my Guide: "Why criest thou too?

22 Do not impede his journey fate-ordained;
It is so willed there where is power to do
That which is willed; and ask no further question."

25 And now begin the dolesome notes to grow
Audible unto me, now am I come
There where much lamentation strikes upon me.

28 I came into a place mute of all light,
Which bellows as the sea does in a tempest,
If by opposing winds 'tis combated.

31 The infernal hurricane that never rests
Hurtles the spirits onward in its rapine;

Whirling them round, and smiting, it molests them.

34 When they arrive before the precipice,
There are the shrieks, the plaints, and the laments,
There they blaspheme the puissance divine.

37 I understood that unto such a torment
The carnal malefactors were condemned,
Who reason subjugate to appetite.

40 And as the wings of starlings bear them on
In the cold season in large band and full,
So doth that blast the spirits maledict;

43 It hither, thither, downward, upward, drives them;
No hope doth comfort them for evermore,
Not of repose, but even of lesser pain.

46 And as the cranes go chanting forth their lays,
Making in air a long line of themselves,
So saw I coming, uttering lamentations,

49 Shadows borne onward by the aforesaid stress.
Whereupon said I: "Master, who are those
People, whom the black air so castigates?"

52 "The first of those, of whom intelligence
Thou fain wouldst have," then said he unto me,
"The empress was of many languages.

55 To sensual vices she was so abandoned,
That lustful she made licit in her law,
To remove the blame to which she had been led.

58 She is Semiramis of whom we read
That she succeeded Ninus, and was his spouse;
She held the land which now the Sultan rules.

61 The next is she who killed herself for love,
And broke faith with the ashes of Sichcaeus;
Then Cleopatra the voluptuous."

64 Helen I saw, for whom so many ruthless
Seasons revolved; and saw the great Achilles,
Who at the last hour combated with Love.

Paris I saw, Tristan; and more than a thousand
Shades did he name and point out with his finger,
Whom Love had separated from our life.

After that I had listened to my Teacher,
Naming the dames of eld and cavaliers,
Pity prevailed, and I was nigh bewildered.

And I began: "O Poet, willingly
Speak would I to those two, who go together,
And seem upon the wind to be so light."

And, he to me: "Thou'lt mark, when they shall be
Nearer to us; and then do thou implore them
By love which leadeth them, and they will come."

Soon as the wind in our direction swayed them,
My voice uplifted I: "O ye weary souls!
Come speak to us, if no one interdicts it."

As turtle-doves, called onward by desire,
With open and steady wings to the sweet nest
Fly through the air by their volition borne,

So came they from the band where Dido is,
Approaching us athwart the air malign,
So strong was the affectionate appeal.

"O living creature gracious and benignant,
Who visiting goest through the purple air
Us, who have stained the world incarnadine,

If were the King of the Universe our friend,
We would pray unto him to give thee peace,
Since thou hast pity on our woe perverse.

Of what it pleases thee to hear and speak,
That will we hear, and we will speak to you,
While silent is the wind, as it is now.

Sitteth the city, wherein I was born,
Upon the sea-shore where the Po descends
To rest in peace with all his retinue.

Love, that on gentle heart doth swiftly seize,

Seized this man for the person beautiful
That was ta'en from me, and still the mode offends me.

103 Love, that exempts no one beloved from loving,
Seized me with pleasure of this man so strongly,
That, as thou seest, it doth not yet desert me;

106 Love has conducted us unto one death;
Caina waiteth him who quenched our life!"
These words were borne along from them to us.

109 As soon as I had heard those souls tormented,
I bowed my face, and so long held it down
Until the Poet said to me: "What thinkest?"

112 When I made answer, I began: "Alas!
How many pleasant thoughts, how much desire,
Conducted these unto the dolorous pass!"

115 Then unto them I turned me, and I spake,
And I began: "Thine agonies, Francesca,
Sad and compassionate to weeping make me.

118 But tell me, at the time of those sweet sighs,
By what and in what manner Love conceded,
That you should know your dubious desires?"

121 And she to me: "There is no greater sorrow
Than to be mindful of the happy time
In misery, and that thy Teacher knows.

124 But, if to recognise the earliest root
Of love in us thou hast so great desire,
I will do even as he who weeps and speaks.

127 One day we reading were for our delight
Of Launcelot, how Love did him enthral.
Alone we were and without any fear.

130 Full many a time our eyes together drew
That reading, and drove the colour from our faces;
But one point only was it that o'ercame us.

133 When as we read of the much-longed-for smile
Being by such a noble lover kissed,

This one, who ne'er from me shall be divided,

136 Kissed me upon the mouth all palpitating.
Galeotto was the book and he who wrote it.
That day no farther did we read therein."

139 And all the while one spirit uttered this,
The other one did weep so, that, for pity,
I swooned away as if I had been dying,

142 And fell, even as a dead body falls.

Canto VI

AT the return of consciousness, that closed
Before the pity of those two relations,
Which utterly with sadness had confused me,

4 New torments I behold, and new tormented
Around me, whichsoever way I move,
And whichsoever way I turn, and gaze.

7 In the third circle am I of the rain
Eternal, maledict, and cold, and heavy;
Its law and quality are never new.

10 Huge hail, and water sombre-hued, and snow,
Athwart the tenebrous air pour down amain;
Noisome the earth is, that receiveth this.

13 Cerberus, monster cruel and uncouth,
With his three gullets like a dog is barking
Over the people that are there submerged.

16 Red eyes he has, and unctuous beard and black,
And belly large, and armed with claws his hands;
He rends the spirits, flays, and quarters them.

19 Howl the rain maketh them like unto dogs;
One side they make a shelter for the other;
Oft turn themselves the wretched reprobates.

When Cerberus perceived us, the great worm!
His mouths he opened, and displayed his tusks;
Not a limb had he that was motionless.

And my Conductor, with his spans extended,
Took of the earth, and with his fists well filled,
He threw it into those rapacious gullets.

Such as that dog is, who by barking craves,
And quiet grows soon as his food he gnaws,
For to devour it he but thinks and struggles,

The like became those muzzles filth-begrimed
Of Cerberus the demon, who so thunders
Over the souls that they would fain be deaf.

We passed across the shadows, which subdues
The heavy rain-storm, and we placed our feet
Upon their vanity that person seems.

They all were lying prone upon the earth,
Excepting one, who sat upright as soon
As he beheld us passing on before him.

"O thou that art conducted through this Hell,"
He said to me, "recall me, if thou canst;
Thyself wast made before I was unmade."

And I to him: "The anguish which thou hast
Perhaps doth draw thee out of my remembrance,
So that it seems not I have ever seen thee.

But tell me who thou art, that in so doleful
A place art put, and in such punishment,
If some are greater, none is so displeasing."

And he to me: "Thy city, which is full
Of envy so that now the sack runs over,
Held me within it in the life serene.

You citizens were wont to call me Ciacco;
For the pernicious sin of gluttony
I as thou seest, am battered by this rain.

And I, sad soul, am not the only one,

For all these suffer the like penalty
For the like sin," and word no more spake he.

58 I answered him: "Ciacco, thy wretchedness
Weighs on me so that it to weep invites me;
But tell me, if thou knowest, to what shall come

61 The citizens of the divided city;
If any there be just; and the occasion
Tell me why so much discord has assailed it."

64 And he to me: "They, after long contention,
Will come to bloodshed; and the rustic party
Will drive the other out with much offence.

67 Then afterwards behoves it this one fall
Within three suns, and rise again the other
By force of him who now is on the coast.

70 High will it hold its forehead a long while,
Keeping the other under heavy burdens,
Howe'er it weeps thereat and is indignant.

73 The just are two, and are not understood there;
Envy and Arrogance and Avarice
Are the three sparks that have all hearts enkindled."

76 Here ended he his tearful utterance;
And I to him: "I wish thee still to teach me,
And make a gift to me of further speech.

79 Farinata and Tegghiaio, once so worthy,
Jacopo Rusticucci, Arrigo, and Mosca,
And others who on good deeds set their thoughts,

82 Say where they are, and cause that I may know them;
For great desire constraineth me to learn
If Heaven doth sweeten them, or Hell envenom."

85 And he: "They are among the blacker souls;
A different sin downweighs them to the bottom;
If thou so far descendest, thou canst see them.

88 But when thou art again in the sweet world,
I pray thee to the mind of others bring me;

No more I tell thee and no more I answer."

91 Then his straightforward eyes he turned askance,
Eyed me a little, and then bowed his head;
He fell therewith prone like the other blind.

94 And the Guide said to me: "He wakes no more
This side the sound of the angelic trumpet;
When shall approach the hostile Potentate,

97 Each one shall find again his dismal tomb,
Shall reassume his flesh and his own figure,
Shall hear what through eternity re-echoes."

100 So we passed onward o'er the filthy mixture
Of shadows and of rain with footsteps slow,
Touching a little on the future life.

103 Wherefore I said: "Master, these torments here,
Will they increase after the mighty sentence,
Or lesser be, or will they be as burning?"

106 And he to me: "Return unto thy science,
Which wills, that as the thing more perfect is,
The more it feels of pleasure and of pain.

109 Albeit that this people maledict
To true perfection never can attain,
Hereafter more than now they look to be."

112 Round in a circle by that road we went,
Speaking much more, which I do not repeat;
We came unto the point where the descent is;

115 There we found Plutus the great enemy.

Canto VII

"PAPE Satan, Pape Satan, Aleppe!"[1]
Thus Plutus with his clucking voice began;
And that benignant Sage, who all things knew,

4 Said, to encourage me: "Let not thy fear
Harm thee; for any power that he may have
Shall not prevent thy going down this crag."

7 Then he turned round unto that bloated lip,
And said: "Be silent, thou accursed wolf;
Consume within thyself with thine own rage.

10 Not causeless is this journey to the abyss;
Thus is it willed on high, where Michael wrought
Vengeance upon the proud adultery."

13 Even as the sails inflated by the wind
Involved together fall when snaps the mast,
So fell the cruel monster to the earth.

16 Thus we descended into the fourth chasm,
Gaining still farther on the dolesome shore
Which all the woe of the universe insacks.

19 Justice of God, ah! who heaps up so many
New toils and sufferings as I beheld?
And why doth our transgression waste us so?

22 As doth the billow there upon Charybdis,
That breaks itself on that which it encounters,
So here the folk must dance their roundelay.

25 Here saw I people, more than elsewhere, many,
On one side and the other, with great howls,
Rolling weights forward by main force of chest.

28 They clashed together, and then at that point
Each one turned backward, rolling retrograde,
Crying, "Why keepest?" and, "Why squanderest thou?"

31 Thus they returned along the lurid circle

1 Possible translation: "O Pope Satan, my god!"

On either hand unto the opposite point,
Shouting their shameful metre evermore.

34 Then each, when he arrived there, wheeled about
Through his half-circle to another joust;
And I, who had my heart pierced as it were,

37 Exclaimed: "My Master, now declare to me
What people these are, and if all were clerks,
These shaven crowns upon the left of us."

40 And he to me: "All of them were asquint
In intellect in the first life, so much
That there with measure they no spending made.

43 Clearly enough their voices bark it forth,
Whene'er they reach the two points of the circle,
Where sunders them the opposite defect.

46 Clerks those were who no hairy covering
Have on the head, and Popes and Cardinals,
In whom doth Avarice practise its excess."

49 And I: "My Master, among such as these
I ought forsooth to recognise some few,
Who were infected with these maladies."

52 And he to me: "Vain thought thou entertainest;
The undiscerning life which made them sordid
Now makes them unto all discernment dim.

55 Forever shall they come to these two buttings;
These from the sepulchre shall rise again
With the fist closed, and these with tresses shorn.

58 Ill giving and ill keeping the fair world
Have ta'en from them, and placed them in this scuffle;
Whate'er it be, no words adorn I for it.

61 Now canst thou, Son, behold the transient farce
Of goods that are committed unto Fortune,
For which the human race each other buffet;

64 For all the gold that is beneath the moon,
Or ever has been, of these weary souls
Could never make a single one repose."

67 "Master," I said to him, "now tell me also
What is this Fortune which thou speakest of,
That has the world's goods so within its clutches?"

70 And he to me: "O creatures imbecile,
What ignorance is this which doth beset you?
Now will I have thee learn my judgment of her.

73 He whose omniscience everything transcends
The heavens created, and gave who should guide them,
That every part to every part may shine,

76 Distributing the light in equal measure;
He in like manner to the mundane splendours
Ordained a general ministress and guide,

79 That she might change at times the empty treasures
From race to race, from one blood to another,
Beyond resistance of all human wisdom.

82 Therefore one people triumphs, and another
Languishes, in pursuance of her judgment,
Which hidden is, as in the grass a serpent.

85 Your knowledge has no counterstand against her;
She makes provision, judges, and pursues
Her governance, as theirs the other gods.

88 Her permutations have not any truce;
Necessity makes her precipitate,
So often cometh who his turn obtains.

91 And this is she who is so crucified
Even by those who ought to give her praise,
Giving her blame amiss, and bad repute.

94 But she is blissful, and she hears it not;
Among the other primal creatures gladsome
She turns her sphere, and blissful she rejoices.

97 Let us descend now unto greater woe;
Already sinks each star that was ascending
When I set out, and loitering is forbidden."

100 We crossed the circle to the other bank,

Near to a fount that boils, and pours itself
Along a gully that runs out of it.

103 The water was more sombre far than perse;
And we, in company with the dusky waves,
Made entrance downward by a path uncouth.

106 A marsh it makes, which has the name of Styx,
This tristful brooklet, when it has descended
Down to the foot of the malign gray shores.

109 And I, who stood intent upon beholding,
Saw people mudbesprent in that lagoon,
All of them naked and with angry look.

112 They smote each other not alone with hands,
But with the head and with the breast and feet,
Tearing each other piecemeal with their teeth.

115 Said the good Master: "Son, thou now beholdest
The souls of those whom anger overcame;
And likewise I would have thee know for certain

118 Beneath the water people are who sigh
And make this water bubble at the surface,
As the eye tells thee wheresoe'er it turns.

121 Fixed in the mire they say, 'We sullen were
In the sweet air, which by the sun is gladdened,
Bearing within ourselves the sluggish reek;

124 Now we are sullen in this sable mire.'
This hymn do they keep gurgling in their throats,
For with unbroken words they cannot say it."

127 Thus we went circling round the filthy fen
A great arc 'twixt the dry bank and the swamp,
With eyes turned unto those who gorge the mire;

130 Unto the foot of a tower we came at last.

Canto VIII

I SAY, continuing, that long before
We to the foot of that high tower had come,
Our eyes went upward to the summit of it,

4 By reason of two flamelets we saw placed there,
And from afar another answered them,
So far, that hardly could the eye attain it.

7 And, to the sea of all discernment turned,
I said: "What sayeth this, and what respondeth
That other fire? And who are they that made it?"

10 And he to me: "Across the turbid waves
What is expected thou canst now discern,
If reek of the morass conceal it not."

13 Cord never shot an arrow from itself
That sped away athwart the air so swift,
As I beheld a very little boat

16 Come o'er the water tow'rds us at that moment,
Under the guidance of a single pilot,
Who shouted, "Now art thou arrived, fell soul?"

19 "Phlegyas, Phlegyas, thou criest out in vain
For this once," said my Lord; "thou shalt not have
Longer than in the passing of the slough."

22 As he who listens to some great deceit
That has been done to him, and then resents it,
Such became Phlegyas, in his gathered wrath.

25 My Guide descended down into the boat,
And then he made me enter after him,
And only when I entered seemed it laden.

28 Soon as the Guide and I were in the boat,
The antique prow goes on its way, dividing
More of the water than 'tis wont with others.

31 While we were running through the dead canal,
Uprose in front of me one full of mire,

And said, "Who art thou that comest ere the hour?"

34 And I to him: "Although I come, I stay not;
But who art thou that hast become so squalid?"
"Thou seest that I am one who weeps," he answered.

37 And I to him: "With weeping and with wailing,
Thou spirit maledict, do thou remain;
For thee I know, though thou art all defiled."

40 Then stretched he both his hands unto the boat;
Whereat my wary Master thrust him back,
Saying, "Away there with the other dogs!"

43 Thereafter with his arms he clasped my neck;
He kissed my face, and said: "Disdainful soul,
Blessed be she who bore thee in her bosom.

46 That was an arrogant person in the world;
Goodness is none, that decks his memory;
So likewise here his shade is furious.

49 How many are esteemed great kings up there,
Who here shall be like unto swine in mire,
Leaving behind them horrible dispraises!"

52 And I: "My Master, much should I be pleased,
If I could see him soused into this broth,
Before we issue forth out of the lake."

55 And he to me: "Ere unto thee the shore
Reveal itself, thou shalt be satisfied;
Such a desire 'tis meet thou shouldst enjoy."

58 A little after that, I saw such havoc
Made of him by the people of the mire,
That still I praise and thank my God for it.

61 They all were shouting, "At Philippo Argenti!"
And that exasperate spirit Florentine
Turned round upon himself with his own teeth.

64 We left him there, and more of him I tell not;
But on mine ears there smote a lamentation,
Whence forward I intent unbar mine eyes.

And the good Master said: "Even now, my Son,
The city draweth near whose name is Dis,
With the grave citizens, with the great throng."

And I: "Its mosques already, Master, clearly
Within there in the valley I discern
Vermilion, as if issuing from the fire

They were." And he to me: "The fire eternal
That kindles them within makes them look red,
As thou beholdest in this nether Hell."

Then we arrived within the moats profound,
That circumvallate that disconsolate city;
The walls appeared to me to be of iron.

Not without making first a circuit wide,
We came unto a place where loud the pilot
Cried out to us, "Debark, here is the entrance."

More than a thousand at the gates I saw
Out of the Heavens rained down, who angrily
Were saying, "Who is this that without death

Goes through the kingdom of the people dead?"
And my sagacious Master made a sign
Of wishing secretly to speak with them.

A little then they quelled their great disdain,
And said: "Come thou alone, and he begone
Who has so boldly entered these dominions.

Let him return alone by his mad road;
Try, if he can; for thou shalt here remain,
Who hast escorted him through such dark regions."

Think, Reader, if I was discomforted
At utterance of the accursed words;
For never to return here I believed.

"O my dear Guide, who more than seven times
Hast rendered me security, and drawn me
From imminent peril that before me stood,

Do not desert me," said I, "thus undone;

And if the going farther be denied us,
Let us retrace our steps together swiftly."

And that Lord, who had led me thitherward,
Said unto me: "Fear not; because our passage
None can take from us, it by Such is given.

But here await me, and thy weary spirit
Comfort and nourish with a better hope;
For in this nether world I will not leave thee."

So onward goes and there abandons me
My Father sweet, and I remain in doubt,
For No and Yes within my head contend.

I could not hear what he proposed to them;
But with them there he did not linger long,
Ere each within in rivalry ran back.

They closed the portals, those our adversaries,
On my Lord's breast, who had remained without
And turned to me with footsteps far between.

His eyes cast down, his forehead shorn had he
Of all its boldness, and he said, with sighs,
"Who has denied to me the dolesome houses?"

And unto me: "Thou, because I am angry,
Fear not, for I will conquer in the trial,
Whatever for defence within be planned.

This arrogance of theirs is nothing new;
For once they used it at less secret gate,
Which finds itself without a fastening still.

O'er it didst thou behold the dead inscription;
And now this side of it descends the steep,
Passing across the circles without escort,

One by whose means the city shall be opened."

Canto IX

THAT hue which cowardice brought out on me,
Beholding my Conductor backward turn,
Sooner repressed within him his new colour.

He stopped attentive, like a man who listens,
Because the eye could not conduct him far
Through the black air, and through the heavy fog.

"Still it behoveth us to win the fight,"
Began he, "else . . . such offered us herself . . .
O how I long that some one here arrive!"

Well I perceived, as soon as the beginning
He covered up with what came afterward,
That they were words quite different from the first;

But none the less his saying gave me fear,
Because I carried out the broken phrase,
Perhaps to a worse meaning than he had.

"Into this bottom of the doleful conch
Doth any e'er descend from the first grade,
Which for its pain has only hope cut off?"

This question put I; and he answered me:
"Seldom it comes to pass that one of us
Maketh the journey upon which I go.

True is it, once before I here below
Was conjured by that pitiless Erictho,
Who summoned back the shades unto their bodies.

Naked of me short while the flesh had been,
Before within that wall she made me enter,
To bring a spirit from the circle of Judas;

That is the lowest region and the darkest,
And farthest from the heaven which circles all.
Well know I the way; therefore be reassured.

This fen, which a prodigious stench exhales,
Encompasses about the city dolent,

Where now we cannot enter without anger."

34 And more he said, but not in mind I have it;
Because mine eye had altogether drawn me
Tow'rds the high tower with the red-flaming summit,

37 Where in a moment saw I swift uprisen
The three infernal Furies stained with blood,
Who had the limbs of women and their mien,

40 And with the greenest hydras were begirt;
Small serpents and cerastes were their tresses,
Wherewith their horrid temples were entwined.

43 And he who well the handmaids of the Queen
Of everlasting lamentation knew,
Said unto me: "Behold the fierce Erinnys.

46 This is Megaera, on the left-hand side;
She who is weeping on the right, Alecto;
Tisiphone is between," and then was silent.

49 Each one her breast was rending with her nails;
They beat them with their palms, and cried so loud,
That I for dread pressed close unto the Poet.

52 "Medusa come, so we to stone will change him!"
All shouted looking down; "in evil hour
Avenged we not on Theseus his assault!"

55 "Turn thyself round, and keep thine eyes close shut,
For if the Gorgon appear, and thou shouldst see it,
No more returning upward would there be."

58 Thus said the Master; and he turned me round
Himself, and trusted not unto my hands
So far as not to blind me with his own.

61 O ye who have undistempered intellects,
Observe the doctrine that conceals itself
Beneath the veil of the mysterious verses!

64 And now there came across the turbid waves
The clangour of a sound with terror fraught,
Because of which both of the margins trembled;

Not otherwise it was than of a wind
Impetuous on account of adverse heats,
That smites the forest, and, without restraint,

The branches rends, beats down, and bears away;
Right onward, laden with dust, it goes superb,
And puts to flight the wild beasts and the shepherds.

Mine eyes he loosed, and said: "Direct the nerve
Of vision now along that ancient foam,
There yonder where that smoke is most intense."

Even as the frogs before the hostile serpent
Across the water scatter all abroad,
Until each one is huddled in the earth,

More than a thousand ruined souls I saw,
Thus fleeing from before one who on foot
Was passing o'er the Styx with soles unwet.

From off his face he fanned that unctuous air,
Waving his left hand oft in front of him,
And only with that anguish seemed he weary.

Well I perceived one sent from Heaven was he,
And to the Master turned; and he made sign
That I should quiet stand, and bow before him.

Ah! how disdainful he appeared to me!
He reached the gate, and with a little rod
He opened it, for there was no resistance.

"O banished out of Heaven, people despised!"
Thus he began upon the horrid threshold;
"Whence is this arrogance within you couched?

Wherefore recalcitrate against that will,
From which the end can never be cut off,
And which has many times increased your pain?

What helpeth it to butt against the fates?
Your Cerberus, if you remember well,
For that still bears his chin and gullet peeled."

Then he returned along the miry road,
And spake no word to us, but had the look

Of one whom other care constrains and goads

Than that of him who in his presence is;
And we our feet directed tow'rds the city,
After those holy words all confident.

Within we entered without any contest;
And I, who inclination had to see
What the condition such a fortress holds,

Soon as I was within, cast round mine eye,
And see on every hand an ample plain,
Full of distress and torment terrible.

Even as at Arles, where stagnant grows the Rhone,
Even as at Pola near to the Quarnaro,
That shuts in Italy and bathes its borders,

The sepulchres make all the place uneven;
So likewise did they there on every side,
Saving that there the manner was more bitter;

For flames between the sepulchres were scattered,
By which they so intensely heated were,
That iron more so asks not any art.

All of their coverings uplifted were,
And from them issued forth such dire laments,
Sooth seemed they of the wretched and tormented.

And I: "My Master, what are all those people
Who, having sepulture within those tombs,
Make themselves audible by doleful sighs?"

And he to me: "Here are the Heresiarchs,
With their disciples of all sects, and much
More than thou thinkest laden are the tombs.

Here like together with its like is buried;
And more and less the monuments are heated."
And when he to the right had turned, we passed

Between the torments and high parapets.

Canto X

NOW onward goes, along a narrow path
Between the torments and the city wall,
My Master, and I follow at his back.

4 "O power supreme, that through these impious circles
Turnest me," I began, "as pleases thee,
Speak to me, and my longings satisfy;

7 The people who are lying in these tombs,
Might they be seen? Already are uplifted
The covers all, and no one keepeth guard."

10 And he to me: "They all will be closed up
When from Jehoshaphat they shall return
Here with the bodies they have left above.

13 Their cemetery have upon this side
With Epicurus all his followers,
Who with the body mortal make the soul;

16 But in the question thou dost put to me,
Within here shalt thou soon be satisfied,
And likewise in the wish thou keepest silent."

19 And I: "Good Leader, I but keep concealed
From thee my heart, that I may speak the less,
Nor only now hast thou thereto disposed me."

22 "O Tuscan, thou who through the city of fire
Goest alive, thus speaking modestly,
Be pleased to stay thy footsteps in this place.

25 Thy mode of speaking makes thee manifest
A native of that noble fatherland,
To which perhaps I too molestful was."

28 Upon a sudden issued forth this sound
From out one of the tombs; wherefore I pressed,
Fearing, a little nearer to my Leader.

31 And unto me he said: "Turn thee; what dost thou?
Behold there Farinata who has risen;
From the waist upwards wholly shalt thou see him."

34 I had already fixed mine eyes on his,
And he uprose erect with breast and front
E'en as if Hell he had in great despite.

37 And with courageous hands and prompt my Leader
Thrust me between the sepulchres towards him,
Exclaiming, "Let thy words explicit be."

40 As soon as I was at the foot of his tomb
Somewhat he eyed me, and, as if disdainful,
Then asked of me, "Who were thine ancestors?"

43 I, who desirous of obeying was,
Concealed it not, but all revealed to him;
Whereat he raised his brows a little upward.

46 Then said he: "Fiercely adverse have they been
To me, and to my fathers, and my party;
So that two several times I scattered them."

49 "If they were banished, they returned on all sides,"
I answered him, "the first time and the second;
But yours have not acquired that art aright."

52 Then there uprose upon the sight, uncovered
Down to the chin, a shadow at his side;
I think that he had risen on his knees.

55 Round me he gazed, as if solicitude
He had to see if some one else were with me,
But after his suspicion was all spent,

58 Weeping, he said to me: "If through this blind
Prison thou goest by loftiness of genius,
Where is my son? And why is he not with thee?"

61 And I to him: "I come not of myself;
He who is waiting yonder leads me here,
Whom in disdain perhaps your Guido had."

64 His language and the mode of punishment
Already unto me had read his name;
On that account my answer was so full.

67 Up starting suddenly, he cried out: "How
Saidst thou, he had? Is he not still alive?
Does not the sweet light strike upon his eyes?"

70 When he became aware of some delay,
Which I before my answer made, supine
He fell again, and forth appeared no more.

73 But the other, magnanimous, at whose desire
I had remained, did not his aspect change,
Neither his neck he moved, nor bent his side.

76 "And if," continuing his first discourse,
"They have that art," he said, "not learned aright,
That more tormenteth me, than doth this bed.

79 But fifty times shall not rekindled be
The countenance of the Lady who reigns here
Ere thou shalt know how heavy is that art;

82 And as thou wouldst to the sweet world return,
Say why that people is so pitiless
Against my race in each one of its laws?"

85 Whence I to him: "The slaughter and great carnage
Which have with crimson stained the Arbia, cause
Such orisons in our temple to be made."

88 After his head he with a sigh had shaken,
"There I was not alone," he said, "nor surely
Without a cause had with the others moved.

91 But there I was alone, where every one
Consented to the laying waste of Florence,
He who defended her with open face."

94 "Ah! so hereafter may your seed repose,"
I him entreated, "solve for me that knot,
Which has entangled my conceptions here.

97 It seems that you can see, if I hear rightly,
Beforehand whatsoe'er time brings with it,
And in the present have another mode."

100 "We see, like those who have imperfect sight,
The things," he said, "that distant are from us;
So much still shines on us the Sovereign Ruler.

103 When they draw near, or are, is wholly vain
Our intellect, and if none brings it to us,

Not anything know we of your human state.

Hence thou canst understand, that wholly dead
Will be our knowledge from the moment when
The portal of the future shall be closed."

Then I, as if compunctious for my fault,
Said: "Now, then, you will tell that fallen one,
That still his son is with the living joined.

And if just now, in answering, I was dumb,
Tell him I did it because I was thinking
Already of the error you have solved me."

And now my Master was recalling me,
Wherefore more eagerly I prayed the spirit
That he would tell me who was with him there.

He said: "With more than a thousand here I lie;
Within here is the second Frederick,
And the Cardinal, and of the rest I speak not."

Thereon he hid himself; and I towards
The ancient poet turned my steps, reflecting
Upon that saying, which seemed hostile to me.

He moved along; and afterward thus going,
He said to me, "Why art thou so bewildered?"
And I in his inquiry satisfied him.

"Let memory preserve what thou hast heard
Against thyself," that Sage commanded me,
"And now attend here;" and he raised his finger.

"When thou shalt be before the radiance sweet
Of her whose beauteous eyes all things behold,
From her thou'lt know the journey of thy life."

Unto the left hand then he turned his feet;
We left the wall, and went towards the middle,
Along a path that strikes into a valley,

Which even up there unpleasant made its stench.

Canto XI

UPON the margin of a lofty bank
Which great rocks broken in a circle made,
We came upon a still more cruel throng;

4 And there, by reason of the horrible
Excess of stench the deep abyss throws out,
We drew ourselves aside behind the cover

7 Of a great tomb, whereon I saw a writing,
Which said: "Pope Anastasius I hold,
Whom out of the right way Photinus drew."

10 "Slow it behoveth our descent to be,
So that the sense be first a little used
To the sad blast, and then we shall not heed it."

13 The Master thus; and unto him I said,
"Some compensation find, that the time pass not
Idly;" and he: "Thou seest I think of that.

16 My son, upon the inside of these rocks,"
Began he then to say, "are three small circles,
From grade to grade, like those which thou art leaving

19 They all are full of spirits maledict;
But that hereafter sight alone suffice thee,
Hear how and wherefore they are in constraint.

22 Of every malice that wins hate in Heaven,
Injury is the end; and all such end
Either by force or fraud afflicteth others.

25 But because fraud is man's peculiar vice,
More it displeases God; and so stand lowest
The fraudulent, and greater dole assails them.

28 All the first circle of the Violent is;
But since force may be used against three persons,
In three rounds 'tis divided and constructed.

31 To God, to ourselves, and to our neighbour can we
Use force; I say on them and on their things,
As thou shalt hear with reason manifest.

We drew ourselves aside behind the cover
Of a great tomb, whereon I saw a writing,
Which said: Pope Anastasius I hold,
Whom out of the right way Photinus drew.

Gustave Doré

34 A death by violence, and painful wounds,
Are to our neighbour given; and in his substance
Ruin, and arson, and injurious levies;

37 Whence homicides, and he who smites unjustly,
Marauders, and freebooters, the first round
Tormenteth all in companies diverse.

40 Man may lay violent hands upon himself
And his own goods; and therefore in the second
Round must perforce without avail repent

43 Whoever of your world deprives himself,
Who games, and dissipates his property,
And weepeth there, where he should jocund be.

46 Violence can be done the Deity,
In heart denying and blaspheming Him,
And by disdaining Nature and her bounty.

49 And for this reason doth the smallest round
Seal with its signet Sodom and Cahors,
And who, disdaining God, speaks from the heart.

52 Fraud, wherewithal is every conscience stung,
A man may practise upon him who trusts,
And him who doth no confidence imburse.

55 This latter mode, it would appear, dissevers
Only the bond of love which Nature makes;
Wherefore within the second circle nestle

58 Hypocrisy, flattery, and who deals in magic,
Falsification, theft, and simony,
Panders, and barrators, and the like-filth.

61 By the other mode, forgotten is that love
Which Nature makes, and what is after added,
From which there is a special faith engendered.

64 Hence in the smallest circle, where the point is
Of the Universe, upon which Dis is seated,
Whoe'er betrays for ever is consumed."

67 And I: "My Master, clear enough proceeds
Thy reasoning, and full well distinguishes

This cavern and the people who possess it.

70 But tell me, those within the fat lagoon,
Whom the wind drives, and whom the rain doth beat,
And who encounter with such bitter tongues,

73 Wherefore are they inside of the red city
Not punished, if God has them in his wrath,
And if he has not, wherefore in such fashion?"

76 And unto me he said: "Why wanders so
Thine intellect from that which it is wont?
Or, sooth, thy mind where is it elsewhere looking?

79 Hast thou no recollection of those words
With which thine Ethics thoroughly discusses
The dispositions three, that Heaven abides not,

82 Incontinence, and Malice, and insane
Bestiality? And how Incontinence
Less God offendeth, and less blame attracts?

85 If thou regardest this conclusion well,
And to thy mind recallest who they are
That up outside are undergoing penance,

88 Clearly wilt thou perceive why from these felons
They separated are, and why less wroth
Justice divine doth smite them with its hammer."

91 "O Sun, that healest all distempered vision,
Thou dost content me so, when thou resolvest,
That doubting pleases me no less than knowing!

94 Once more a little backward turn thee," said I,
"There where thou sayest that usury offends
Goodness divine, and disengage the knot."

97 "Philosophy," he said, "to him who heeds it,
Noteth, not only in one place alone,
After what manner Nature takes her course

100 From Intellect Divine, and from its art;
And if thy Physics carefully thou notest,
After not many pages shalt thou find,

103 That this your art as far as possible
Follows, as the disciple doth the master;
So that your art is, as it were, God's grandchild.

106 From these two, if thou bringest to thy mind
Genesis at the beginning, it behoves
Mankind to gain their life and to advance;

109 And since the usurer takes another way,
Nature herself and in her follower
Disdains he, for elsewhere he puts his hope.

112 But follow, now, as I would fain go on,
For quivering are the Fishes on the horizon,
And the Wain wholly over Caurus lies,

115 And far beyond there we descend the crag."

Canto XII

THE place where to descend the bank we came
Was alpine, and from what was there, moreover,
Of such a kind that every eye would shun it.

4 Such as that ruin is which in the flank
Smote, on this side of Trent, the Adige,
Either by earthquake or by failing stay,

7 For from the mountain's top, from which it moved,
Unto the plain the cliff is shattered so,
Some path 'twould give to him who was above;

10 Even such was the descent of that ravine,
And on the border of the broken chasm
The infamy of Crete was stretched along,

13 Who was conceived in the fictitious cow;
And when he us beheld, he bit himself,
Even as one whom anger racks within.

16 My Sage towards him shouted: "Peradventure
Thou think'st that here may be the Duke of Athens,

Who in the world above brought death to thee?

19 Get thee gone, beast, for this one cometh not
Instructed by thy sister, but he comes
In order to behold your punishments."

22 As is that bull who breaks loose at the moment
In which he has received the mortal blow,
Who cannot walk, but staggers here and there,

25 The Minotaur beheld I do the like;
And he, the wary, cried: "Run to the passage;
While he wroth, 'tis well thou shouldst descend."

28 Thus down we took our way o'er that discharge
Of stones, which oftentimes did move themselves
Beneath my feet, from the unwonted burden.

31 Thoughtful I went and he said: "Thou art thinking
Perhaps upon this ruin, which is guarded
By that brute anger which just now I quenched.

34 Now will I have thee know, the other time
I here descended to the nether Hell,
This precipice had not yet fallen down.

37 But truly, if I well discern, a little
Before His coming who the mighty spoil
Bore off from Dis, in the supernal circle,

40 Upon all sides the deep and loathsome valley
Trembled so, that I thought the Universe
Was thrilled with love, by which there are who think

43 The world ofttimes converted into chaos;
And at that moment this primeval crag
Both here and elsewhere made such overthrow.

46 But fix thine eyes below; for draweth near
The river of blood, within which boiling is
Whoe'er by violence doth injure others."

49 O blind cupidity, O wrath insane,
That spurs us onward so in our short life,
And in the eternal then so badly steeps us!

52 I saw an ample moat bent like a bow,
As one which all the plain encompasses,
Conformable to what my Guide had said.

55 And between this and the embankment's foot
Centaurs in file were running, armed with arrows,
As in the world they used the chase to follow.

58 Beholding us descend, each one stood still,
And from the squadron three detached themselves,
With bows and arrows in advance selected;

61 And from afar one cried: "Unto what torment
Come ye, who down the hillside are descending?
Tell us from there; if not, I draw the bow."

64 My Master said: "Our answer will we make
To Chiron, near you there; in evil hour,
That will of thine was evermore so hasty."

67 Then touched he me, and said: "This one is Nessus,
Who perished for the lovely Dejanira,
And for himself, himself did vengeance take.

70 And he in the midst, who at his breast is gazing,
Is the great Chiron, who brought up Achilles;
That other Pholus is, who was so wrathful.

73 Thousands and thousands go about the moat
Shooting with shafts whatever soul emerges
Out of the blood, more than his crime allots."

76 Near we approached unto those monsters fleet;
Chiron an arrow took, and with the notch
Backward upon his jaws he put his beard.

79 After he had uncovered his great mouth,
He said to his companions: "Are you ware
That he behind moveth whate'er he touches?

82 Thus are not wont to do the feet of dead men."
And my good Guide, who now was at his breast,
Where the two natures are together joined,

85 Replied: "Indeed he lives, and thus alone

Me it behoves to show him the dark valley;
Necessity, and not delight, impels us.

88 Some one withdrew from singing Halleluja,
Who unto me committed this new office;
No thief is he, nor I a thievish spirit.

91 But by that virtue through which I am moving
My steps along this savage thoroughfare,
Give us some one of thine, to be with us,

94 And who may show us where to pass the ford,
And who may carry this one on his back;
For 'tis no spirit that can walk the air."

97 Upon his right breast Chiron wheeled about,
And said to Nessus: "Turn and do thou guide them,
And warn aside, if other band may meet you."

100 We with our faithful escort onward moved
Along the brink of the vermilion boiling,
Wherein the boiled were uttering loud laments.

103 People I saw within up to the eyebrows,
And the great Centaur said: "Tyrants are these,
Who dealt in bloodshed and in pillaging.

106 Here they lament their pitiless mischiefs; here
Is Alexander, and fierce Dionysius
Who upon Sicily brought dolorous years.

109 That forehead there which has the hair so black
Is Azzolin; and the other who is blond,
Obizzo is of Esti, who, in truth,

112 Up in the world was by his stepson slain."
Then turned I to the Poet; and he said,
"Now he be first to thee, and second I."

115 A little farther on the Centaur stopped
Above a folk, who far down as the throat
Seemed from that boiling stream to issue forth.

118 A shade he showed us on one side alone,
Saying: "He cleft asunder in God's bosom
The heart that still upon the Thames is honoured."

Then people saw I, who from out the river
Lifted their heads and also all the chest;
And many among these I recognised.

Thus ever more and more grew shallower
That blood, so that the feet alone it covered;
And there across the moat our passage was.

"Even as thou here upon this side beholdest
The boiling stream, that aye diminishes,"
The Centaur said, "I wish thee to believe

That on this other more and more declines
Its bed, until it reunites itself
Where it behoveth tyranny to groan.

Justice divine, upon this side, is goading
That Attila, who was a scourge on earth,
And Pyrrhus, and Sextus; and for ever milks

The tears which with the boiling it unseals
In Rinier da Corneto and Rinier Pazzo,
Who made upon the highways so much war."

Then back he turned, and passed again the ford.

Canto XIII

NOT yet had Nessus reached the other side,
When we had put ourselves within a wood,
That was not marked by any path whatever.

4 Not foliage green, but of a dusky colour,
Not branches smooth, but gnarled and intertangled,
Not apple-trees were there, but thorns with poison.

7 Such tangled thickets have not, nor so dense,
Those savage wild beasts, that in hatred hold
'Twixt Cecina and Corneto the tilled places.

10 There do the hideous Harpies make their nests,
Who chased the Trojans from the Strophades,
With sad announcement of impending doom;

13 Broad wings have they, and necks and faces human,
And feet with claws, and their great bellies fledged;
They make laments upon the wondrous trees.

16 And the good Master: "Ere thou enter farther,
Know that thou art within the second round,"
Thus he began to say, "and shalt be, till

19 Thou comest out upon the horrible sand;
Therefore look well around, and thou shalt see
Things that will credence give unto my speech."

22 I heard on all sides lamentations uttered,
And person none beheld I who might make them,
Whence, utterly bewildered, I stood still.

25 I think he thought that I perhaps might think
So many voices issued through those trunks
From people who concealed themselves from us;

28 Therefore the Master said: "If thou break off
Some little spray from any of these trees,
The thoughts thou hast will wholly be made vain."

31 Then stretched I forth my hand a little forward,
And plucked a branchlet off from a great thorn,

And the trunk cried, "Why dost thou mangle me?"

34 After it had become embrowned with blood,
It recommenced its cry: "Why dost thou rend me
Hast thou no spirit of pity whatsoever?

37 Men once we were, and now are changed to trees;
Indeed, thy hand should be more pitiful,
Even if the souls of serpents we had been."

40 As out of a green brand, that is on fire
At one of the ends, and from the other drips
And hisses with the wind that is escaping;

43 So from that splinter issued forth together
Both words and blood; whereat I let the tip
Fall, and stood like a man who is afraid.

46 "Had he been able sooner to believe,"
My Sage made answer, "O thou wounded soul,
What only in my verses he has seen,

49 Not upon thee had he stretched forth his hand;
Whereas the thing incredible has caused me
To put him to an act which grieveth me.

52 But tell him who thou wast, so that by way
Of some amends thy fame he may refresh
Up in the world, to which he can return."

55 And the trunk said: "So thy sweet words allure me,
I cannot silent be; and you be vexed not,
That I a little to discourse am tempted.

58 I am the one who both keys had in keeping
Of Frederick's heart, and turned them to and fro
So softly in unlocking and in locking,

61 That from his secrets most men I withheld;
Fidelity I bore the glorious office
So great, I lost thereby my sleep and pulses.

64 The courtesan who never from the dwelling
Of Caesar turned aside her strumpet eyes,
Death universal and the vice of courts,

Why dost thou rend me
Hast thou no spirit of pity whatsoever?
Men once we were, and now are changed to trees;
Indeed, thy hand should be more pitiful,
Even if the souls of serpents we had been.

Gustave Doré

67 Inflamed against me all the other minds,
And they, inflamed, did so inflame Augustus,
That my glad honours turned to dismal mournings.

70 My spirit, in disdainful exultation,
Thinking by dying to escape disdain,
Made me unjust against myself, the just.

73 I, by the roots unwonted of this wood,
Do swear to you that never broke I faith
Unto my lord, who was so worthy of honour;

76 And to the world if one of you return,
Let him my memory comfort, which is lying
Still prostrate from the blow that envy dealt it."

79 Waited awhile, and then: "Since he is silent,"
The Poet said to me, "lose not the time,
But speak, and question him, if more may please thee."

82 Whence I to him: "Do thou again inquire
Concerning what thou thinks't will satisfy me;
For I cannot, such pity is in my heart."

85 Therefore he recommenced: "So may the man
Do for thee freely what thy speech implores,
Spirit incarcerate, again be pleased

88 To tell us in what way the soul is bound
Within these knots; and tell us, if thou canst
If any from such members e'er is freed."

91 Then blew the trunk amain, and afterward
The wind was into such a voice converted:
"With brevity shall be replied to you.

94 When the exasperated soul abandons
The body whence it rent itself away,
Minos consigns it to the seventh abyss.

97 It falls into the forest, and no part
Is chosen for it; but where Fortune hurls it,
There like a grain of spelt it germinates.

100 It springs a sapling, and a forest tree;
The Harpies, feeding then upon its leaves,

Do pain create, and for the pain an outlet.

103 Like others for our spoils shall we return;
But not that any one may them revest,
For 'tis not just to have what one casts off.

106 Here we shall drag them, and along the dismal
Forest our bodies shall suspended be,
Each to the thorn of his molested shade."

109 We were attentive still unto the trunk,
Thinking that more it yet might wish to tell us,
When by a tumult we were overtaken,

112 In the same way as he is who perceives
The boar and chase approaching to his stand,
Who hears the crashing of the beasts and branches;

115 And two behold! upon our left-hand side,
Naked and scratched, fleeing so furiously,
That of the forest, every fan they broke.

118 He who was in advance: "Now help, Death, help!"
And the other one, who seemed to lag too much,
Was shouting: "Lano, were not so alert

121 Those legs of thine at joustings of the Toppo!"
And then, perchance because his breath was failing,
He grouped himself together with a bush.

124 Behind them was the forest full of black
She-mastiffs, ravenous, and swift of foot
As greyhounds, who are issuing from the chain.

127 On him who had crouched down they set their teeth,
And him they lacerated piece by piece,
Thereafter bore away those aching members.

130 Thereat my Escort took me by the hand,
And led me to the bush, that all in vain
Was weeping from its bloody lacerations.

133 "O Jacopo," it said, "of Sant Andrea,
What helped it thee of me to make a screen?
What blame have I in thy nefarious life?"

136 When near him had the Master stayed his steps,
He said: “Who wast thou, that through wounds so many
Art blowing out with blood thy dolorous speech?”

139 And he to us: “O souls, that hither come
To look upon the shameful massacre
That has so rent away from me my leaves,

142 Gather them up beneath the dismal bush;
I of that city was which to the Baptist
Changed its first patron, wherefore he for this

145 Forever with his art will make it sad.
And were it not that on the pass of Arno
Some glimpses of him are remaining still,

148 Those citizens, who afterwards rebuilt it
Upon the ashes left by Attila,
In vain had caused their labour to be done.

151 Of my own house I made myself a gibbet.”

Canto XIV

BECAUSE the charity of my native place
Constrained me, gathered I the scattered leaves,
And gave them back to him, who now was hoarse.

4 Then came we to the confine, where disparted
The second round is from the third, and where
A horrible form of Justice is beheld.

7 Clearly to manifest these novel things,
I say that we arrived upon a plain,
Which from its bed rejecteth every plant;

10 The dolorous forest is a garland to it
All round about, as the sad moat to that;
There close upon the edge we stayed our feet.

13 The soil was of an arid and thick sand,
Not of another fashion made than that
Which by the feet of Cato once was pressed.

16 Vengeance of God, O how much oughtest thou
By each one to be dreaded, who doth read
That which was manifest unto mine eyes!

19 Of naked souls beheld I many herds,
Who all were weeping very miserably,
And over them seemed set a law diverse.

22 Supine upon the ground some folk were lying;
And some were sitting all drawn up together,
And others went about continually.

25 Those who were going round were far the more,
And those were less who lay down to their torment,
But had their tongues more loosed to lamentation.

28 O'er all the sand-waste, with a gradual fall,
Were raining down dilated flakes of fire,
As of the snow on Alp without a wind.

31 As Alexander, in those torrid parts
Of India, beheld upon his host

Flames fall unbroken till they reached the ground,

34 Whence he provided with his phalanxes
To trample down the soil, because the vapour
Better extinguished was while it was single;

37 Thus was descending the eternal heat,
Whereby the sand was set on fire, like tinder
Beneath the steel, for doubling of the dole.

40 Without repose forever was the dance
Of miserable hands, now there, now here,
Shaking away from off them the fresh gleeds.

43 "Master," began I, "thou who overcomest
All things except the demons dire, that issued
Against us at the entrance of the gate,

46 Who is that mighty one who seems to heed not
The fire, and lieth lowering and disdainful,
So that the rain seems not to ripen him?"

49 And he himself, who had become aware
That I was questioning my Guide about him,
Cried: "Such as I was living, am I dead.

52 If Jove should weary out his smith, from whom
He seized in anger the sharp thunderbolt,
Wherewith upon the last day I was smitten,

55 And if he wearied out by turns the others
In Mongibello at the swarthy forge,
Vociferating, 'Help, good Vulcan, help!'

58 Even as he did there at the fight of Phlegra,
And shot his bolts at me with all his might,
He would not have thereby a joyous vengeance."

61 Then did my Leader speak with such great force,
That I had never heard him speak so loud:
"O Capaneus, in that is not extinguished

64 Thine arrogance, thou punished art the more;
Not any torment, saving thine own rage,
Would be unto thy fury pain complete."

67 Then he turned round to me with better lip,
Saying: "One of the Seven Kings was he
Who Thebes besieged, and held, and seems to hold

70 God in disdain, and little seems to prize him;
But, as I said to him, his own despites
Are for his breast the fittest ornaments.

73 Now follow me, and mind thou do not place
As yet thy feet upon the burning sand,
But always keep them close unto the wood."

76 Speaking no word, we came to where there gushes
Forth from the wood a little rivulet,
Whose redness makes my hair still stand on end.

79 As from the Bulicame springs the brooklet,
The sinful women later share among them,
So downward through the sand it went its way.

82 The bottom of it, and both sloping banks,
Were made of stone, and the margins at the side;
Whence I perceived that there the passage was.

85 "In all the rest which I have shown to thee
Since we have entered in within the gate
Whose threshold unto no one is denied,

88 Nothing has been discovered by thine eyes
So notable as is the present river,
Which all the little dames above it quenches."

91 These words were of my Leader; whence I prayed him
That he would give me largess of the food,
For which he had given me largess of desire.

94 "In the mid-sea there sits a wasted land,"
Said he thereafterward, "whose name is Crete,
Under whose king the world of old was chaste.

97 There is a mountain there, that once was glad
With waters and with leaves, which was called Ida;
Now 'tis deserted, as a thing worn out.

100 Rhea once chose it for the faithful cradle
Of her own son; and to conceal him better,

Whene'er he cried, she there had clamours made.

103 A grand old man stands in the mount erect,
Who holds his shoulders turned tow'rds Damietta,
And looks at Rome as if it were his mirror.

106 His head is fashioned of refined gold,
And of pure silver are the arms and breast;
Then he is brass as far down as the fork.

109 From that point downward all is chosen iron,
Save that the right foot is of kiln-baked clay,
And more he stands on that than on the other.

112 Each part, except the gold, is by a fissure
Asunder cleft, that dripping is with tears,
Which gathered together perforate that cavern.

115 From rock to rock they fall into this valley;
Acheron, Styx, and Phlegethon they form;
Then downward go along this narrow sluice

118 Unto that point where is no more descending.
They form Cocytus; what that pool may be
Thou shalt behold, so here 'tis not narrated."

121 And I to him: "If so the present runnel
Doth take its rise in this way from our world,
Why only on this verge appears it to us?"

124 And he to me: "Thou knowest the place is round
And notwithstanding thou hast journeyed far,
Still to the left descending to the bottom,

127 Thou hast not yet through all the circle turned.
Therefore if something new appear to us,
It should not bring amazement to thy face."

130 And I again: "Master, where shall be found
Lethe and Phlegethon, for of one thou'rt silent,
And sayest the other of this rain is made?"

133 "In all thy questions truly thou dost please me,"
Replied he; "but the boiling of the red
Water might well solve one of them thou makest.

136 Thou shalt see Lethe, but outside this moat,
There where the souls repair to lave themselves,
When sin repented of has been removed."

139 Then said he: "It is time now to abandon
The wood; take heed that thou come after me;
A way the margins make that are not burning,

142 And over them all vapours are extinguished."

Canto XV

NOW bears us onward one of the hard margins,
And so the brooklet's mist o'ershadows it,
From fire it saves the water and the dikes.

4 Even as the Flemings, 'twixt Cadsand and Bruges,
Fearing the flood that tow'rds them hurls itself,
Their bulwarks build to put the sea to flight;

7 And as the Paduans along the Brenta,
To guard their villas and their villages,
Or ever Chiarentana feel the heat;

10 In such similitude had those been made,
Albeit not so lofty nor so thick,
Whoever he might be, the master made them.

13 Now were we from the forest so remote,
I could not have discovered where it was,
Even if backward I had turned myself,

16 Then we a company of souls encountered,
Who came beside the dike, and every one
Gazed at us, as at evening we are wont

19 To eye each other under a new moon,
And so towards us sharpened they their brows
As an old tailor at the needle's eye.

22 Thus scrutinised by such a family,
By some one I was recognised, who seized

My garment's hem, and cried out, "What a marvel!"

25 And I, when he stretched forth his arm to me,
On his baked aspect fastened so mine eyes,
That the scorched countenance prevented not

28 His recognition by my intellect;
And bowing down my face unto his own,
I made reply, "Are you here, Ser Brunetto?"

31 And he: "May't not displease thee, O my son,
If a brief space with thee Brunetto Latini
Backward return and let the trail go on."

34 I said to him: "With all my power I ask it;
And if you wish me to sit down with you,
I will, if he please, for I go with him."

37 "O son," he said, "whoever of this herd
A moment stops, lies then a hundred years,
Nor fans himself when smiteth him the fire.

40 Therefore go on; I at thy skirts will come,
And afterward will I rejoin my band,
Which goes lamenting its eternal doom."

43 I did not dare to go down from the road
Level to walk with him; but my head bowed
I held as one who goeth reverently.

46 And he began: "What fortune or what fate
Before the last day leadeth thee down here?
And who is this that showeth thee the way?"

49 "Up there above us in the life serene,"
I answered him, "I lost me in a valley,
Or ever yet my age had been completed.

52 But yestermorn I turned my back upon it;
This one appeared to me, returning thither,
And homeward leadeth me along this road."

55 And he to me: "If thou thy star do follow,
Thou canst not fail thee of a glorious port,
If well I judged in the life beautiful.

58 And if I had not died so prematurely,
Seeing Heaven thus benignant unto thee,
I would have given thee comfort in the work.

61 But that ungrateful and malignant people,
Which of old time from Fesole descended,
And smacks still of the mountain and the granite,

64 Will make itself, for thy good deeds, thy foe;
And it is right; for among crabbed sorbs
It ill befits the sweet fig to bear fruit.

67 Old rumour in the world proclaims them blind;
A people avaricious, envious, proud;
Take heed that of their customs thou do cleanse thee.

70 Thy fortune so much honour doth reserve thee,
One party and the other shall be hungry
For thee; but far from goat shall be the grass.

73 Their litter let the beasts of Fesole
Make of themselves, nor let them touch the plant,
If any still upon their dunghill rise,

76 In which may yet revive the consecrated
Seed of those Romans, who remained there when
The nest of such great malice it became."

79 "If my entreaty wholly were fulfilled,"
Replied I to him, "not yet would you be
In banishment from human nature placed;

82 For in my mind is fixed, and touches now
My heart the dear and good paternal image
Of you, when in the world from hour to hour

85 You taught me how a man becomes eternal;
And how much I am grateful, while I live
Behoves that in my language be discerned.

88 What you narrate of my career I write,
And keep it to be glossed with other text
By a Lady who can do it, if I reach her.

91 This much will I have manifest to you;

Provided that my conscience do not chide me,
For whatsoever Fortune I am ready.

94 Such handsel is not new unto mine ears;
Therefore let Fortune turn her wheel around
As it may please her, and the churl his mattock."

97 My Master thereupon on his right cheek
Did backward turn himself, and looked at me;
Then said: "He listeneth well who noteth it."

100 Nor speaking less on that account, I go
With Ser Brunetto, and I ask who are
His most known and most eminent companions.

103 And he to me: "To know of some is well;
Of others it were laudable to be silent,
For short would be the time for so much speech.

106 Know them in sum, that all of them were clerks,
And men of letters great and of great fame,
In the world tainted with the selfsame sin.

109 Priscian goes yonder with that wretched crowd,
And Francis of Accorso; and thou hadst seen there
If thou hadst had a hankering for such scurf,

112 That one, who by the Servant of the Servants
From Arno was transferred to Bacchiglione,
Where he has left his sin-excited nerves.

115 More would I say, but coming and discoursing
Can be no longer; for that I behold
New smoke uprising yonder from the sand.

118 A people comes with whom I may not be;
Commended unto thee be my Tesoro,
In which I still live, and no more I ask."

121 Then he turned round, and seemed to be of those
Who at Verona run for the Green Mantle
Across the plain; and seemed to be among them

124 The one who wins, and not the one who loses.

Canto XVI

NOW was I where was heard the reverberation
Of water falling into the next round,
Like to that humming which the beehives make,

4 When shadows three together started forth,
Running, from out a company that passed
Beneath the rain of the sharp martyrdom.

7 Towards us came they, and each one cried out:
"Stop, thou; for by thy garb to us thou seemest
To be some one of our depraved city."

10 Ah me! what wounds I saw upon their limbs,
Recent and ancient by the flames burnt in!
It pains me still but to remember it.

13 Unto their cries my Teacher paused attentive;
He turned his face towards me, and "Now wait,"
He said; "to these we should be courteous.

16 And if it were not for the fire that darts
The nature of this region, I should say
That haste were more becoming thee than them."

19 As soon as we stood still, they recommenced
The old refrain, and when they overtook us,
Formed of themselves a wheel, all three of them.

22 As champions stripped and oiled are wont to do,
Watching for their advantage and their hold,
Before they come to blows and thrusts between them,

25 Thus, wheeling round, did every one his visage
Direct to me, so that in opposite wise
His neck and feet continual journey made.

28 And, "If the misery of this soft place
Bring in disdain ourselves and our entreaties,"
Began one, "and our aspect black and blistered.

31 Let the renown of us thy mind incline
To tell us who thou art, who thus securely
Thy living feet dost move along through Hell.

34 He in whose footprints thou dost see me treading,
Naked and skinless though he now may go,
Was of a greater rank than thou dost think;

37 He was the grandson of the good Gualdrada;
His name was Guidoguerra, and in life
Much did he with his wisdom and his sword.

40 The other, who close by me treads the sand,
Tegghiaio Aldobrandi is, whose fame
Above there in the world should welcome be.

43 And I, who with them on the cross am placed,
Jacopo Rusticucci was; and truly
My savage wife, more than aught else, doth harm me."

46 Could I have been protected from the fire,
Below I should have thrown myself among them,
And think the Teacher would have suffered it;

49 But as I should have burned and baked myself,
My terror overmastered my good will,
Which made me greedy of embracing them.

52 Then I began: "Sorrow and not disdain
Did your condition fix within me so,
That tardily it wholly is stripped off,

55 As soon as this my Lord said unto me
Words, on account of which I thought within me
That people such as you are were approaching.

58 I of your city am; and evermore
Your labours and your honourable names
I with affection have retraced and heard.

61 I leave the gall, and go for the sweet fruits
Promised to me by the veracious Leader;
But to the centre first I needs must plunge."

64 "So may the soul for a long while conduct
Those limbs of thine," did he make answer
"And so may thy renown shine after thee,

67 Valour and courtesy, say if they dwell
Within our city, as they used to do,
Or if they wholly have gone out of it;

70 For Guglielmo Borsier, who is in torment
With us of late, and goes there with his comrades,
Doth greatly mortify us with his words."

73 "The new inhabitants and the sudden gains,
Pride and extravagance have in thee engendered,
Florence, so that thou weep'st thereat already!"

76 In this wise I exclaimed with face uplifted;
And the three, taking that for my reply,
Looked at each other, as one looks at truth.

79 "If other times so little it doth cost thee,"
Replied they all, "to satisfy another,
Happy art thou, thus speaking at thy will!

82 Therefore, if thou escape from these dark places,
And come to rebehold the beauteous stars,
When it shall pleasure thee to say, 'I was,'

85 See that thou speak of us unto the people."
Then they broke up the wheel, and in their flight
It seemed as if their agile legs were wings.

88 Not an Amen could possibly be said
So rapidly as they had disappeared;
Wherefore the Master deemed best to depart.

91 I followed him, and little had we gone,
Before the sound of water was so near us,
That speaking we should hardly have been heard.

94 Even as that stream which holdeth its own course
The first from Monte Veso tow'rds the East,
Upon the left-hand slope of Apennine,

97 Which is above called Acquacheta, ere
It down descendeth into its low bed,
And at Forli is vacant of that name,

100 Reverberates there above San Benedetto
From Alps, by falling at a single leap,
Where for a thousand there were room enough;

103 Thus downward from a bank precipitate,

We found resounding that dark-tinted water,
So that it soon the ear would have offended.

106 I had a cord around about me girt,
And therewithal I whilom had designed
To take the panther with the painted skin.

109 After I this had all from me unloosed,
As my Conductor had commanded me,
I reached it to him, gathered up and coiled

112 Whereat he turned himself to the right side,
And at a little distance from the verge,
He cast it down into that deep abyss.

115 "It must needs be some novelty respond,"
I said within myself, "to the new signal
The Master with his eye is following so."

118 Ah me! How very cautious men should be
With those who not alone behold the act,
But with their wisdom look into the thoughts!

121 He said to me: "Soon there will upward come
What I await; and what thy thought is dreaming
Must soon reveal itself unto thy sight."

124 Aye to that truth which has the face of falsehood,
A man should close his lips as far as may be,
Because without his fault it causes shame;

127 But here I cannot; and, Reader, by the notes
Of this my Comedy to thee I swear,
So may they not be void of lasting favour,

130 Athwart that dense and darksome atmosphere
I saw a figure swimming upward come,
Marvellous unto every steadfast heart,

133 Even as he returns who goeth down
Sometimes to clear an anchor, which has grappled
Reef,or aught else that in the sea is hidden,

136 Who upward stretches, and draws in his feet.

Canto XVII

"BEHOLD the monster with the pointed tail,
Who cleaves the hills, and breaketh walls and weapons,
Behold him who infecteth all the world."

4 Thus unto me my Guide began to say,
And beckoned him that he should come to shore,
Near to the confine of the trodden marble;

7 And that uncleanly image of deceit
Came up and thrust ashore its head and bust,
But on the border did not drag its tail.

10 The face was as the face of a just man,
Its semblance outwardly was so benign,
And of a serpent all the trunk beside.

13 Two paws it had, hairy unto the armpits;
The back, and breast, and both the sides it had
Depicted o'er with nooses and with shields.

16 With colours more, groundwork or broidery
Never in cloth did Tartars make nor Turks,
Nor were such tissues by Arachne laid.

19 As sometimes wherries lie upon the shore,
That part are in the water, part on land;
And as among the guzzling Germans there,

22 The beaver plants himself to wage his war;
So that vile monster lay upon the border,
Which is of stone, and shutteth in the sand.

25 His tail was wholly quivering in the void,
Contorting upwards the envenomed fork,
That in the guise of scorpion armed its point.

28 The Guide said: "Now perforce must turn aside
Our way a little, even to that beast
Malevolent, that yonder coucheth him."

31 We therefore on the right side descended,
And made ten steps upon the outer verge,
Completely to avoid the sand and flame;

34 And after we are come to him, I see
A little farther off upon the sand
A people sitting near the hollow place.

37 Then said to me the Master: “So that full
Experience of this round thou bear away,
Now go and see what their condition is.

40 There let thy conversation be concise;
Till thou returnest I will speak with him,
That he concede to us his stalwart shoulders.”

43 Thus farther still upon the outermost
Head of that seventh circle all alone
I went, where sat the melancholy folk.

46 Out of their eyes was gushing forth their woe;
This way, that way, they helped them with their hands
Now from the flames and now from the hot soil.

49 Not otherwise in summer do the dogs,
Now with the foot, now with the muzzle, when so
By fleas, or flies, or gadflies, they are bitten.

52 When I had turned mine eyes upon the faces
Of some, on whom the dolorous fire is falling,
Not one of them I knew; but I perceived

55 That from the neck of each there hung a pouch,
Which certain colour had, and certain blazon;
And thereupon it seems their eyes are feeding.

58 And as I gazing round me came among them,
Upon a yellow pouch I azure saw
That had the face and posture of a lion.

61 Proceeding then the current of my sight,
Another of them saw I, red as blood,
Display a goose more white than butter is.

64 And one, who with an azure sow and gravid
Emblazoned had his little pouch of white,
Said unto me: “What dost thou in this moat?

67 Now get thee gone; and since thou’rt still alive,
Know that a neighbour of mine, Vitaliano,

Will have his seat here on my left-hand side.

70 A Paduan am I with these Florentines;
Full many a time they thunder in mine ears,
Exclaiming, 'Come the sovereign cavalier,

73 He who shall bring the satchel with three goats;'"
Then twisted he his mouth, and forth he thrust
His tongue, like to an ox that licks its nose.

76 And fearing lest my longer stay might vex
Him who had warned me not to tarry long,
Backward I turned me from those weary souls.

79 I found my Guide, who had already mounted
Upon the back of that wild animal,
And said to me: "Now be both strong and bold.

82 Now we descend by stairways such as these;
Mount thou in front, for I will be midway,
So that the tail may have no power to harm thee."

85 Such as he is who has so near the ague
Of quartan that his nails are blue already,
And trembles all, but looking at the shade;

88 Even such became I at those proffered words;
But shame in me his menaces produced,
Which maketh servant strong before good master.

91 I seated me upon those monstrous shoulders;
I wished to say, and yet the voice came not
As I believed, "Take heed that thou embrace me."

94 But he, who other times had rescued me
In other peril, soon as I had mounted,
Within his arms encircled and sustained me,

97 And said: "Now, Geryon, bestir thyself;
The circles large, and the descent be little;
Think of the novel burden which thou hast."

100 Even as the little vessel shoves from shore,
Backward, still backward, so he thence withdrew;
And when he wholly felt himself afloat,

103 There where his breast had been he turned his tail,
And that extended like an eel he moved,
And with his paws drew to himself the air.

106 A greater fear I do not think there was
What time abandoned Phaeton the reins,
Whereby the heavens, as still appears, were scorched;

109 Nor when the wretched Icarus his flanks
Felt stripped of feathers by the melting wax,
His father crying, "An ill way thou takest!"

112 Than was my own, when I perceived myself
On all sides in the air, and saw extinguished
The sight of everything but of the monster.

115 Onward he goeth, swimming slowly, slowly;
Wheels and descends, but I perceive it only
By wind upon my face and from below.

118 I heard already on the right the whirlpool
Making a horrible crashing under us;
Whence I thrust out my head with eyes cast downward.

121 Then was I still more fearful of the abyss;
Because I fires beheld, and heard laments,
Whereat I, trembling, all the closer clung.

124 I saw then, for before I had not seen it,
The turning and descending, by great horrors
That were approaching upon divers sides.

127 As falcon who has long been on the wing,
Who, without seeing either lure or bird,
Maketh the falconer say, "Ah me, thou stoopest,"

130 Descendeth weary, whence he started swiftly,
Through a hundred circles, and alights
Far from his master, sullen and disdainful;

133 Even thus did Geryon place us on the bottom,
Close to the bases of the rough-hewn rock,
And being disencumbered of our persons,

136 He sped away as arrow from the string.

Canto XVIII

THERE is a place in Hell called Malebolge,
Wholly of stone and of an iron colour,
As is the circle that around it turns.

4 Right in the middle of the field malign
There yawns a well exceeding wide and deep,
Of which its place the structure will recount.

7 Round, then, is that enclosure which remains
Between the well and foot of the high, hard bank,
And has distinct in valleys ten its bottom.

10 As where for the protection of the walls
Many and many moats surround the castles,
The part in which they are a figure forms,

13 Just such an image those presented there;
And as about such strongholds from their gates
Unto the outer bank are little bridges,

16 So from the precipice's base did crags
Project, which intersected dikes and moats,
Unto the well that truncates and collects them.

19 Within this place, down shaken from the back
Of Geryon, we found us; and the Poet
Held to the left, and I moved on behind.

22 Upon my right hand I beheld new anguish,
New torments, and new wielders of the lash,
Wherewith the foremost Bolgia was replete.

25 Down at the bottom were the sinners naked;
This side the middle came they facing us,
Beyond it, with us, but with greater steps;

28 Even as the Romans, for the mighty host,
The year of Jubilee, upon the bridge,
Have chosen a mode to pass the people over;

31 For all upon one side towards the Castle
Their faces have, and go unto St. Peter's;
On the other side they go towards the Mountain.

34 This side and that, along the livid stone
Beheld I horned demons with great scourges,
Who cruelly were beating them behind.

37 Ah me! how they did make them lift their legs
At the first blows! And sooth not any one
The second waited for, nor for the third.

40 While I was going on, mine eyes by one
Encountered were; and straight I said: "Already
With sight of this one I am not unfed."

43 Therefore I stayed my feet to make him out,
And with me the sweet Guide came to a stand,
And to my going somewhat back assented;

46 And he, the scourged one, thought to hide himself,
Lowering his face, but little it availed him;
For said I: "Thou that castest down thine eyes

49 If false are not the features which thou bearest;
Thou art Venedico Caccianimico;
But what doth bring thee to such pungent sauces?"

52 And he to me: "Unwillingly I tell it;
But forces me thine utterance distinct,
Which makes me recollect the ancient world.

55 I was the one who the fair Ghisola
Induced to grant the wishes of the Marquis,
Howe'er the shameless story may be told.

58 Not the sole Bolognese am I who weeps here;
Nay, rather is this place so full of them,
That not so many tongues to-day are taught

61 'Twixt Reno and Savena to say 'sipa;'
And if thereof thou wishest pledge or proof,
Bring to thy mind our avaricious heart."

64 While speaking in this manner, with his scourge
A demon smote him, and said: "Get thee
Pander, there are no women here for coin."

67 I joined myself again unto mine Escort;
Thereafterward with footsteps few we came

To where a crag projected from the bank.

This very easily did we ascend,
And turning to the right along its ridge,
From those eternal circles we departed.

When we were there, where it is hollowed out
Beneath, to give a passage to the scourged,
The Guide said: "Wait, and see that on thee strike

The vision of those others evil-born,
Of whom thou hast not yet beheld the faces,
Because together with us they have gone."

From the old bridge we looked upon the train
Which tow'rds us came upon the other border,
And which the scourges in like manner smite.

And the good Master, without my inquiring,
Said to me: "See that tall one who is coming,
And for his pain seems not to shed a tear;

Still what a royal aspect he retains!
That Jason is, who by his heart and cunning
The Colchians of the Ram made destitute.

He by the isle of Lemnos passed along
After the daring women pitiless
Had unto death devoted all their males.

There with his tokens and with ornate words
Did he deceive Hypsipyle, the maiden
Who first, herself, had all the rest deceived.

There did he leave her pregnant and forlorn;
Such sin unto such punishment condemns him,
And also for Medea is vengeance done.

With him go those who in such wise deceive;
And this sufficient be of the first valley
To know, and those that in its jaws it holds."

We were already where the narrow path
Crosses athwart the second dike, and forms
Of that a buttress for another arch.

Thence we heard people, who are making moan
In the next Bolgia, snorting with their muzzles,
And with their palms beating upon themselves.

The margins were incrusted with a mould
By exhalation from below, that sticks there,
And with the eyes and nostrils wages war.

The bottom was so deep, no place sufficed
To give us sight of it, without ascending
The arch's back, where most the crag impends.

Thither we came, and thence down in the moat
I saw a people smothered in a filth
That out of human privies seemed to flow.

And whilst below there with mine eye I searched,
I saw one with his head so foul with ordure,
It was not clear if he were clerk or layman.

He screamed to me: "Wherefore art thou so eager
To look at me more than the other foul ones?"
And I to him: "Because, if I remember,

I have already seen thee with dry hair,
And thou'rt Alessio Interminei of Lucca;
Therefore I eye thee more than all the others."

And he thereon, belabouring his pumpkin:[2]
"The flatteries have submerged me here below,
Wherewith my tongue was never surfeited."

Then said to me the Guide: "See that thou thrust
Thy visage somewhat farther in advance,
That with thine eyes thou well the face attain

Of that uncleanly and dishevelled drab,
Who there doth scratch herself with filthy nails,
And crouches now, and now on foot is standing.

Thais the harlot is it, who replied
Unto her paramour, when he said, 'Have I
Great gratitude from thee ?'—'Nay, marvellous;'

And herewith let our sight be satisfied."

2 "beating his head"

Canto XIX

O SIMON Magus, O forlorn disciples,
Ye who the things of God, which ought to be
The brides of holiness, rapaciously

4 For silver and for gold do prostitute,
Now it behoves for you the trumpet sound,
Because in this third Bolgia ye abide.

7 We had already on the following tomb
Ascended to that portion of the crag
Which o'er the middle of the moat hangs plumb.

10 Wisdom supreme, O how great art thou showest
In heaven, in earth, and in the evil world,
And with what justice doth thy power distribute!

13 I saw upon the sides and on the bottom
The livid stone with perforations filled,
All of one size, and every one was round.

16 To me less ample seemed they not, nor greater
Than those that in my beautiful Saint John
Are fashioned for the place of the baptisers,

19 And one of which, not many years ago,
I broke for some one, who was drowning in it;
Be this a seal all men to undeceive.

22 Out of the mouth of each one there protruded
The feet of a transgressor, and the legs
Up to the calf, the rest within remained.

25 In all of them the soles were both on fire;
Wherefore the joints so violently quivered,
They would have snapped asunder withes and bands.

28 Even as the flame of unctuous things is wont
To move upon the outer surface only,
So likewise was it there from heel to point.

31 "Master, who is that one who writhes himself,
More than his other comrades quivering,"
I said. "and whom a redder flame is sucking?"

34 And he to me: "If thou wilt have me bear thee
Down there along that bank which lowest lies,
From him thou'lt know his errors and himself."

37 And I: "What pleases thee, to me is pleasing;
Thou art my Lord, and knowest that I depart not
From thy desire, and knowest what is not spoken."

40 Straightway upon the fourth dike we arrived;
We turned, and on the left-hand side descended
Down to the bottom full of holes and narrow.

43 And the good Master yet from off his haunch
Deposed me not, till to the hole he brought me
Of him who so lamented with his shanks.

46 "Whoe'er thou art, that standest upside down,
O doleful soul, implanted like a stake,"
To say began I, "if thou canst, speak out."

49 I stood even as the friar who is confessing
The false assassin, who, when he is fixed,
Recalls him, so that death may be delayed.

52 And he cried out: "Dost thou stand there already,
Dost thou stand there already, Boniface?
By many years the record lied to me.

55 Art thou so early satiate with that wealth,
For which thou didst not fear to take by fraud
The beautiful Lady, and then work her woe?"

58 Such I became, as people are who stand,
Not comprehending what is answered them,
As if bemocked, and know not how to answer.

61 Then said Virgilius: "Say to him straightway,
'I am not he, I am not he thou thinkest.'"
And I replied as was imposed on me.

64 Whereat the spirit writhed with both his feet,
Then, sighing, with a voice of lamentation
Said to me: "Then what wantest thou of me?

67 If who I am thou carest so much to know,
That thou on that account hast crossed the bank,
Know that I vested was with the great mantle;

70 And truly was I son of the She-bear,
So eager to advance the cubs, that wealth
Above, and here myself, I pocketed.

73 Beneath my head the others are dragged down
Who have preceded me in simony,
Flattened along the fissure of the rock.

76 Below there I shall likewise fall, whenever
That one shall come who I believed thou wast,
What time the sudden question I proposed.

79 But longer I my feet already toast,
And here have been in this way upside down,
Than he will planted stay with reddened feet;

82 For after him shall come of fouler deed
From tow'rds the west a Pastor without law,
Such as befits to cover him and me.

85 New Jason will he be, of whom we read
In Maccabees; and as his king was pliant,
So he who governs France shall be to this one."

88 I do not know if I were here too bold,
That him I answered only in this metre:
"I pray thee tell me now how great a treasure

91 Our Lord demanded of Saint Peter first,
Before he put the keys into his keeping?
Truly he nothing asked but 'Follow me.'

94 Nor Peter nor the rest asked of Matthias
Silver or gold, when he by lot was chosen
Unto the place the guilty soul had lost.

97 Therefore stay here, for thou art justly punished,
And keep safe guard o'er the ill-gotten money,
Which caused thee to be valiant against Charles.

100 And were it not that still forbids it me
The reverence for the keys superlative
Thou hadst in keeping in the gladsome life,

103 I would make use of words more grievous still;
Because your avarice afflicts the world,
Trampling the good and lifting the depraved.

Beneath my head the others are dragged down
Who have preceded me in simony,
Flattened along the fissure of the rock.

Gustave Doré

106 The Evangelist you Pastors had in mind,
When she who sitteth upon many waters
To fornicate with kings by him was seen;

109 The same who with the seven heads was born,
And power and strength from the ten horns received,
So long as virtue to her spouse was pleasing.

112 Ye have made yourselves a god of gold and silver;
And from the idolater how differ ye,
Save that he one, and ye a hundred worship?

115 Ah, Constantine! of how much ill was mother,
Not thy conversion, but that marriage dower
Which the first wealthy Father took from thee!"

118 And while I sang to him such notes as these.
Either that anger or that conscience stung him,
He struggled violently with both his feet.

121 I think in sooth that it my Leader pleased,
With such contented lip he listened ever
Unto the sound of the true words expressed.

124 Therefore with both his arms he took me up,
And when he had me all upon his breast,
Remounted by the way where he descended.

127 Nor did he tire to have me clasped to him;
But bore me to the summit of the arch
Which from the fourth dike to the fifth is passage.

130 There tenderly he laid his burden down,
Tenderly on the crag uneven and steep,
That would have been hard passage for the goats:

133 Thence was unveiled to me another valley.

Canto XX

OF a new pain behoves me to make verses
And give material to the twentieth Canto
Of the first song, which is of the submerged.

4 I was already thoroughly disposed
To peer down into the uncovered depth,
Which bathed itself with tears of agony;

7 And people saw I through the circular valley,
Silent and weeping, coming at the pace
Which in this world the Litanies assume.

10 As lower down my sight descended on them,
Wondrously each one seemed to be distorted
From chin to the beginning of the chest;

13 For tow'rds the reins the countenance was turned,
And backward it behoved them to advance,
As to look forward had been taken from them.

16 Perchance indeed by violence of palsy
Some one has been thus wholly turned awry;
But I ne'er saw it nor believe it can be.

19 As God may let thee, Reader, gather fruit
From this thy reading, think now for thyself
How I could ever keep my face unmoistened,

22 When our own image near me I beheld
Distorted so, the weeping of the eyes
Along the fissure bathed the hinder parts.

25 Truly I wept, leaning upon a peak
Of the hard crag, so that my Escort said
To me: "Art thou, too, of the other fools?

28 Here pity lives when it is wholly dead;
Who is a greater reprobate than he
Who feels compassion at the doom divine?

31 Lift up, lift up thy head, and see for whom
Opened the earth before the Thebans' eyes;

Wherefore they all cried: 'Whither rushest thou,

34 Amphiaraus? Why dost leave the war?'
And downward ceased he not to fall amain
As far as Minos, who lays hold on all.

37 See, he has made a bosom of his shoulders!
Because he wished to see too far before him
Behind he looks, and backward goes his way:

40 Behold Tiresias, who his semblance changed,
When from a male a female he became,
His members being all of them transformed;

43 And afterwards was forced to strike once more
The two entangled serpents with his rod,
Ere he could have again his manly plumes.

46 That Aruns is, who backs the other's belly,
Who in the hills of Luni, there where grubs
The Carrarese who houses underneath,

49 Among the marbles white a cavern had
For his abode; whence to behold the stars
And sea, the view was not cut off from him.

52 And she there, who is covering up her breasts,
Which thou beholdest not, with loosened tresses,
And on that side has all the hairy skin,

55 Was Manto, who made quest through many lands,
Afterwards tarried there where I was born;
Whereof I would thou list to me a little.

58 After her father had from life departed,
And the city of Bacchus had become enslaved,
She a long season wandered through the world.

61 Above in beauteous Italy lies a lake
At the Alp's foot that shuts in Germany
Over Tyrol, and has the name Benaco.

64 By a thousand springs, I think, and more, is bathed,
'Twixt Garda and Val Camonica, Pennino,
With water that grows stagnant in that lake.

67 Midway a place is where the Trentine Pastor,
And he of Brescia, and the Veronese
Might give his blessing, if he passed that way.

70 Sitteth Peschiera, fortress fair and strong,
To front the Brescians and the Bergamasks,
Where round about the bank descendeth lowest.

73 There of necessity must fall whatever
In bosom of Benaco cannot stay,
And grows a river down through verdant pastures.

76 Soon as the water doth begin to run
No more Benaco is it called, but Mincio,
Far as Governo, where it falls in Po.

79 Not far it runs before it finds a plain
In which it spreads itself, and makes it marshy,
And oft 'tis wont in summer to be sickly.

82 Passing that way the virgin pitiless
Land in the middle of the fen descried,
Untilled and naked of inhabitants;

85 There to escape all human intercourse,
She with her servants stayed, her arts to practise
And lived, and left her empty body there.

88 The men, thereafter, who were scattered round,
Collected in that place, which was made strong
By the lagoon it had on every side;

91 They built their city over those dead bones,
And, after her who first the place selected,
Mantua named it, without other omen.

94 Its people once within more crowded were,
Ere the stupidity of Casalodi
From Pinamonte had received deceit.

97 Therefore I caution thee, if e'er thou hearest
Originate my city otherwise,
No falsehood may the verity defraud."

100 And I: "My Master, thy discourses are

To me so certain, and so take my faith,
That unto me the rest would be spent coals.

103 But tell me of the people who are passing,
If any one note-worthy thou beholdest,
For only unto that my mind reverts."

106 Then said he to me: "He who from the cheek
Thrusts out his beard upon his swarthy shoulders
Was, at the time when Greece was void of males,

109 So that there scarce remained one in the cradle,
An augur, and with Calchas gave the moment,
In Aulis, when to sever the first cable.

112 Eryphylus his name was, and so sings
My lofty Tragedy in some part or other;
That knowest thou well, who knowest the whole of it.

115 The next, who is so slender in the flanks,
Was Michael Scott, who of a verity
Of magical illusions knew the game.

118 Behold Guido Bonatti, behold Asdente
Who now unto his leather and his thread
Would fain have stuck, but he too late repents.

121 Behold the wretched ones, who left the needle,
The spool and rock, and made them fortune-tellers;
They wrought their magic spells with herb and image.

124 But come now, for already holds the confines
Of both the hemispheres, and under Seville
Touches the ocean-wave, Cain and the thorns,

127 And yesternight the moon was round already;
Thou shouldst remember well it did not harm thee
From time to time within the forest deep."

130 Thus spake he to me, and we walked the while.

Canto XXI

FROM bridge to bridge thus, speaking other things
Of which my Comedy cares not to sing,
We came along, and held the summit, when

4 We halted to behold another fissure
Of Malebolge and other vain laments;
And I beheld it marvellously dark.

7 As in the Arsenal of the Venetians
Boils in the winter the tenacious pitch
To smear their unsound vessels o'er again,

10 For sail they cannot; and instead thereof
One makes his vessel new, and one recaulks
The ribs of that which many a voyage has made;

13 One hammers at the prow, one at the stern,
This one makes oars, and that one cordage twists,
Another mends the mainsail and the mizzen;

16 Thus, not by fire, but by the art divine,
Was boiling down below there a dense pitch
Which upon every side the bank belimed.

19 I saw it, but I did not see within it
Aught but the bubbles that the boiling raised,
And all swell up and resubside compressed.

22 The while below there fixedly I gazed,
My Leader, crying out: "Beware, beware!"
Drew me unto himself from where I stood.

25 Then I turned round, as one who is impatient
To see what it behoves him to escape,
And whom a sudden terror doth unman,

28 Who, while he looks, delays not his departure.
And I beheld behind us a black devil,
Running along upon the crag, approach.

31 Ah, how ferocious was he in his aspect!
And how he seemed to me in action ruthless,
With open wings and light upon his feet!

His shoulders, which sharp-pointed were and high,
A sinner did encumber with both haunches,
And he held clutched the sinews of the feet.

From off our bridge, he said: "O Malebranche,
Behold one of the elders of Saint Zita;
Plunge him beneath, for I return for others

Unto that town, which is well furnished with them.
All there are barrators, except Bonturo;
No into Yes for money there is changed."

He hurled him down, and over the hard crag
Turned round, and never was a mastiff loosened
In so much hurry to pursue a thief.

The other sank, and rose again face downward;
But the demons, under cover of the bridge,
Cried: "Here the Santo Volto has no place!

Here swims one otherwise than in the Serchio;
Therefore, if for our gaffs thou wishest not,
Do not uplift thyself above the pitch."

They seized him then with more than a hundred rakes;
They said: "It here behoves thee to dance covered,
That, if thou canst, thou secretly mayest pilfer."

Not otherwise the cooks their scullions make
Immerse into the middle of the caldron
The meat with hooks, so that it may not float.

Said the good Master to me: "That it be not
Apparent thou art here, crouch thyself down
Behind a jag, that thou mayest have some screen;

And for no outrage that is done to me
Be thou afraid, because these things I know,
For once before was I in such a scuffle."

Then he passed on beyond the bridge's head,
And as upon the sixth bank he arrived,
Need was for him to have a steadfast front.

With the same fury, and the same uproar,

As dogs leap out upon a mendicant,
Who on a sudden begs, where'er he stops,

70 They issued from beneath the little bridge,
And turned against him all their grappling-irons;
But he cried out: "Be none of you malignant!

73 Before those hooks of yours lay hold of me,
Let one of you step forward, who may hear me,
And then take counsel as to grappling me."

76 They all cried out: "Let Malacoda go;"
Whereat one started, and the rest stood still,
And he came to him, saying: "What avails it?"

79 "Thinkest thou, Malacoda, to behold me
Advanced into this place," my Master said,
"Safe hitherto from all your skill of fence,

82 Without the will divine, and fate auspicious?
Let me go on, for it in Heaven is willed
That I another show this savage road."

85 Then was his arrogance so humbled in him,
That he let fall his grapnel at his feet,
And to the others said: "Now strike him not."

88 And unto me my Guide: "O thou, who sittest
Among the splinters of the bridge crouched down,
Securely now return to me again."

91 Wherefore I started and came swiftly to him;
And all the devils forward thrust themselves,
So that I feared they would not keep their compact.

94 And thus beheld I once afraid the soldiers
Who issued under safeguard from Caprona,
Seeing themselves among so many foes.

97 Close did I press myself with all my person
Beside my Leader, and turned not mine eyes
From off their countenance, which was not good.

100 They lowered their rakes, and "Wilt thou have me hit him,"
They said to one another, "on the rump?"
And answered: "Yes; see that thou nick him with it."

103 But the same demon who was holding parley
With my Conductor turned him very quickly,
And said: "Be quiet, be quiet, Scarmiglione;"

106 Then said to us: "You can no farther go
Forward upon this crag, because is lying
All shattered, at the bottom, the sixth arch.

109 And if it still doth please you to go onward,
Pursue your way along upon this rock;
Near is another crag that yields a path.

112 Yesterday, five hours later than this hour,
One thousand and two hundred sixty-six
Years were complete, that here the way was broken.

115 I send in that direction some of mine
To see if any one doth air himself;
Go ye with them; for they will not be vicious.

118 Step forward, Alichino and Calcabrina,"
Began he to cry out, "and thou, Cagnazzo;
And Barbariccia, do thou guide the ten.

121 Come forward, Libicocco and Draghignazzo,
And tusked Ciriatto and Graffiacane,
And Farfarello and mad Rubicante;

124 Search ye all round about the boiling pitch;
Let these be safe as far as the next crag,
That all unbroken passes o'er the dens."

127 "O me! what is it, Master, that I see?
Pray let us go," I said, "without an escort,
If thou knowest how, since for myself I ask none.

130 If thou art as observant as thy wont is,
Dost thou not see that they do gnash their teeth,
And with their brows are threatening woe to us?"

133 And he to me: "I will not have thee fear;
Let them gnash on, according to their fancy,
Because they do it for those boiling wretches."

136 Along the left-hand dike they wheeled about;

But first had each one thrust his tongue between
His teeth towards their leader for a signal;

139 And he had made a trumpet of his rump.

Canto XXII

I HAVE erewhile seen horsemen moving camp,
Begin the storming, and their muster make,
And sometimes starting off for their escape;

4 Vaunt-couriers have I seen upon your land,
O Aretines, and foragers go forth,
Tournaments stricken, and the joustings run,

7 Sometimes with trumpets and sometimes with bells,
With kettle-drums, and signals of the castles,
And with our own, and with outlandish things,

10 But never yet with bagpipe so uncouth
Did I see horsemen move, nor infantry,
Nor ship by any sign of land or star.

13 We went upon our way with the ten demons:
Ah, savage company! But in the church
With saints, and in the tavern with the gluttons!

16 Ever upon the pitch was my intent,
To see the whole condition of that Bolgia,
And of the people who therein were burned.

19 Even as the dolphins, when they make a sign
To mariners by arching of the back,
That they should counsel take to save their vessel,

22 Thus sometimes, to alleviate his pain,
One of the sinners would display his back,
And in less time conceal it than it lightens.

25 As on the brink of water in a ditch
The frogs stand only with their muzzles out,
So that they hide their feet and other bulk.

28 So upon every side the sinners stood;
But ever as Barbariccia near them came,
Thus underneath the boiling they withdrew.

31 I saw, and still my heart doth shudder at it,
One waiting thus, even as it comes to pass
One frog remains, and down another dives;

34 And Graffiacan, who most confronted him,
Grappled him by his tresses smeared with pitch,
And drew him up, so that he seemed an otter.

37 I knew, before, the names of all of them,
So had I noted them when they were chosen,
And when they called each other, listened how.

40 "O Rubicante, see that thou do lay
Thy claws upon him, so that thou mayst flay him,"
Cried all together the accursed ones.

43 And I: "My Master, see to it, if thou canst,
That thou mayst know who is the luckless wight,
Thus come into his adversaries' hands."

46 Near to the side of him my Leader drew,
Asked of him whence he was; and he replied:
"I in the kingdom of Navarre was born;

49 My mother placed me servant to a lord,
For she had borne me to a ribald knave,
Destroyer of himself and of his things.

52 Then I domestic was of good King Thibault;
I set me there to practise barratry,
For which I pay the reckoning in this heat."

55 And Ciriatto, from whose mouth projected,
On either side, a tusk, as in a boar,
Caused him to feel how one of them could rip.

58 Among malicious cats the mouse had come;
But Barbariccia clasped him in his arms,
And said: "Stand ye aside, while I enfork him."

61 And to my Master he turned round his head;

"Ask him again," he said, "if more thou wish
To know from him, before some one destroy him."

64 The Guide: "Now tell then of the other culprits;
Knowest thou any one who is a Latian,
Under the pitch?" And he: "I separated

67 Lately from one who was a neighbour to it;
Would that I still were covered up with him,
For I should fear not either claw nor hook!"

70 And Libicocco: "We have borne too much;"
And with his grapnel seized him by the arm,
So that, by rending, he tore off a tendon.

73 Eke Draghignazzo wished to pounce upon him
Down at the legs; whence their Decurion
Turned round and round about with evil look.

76 When they again somewhat were pacified,
Of him, who still was looking at his wound,
Demanded my Conductor without stay:

79 "Who was that one, from whom a luckless parting
Thou sayest thou hast made, to come ashore?"
And he replied, "It was the Friar Gomita,

82 He of Gallura, vessel of all fraud,
Who had the enemies of his Lord in hand,
And dealt so with them each exults thereat;

85 Money he took, and let them smoothly off,
As he says; and in other offices
A barrator was he, not mean but sovereign.

88 Foregathers with him one Don Michael Zanche
Of Logodoro; and of Sardinia
To gossip never do their tongues feel tired.

91 O me! see that one, how he grinds his teeth;
Still farther would I speak, but am afraid
Lest he to scratch my itch be making ready."

94 And the grand Provost, turned to Farfarello,
Who rolled his eyes about as if to strike,

Said: "Stand aside there, thou malicious bird."

"If you desire either to see or hear,"
The terror-stricken recommenced thereon,
"Tuscans or Lombards, I will make them come.

But let the Malebranche cease a little,
So that these may not their revenges fear,
And I, down sitting in this very place,

For one that I am will make seven come,
When I shall whistle, as our custom is
To do whenever one of us comes out."

Cagnazzo at these words his muzzle lifted,
Shaking his head, and said: "Just hear the trick
Which he has thought of, down to throw himself!"

Whence he, who snares in great abundance had,
Responded: "I by far too cunning am,
When I procure for mine a greater sadness."

Alichin held not in, but running counter
Unto the rest, said to him: "If thou dive,
I will not follow thee upon the gallop,

But I will beat my wings above the pitch;
The height be left, and be the bank a shield
To see if thou alone dost countervail us."

O thou who readest, thou shalt hear new sport!
Each to the other side his eyes averted;
He first, who most reluctant was to do it.

The Navarrese selected well his time;
Planted his feet on land, and in a moment
Leaped, and released himself from their design.

Whereat each one was suddenly stung with shame,
But he most who was cause of the defeat;
Therefore he moved, and cried: "Thou art o'ertaken."

But little it availed, for wings could not
Outstrip the fear; the other one went under,
And, flying, upward he his breast directed;

Not otherwise the duck upon a sudden
Dives under, when the falcon is approaching,
And upward he returneth cross and weary.

Infuriate at the mockery, Calcabrina
Flying behind him followed close, desirous
The other should escape, to have a quarrel.

And when the barrator had disappeared,
He turned his talons upon his companion,
And grappled with him right above the moat.

But sooth the other was a doughty sparhawk
To clapperclaw him well; and both of them
Fell in the middle of the boiling pond.

A sudden intercessor was the heat;
But ne'ertheless of rising there was naught,
To such degree they had their wings belimed.

Lamenting with the others, Barbariccia
Made four of them fly to the other side
With all their gaffs, and very speedily.

This side and that they to their posts descended;
They stretched their hooks towards the pitch-ensnared,
Who were already baked within the crust,

And in this manner busied did we leave them.

Canto XXIII

SILENT, alone, and without company
We went, the one in front, the other after,
As go the Minor Friars along their way.

4 Upon the fable of Aesop was directed
My thought, by reason of the present quarrel,
Where he has spoken of the frog and mouse;

7 For 'mo' and 'issa' are not more alike
Than this one is to that, if well we couple
End and beginning with a steadfast mind.

10 And even as one thought from another springs,
So afterward from that was born another,
Which the first fear within me double made.

13 Thus did I ponder: "These on our account
Are laughed to scorn, with injury and scoff
So great, that much I think it must annoy them.

16 If anger be engrafted on ill-will,
They will come after us more merciless
Than dog upon the leveret which he seizes."

19 I felt my hair stand all on end already
With terror, and stood backwardly intent,
When said I: "Master, if thou hidest not

22 Thyself and me forthwith, of Malebranche
I am in dread; we have them now behind us;
I so imagine them, I already feel them."

25 And he: "If I were made of leaded glass
Thine outward image I should not attract
Sooner to me than I imprint the inner.

28 Just now thy thoughts came in among my own,
With similar attitude and similar face,
So that of both one counsel sole I made.

31 If peradventure the right bank so slope
That we to the next Bolgia can descend.
We shall escape from the imagined chase."

34 Not yet he finished rendering such opinion,
When I beheld them come with outstretched wings,
Not far remote, with will to seize upon us.

37 My Leader on a sudden seized me up,
Even as a mother who by noise is wakened,
And close beside her sees the enkindled flames,

40 Who takes her son, and flies, and does not stop,
Having more care of him than of herself,
So that she clothes her only with a shift;

43 And downward from the top of the hard bank
Supine he gave him to the pendent rock,
That one side of the other Bolgia walls.

46 Ne'er ran so swiftly water through a sluice
To turn the water of any land-built mill,
When nearest to the paddles it approaches,

49 As did my Master down along that border,
Bearing me with him on his breast away,
As his own son, and not as a companion.

52 Hardly the bed of the ravine below
His feet had reached, ere they had reached the hill
Right over us; but he was not afraid;

55 For the high Providence, which had ordained
To place them ministers of the fifth moat,
The power of thence departing took from all.

58 A painted people there below we found,
Who went about with footsteps very slow,
Weeping and in their semblance tired and vanquished.

61 They had on mantles with the hoods low down
Before their eyes, and fashioned of the cut
That in Cologne they for the monks are made.

64 Without, they gilded are so that it dazzles;
But inwardly all leaden and so heavy
That Frederick used to put them on of straw.

67 O everlastingly fatiguing mantle!

Again we turned us, still to the left hand
Along with them, intent on their sad plaint;

70 But owing to the weight, that weary folk
Came on so tardily, that we were new
In company at each motion of the haunch.

73 Whence I unto my Leader: "See thou find
Some one who may by deed or name be known,
And thus in going move thine eye about."

76 And one, who understood the Tuscan speech
Cried to us from behind: "Stay ye your feet
Ye, who so run athwart the dusky air

79 Perhaps thou'lt have from me what thou demandest."
Whereat the Leader turned him, and said: "Wait,
And then according to his pace proceed."

82 I stopped, and two beheld I show great haste
Of spirit, in their faces, to be with me;
But the burden and the narrow way delayed them.

85 When they came up, long with an eye askance
They scanned me without uttering a word.
Then to each other turned, and said together:

88 "He by the action of his throat seems living;
And if they dead are, by what privilege
Go they uncovered by the heavy stole?"

91 Then said to me: "Tuscan, who to the college
Of miserable hypocrites art come,
Do not disdain to tell us who thou art."

94 And I to them: "Born was I, and grew up
In the great town on the fair river of Arno,
And with the body I've always had.

97 But who are ye, in whom there trickles down
Along your cheeks such grief as I behold?
And what pain is upon you, that so sparkles?"

100 And one replied to me: "These orange cloaks
Are made of lead so heavy, that the weights

Cause in this way their balances to creak.

103 Frati Gaudenti were we, and Bolognese;
I Catalano, and he Loderingo
Named, and together taken by thy city,

106 As the wont is to take one man alone,
For maintenance of its peace; and we were such
That still it is apparent round Gardingo."

109 "O Friars," began I, "your iniquitous ..."
But said no more; for to mine eyes there rushed
One crucified with three stakes on the ground.

112 When me he saw, he writhed himself all over,
Blowing into his beard with suspirations;
And the Friar Catalan, who noticed this,

115 Said to me: "This transfixed one, whom thou seest,
Counselled the Pharisees that it was meet
To put one man to torture for the people.

118 Crosswise and naked is he on the path,
As thou perceivest; and he needs must feel,
Whoever passes, first how much he weighs;

121 And in like mode his father-in-law is punished
Within this moat, and the others of the council,
Which for the Jews was a malignant seed."

124 And thereupon I saw Virgilius marvel
O'er him who was extended on the cross
So vilely in eternal banishment.

127 Then he directed to the Friar this voice:
"Be not displeased, if granted thee, to tell us
If to the right hand any pass slopes down

130 By which we two may issue forth from here,
Without constraining some of the black angels
To come and extricate us from this deep."

133 Then he made answer: "Nearer than thou hopest
There is a rock, that forth from the great circle
Proceeds, and crosses all the cruel valleys,

136 Save that at this 'tis broken, and does not bridge it;
You will be able to mount up the ruin,
That sidelong slopes and at the bottom rises."

139 The Leader stood awhile with head bowed down;
Then said: "The business badly he recounted
Who grapples with his hook the sinners yonder."

142 And the Friar: "Many of the Devil's vices
Once heard I at Bologna, and among them,
That he's a liar and the father of lies."

145 Thereat my Leader with great strides went on,
Somewhat disturbed with anger in his looks;
Whence from the heavy-laden I departed

148 After the prints of his beloved feet.

Canto XXIV

IN that part of the youthful year wherein
The Sun his locks beneath Aquarius tempers,
And now the nights draw near to half the day,

4 What time the hoar-frost copies on the ground
The outward semblance of her sister white,
But little lasts the temper of her pen,

7 The husbandman, whose forage faileth him,
Rises, and looks, and seeth the champaign
All gleaming white, whereat he beats his flank,

10 Returns in doors, and up and down laments,
Like a poor wretch, who knows not what to do;
Then he returns and hope revives again,

13 Seeing the world has changed its countenance
In little time, and takes his shepherd's crook,
And forth the little lambs to pasture drives.

16 Thus did the Master fill me with alarm
When I beheld his forehead so disturbed,

And to the ailment came as soon the plaster.

For as we came unto the ruined bridge
The Leader turned to me with that sweet look
Which at the mountain's foot I first beheld.

His arms he opened, after some advisement
Within himself elected, looking first
Well at the ruin, and laid hold of me.

And even as he who acts and meditates,
For aye it seems that he provides beforehand,
So upward lifting me towards the summit

Of a huge rock, he scanned another crag,
Saying: "To that one grapple afterwards,
But try first if 'tis such that it will hold thee."

This was no way for one clothed with a cloak;
For hardly we, he light, and I pushed upward,
Were able to ascend from jag to jag.

And had it not been, that upon that precinct
Shorter was the ascent than on the other,
He I know not, but I had been dead beat.

But because Malebolge tow'rds the mouth
Of the profoundest well is all inclining,
The structure of each valley doth import

That one bank rises and the other sinks.
Still we arrived at length upon the point
Wherefrom the last stone breaks itself asunder.

The breath was from my lungs so milked away,
When I was up, that I could go no farther,
Nay, I sat down upon my first arrival.

"Now it behoves thee thus to put off sloth,"
My Master said; "for sitting upon down,
Or under quilt, one cometh not to fame,

Withouten which whoso his life consumes
Such vestige leaveth of himself on earth.
As smoke in air or in the water foam.

52 And therefore raise thee up, o'ercome the anguish
With spirit that o'ercometh every battle,
If with its heavy body it sink not.

55 A longer stairway it behoves thee mount;
'Tis not enough from these to have departed;
Let it avail thee, if thou understand me."

58 Then I uprose, showing myself provided
Better with breath than I did feel myself,
And said: "Go on, for I am strong and bold."

61 Upward we took our way along the crag,
Which jagged was, and narrow, and difficult,
And more precipitous far than that before.

64 Speaking I went, not to appear exhausted;
Whereat a voice from the next moat came forth,
Not well adapted to articulate words.

67 I know not what it said, though o'er the back
I now was of the arch that passes there;
But he seemed moved to anger who was speaking.

70 I was bent downward, but my living eyes
Could not attain the bottom, for the dark;
Wherefore I: "Master, see that thou arrive

73 At the next round, and let us descend the wall;
For as from hence I hear and understand not,
So I look down and nothing I distinguish."

76 "Other response," he said, "I make thee not,
Except the doing; for the modest asking
Ought to be followed by the deed in silence."

79 We from the bridge descended at its head,
Where it connects itself with the eighth bank,
And then was manifest to me the Bolgia;

82 And I beheld therein a terrible throng
Of serpents, and of such a monstrous kind,
That the remembrance still congeals my blood

85 Let Libya boast no longer with her sand;

For if Chelydri, Jaculi, and Pharae
She breeds, with Cenchri and with Ammhisbaena,

88 Neither so many plagues nor so malignant
E'er showed she with all Ethiopia,
Nor with whatever on the Red Sea is!

91 Among this cruel and most dismal throng
People were running naked and affrighted.
Without the hope of hole or heliotrope.

94 They had their hands with serpents bound behind them;
These riveted upon their reins the tail
And head, and were in front of them entwined.

97 And lo! At one who was upon our side
There darted forth a serpent, which transfixed him
There where the neck is knotted to the shoulders.

100 Nor 'O' so quickly e'er, nor 'I' was written,
As he took fire, and burned; and ashes wholly
Behoved it that in falling he became.

103 And when he on the ground was thus destroyed,
The ashes drew together, and of themselves
Into himself they instantly returned.

106 Even thus by the great sages 'tis confessed
The phoenix dies, and then is born again,
When it approaches its five-hundredth year;

109 On herb or grain it feeds not in its life,
But only on tears of incense and amomum,
And nard and myrrh are its last winding-sheet.

112 And as he is who falls, and knows not how,
By force of demons who to earth down drag him,
Or other oppilation that binds man,

115 When he arises and around him looks,
Wholly bewildered by the mighty anguish
Which he has suffered, and in looking sighs;

118 Such was that sinner after he had risen.
Justice of God! O how severe it is,
That blows like these in vengeance poureth down!

Among this cruel and most dismal throng
People were running naked and affrighted.
Without the hope of hole or heliotrope.

Gustave Doré

The Guide thereafter asked him who he was;
Whence he replied: "I rained from Tuscany
A short time since into this cruel gorge.

A bestial life, and not a human, pleased me,
Even as the mule I was; I'm Vanni Fucci,
Beast, and Pistoia was my worthy den."

And I unto the Guide: "Tell him to stir not,
And ask what crime has thrust him here below,
For once a man of blood and wrath I saw him."

And the sinner, who had heard, dissembled not,
But unto me directed mind and face,
And with a melancholy shame was painted.

Then said: "It pains me more that thou hast caught me
Amid this misery where thou seest me,
Than when I from the other life was taken.

What thou demandest I cannot deny;
So low am I put down because I robbed
The sacristy of the fair ornaments,

And falsely once 'twas laid upon another;
But that thou mayst not such a sight enjoy,
If thou shalt e'er be out of the dark places,

Thine ears to my announcement ope and hear:
Pistoia first of Neri groweth meagre;
Then Florence doth renew her men and manners;

Mars draws a vapour up from Val di Magra,
Which is with turbid clouds enveloped round,
And with impetuous and bitter tempest

Over Campo Picen shall be the battle;
When it shall suddenly rend the mist asunder,
So that each Bianco shall thereby be smitten

And this I've said that it may give thee pain."

Canto XXV

AT the conclusion of his words, the thief
Lifted his hands aloft with both the figs,
Crying: "Take that, God, for at thee I aim them."

4 From that time forth the serpents were my friends;
For one entwined itself about his neck
As if it said: "I will not thou speak more;"

7 And round his arms another, and rebound him,
Clinching itself together so in front,
That with them he could not a motion make,

10 Pistoia, ah, Pistoia! why resolve not
To burn thyself to ashes and so perish,
Since in ill-doing thou thy seed excellest?

13 Through all the sombre circles of this Hell,
Spirit I saw not against God so proud,
Not he who fell at Thebes down from the walls!

16 He fled away, and spake no further word;
And I beheld a Centaur full of rage
Come crying out: "Where is, where is the scoffer?"

19 I do not think Maremma has so many
Serpents as he had all along his back,
As far as where our countenance begins.

22 Upon the shoulders, just behind the nape,
With wings wide open was a dragon lying,
And he sets fire to all that he encounters.

25 My Master said: "That one is Cacus, who
Beneath the rock upon Mount Aventine
Created oftentimes a lake of blood.

28 He goes not on the same road with his brothers,
By reason of the fraudulent theft he made
Of the great herd, which he had near to him;

31 Whereat his tortuous actions ceased beneath
The mace of Hercules, who peradventure

Gave him a hundred, and he felt not ten."

34 While he was speaking thus, he had passed by,
And spirits three had underneath us come,
Of which nor I aware was, nor my Leader

37 Until what time they shouted: "Who are you?"
On which account our story made a halt
And then we were intent on them alone.

40 I did not know them; but it came to pass,
As it is wont to happen by some chance,
That one to name the other was compelled,

43 Exclaiming: "Where can Cianfa have remained?"
Whence I, so that the Leader might attend,
Upward from chin to nose my finger laid.

46 If thou art, Reader, slow now to believe
What I shall say, it will no marvel be,
For I who saw it hardly can admit it.

49 As I was holding raised on them my brows,
Behold! a serpent with six feet darts forth
In front of one, and fastens wholly on him.

52 With middle feet it bound him round the paunch,
And with the forward ones his arms it seized;
Then thrust its teeth through one cheek and the other;

55 The hindermost it stretched upon his thighs,
And put its tail through in between the two,
And up behind along the reins outspread it.

58 Ivy was never fastened by its barbs
Unto a tree so, as this horrible reptile
Upon the other's limbs entwined its own.

61 Then they stuck close, as if of heated wax
They had been made, and intermixed their colour;
Nor one nor other seemed now what he was;

64 E'en as proceedeth on before the flame
Upward along the paper a brown colour,
Which is not black as yet, and the white dies.

67 The other two looked on, and each of them
Cried out: "O me, Agnello, how thou changest!
Behold, thou now art neither two nor one."

70 Already the two heads had one become,
When there appeared to us two figures mingled
Into one face, wherein the two were lost.

73 Of the four lists were fashioned the two arms,
The thighs and legs, the belly and the chest
Members became that never yet were seen.

76 Every original aspect there was cancelled;
Two and yet none did the perverted image
Appear, and such departed with slow pace.

79 Even as a lizard, under the great scourge
Of days canicular, exchanging hedge,
Lightning appeareth if the road it cross;

82 Thus did appear, coming towards the bellies
Of the two others, a small fiery serpent,
Livid and black as is a peppercorn.

85 And in that part whereat is first received
Our aliment, it one of them transfixed;
Then downward fell in front of him extended.

88 The one transfixed looked at it, but said naught;
Nay, rather with feet motionless he yawned,
Just as if sleep or fever had assailed him.

91 He at the serpent gazed, and it at him;
One through the wound, the other through the mouth
Smoked violently, and the smoke commingled.

94 Henceforth be silent Lucan, where he mentions
Wretched Sabellus and Nassidius,
And wait to hear what now shalle be shot forth.

97 Be silent ovid, of Cadmus and Arethusa;
For if him to a snake, her to a fountain,
Converts he fabling, that I grudge him not;

100 Because two natures never front to front

Has he transmuted, so that both the forms
To interchange their matter ready were.

103 Together they responded in such wise,
That to a fork the serpent cleft his tail,
And eke the wounded drew his feet together.

106 The legs together with the thighs themselves
Adhered so, that in little time the juncture
No sign whatever made that was apparent.

109 He with the cloven tail assumed the figure
The other one was losing, and his skin
Became elastic, and the other's hard.

112 I saw the arms draw inward at the armpits,
And both feet of the reptile, that were short,
Lengthen as much as those contracted were.

115 Thereafter the hind feet, together twisted,
Became the member that a man conceals,
And of his own the wretch had two created.

118 While both of them the exhalation veils
With a new colour, and engenders hair
On one of them and depilates the other,

121 The one uprose and down the other fell,
Though turning not away their impious lamps,
Underneath which each one his muzzle changed.

124 He who was standing drew it tow'rds the temples,
And from excess of matter, which came thither,
Issued the ears from out the hollow cheeks;

127 What did not backward run and was retained
Of that excess made to the face a nose,
And the lips thickened far as was befitting.

130 He who lay prostrate thrusts his muzzle forward,
And backward draws the ears into his head,
In the same manner as the snail its horns

133 And so the tongue, which was entire and apt
For speech before, is cleft, and the bi-forked

In the other closes up, and the smoke ceases.

The soul,which to a reptile had been changed,
Along the valley hissing takes to flight,
And after him the other speaking sputters.

Then did he turn upon him his new shoulders,
And said to the other: “I’ll have Buoso run,
Crawling as I have done, along this road.”

In this way I beheld the seventh ballast
Shift and reshift, and here be my excuse
The novelty, if aught my pen transgress.

And notwithstanding that mine eyes might be
Somewhat bewildered, and my mind dismayed,
They could not flee away so secretly

But that I plainly saw Puccio Sciancato;
And he it was who sole of three companions,
Which came in the beginning, was not changed;

The other was he whom thou, Gaville, weepest.

Canto XXVI

REJOICE, O Florence, since thou art so great,
That over sea and land thou beatest thy wings,
And throughout Hell thy name is spread abroad!

4 Among the thieves five citizens of thine
Like these I found, whence shame comes unto me,
And thou thereby to no great honour risest.

7 But if when morn is near our dreams are true,
Feel shalt thou in a little time from now
What Prato, if none other, craves for thee.

10 And if it now were, it were not too soon;
Would that it were, seeing it needs must be,
For 'twill aggrieve me more the more I age.

13 We went our way, and up along the stairs
The bourns had made us to descend before,
Remounted my Conductor and drew me.

16 And following the solitary path
Among the rocks and ridges of the crag,
The foot without the hand sped not at all.

19 Then sorrowed I, and sorrow now again,
When I direct my mind to what I saw,
And more my genius curb than I am wont,

22 That it may run not unless virtue guide it;
So that if some good star, or better thing,
Have given me good, I may myself not grudge it.

25 As many as the hind (who on the hill
Rests at the time when he who lights the world
His countenance keeps least concealed from us,

28 While as the fly gives place unto the gnat)
Seeth the glow-worms down along the valley,
Perchance there where he ploughs and makes his vintage

31 With flames as manifold resplendent all
Was the eighth Bolgia, as I grew aware

As soon as I was where the depth appeared.

34 And such as he who with the bears avenged him
Beheld Elijah's chariot at departing,
What time the steeds to heaven erect uprose

37 For with his eye he could not follow it
So as to see aught else than flame alone,
Even as a little cloud ascending upward,

40 Thus each along the gorge of the intrenchment
Was moving; for not one reveals the theft,
And every flame a sinner steals away.

43 I stood upon the bridge uprisen to see,
So that, if I had seized not on a rock,
Down had I fallen without being pushed.

46 And the Leader, who beheld me so attent
Exclaimed: "Within the fires the spirits are;
Each swathes himself with that wherewith he burns."

49 "My Master," I replied, "by hearing thee
I am more sure; but I surmised already
It might be so, and already wished to ask thee

52 Who is within that fire, which comes so cleft
At top, it seems uprising from the pyre
Where was Eteocles with his brother placed."

55 He answered me: "Within there are tormented
Ulysses and Diomed, and thus together
They unto vengeance run as unto wrath.

58 And there within their flame do they lament
The ambush of the horse, which made the door
Whence issued forth the Romans' gentle seed;

61 Therein is wept the craft, for which being dead
Deidamia still deplores Achilles,
And pain for the Palladium there is borne."

64 "If they within those sparks possess the power
To speak," I said, "thee, Master, much I pray,
And re-pray, that the prayer be worth a thousand,

67 That thou make no denial of awaiting
Until the horned flame shall hither come;
Thou seest that with desire I lean towards it."

70 And he to me: "Worthy is thy entreaty
Of much applause, and therefore I accept it;
But take heed that thy tongue restrain itself.

73 Leave me to speak, because I have conceived
That which thou wishest; for they might disdain
Perchance, since they were Greeks, discourse of thine."

76 When now the flame had come unto that point,
Where to my Leader it seemed time and place,
After this fashion did I hear him speak:

79 "O ye, who are twofold within one fire,
If I deserved of you, while I was living,
If I deserved of you or much or little

82 When in the world I wrote the lofty verses,
Do not move on, but one of you declare
Whither, being lost, he went away to die."

85 Then of the antique flame the greater horn,
Murmuring, began to wave itself about
Even as a flame doth which the wind fatigues.

88 Thereafterward, the summit to and fro
Moving as if it were the tongue that spake
It uttered forth a voice, and said: "When I

91 From Circe had departed, who concealed me
More than a year there near unto Gaeta,
Or ever yet Aeneas named it so,

94 Nor fondness for my son, nor reverence
For my old father, nor the due affection
Which joyous should have made Penelope,

97 Could overcome within me the desire
I had to be experienced of the world,
And of the vice and virtue of mankind;

100 But I put forth on the high open sea

With one sole ship, and that small company
By which I never had deserted been.

103 Both of the shores I saw as far as Spain,
Far as Morocco. and the isle of Sardes,
And the others which that sea bathes round about.

106 I and my company were old and slow
When at that narrow passage we arrived
Where Hercules his landmarks set as signals,

109 That man no farther onward should adventure.
On the right hand behind me left I Seville,
And on the other already had left Ceuta.

112 'O brothers, who amid a hundred thousand
Perils,' I said, 'have come unto the West,
To this so inconsiderable vigil

115 Which is remaining of your senses still
Be ye unwilling to deny the knowledge,
Following the sun, of the unpeopled world.

118 Consider ye the seed from which ye sprang;
Ye were not made to live like unto brutes,
But for pursuit of virtue and of knowledge.'

121 So eager did I render my companions,
With this brief exhortation, for the voyage,
That then I hardly could have held them back.

124 And having turned our stern unto the morning,
We of the oars made wings for our mad flight,
Evermore gaining on the larboard side.

127 Already all the stars of the other pole
The night beheld, and ours so very low
It did not rise above the ocean floor.

130 Five times rekindled and as many quenched
Had been the splendour underneath the moon,
Since we had entered into the deep pass,

133 When there appeared to us a mountain, dim
From distance, and it seemed to me so high

As I had never any one beheld.

Joyful were we, and soon it turned to weeping;
For out of the new land a whirlwind rose,
And smote upon the fore part of the ship.

Three times it made her whirl with all the waters,
At the fourth time it made the stern uplift,
And the prow downward go, as pleased Another,

Until the sea above us closed again."

Canto XXVII

ALREADY was the flame erect and quiet,
To speak no more, and now departed from us
With the permission of the gentle Poet;

When yet another, which behind it came,
Caused us to turn our eyes upon its top
By a confused sound that issued from it.

As the Sicilian bull (that bellowed first
With the lament of him, and that was right,
Who with his file had modulated it)

Bellowed so with the voice of the afflicted,
That, notwithstanding it was made of brass,
Still it appeared with agony transfixed;

Thus, by not having any way or issue
At first from out the fire, to its own language
Converted were the melancholy words.

But afterwards, when they had gathered way
Up through the point, giving it that vibration
The tongue had given them in their passage out,

We heard it said: "O thou, at whom I aim
My voice, and who but now wast speaking Lombard,
Saying, 'Now go thy way, no more I urge thee,'

Because I come perchance a little late,

To stay and speak with me let it not irk thee;
Thou seest it irks not me, and I am burning.

25 If thou but lately into this blind world
Hast fallen down from that sweet Latian land,
Wherefrom I bring the whole of my transgression,

28 Say, if the Romagnuols have peace or war,
For I was from the mountains there between
Urbino and the yoke whence Tiber bursts."

31 I still was downward bent and listening,
When my Conductor touched me on the side,
Saying: "Speak thou: this one a Latian is."

34 And I, who had beforehand my reply
In readiness, forthwith began to speak:
"O soul, that down below there art concealed,

37 Romagna thine is not and never has been
Without war in the bosom of its tyrants;
But open war I none have left there now.

40 Ravenna stands as it long years has stood;
The Eagle of Polenta there is brooding,
So that she covers Cervia with her vans.

43 The city which once made the long resistance,
And of the French a sanguinary heap,
Beneath the Green Paws finds itself again;

46 Verrucchio's ancient Mastiff and the new,
Who made such bad disposal of Montagna,
Where they are wont make wimbles of their teeth.

49 The cities of Lamone and Santerno
Governs the Lioncel of the white lair,
Who changes sides 'twixt summer-time and winter;

52 And that of which the Savio bathes the flank,
Even as it lies between the plain and mountain,
Lives between tyranny and a free state.

55 Now I entreat thee tell us who thou art;
Be not more stubborn than the rest have been,
So may thy name hold front there in the world."

58 After the fire a little more had roared
In its own fashion, the sharp point it moved
This way and that, and then gave forth such breath:

61 "If I believed that my reply were made
To one who to the world would e'er return,
This flame without more flickering would stand still;

64 But inasmuch as never from this depth
Did any one return, if I hear true,
Without the fear of infamy I answer,

67 I was a man of arms, then Cordelier,
Believing thus begirt to make amends;
And truly my belief had been fulfilled

70 But for the High Priest, whom may ill betide,
Who put me back into my former sins;
And how and wherefore I will have thee hear.

73 While I was still the form of bone and pulp
My mother gave to me, the deeds I did
Were not those of a lion, but a fox.

76 The machinations and the covert ways
I knew them all, and practised so their craft,
That to the ends of earth the sound went forth.

79 When now unto that portion of mine age
I saw myself arrived, when each one ought
To lower the sails, and coil away the ropes,

82 That which before had pleased me then displeased me;
And penitent and confessing I surrendered,
Ah woe is me! And it would have bestead me;

85 The Leader of the modern Pharisees
Having a war near unto Lateran,
And not with Saracens nor with the Jews,

88 For each one of his enemies was Christian,
And none of them had been to conquer Acre,
Nor merchandising in the Sultan's land,

91 Nor the high office, nor the sacred orders,
In him regarded, nor in me that cord

Which used to make those girt with it more meagre;

But even as Constantine sought out Sylvester
To cure his leprosy, within Soracte,
So this one sought me out as an adept

To cure him of the fever of his pride.
Counsel he asked of me, and I was silent,
Because his words appeared inebriate.

And then he said: ‘Be not thy heart afraid;
Henceforth I thee absolve; and thou instruct me
How to raze Palestrina to the ground.

Heaven have I power to lock and to unlock,
As thou dost know; therefore the keys are two,
The which my predecessor held not dear.’

Then urged me on his weighty arguments
There, where my silence was the worst advice;
And said I: ‘Father, since thou washest me

Of that sin into which I now must fall,
The promise long with the fulfilment short
Will make thee triumph in thy lofty seat.’

Francis came afterward, when I was dead,
For me; but one of the black Cherubim
Said to him: ‘Take him not; do me no wrong;

He must come down among my servitors,
Because he gave the fraudulent advice
From which time forth I have been at his hair;

For who repents not cannot be absolved,
Nor can one both repent and will at once,
Because of the contradiction which consents not.’

O miserable me! How I did shudder
When he seized on me, saying: ‘Peradventure
Thou didst not think that I was a logician!’

He bore me unto Minos, who entwined
Eight times his tail about his stubborn back,
And after he had bitten it in great rage,

127 Said: 'Of the thievish fire a culprit this;'
Wherefore, here where thou seest, am I lost,
And vested thus in going I bemoan me."

130 When it had thus completed its recital,
The flame departed uttering lamentations,
Writhing and flapping its sharp-pointed horn.

133 Onward we passed, both I and my Conductor,
Up o'er the crag above another arch,
Which the moat covers, where is paid the fee

136 By those who, sowing discord, win their burden.

Canto XXVIII

WHO ever could, e'en with untrammelled words,
Tell of the blood and of the wounds in full
Which now I saw, by many times narrating?

4 Each tongue would for a certainty fall short
By reason of our speech and memory,
That have small room to comprehend so much

7 If were again assembled all the people
Which formerly upon the fateful land
Of Puglia were lamenting for their blood

10 Shed by the Romans and the lingering war
That of the rings made such illustrious spoils,
As Livy has recorded, who errs not,

13 With those who felt the agony of blows
By making counterstand to Robert Guiscard,
And all the rest, whose bones are gathered still

16 At Ceperano, where a renegade
Was each Apulian, and at Tagliacozzo,
Where without arms the old Alardo conquered,

19 And one his limb transpierced, and one lopped off,
Should show, it would be nothing to compare

With the disgusting mode of the ninth Bolgia.

22 A cask by losing centre-piece or cant
Was never shattered so, as I saw one
Rent from the chin to where one breaketh wind.

25 Between his legs were hanging down his entrails;
His heart was visible, and the dismal sack
That maketh excrement of what is eaten.

28 While I was all absorbed in seeing him,
He looked at me, and opened with his hands
His bosom, saying: "See now how I rend me;

31 How mutilated, see, is Mahomet;
In front of me doth Ali weeping go,
Cleft in the face from forelock unto chin;

34 And all the others whom thou here beholdest,
Disseminators of scandal and of schism
While living were, and therefore are cleft thus.

37 A devil is behind here, who doth cleave us
Thus cruelly, unto the falchion's edge
Putting again each one of all this ream,

40 When we have gone around the doleful road;
By reason that our wounds are closed again
Ere any one in front of him repass.

43 But who art thou, that musest on the crag,
Perchance to postpone going to the pain
That is adjudged upon thine accusations?"

46 "Nor death hath reached him yet, nor guilt doth bring him,"
My Master made reply, "to be tormented;
But to procure him full experience,

49 Me, who am dead, behoves it to conduct him
Down here through Hell, from circle unto circle;
And this is true as that I speak to thee."

52 More than a hundred were there when they heard him,
Who in the moat stood still to look at me,
Through wonderment oblivious of their torture.

55 "Now say to Fra Dolcino, then, to arm him,
Thou, who perhaps wilt shortly see the sun,
If soon he wish not here to follow me,

58 So with provisions, that no stress of snow
May give the victory to the Novarese,
Which otherwise to gain would not be easy."

61 After one foot to go away he lifted,
This word did Mahomet say unto me,
Then to depart upon the ground he stretched it.

64 Another one, who had his throat pierced through,
And nose cut off close underneath the brows,
And had no longer but a single ear,

67 Staying to look in wonder with the others,
Before the others did his gullet open,
Which outwardly was red in every part,

70 And said: "O thou, whom guilt doth not condemn,
And whom I once saw up in Latian land,
Unless too great similitude deceive me,

73 Call to remembrance Pier da Medicina,
If e'er thou see again the lovely plain
That from Vercelli slopes to Marcabo,

76 And make it known to the best two of Fano,
To Messer Guido and Angiolello likewise,
That if foreseeing here be not in vain,

79 Cast over from their vessel shall they be,
And drowned near unto the Cattolica,
By the betrayal of a tyrant fell.

82 Between the isles of Cyprus and Majorca
Neptune ne'er yet beheld so great a crime
Neither of pirates nor Argolic people.

85 That traitor, who sees only with one eye,
And holds the land, which some one here with me
Would fain be fasting from the vision of,

88 Will make them come unto a parley with him;

Then will do so, that to Focara's wind
They will not stand in need of vow or prayer."

91 And I to him: "Show to me and declare,
If thou wouldst have me bear up news of thee,
Who is this person of the bitter vision."

94 Then did he lay his hand upon the jaw
Of one of his companions, and his mouth
Oped, crying: "This is he, and he speaks not.

97 This one, being banished, every doubt submerged
In Caesar by affirming the forearmed
Always with detriment allowed delay."

100 O how bewildered unto me appeared,
With tongue asunder in his windpipe slit,
Curio, who in speaking was so bold!

103 And one, who both his hands dissevered had,
The stumps uplifting through the murky air,
So that the blood made horrible his face,

106 Cried out: "Thou shalt remember Mosca also,
Who said, alas! 'a thing done has an end!'
Which was an ill seed for the Tuscan people."

109 "And death unto thy race," thereto I added;
Whence he, accumulating woe on woe,
Departed, like a person sad and crazed.

112 But I remained to look upon the crowd;
And saw a thing which I should be afraid,
Without some further proof, even to recount,

115 If it were not that conscience reassures me,
That good companion which emboldens man
Beneath the hauberk of its feeling pure.

118 I truly saw, and still I seem to see it,
A trunk without a head walk in like manner
As walked the others of the mournful herd.

121 And by the hair it held the head dissevered,
Hung from the hand in fashion of a lantern,

And that upon us gazed and said: "O me!"

124 It of itself made to itself a lamp,
And they were two in one, and one in two;
How that can be, He knows who so ordains it.

127 When it was come close to the bridge's foot,
It lifted high its arm with all the head,
To bring more closely unto us its words,

130 Which were: "Behold now the sore penalty,
Thou, who dost breathing go the dead beholding;
Behold if any be as great as this.

133 And so that thou may carry news of me,
Know that Bertram de Born am I, the same
Who gave to the Young King the evil comfort.

136 I made the father and the son rebellious;
Achitophel not more with Absalom
And David did with his accursed goadings.

139 Because I parted persons so united,
Parted do I now bear my brain, alas!
From its beginning, which is in this trunk.

142 Thus is observed in me the counterpoise."

Canto XXIX

THE many people and the divers wounds
These eyes of mine had so inebriated,
That they were wishful to stand still and weep;

4 But said Virgilius: "What dost thou still gaze at?
Why is thy sight still riveted down there
Among the mournful, mutilated shades?

7 Thou hast not done so at the other Bolge;
Consider, if to count them thou believest,
That two-and-twenty miles the valley winds,

10 And now the moon is underneath our feet;
Henceforth the time allotted us is brief,
And more is to be seen than what thou seest."

13 "If thou hadst," I made answer thereupon
"Attended to the cause for which I looked,
Perhaps a longer stay thou wouldst have pardoned."

16 Meanwhile my Guide departed, and behind him
I went, already making my reply,
And superadding: "In that cavern where

19 I held mine eyes with such attention fixed,
I think a spirit of my blood laments
The sin which down below there costs so much."

22 Then said the Master: "Be no longer broken
Thy thought from this time forward upon him;
Attend elsewhere, and there let him remain;

25 For him I saw below the little bridge,
Pointing at thee, and threatening with his finger
Fiercely, and heard him called Geri del Bello.

28 So wholly at that time wast thou impeded
By him who formerly held Altaforte,
Thou didst not look that way; so he departed."

31 "O my Conductor, his own violent death,
Which is not yet avenged for him," I said,

"By any who is sharer in the shame,

34 Made him disdainful; whence he went away,
As I imagine, without speaking to me,
And thereby made me pity him the more."

37 Thus did we speak as far as the first place
Upon the crag, which the next valley shows
Down to the bottom, if there were more light.

40 When we were now right over the last cloister
Of Malebolge, so that its lay-brothers
Could manifest themselves unto our sight,

43 Divers lamentings pierced me through and through,
Which with compassion had their arrows barbed,
Whereat mine ears I covered with my hands.

46 What pain would be, if from the hospitals
Of Valdichiana, 'twixt July and September,
And of Maremma and Sardinia

49 All the diseases in one moat were gathered,
Such was it here, and such a stench came from it
As from putrescent limbs is wont to issue.

52 We had descended on the furthest bank
From the long crag, upon the left hand still,
And then more vivid was my power of sight

55 Down tow'rds the bottom, where the ministress
Of the high Lord, Justice infallible,
Punishes forgers, which she here records.

58 I do not think a sadder sight to see
Was in Aegina the whole people sick,
(When was the air so full of pestilence,

61 The animals, down to the little worm,
All fell, and afterwards the ancient people,
According as the poets have affirmed,

64 Were from the seed of ants restored again)
Than was it to behold through that dark
The spirits languishing in divers heaps.

67 This on the belly, that upon the back
One of the other lay, and others crawling
Shifted themselves along the dismal road.

70 We step by step went onward without speech,
Gazing upon and listening to the sick
Who had not strength enough to lift their bodies.

73 I saw two sitting leaned against each other,
As leans in heating platter against platter,
From head to foot bespotted o'er with scabs;

76 And never saw I plied a currycomb
By stable-boy for whom his master waits,
Or him who keeps awake unwillingly,

79 As every one was plying fast the bite
Of nails upon himself, for the great rage
Of itching which no other succour had.

82 And the nails downward with them dragged the scab,
In fashion as a knife the scales of bream,
Or any other fish that has them largest.

85 "O thou, that with thy fingers dost dismail thee,"
Began my Leader unto one of them,
"And makest of them pincers now and then,

88 Tell me if any Latian is with those
Who are herein; so may thy nails suffice thee
To all eternity unto this work."

91 "Latians are we, whom thou so wasted seest,
Both of us here", one weeping made reply;
"But who art thou, that questionest about us?"

94 And said the Guide: "One am I who descends
Down with this living man from cliff to cliff,
And I intend to show Hell unto him."

97 Then broken was their mutual support,
And trembling each one turned himself to me,
With others who had heard him by rebound.

100 Wholly to me did the good Master gather,

Saying: "Say unto them whate'er thou wishest."
And I began, since he would have it so:

103 "So may your memory not steal away
In the first world from out the minds of men,
But so may it survive 'neath many suns,

106 Say to me who ye are, and of what people;
Let not your foul and loathsome punishment
Make you afraid to show yourselves to me."

109 "I of Arezzo was," one made reply,
"And Albert of Siena had me burned;
But what I died for does not bring me here.

112 'Tis true I said to him, speaking in jest,
That I could rise by flight into the air,
And he who had conceit, but little wit,

115 Would have me show to him the art; and only
Because no Daedelus I made him, made me
Be burned by one who held him as his son.

118 But unto the last Bolgia of the ten,
For alchemy, which in the world I practised,
Minos, who cannot err, has me condemned."

121 And to the Poet said I: "Now was ever
So vain a people as the Sienese?
Not for a certainty the French by far."

124 Whereat the other leper, who had heard me,
Replied unto my speech: "Taking out Stricca,
Who knew the art of moderate expenses,

127 And Niccolo, who the luxurious use
Of cloves discovered earliest of all
Within that garden where such seed takes root;

130 And taking out the band, among whom squandered
Caccia d'Ascian his vineyards and vast woods,
And where his wit the Abbagliato proffered!

133 But, that thou know who thus doth second thee
Against the Sienese, make sharp thine eye

Tow'rds me, so that my face well answer thee,

136 And thou shalt see I am Capocchio's shade,
Who metals falsified by alchemy;
Thou must remember, if I well descry thee,

139 How I a skilful ape of nature was."

Canto XXX

'TWAS at the time when Juno was enraged,
For Semele, against the Theban blood,
As she already more than once had shown,

4 So reft of reason Arthamas became,
That, seeing his own wife with children twain
Walking encumbered upon either hand,

7 He cried: "Spread out the nets, that I may take
The lioness and her whelps upon the passage;"
And then extended his unpitying claws,

10 Seizing the first, who had the name Learchus,
And whirled him round, and dashed him on a rock;
And she, with the other burthen, drowned herself;—

13 And at the time when fortune downward hurled
The Trojan's arrogance, that all things dared,
So that the king was with his kingdom crushed,

16 Hecuba sad, disconsolate, and captive,
When lifeless she beheld Polyxena,
And of her Polydorus on the shore

19 Of ocean was the dolorous one aware,
Out of her senses like a dog she barked,
So much the anguish had her mind distorted;

22 But not of Thebes the furies nor the Trojan
Were ever seen in any one so cruel
In goading beasts, and much more human members,

As I beheld two shadows pale and naked,
Who, biting, in the manner ran along
That a boar does, when from the sty turned loose.

One to Capocchio came, and by the nape
Seized with its teeth his neck, so that in dragging
It made his belly grate the solid bottom.

And the Aretine, who trembling had remained,
Said to me: "That mad sprite is Gianni Schicchi,
And raving goes thus harrying other people."

"O," said I to him, "so may not the other
Set teeth on thee, let it not weary thee
To tell us who it is, ere it dart hence."

And he to me: "That is the ancient ghost
Of the nefarious Myrrha, who became
Beyond all rightful love her father's lover.

She came to sin with him after this manner,
By counterfeiting of another's form;
As he who goeth yonder undertook,

That he might gain the lady of the herd,
To counterfeit in himself Buoso Donati,
Making a will and giving it due form."

And after the two maniacs had passed
On whom I held mine eye, I turned it back
To look upon the other evil-born.

I saw one made in fashion of a lute,
If he had only had the groin cut off
Just at the point at which a man is forked.

The heavy dropsy, that so disproportions
The limbs with humours, which it ill concocts,
That the face corresponds not to the belly,

Compelled him so to hold his lips apart
As does the hectic, who because of thirst
One tow'rds the chin, the other upward turns.

"O ye, who without any torment are,

And why I know not, in the world of woe,"
He said to us, "behold, and be attentive

61 Unto the misery of Master Adam;
I had while living much of what I wished,
And now, alas! a drop of water crave.

64 The rivulets, that from the verdant hills
Of Cassentin descend down into Arno,
Making their channels to be cold and moist,

67 Ever before me stand, and not in vain;
For far more doth their image dry me up
Than the disease which strips my face of flesh.

70 The rigid justice that chastises me
Draweth occasion from the place in which
I sinned, to put the more my sighs in flight.

73 There is Romena, where I counterfeited
The currency imprinted with the Baptist,
For which I left my body burned above.

76 But if I here could see the tristful soul
Of Guido, or Alessandro, or their brother,
For Branda's fount I would Dot give the sight.

79 One is within already, if the raving
Shades that are going round about speak truth;
But what avails it me, whose limbs are tied?

82 If I were only still so light, that in
A hundred years I could advance one inch,
I had already started on the way,

85 Seeking him out among this squalid folk,
Although the circuit be eleven miles,
And be not less than half a mile across.

88 For them am I in such a family;
They did induce me into coining florins,
Which had three carats of impurity."

91 And I to him: "Who are the two poor wretches
That smoke like unto a wet hand in winter,

Lying there close upon thy right-hand confines?"

94 "I found them here," replied he, "when I rained
Into this chasm, and since they have not turned,
Nor do I think they will for evermore.

97 One the false woman is who accused Joseph,
The other the false Sinon, Greek of Troy;
From acute fever they send forth such reek."

100 And one of them, who felt himself annoyed
At being, peradventure, named so darkly,
Smote with the fist upon his hardened paunch.

103 It gave a sound, as if it were a drum;
And Master Adam smote him in the face,
With arm that did not seem to be less hard,

106 Saying to him: "Although be taken from me
All motion, for my limbs that heavy are,
I have an arm unfettered for such need."

109 Whereat he answer made: "When thou didst go
Unto the fire, thou hadst it not so ready:
But hadst it so and more when thou wast coining."

112 The dropsical: "Thou sayest true in that;
But thou wast not so true a witness there,
Where thou wast questioned of the truth at Troy."

115 "If I spake false, thou falsifiedst the coin,"
Said Sinon; "and for one fault I am here,
And thou for more than any other demon."

118 "Remember, perjurer, about the horse,"
He made reply who had the swollen belly,
"And rueful be it thee the whole world knows it."

121 "Rueful to thee the thirst be wherewith cracks
Thy tongue," the Greek said, "and the putrid water
That hedges so thy paunch before thine eyes."

124 Then the false-coiner: "So is gaping wide
Thy mouth for speaking evil, as 'tis wont;
Because if I have thirst, and humour stuff me

Thou hast the burning and the head that aches,
And to lick up the mirror of Narcissus
Thou wouldst not want words many to invite thee."

In listening to them was I wholly fixed,
When said the Master to me: "Now just look,
For little wants it that I quarrel with thee."

When him I heard in anger speak to me,
I turned me round towards him with such shame
That still it eddies through my memory.

And as he is who dreams of his own harm,
Who dreaming wishes it may be a dream,
So that he craves what is, as if it were not;

Such I became, not having power to speak,
For to excuse myself I wished, and still
Excused myself, and did not think I did it.

"Less shame doth wash away a greater fault,"
The Master said, "than this of thine has been;
Therefore thyself disburden of all sadness,

And make account that I am aye beside thee,
If e'er it come to pass that fortune bring thee
Where there are people in a like dispute;

For a base wish it is to wish to hear it."

Canto XXXI

ONE and the selfsame tongue first wounded me,
So that it tinged the one cheek and the other,
And then held out to me the medicine;

4 Thus do I hear that once Achilles' spear,
His and his father's, used to be the cause
First of a sad and then a gracious boon.

7 We turned our backs upon the wretched valley,
Upon the bank that girds it round about,
Going across it without any speech.

10 There it was less than night, and less than day,
So that my sight went little in advance;
But I could hear the blare of a loud horn,

13 So loud it would have made each thunder faint,
Which, counter to it following its way,
Mine eyes directed wholly to one place.

16 After the dolorous discomfiture
When Charlemagne the holy emprise lost,
So terribly Orlando sounded not.

19 Short while my head turned thitherward I held
When many lofty towers I seemed to see,
Whereat I: "Master, say, what town is this?"

22 And he to me: "Because thou peerest forth
Athwart the darkness at too great a distance,
It happens that thou errest in thy fancy.

25 Well shalt thou see, if thou arrivest there,
How much the sense deceives itself by distance;
Therefore a little faster spur thee on."

28 Then tenderly he took me by the hand,
And said: "Before we farther have advanced,
That the reality may seem to thee

31 Less strange, know that these are not towers, but giants,
And they are in the well, around the bank,

From navel downward, one and all of them."

34 As, when the fog is vanishing away,
Little by little doth the sight refigure
Whate'er the mist that crowds the air conceals,

37 So, piercing through the dense and darksome air,
More and more near approaching tow'rd the verge,
My error fled, and fear came over me;

40 Because as on its circular parapets
Montereggione crowns itself with towers,
E'en thus the margin which surrounds the well

43 With one half of their bodies turreted
The horrible giants, whom Jove menaces
E'en now from out the heavens when he thunders.

46 And I of one already saw the face,
Shoulders, and breast, and great part of the belly,
And down along his sides both of the arms.

49 Certainly Nature, when she left the making
Of animals like these, did well indeed,
By taking such executors from Mars;

52 And if of elephants and whales she doth not
Repent her, whosoever looketh subtly
More just and more discreet will hold her for it;

55 For where the argument of intellect
Is added unto evil will and power,
No rampart can the people make against it.

58 His face appeared to me as long and large
As is at Rome the pine-cone of Saint Peter's,
And in proportion were the other bones;

61 So that the margin, which an apron was
Down from the middle, showed so much of him
Above it, that to reach up to his hair

64 Three Frieslanders in vain had vaunted them;
For I beheld thirty great palms of him
Down from the place where man his mantle buckles.

"Raphael mai amech izabi almi,"[3]
Began to clamour the ferocious mouth,
To which were not befitting sweeter psalms.

And unto him my Guide: "Soul idiotic,
Keep to thy horn, and vent thyself with that,
When wrath or other passion touches thee.

Search round thy neck, and thou wilt find the belt
Which keeps it fastened, O bewildered soul
And see it, where it bars thy mighty breast."

Then said to me: "He doth himself accuse;
This one is Nimrod, by whose evil thought
One language in the world is not still used.

Here let us leave him and not speak in vain;
For even such to him is every language
As his to others, which to none is known."

Therefore a longer journey did we make,
Turned to the left, and a crossbow-shot oft
We found another far more fierce and large.

In binding him, who might the master be
I cannot say; but he had pinioned close
Behind the right arm, and in front the other,

With chains, that held him so begirt about
From the neck down, that on the part uncovered
It wound itself as far as the fifth gyre.

"This proud one wished to make experiment
Of his own power against the Supreme Jove,"
My Leader said, "whence he has such a guerdon.

Ephialtes is his name; he showed great prowess.
What time the giants terrified the gods;
The arms he wielded never more he moves."

And I to him: "If possible, I should wish
That of the measureless Briareus
These eyes of mine might have experience."

3 There is no clear translation for this; it appears to be gibberish or a garbled form of various words.

Whence he replied: "Thou shalt behold Antaeus
Close by here, who can speak and is unbound,
Who at the bottom of all crime shall place us.

Much farther yon is he whom thou wouldst see,
And he is bound, and fashioned like to this one,
Save that he seems in aspect more ferocious."

There never was an earthquake of such might
That it could shake a tower so violently,
As Ephialtes suddenly shook himself.

Then was I more afraid of death than ever,
For nothing more was needful than the fear,
If I had not beheld the manacles.

Then we proceeded farther in advance,
And to Antaeus came, who, full five ells
Without the head, forth issued from the cavern.

"O thou, who in the valley fortunate,
Which Scipio the heir of glory made,
When Hannibal turned back with all his hosts,

Once brought'st a thousand lions for thy prey,
And who, hadst thou been at the mighty war
Among thy brothers, some it seems still think

The sons of Earth the victory would have gained:
Place us below, nor be disdainful of it,
There where the cold doth lock Cocytus up.

Make us not go to Tityus nor Typhoeus;
This one can give of that which here is longed for;
Therefore stoop down, and do not curl thy lip.

Still in the world can he restore thy fame;
Because he lives, and still expects long life,
If to itself Grace call him not untimely."

So said the Master; and in haste the other
His hands extended and took up my Guide,—
Hands whose great pressure Hercules once felt.

Virgilius, when he felt himself embraced,
Said unto me: "Draw nigh, that I may take thee;"

Then of himself and me one bundle made.

136 As seems the Carisenda, to behold
Beneath the leaning side, when goes a cloud
Above it so that opposite it hangs;

139 Such did Antaeus seem to me, who stood
Watching to see him stoop, and then it was
I could have wished to go some other way.

142 But lightly in the abyss, which swallows up
Judas with Lucifer, he put us down;
Nor thus bowed downward made he there delay,

145 But, as a mast does in a ship, uprose.

Canto XXXII

IF I had rhymes both rough and stridulous,
As were appropriate to the dismal hole
Down upon which thrust all the other rocks,

4 I would press out the juice of my conception
More fully; but because I have them not,
Not without fear I bring myself to speak;

7 For 'tis no enterprise to take in jest,
To sketch the bottom of all the universe,
Nor for a tongue that cries "Mamma" and "Babbo."

10 But may those Ladies help this verse of mine,
Who helped Amphion in enclosing Thebes,
That from the fact the word be not diverse.

13 O rabble ill-begotten above all,
Who're in the place to speak of which is hard,
'Twere better ye had here been sheep or goats!

16 When we were down within the darksome well,
Beneath the giant's feet, but lower far,
And I was scanning still the lofty wall,

19 Heard it said to me: "Look how thou steppest!
Take heed thou do not trample with thy feet
The heads of the tired, miserable brothers!"

22 Whereat I turned me round, and saw before me
And underfoot a lake, that from the frost
The semblance had of glass, and not of water.

25 So thick a veil ne'er made upon its current
In winter-time Danube in Austria,
Nor there beneath the frigid sky the Don,

28 As there was here; so that if Tambernich
Had fallen upon it, or Pietrapana,
E'en at the edge 'twould not have given a creak.

31 And as to croak the frog doth place himself
With muzzle out of water,—when is dreaming
Of gleaning oftentimes the peasant-girl,—

34 Livid, as far down as where shame appears,
Were the disconsolate shades within the ice,
Setting their teeth unto the note of storks.

37 Each one his countenance held downward bent:
From mouth the cold, from eyes the doeful heart
Among them witness of itself procures.

40 When round about me somewhat I had looked,
I downward turned me, and saw two so close,
The hair upon their heads together mingled.

43 "Ye who so strain your breasts together, tell me,"
I said, "who are you;" and they bent their necks,
And when to me their faces they had lifted,

46 Their eyes, which first were only moist within,
Gushed o'er the eyelids, and the frost congealed
The tears between, and locked them up again.

49 Clamp never bound together wood with wood
So strongly; whereat they, like two he-goats,
Butted together, so much wrath o'ercame them.

52 And one, who had by reason of the cold

Lost both his ears, still with his visage downward,
Said: "Why dost thou so mirror thyself in us?

55 If thou desire to know who these two are,
The valley whence Bisenzio descends
Belonged to them and to their father Albert.

58 They from one body came, and all Caina
Thou shalt search through, and shalt not find a shade
More worthy to be fixed in gelatine;

61 Not he in whom were broken breast and shadow
At one and the same blow by Arthur's hand;
Focaccia not; not he who me encumbers

64 So with his head I see no farther forward,
And bore the name of Sassol Mascheroni;
Well knowest thou who he was, if thou art Tuscan.

67 And that thou put me not to further speech,
Know that I Camicion de' Pazzi was,
And wait Carlino to exonerate me."

70 Then I beheld a thousand faces, made
Purple with cold; whence o'er me comes a shudder,
And evermore will come, at frozen ponds.

73 And while we were advancing tow'rds the middle,
Where everything of weight unites together,
And I was shivering in the eternal shade,

76 Whether 'twere will, or destiny, or chance,
I know not; but in walking 'mong the heads
I struck my foot hard in the face of one.

79 Weeping he growled: "Why dost thou trample me?
Unless thou comest to increase the vengeance
of Montaperti, why dost thou molest me?"

82 And I: "My Master, now wait here for me,
That I through him may issue from a doubt;
Then thou mayst hurry me, as thou shalt wish."

85 The Leader stopped; and to that one I said
Who was blaspheming vehemently still:

"Who art thou, that thus reprehendest others?"

88 "Now who art thou, that goest through Antenora
Smiting," replied he, "other people's cheeks,
So that, if thou wert living, 'twere too much?"

91 "Living I am, and dear to thee it may be,"
Was my response, "if thou demandest fame,
That 'mid the other notes thy name I place."

94 And he to me: "For the reverse I long;
Take thyself hence, and give me no more trouble;
For ill thou knowest to flatter in this hollow."

97 Then by the scalp behind I seized upon him,
And said: "It must needs be thou name thyself,
Or not a hair remain upon thee here."

100 Whence he to me: "Though thou strip off my hair,
I will not tell thee who I am, nor show thee,
If on my head a thousand times thou fall."

103 I had his hair in hand already twisted,
And more than one shock of it had pulled out,
He barking, with his eyes held firmly down,

106 When cried another: "What doth ail thee, Bocca?
Is't not enough to clatter with thy jaws,
But thou must bark ? What devil touches thee?"

109 "Now," said I, "I care not to have thee speak,
Accursed traitor; for unto thy shame
I will report of thee veracious news."

112 "Begone," replied he,"and tell what thou wilt,
But be not silent, if thou issue hence,
Of him who had just now his tongue so prompt;

115 He weepeth here the silver of the French;
'I saw,' thus canst thou phrase it, 'him of Duera
There where the sinners stand out in the cold.'

118 If thou shouldst questioned be who else was there,
Thou hast beside thee him of Beccaria,
Of whom the gorget Florence slit asunder;

121 Gianni del Soldanier, I think, may be
Yonder with Ganellon, and Tebaldello
Who oped Faenza when the people slept."

124 Already we had gone away from him,
When I beheld two frozen in one hole,
So that one head a hood was to the other;

127 And even as bread through hunger is devoured,
The uppermost on the other set his teeth,
There where the brain is to the nape united.

130 Not in another fashion Tydeus gnawed
The temples of Menalippus in disdain,
Than that one did the skull and the other things.

133 "O thou, who showest by such bestial sign
Thy hatred against him whom thou art eating,
Tell me the wherefore," said I, "with this compact, us

136 That if thou rightfully of him complain,
In knowing who ye are, and his transgression,
I in the world above repay thee for it,

139 If that wherewith I speak be not dried up."

Canto XXXIII

HIS mouth uplifted from his grim repast,
That sinner, wiping it upon the hair
Of the same head that he behind had wasted.

4 Then he began: "Thou wilt that I renew
The desperate grief, which wrings my heart already
To think of only, ere I speak of it;

7 But if my words be seed that may bear fruit
Of infamy to the traitor whom I gnaw,
Speaking and weeping shalt thou see together.

10 I know not who thou art, nor by what mode
Thou hast come down here; but a Florentine
Thou seemest to me truly, when I hear thee.

13 Thou hast to know I was Count Ugolino,
And this one was Ruggieri the Archbishop;
Now I will tell thee why I am such a neighbour.

16 That, by effect of his malicious thoughts
Trusting in him I was made prisoner,
And after put to death, I need not say;

19 But ne'ertheless what thou canst not have heard,
That is to say, how cruel was my death,
Hear shalt thou, and shalt know if he has wronged me.

22 A narrow perforation in the mew,
Which bears because of me the title of Famine,
And in which others still must be locked up,

25 Had shown me through its opening many moons
Already, when I dreamed the evil dream
Which of the future rent for me the veil.

28 This one appeared to me as lord and master,
Hunting the wolf and whelps upon the mountain
For which the Pisans cannot Lucca see.

31 With sleuth-hounds gaunt, and eager, and well trained,
Gualandi with Sismondi and Lanfranchi

He had sent out before him to the front.

34 After brief course seemed unto me forespent
The father and the sons, and with sharp tushes
It seemed to me I saw their flanks ripped open.

37 When I before the morrow was awake,
Moaning amid their sleep I heard my sons
Who with me were, and asking after bread.

40 Cruel indeed art thou, if yet thou grieve not,
Thinking of what my heart foreboded me,
And weep'st thou not, what art thou wont to weep at?

43 They were awake now, and the hour drew nigh
At which our food used to be brought to us,
And through his dream was each one apprehensive;

46 And I heard locking up the under door
Of the horrible tower; whereat without a word
I gazed into the faces of my sons.

49 I wept not, I within so turned to stone;
They wept; and darling little Anselm mine
Said: 'Thou dost gaze so, father, what doth ail thee?'

52 Still not a tear I shed, nor answer made
All of that day, nor yet the night thereafter,
Until another sun rose on the world.

55 As now a little glimmer made its way
Into the dolorous prison, and I saw
Upon four faces my own very aspect

58 Both of my hands in agony I bit,
And, thinking that I did it from desire
Of eating, on a sudden they uprose,

61 And said they: 'Father, much less pain 'twill give us
If thou do eat of us; thyself didst clothe us
With this poor flesh, and do thou strip it off.'

64 I calmed me then, not to make them more sad.
That day we all were silent, and the next.
Ah! obdurate earth, wherefore didst thou not open?

67 When we had come unto the fourth day, Gaddo
Threw himself down outstretched before my feet,
Saying, 'My father, why dost thou not help me?'

70 And there he died; and, as thou seest me,
I saw the three fall, one by one, between
The fifth day and the sixth; whence I betook me,

73 Already blind, to groping over each,
And three days called them after they were dead;
Then hunger did what sorrow could not do."

76 When he had said this, with his eyes distorted,
The wretched skull resumed he with his teeth,
Which, as a dog's, upon the bone were strong.

79 Ah! Pisa, thou opprobrium of the people
Of the fair land there where the 'Si' doth sound,
Since slow to punish thee thy neighbours are,

82 Let the Capraia and Gorgona move,
And make a hedge across the mouth of Arno
That every person in thee it may drown!

85 For if Count Ugolino had the fame
Of having in thy castles thee betrayed,
Thou shouldst not on such cross have put his sons.

88 Guiltless of any crime, thou modern Thebes!
Their youth made Uguccione and Brigata,
And the other two my song doth name above!

91 We passed still farther onward, where the ice
Another people ruggedly enswathes,
Not downward turned, but all of them reversed.

94 Weeping itself there does not let them weep,
And grief that finds a barrier in the eyes
Turns itself inward to increase the anguish;

97 Because the earliest tears a cluster form,
And, in the manner of a crystal visor,
Fill all the cup beneath the eyebrow full.

100 And notwithstanding that, as in a callus,

Because of cold all sensibility
Its station had abandoned in my face,

103 Still it appeared to me I felt some wind;
Whence I: "My Master, who sets this in motion?
Is not below here every vapour quenched?"

106 Whence he to me: "Full soon shalt thou be where
Thine eye shall answer make to thee of this,
Seeing the cause which raineth down the blast."

109 And one of the wretches of the frozen crust
Cried out to us: "O souls so merciless
That the last post is given unto you,

112 Lift from mine eyes the rigid veils, that I
May vent the sorrow which impregns my heart
A little, e'er the weeping recongeal."

115 Whence I to him: "If thou wouldst have me help thee
Say who thou wast; and if I free thee not,
May I go to the bottom of the ice."

118 Then he replied: "I am Friar Alberigo;
He am I of the fruit of the bad garden,
Who here a date am getting for my fig."

121 "O," said I to him, "now art thou, too, dead?"
And he to me: "How may my body fare
Up in the world, no knowledge I possess.

124 Such an advantage has this Ptolomaea,
That oftentimes the soul descendeth here
Sooner than Atropos in motion sets it.

127 And, that thou mayest more willingly remove
From off my countenance these glassy tears,
Know that as soon as any soul betrays

130 As I have done, his body by a demon
Is taken from him, who thereafter rules it,
Until his time has wholly been revolved.

133 Itself down rushes into such a cistern;
And still perchance above appears the body

Of yonder shade, that winters here behind me.

136 This thou shouldst know, if thou hast just come down;
It is Ser Branca d' Oria, and many years
Have passed away since he was thus locked up."

139 "I think," said I to him, "thou dost deceive me;
For Branca d' Oria is not dead as yet,
And eats, and drinks, and sleeps, and puts on clothes."

142 "In moat above," said he, "of Malebranche,
There where is boiling the tenacious pitch,
As yet had Michel Zanche not arrived,

145 When this one left a devil in his stead
In his own body and one near of kin,
Who made together with him the betrayal.

148 But hitherward stretch out thy hand forthwith,
Open mine eyes;"—and open them I did not,
And to be rude to him was courtesy.

151 Ah, Genoese! ye men at variance
With every virtue, full of every vice
Wherefore are ye not scattered from the world

154 For with the vilest spirit of Romagna
I found of you one such, who for his deeds
In soul already in Cocytus bathes,

157 And still above in body seems alive!

Canto XXXIV

"VEXILLA Regis prodeunt Inferni[4]
Towards us; therefore look in front of thee,"
My Master said, "if thou discernest him."

4 As when there breathes a heavy fog, or when
Our hemisphere is darkening into night,
Appears far off a mill the wind is turning,

7 Methought that such a building then I saw;
And, for the wind, I drew myself behind
My Guide, because there was no other shelter.

10 Now was I, and with fear in verse I put it,
There where the shades were wholly covered up,
And glimmered through like unto straws in glass.

13 Some prone are lying, others stand erect,
This with the head, and that one with the soles;
Another, bow-like, face to feet inverts.

16 When in advance so far we had proceeded,
That it my Master pleased to show to me
The creature who once had the beauteous semblance,

19 He from before me moved and made me stop,
Saying: "Behold Dis, and behold the place
Where thou with fortitude must arm thyself."

22 How frozen I became and powerless then,
Ask it not, Reader, for I write it not,
Because all language would be insufficient.

25 I did not die, and I alive remained not;
Think for thyself now, hast thou aught of wit,
What I became, being of both deprived.

28 The Emperor of the kingdom dolorous
From his mid-breast forth issued from the ice,
And better with a giant I compare

31 Than do the giants with those arms of his;

4 "The banner of the king of hell"

Consider now how great must be that whole,
Which unto such a part conforms itself.

34 Were he as fair once, as he now is foul,
And lifted up his brow against his Maker,
Well may proceed from him all tribulation.

37 O, what a marvel it appeared to me,
When I beheld three faces on his head!
The one in front, and that vermilion was;

40 Two were the others, that were joined with this
Above the middle part of either shoulder,
And they were joined together at the crest;

43 And the right-hand one seemed 'twixt white and yellow
The left was such to look upon as those
Who come from where the Nile falls valley-ward.

46 Underneath each came forth two mighty wings,
Such as befitting were so great a bird;
Sails of the sea I never saw so large.

49 No feathers had they, but as of a bat
Their fashion was; and he was waving them,
So that three winds proceeded forth therefrom.

52 Thereby Cocytus wholly was congealed.
With six eyes did he weep, and down three chins
Trickled the tear-drops and the bloody drivel.

55 At every mouth he with his teeth was crunching
A sinner, in the manner of a brake,
So that he three of them tormented thus.

58 To him in front the biting was as naught
Unto the clawing, for sometimes the spine
Utterly stripped of all the skin remained.

61 "That soul up there which has the greatest pain,"
The Master said, "is Judas Iscariot;
With head inside, he plies his legs without.

64 Of the two others, who head downward are,
The one who hangs from the black jowl is Brutus;
See how he writhes himself, and speaks no word.

And the other, who so stalwart seems, is Cassius.
But night is reascending, and 'tis time
That we depart, for we have seen the whole."

As seemed him good, I clasped him round the neck,
And he the vantage seized of time and place,
And when the wings were opened wide apart,

He laid fast hold upon the shaggy sides;
From fell to fell descended downward then
Between the thick hair and the frozen crust.

When we were come to where the thigh revolves
Exactly on the thickness of the haunch,
The Guide, with labour and with hard-drawn breath,

Turned round his head where he had had his legs,
And grappled to the hair, as one who mounts,
So that to Hell I thought we were returning.

"Keep fast thy hold, for by such stairs as these,"
The Master said, panting as one fatigued,
"Must we perforce depart from so much evil."

Then through the opening of a rock he issued,
And down upon the margin seated me;
Then tow'rds me he outstretched his wary step.

I lifted up mine eyes and thought to see
Lucifer in the same way I had left him;
And I beheld him upward hold his legs.

And if I then became disquieted,
Let stolid people think who do not see
What the point is beyond which I had passed.

"Rise up," the Master said, "upon thy feet;
The way is long, and difficult the road,
And now the sun to middle-tierce returns."[5]

It was not any palace corridor
There where we were, but dungeon natural,
With floor uneven and unease of light.

5 "And already the sun is half a third of the way up."

100 "Ere from the abyss I tear myself away,
My Master," said I when I had arisen,
"To draw me from an error speak a little;

103 Where is the ice? And how is this one fixed
Thus upside down? And how in such short time
From eve to morn has the sun made his transit?"

106 And he to me: "Thou still imaginest
Thou art beyond the centre, where I grasped
The hair of the fell worm, who mines the world.

109 That side thou wast, so long as I descended;
When round I turned me, thou didst pass the point
To which things heavy draw from every side,

112 And now beneath the hemisphere art come
Opposite that which overhangs the vast
Dry-land, and 'neath whose cope was put to death

115 The Man who without sin was born and lived.
Thou hast thy feet upon the little sphere
Which makes the other face of the Judecca.

118 Here it is morn when it is evening there;
And he who with his hair a stairway made us
Still fixed remaineth as he was before.

121 Upon this side he fell down out of heaven;
And all the land, that whilom here emerged,
For fear of him made of the sea a veil,

124 And came to our hemisphere; and peradventure
To flee from him, what on this side appears
Left the place vacant here, and back recoiled."

127 A place there is below, from Beelzebub
As far receding as the tomb extends,
Which not by sight is known, but by the sound

130 Of a small rivulet, that there descendeth
Through chasm within the stone, which it has gnawed
With course that winds about and slightly falls.

133 The Guide and I into that hidden road

Now entered, to return to the bright world;
And without care of having any rest

136 We mounted up, the first and I the second,
Till I beheld through a round aperture
Some of the beauteous things that Heaven doth bear;

139 Thence we came forth to rebehold the stars.

I saw beside me an old man alone,
Worthy of so much reverence in his look,
That more owes not to father any son.

Gustave Doré

Purgatorio

Canto I

TO run o'er better waters hoists its sail
The little vessel of my genius now,
That leaves behind itself a sea so cruel;

4 And of that second kingdom will I sing
Wherein the human spirit doth purge itself,
And to ascend to heaven becometh worthy.

7 Let dead Poesy here rise again,
O holy Muses, since that I am yours,
And here Calliope somewhat ascend,

10 My song accompanying with that sound,
Of which the miserable magpies felt
The blow so great, that they despaired of pardon.

13 Sweet colour of the oriental sapphire,
That was upgathered in the cloudless aspect
Of the pure air, as far as the first circle,

16 Unto mine eyes did recommence delight
Soon as I issued forth from the dead air,
Which had with sadness filled mine eyes and breast.

19 The beauteous planet, that to love incites,
Was making all the orient to laugh,
Veiling the Fishes that were in her escort.

22 To the right hand I turned, and fixed my mind
Upon the other pole, and saw four stars
Ne'er seen before save by the primal people.

25 Rejoicing in their flamelets seemed the heaven.
O thou septentrional and widowed site,

Because thou art deprived of seeing these!

When from regarding them I had withdrawn,
Turning a little to the other pole,
There where the Wain had disappeared already,

I saw beside me an old man alone,
Worthy of so much reverence in his look,
That more owes not to father any son.

A long beard and with white hair intermingled
He wore, in semblance like unto the tresses,
Of which a double list fell on his breast.

The rays of the four consecrated stars
Did so adorn his countenance with light,
That him I saw as were the sun before him.

"Who are you? ye who, counter the blind river,
Have fled away from the eternal prison?"
Moving those venerable plumes, he said:

"Who guided you? or who has been your lamp
In issuing forth out of the night profound,
That ever black makes the infernal valley?

The laws of the abyss, are they thus broken?
Or is there changed in heaven some council new,
That being damned ye come unto my crags?"

Then did my Leader lay his grasp upon me,
And with his words, and with his hands and signs, so
Reverent he made in me my knees and brow:

Then answered him: "I came not of myself;
A Lady from Heaven descended, at whose prayers
I aided this one with my company.

But since it is thy will more be unfolded
Of our condition, how it truly is,
Mine cannot be that this should be denied thee.

This one has never his last evening seen,
But by his folly was so near to it
That very little time was there to turn.

61 As I have said, I unto him was sent
To rescue him, and other way was none
Than this to which I have myself betaken.

64 I've shown him all the people of perdition
And now those spirits I intend to show
Who purge themselves beneath thy guardianship.

67 How I have brought him would be long to tell thee.
Virtue descendeth from on high that aids me
To lead him to behold thee and to hear thee.

70 Now may it please thee to vouchsafe his coming;
He seeketh Liberty, which is so dear,
As knoweth he who life for her refuses.

73 Thou know'st it; since, for her, to thee not bitter
Was death in Utica, where thou didst leave
The vesture, that will shine so, the great day.

76 By us the eternal edicts are not broken;
Since this one lives, and Minos binds not me;
But of that circle I, where are the chaste

79 Eyes of thy Marcia, who in looks still prays thee,
O holy breast, to hold her as thine own;
For her love, then, incline thyself to us.

82 Permit us through thy sevenfold realm to go;
I will take back this grace from thee to her,
If to be mentioned there below thou deignest."

85 "Marcia so pleasing was unto mine eyes
While I was on the other side," then said he,
"That every grace she wished of me I granted;

88 Now that she dwells beyond the evil river,
She can no longer move me, by that law
Which, when I issued forth from there, was made.

91 But if a Lady of Heaven do move and rule thee,
As thou dost say, no flattery is needful;
Let it suffice thee that for her thou ask me.

94 Go, then, and see thou gird this one about

With a smooth rush, and that thou wash his face,
So that thou cleanse away all stain therefrom,

For 'twere not fitting that the eye o'ercast
By any mist should go before the first
Angel, who is of those of Paradise.

This little island round about its base
Below there, yonder, where the billow beats it,
Doth rushes bear upon its washy ooze;

No other plant that putteth forth the leaf,
Or that doth indurate, can there have life,
Because it yieldeth not unto the shocks.

Thereafter be not this way your return;
The sun, which now is rising, will direct you
To take the mount by easier ascent."

With this he vanished; and I raised me up
Without a word, and wholly drew myself
Unto my Guide, and turned mine eyes to him.

And he began: "Son, follow thou my steps;
Let us turn back, for on this side declines
The plain unto its lower boundaries."

The dawn was vanquishing the matin hour
Which fled before it, so that from afar
I recognised the trembling of the sea.

Along the solitary plain we went
As one who unto the lost road returns,
And till he finds it seems to go in vain.

As soon as we were come to where the dew
Fights with the sun, and, being in a part
Where shadow falls, little evaporates,

Both of his hands upon the grass outspread
In gentle manner did my Master place;
Whence I, who of his action was aware,

Extended unto him my tearful cheeks;
There did he make in me uncovered wholly
That hue which Hell had covered up in me.

130 Then came we down upon the desert shore
Which never yet saw navigate its waters
Any that afterward had known return.

133 There he begirt me as the other pleased
O marvellous! for even as he culled
The humble plant, such it sprang up again

136 Suddenly there where he uprooted it.

Canto II

ALREADY had the sun the horizon reached
Whose circle of meridian covers o'er
Jerusalem with its most lofty point,

4 And night that opposite to him revolves
Was issuing forth from Ganges with the Scales
That fall from out her hand when she exceedeth;

7 So that the white and the vermilion cheeks
Of beautiful Aurora, where I was,
By too great age were changing into orange.

10 We still were on the border of the sea,
Like people who are thinking of their road,
Who go in heart and with the body stay;

13 And lo! as when, upon the approach of morning,
Through the gross vapours Mars grows fiery red
Down in the West upon the ocean floor,

16 Appeared to me—may I again behold it!—
A light along the sea so swiftly coming,
Its motion by no flight of wing is equalled;

19 From which when I a little had withdrawn
Mine eyes, that I might question my Conductor,
Again I saw it brighter grown and larger.

22 Then on each side of it appeared to me
I knew not what of white, and underneath
Little by little there came forth another.

25 My Master yet had uttered not a word
While the first whiteness into wings unfolded;
But when he clearly recognised the pilot,

28 He cried: "Make haste, make haste to bow the knee!
Behold the Angel of God! fold thou thy hands!
Henceforward shalt thou see such officers!

31 See how he scorneth human arguments,
So that nor oar he wants, nor other sail
Than his own wings, between so distant shores.

34 See how he holds them pointed up to heaven,
Fanning the air with the eternal pinions,
That do not moult themselves like mortal hair!"

37 Then as still nearer and more near us came
The Bird Divine, more radiant he appeared
So that near by the eye could not endure him,

40 But down I cast it; and he came to shore
With a small vessel, very swift and light,
So that the water swallowed naught thereof.

43 Upon the stern stood the Celestial Pilot;
Beatitude seemed written in his face,
And more than a hundred spirits sat within.

46 "In exitu Israel de Aegypto!"[1]
They chanted all together in one voice,
With whatso in that psalm is after written.

49 Then made he sign of holy rood upon them,
Whereat all cast themselves upon the shore,
And he departed swiftly as he came.

52 The throng which still remained there unfamiliar
Seemed with the place, all round about them gazing,
As one who in new matters makes essay.

55 On every side was darting forth the day
The sun, who had with his resplendent shafts
From the mid-heaven chased forth the Capricorn,

1 "When the Israelites went out of Egypt!"

Upon the stern stood the Celestial Pilot;
Beatitude seemed written in his face,
And more than a hundred spirits sat within.

Gustave Doré

When the new people lifted up their faces
Towards us, saying to us: "If ye know,
Show us the way to go unto the mountain."

And answer made Virgilius: "Ye believe
Perchance that we have knowledge of this place,
But we are strangers even as yourselves.

Just now we came, a little while before you,
Another way, which was so rough and steep,
That mounting will henceforth seem sport to us."

The souls who had, from seeing me draw breath,
Become aware that I was still alive,
Pallid in their astonishment became;

And as to messenger who bears the olive
The people throng to listen to the news,
And no one shows himself afraid of crowding,

So at the sight of me stood motionless
Those fortunate spirits, all of them, as if
Oblivious to go and make them fair.

One from among them saw I coming forward,
As to embrace me, with such great affection,
That it incited me to do the like.

O empty shadows, save in aspect only!
Three times behind it did I clasp my hands,
As oft returned with them to my own breast!

I think with wonder I depicted me;
Whereat the shadow smiled and backward drew;
And I, pursuing it, pressed farther forward.

Gently it said that I should stay my steps;
Then knew I who it was, and I entreated
That it would stop awhile to speak with me.

It made reply to me: "Even as I loved thee
In mortal body, so I love thee free;
Therefore I stop; but wherefore goest thou?"

"My own Casella! to return once more

There where I am, I make this journey," said I;
"But how from thee has so much time be taken?"

94 And he to me: "No outrage has been done me,
If he who takes both when and whom he pleases
Has many times denied to me this passage,

97 For of a righteous will his own is made.
He, sooth to say, for three months past has taken
Whoever wished to enter with all peace;

100 Whence I, who now had turned unto that shore
Where salt the waters of the Tiber grow,
Benignantly by him have been received.

103 Unto that outlet now his wing is pointed,
Because for evermore assemble there
Those who tow'rds Acheron do not descend."

106 And I: "If some new law take not from thee
Memory or practice of the song of love,
Which used to quiet in me all my longings,

109 Then may it please to comfort therewithal
Somewhat this soul of mine, that with its body
Hitherward coming is so much distressed."

112 "Love, that within my mind discourses with me,"
Forthwith began he so melodiously,
The melody within me still is sounding.

115 My Master, and myself, and all that people
Which with him were, appeared as satisfied
As if naught else might touch the mind of any;

118 We all of us were moveless and attentive
Unto his notes; and lo! the grave old man,
Exclaiming: "What is this, ye laggard spirits

121 What negligence, what standing still is this?
Run to the mountain to strip off the slough,
That lets not God be manifest to you."

124 Even as when, collecting grain or tares,
The doves, together at their pasture met,

Quiet, nor showing their accustomed pride

127 If aught appear of which they are afraid,
Upon a sudden leave their food alone,
Because they are assailed by greater care;

130 So that fresh company did I behold
The song relinquish, and go tow'rds the hill,
As one who goes, and knows not whitherward;

133 Nor was our own departure less in haste.

Canto III

INASMUCH as the instantaneous flight
Had scattered them asunder o'er the plain,
Turned to the mountain whither reason spurs us,

4 I pressed me close unto my faithful comrade,
And how without him had I kept my course?
Who would have led me up along the mountain?

7 He seemed to me within himself remorseful;
O noble conscience, and without a stain,
How sharp a sting is trivial fault to thee!

10 After his feet had laid aside the haste
Which mars the dignity of every act,
My mind, that hitherto had been restrained,

13 Let loose its faculties as if delighted,
And I my sight directed to the hill
That highest tow'rds the heaven uplifts itself

16 The sun, that in our rear was flaming red,
Was broken in front of me into the figure
Which had in me the stoppage of its rays;

19 Unto one side I turned me with the fear
Of being left alone, when I beheld
Only in front of me the ground obscured.

22 "Why dost thou still mistrust?" my Comforter
Began to say to me turned wholly round;
"Dost thou not think me with thee, and that I guide thee?

25 'Tis evening there already where is buried
The body within which I cast a shadow;
'Tis from Brundusium ta'en, and Naples has it.

28 Now if in front of me no shadow fall,
Marvel not at it more than at the heavens,
Because one ray impedeth not another

31 To suffer torments, both of cold and heat,
Bodies like this that Power provides, which wills
That how it works be not unveiled to us.

34 Insane is he who hopeth that our reason
Can traverse the illimitable way,
Which the one Substance in three Persons follows!

37 Mortals, remain contented at the 'Quia;'
For if ye had been able to see all,
No need there were for Mary to give birth;

40 And ye have seen desiring without fruit,
Those whose desire would have been quieted,
Which evermore is given them for a grief.

43 I speak of Aristotle and of Plato,
And many others;"—and here bowed his head,
And more he said not, and remained disturbed.

46 We came meanwhile unto the mountain's foot;
There so precipitate we found the rock,
That nimble legs would there have been in vain.

49 'Twixt Lerici and Turbia, the most desert,
The most secluded pathway is a stair
Easy and open, if compared with that.

52 "Who knoweth now upon which hand the hill
Slopes down," my Master said, his footsteps staying,
"So that who goeth without wings may mount?"

55 And while he held his eyes upon the ground

Examining the nature of the path,
And I was looking up around the rock,

58 On the left hand appeared to me a throng
Of souls, that moved their feet in our direction,
And did not seem to move, they came so slowly.

61 "Lift up thine eyes," I to the Master said;
"Behold, on this side, who will give us counsel,
If thou of thine own self can have it not."

64 Then he looked at me, and with frank expression
Replied: "Let us go there, for they come slowly,
And thou be steadfast in thy hope, sweet son."

67 Still was that people as far off from us,
After a thousand steps of ours I say,
As a good thrower with his hand would reach,

70 When they all crowded unto the hard masses
Of the high bank, and motionless stood and close,
As he stands still to look who goes in doubt.

73 "O happy dead! O spirits elect already!"
Virgilius made beginning, "by that peace
Which I believe is waiting for you all,

76 Tell us upon what side the mountain slopes,
So that the going up be possible,
For to lose time irks him most who most knows."

79 As sheep come issuing forth from out the fold
By ones and twos and threes, and the others stand
Timidly, holding down their eyes and nostrils,

82 And what the foremost does the others do,
Huddling themselves against her, if she stop,
Simple and quiet and the wherefore know not;

85 So moving to approach us thereupon
I saw the leader of that fortunate flock,
Modest in face and dignified in gait.

88 As soon as those in the advance saw broken
The light upon the ground at my right side,

So that from me the shadow reached the rock,

91 They stopped, and backward drew themselves somewhat;
And all the others, who came after them,
Not knowing why nor wherefore, did the same.

94 "Without your asking, I confess to you
This is a human body which you see,
Whereby the sunshine on the ground is cleft.

97 Marvel ye not thereat, but be persuaded
That not without a power which comes from Heaven
Doth he endeavour to surmount this wall."

100 The Master thus; and said those worthy people:
"Return ye then, and enter in before us,"
Making a signal with the back o' the hand

103 And one of them began: "Whoe'er thou art,
Thus going turn thine eyes, consider well
If e'er thou saw me in the other world."

106 I turned me tow'rds him, and looked at him closely;
Blond was he, beautiful, and of noble aspect,
But one of his eyebrows had a blow divided.

109 When with humility I had disclaimed
E'er having seen him, "Now behold!" he said,
And showed me high upon his breast a wound.

112 Then said he with a smile: "I am Manfredi,
The grandson of the Empress Costanza;
Therefore, when thou returnest, I beseech thee

115 Go to my daughter beautiful, the mother
Of Sicily's honour and of Aragon's,
And the truth tell her, if aught else be told.

118 After I had my body lacerated
By these two mortal stabs, I gave myself
Weeping to Him, who willingly doth pardon.

121 Horrible my iniquities had been;
But Infinite Goodness hath such ample arms,
That it receives whatever turns to it.

124 Had but Cosenza's pastor, who in chase
Of me was sent by Clement at that time,
In God read understandingly this page,

127 The bones of my dead body still would be
At the bridge-head, near unto Benevento,
Under the safeguard of the heavy cairn.

130 Now the rain bathes and moveth them the wind,
Beyond the realm, almost beside the Verde,
Where he transported them with tapers quenched.

133 By malison[2] of theirs is not so lost
Eternal Love, that it cannot return,
So long as hope has anything of green.

136 True is it, who in contumacy[3] dies
Of Holy Church, though penitent at last,
Must wait upon the outside this bank

139 Thirty times told the time that he has been
In his presumption, unless such decree
Shorter by means of righteous prayers become.

142 See now if thou hast power to make me happy,
By making known unto my good Costanza
How thou hast seen me, and this ban beside,

145 For those on earth can much advance us here."

---

2 A curse.

3 Stubborn refusal to obey or comply with authority.

Canto IV

WHENEVER by delight or else by pain,
That seizes any faculty of ours,
Wholly to that the soul collects itself,

4 It seemeth that no other power it heeds;
And this against that error is which thinks
One soul above another kindles in us.

7 And hence, whenever aught is heard or seen
Which keeps the soul intently bent upon it,
Time passes on, and we perceive it not,

10 Because one faculty is that which listens,
And other that which the soul keeps entire;
This is as if in bonds, and that is free.

13 Of this I had experience positive
In hearing and in gazing at that spirit;
For fifty full degrees uprisen was

16 The sun, and I had not perceived it, when
We came to where those souls with one accord
Cried out unto us: "Here is what you ask."

19 A greater opening ofttimes hedges up
With but a little forkful of his thorns
The villager, what time the grape imbrowns,

22 Than was the passage-way through which ascended
Only my Leader and myself behind him,
After that company departed from us.

25 One climbs Sanleo and descends in Noli,
And mounts the summit of Bismantova,
With feet alone; but here one needs must fly;

28 With the swift pinions and the plumes I say
Of great desire, conducted after him
Who gave me hope, and made a light for me.

31 We mounted upward through the rifted rock,
And on each side the border pressed upon us,

And feet and hands the ground beneath required.

34 When we were come upon the upper rim
Of the high bank, out on the open slope,
"My Master," said I, "what way shall we take?"

37 And he to me: "No step of thine descend;
Still up the mount behind me win thy way,
Till some sage escort shall appear to us."

40 The summit was so high it vanquished sight,
And the hillside precipitous far more
Than line from middle quadrant to the centre.

43 Spent with fatigue was I, when I began:
"O my sweet Father! turn thee and behold
How I remain alone, unless thou stay!"

46 "O son," he said, "up yonder drag thyself,"
Pointing me to a terrace somewhat higher,
Which on that side encircles all the hill.

49 These words of his so spurred me on, that I
Strained every nerve, behind him scrambling up,
Until the circle was beneath my feet.

52 Thereon ourselves we seated both of us
Turned to the East, from which we had ascended,
For all men are delighted to look back.

55 To the low shores mine eyes I first directed,
Then to the sun uplifted them, and wondered
That on the left hand we were smitten by it.

58 The Poet well perceived that I was wholly
Bewildered at the chariot of the light,
Where 'twixt us and the Aquilon it entered.

61 Whereon he said to me: "If Castor and Pollux
Were in the company of yonder mirror,
That up and down conducteth with its light,

64 Thou wouldst behold the zodiac's jagged wheel
Revolving still more near unto the Bears,
Unless it swerved aside from its old track.

67 How that may be wouldst thou have power to think,
Collected in thyself, imagine Zion
Together with this mount on earth to stand,

70 So that they both one sole horizon have,
And hemispheres diverse; whereby the road
Which Phaeton, alas! knew not to drive,

73 Thou'lt see how of necessity must pass
This on one side, when that upon the other,
If thine intelligence right clearly heed."

76 "Truly, my Master," said I, "never yet
Saw I so clearly as I now discern,
There where my wit appeared incompetent,

79 That the mid-circle of supernal motion,
Which in some art is the Equator called
And aye remains between the Sun and Winter,

82 For reason which thou sayest, departeth hence
Tow'rds the Septentrion, what time the Hebrews
Beheld it tow'rds the region of the heat.

85 But, if it pleaseth thee, I fain would learn
How far we have to go; for the hill rises
Higher than eyes of mine have power to rise."

88 And he to me: "This mount is such that ever
At the beginning down below 'tis tiresome,
And aye the more one climbs, the less it hurts.

91 Therefore, when it shall seem so pleasant to thee,
That going up shall be to thee as easy
As going down the current in a boat,

94 Then at this pathway's ending thou wilt be;
There to repose thy panting breath expect;
No more I answer; and this I know for true."

97 And as he finished uttering these words,
A voice close by us sounded: "Peradventure
Thou wilt have need of sitting down ere that."

100 At sound thereof each one of us turned round,

And saw upon the left hand a great rock,
Which neither I nor he before had noticed.

Thither we drew; and there were persons there
Who in the shadow stood behind the rock,
As one through indolence is wont to stand.

And one of them, who seemed to me fatigued,
Was sitting down, and both his knees embraced,
Holding his face low down between them bowed.

"O my sweet Lord," I said, "do turn thine eye
On him who shows himself more negligent
Then even Sloth herself his sister were."

Then he turned round to us, and he gave heed,
Just lifting up his eyes above his thigh,
And said: "Now go thou up, for thou art valiant."

Then knew I who he was; and the distress,
That still a little did my breathing quicken,
My going to him hindered not; and after

I came to him he hardly raised his head,
Saying: "Hast thou seen clearly how the sun
O'er thy left shoulder drives his chariot?"

His sluggish attitude and his curt words
A little unto laughter moved my lips;
Then I began: "Belacqua, I grieve not

For thee henceforth; but tell me, wherefore seated
In this place art thou? Waitest thou an escort?
Or has thy usual habit seized upon thee?"

And he: "O brother, what's the use of climbing?
Since to my torment would not let me go
The Angel of God, who sitteth at the gate.

First heaven must needs so long revolve me round
Outside thereof, as in my life it did,
Since the good sighs I to the end postponed,

Unless, e'er that, some prayer may bring me aid
Which rises from a heart that lives in grace;

What profit others that in heaven are heard not?"

136 Meanwhile the Poet was before me mounting,
And saying: "Come now; see the sun has touched
Meridian, and from the shore the night

139 Covers already with her foot Morocco."

Canto V

I HAD already from those shades departed,
And followed in the footsteps of my Guide,
When from behind, pointing his finger at me,

4 One shouted: "See, it seems as if shone not
The sunshine on the left of him below,
And like one living seems he to conduct him."

7 Mine eyes I turned at utterance of these words,
And saw them watching with astonishment
But me, but me, and the light which was broken!

10 "Why doth thy mind so occupy itself,"
The Master said, "that thou thy pace dost slacken?
What matters it to thee what here is whispered?

13 Come after me, and let the people talk;
Stand like a steadfast tower, that never wags
Its top for all the blowing of the winds;

16 For evermore the man in whom is springing
Thought upon thought, removes from him the mark,
Because the force of one the other weakens."

19 What could I say in answer but "I come"?
I said it somewhat with that colour tinged
Which makes a man of pardon sometimes worthy.

22 Meanwhile along the mountain-side across
Came people in advance of us a little,
Singing the Miserere verse by verse.

25 When they became aware I gave no place
For passage of the sunshine through my body
They changed their song into a long, hoarse "Oh!"

28 And two of them, in form of messengers,
Ran forth to meet us, and demanded of us,
"Of your condition make us cognisant."

31 And said my Master: "Ye can go your way
And carry back again to those who sent you,
That this one's body is of very flesh.

34 If they stood still because they saw his shadow,
As I suppose, enough is answered them;
Him let them honour, it may profit them."

37 Vapours enkindled saw I ne'er so swiftly
At early nightfall cleave the air serene,
Nor, at the set of sun, the clouds of August,

40 But upward they returned in briefer time,
And, on arriving, with the others wheeled
Tow'rds us, like troops that run without a rein.

43 "This folk that presses unto us is great,
And cometh to implore thee," said the Poet;
"So still go onward, and in going listen."

46 "O soul that goest to beatitude
With the same members wherewith thou wast born,"
Shouting they came, "a little stay thy steps,

49 Look, if thou e'er hast any of us seen,
So that o'er yonder thou bear news of him;
Ah, why dost thou go on? Ah, why not stay?

52 Long since we all were slain by violence,
And sinners even to the latest hour;
Then did a light from heaven admonish us,

55 So that, both penitent and pardoning, forth
From life we issued reconciled to God,
Who with desire to see Him stirs our hearts."

58 And I: "Although I gaze into your faces,
No one I recognize; but if may please you

Aught I have power to do, ye well-born spirits,

61 Speak ye, and I will do it, by that peace
Which, following the feet of such a Guide,
From world to world makes itself sought by me."

64 And one began: "Each one has confidence
In thy good offices without an oath,
Unless the 'I' cannot cut off the 'I will;'

67 Whence I, who speak alone before the others,
Pray thee, if ever thou dost see the land
That 'twixt Romagna lies and that of Charles,

70 Thou be so courteous to me of thy prayers
In Fano, that they pray for me devoutly,
That I may purge away my grave offences.

73 From thence was I; but the deep wounds, through which
Issued the blood wherein I had my seat,
Were dealt me in bosom of the Antenori,

76 There where I thought to be the most secure;
'Twas he of Este had it done, who held me
In hatred far beyond what justice willed.

79 But if towards the Mira I had fled,
When I was overtaken at Oriaco,
I still should be o'er yonder where men breathe.

82 I ran to the lagoon, and reeds and mire
Did so entangle me I fell, and saw there
A lake made from my veins upon the ground."

85 Then said another: "Ah, be that desire
Fulfilled that draws thee to the lofty mountain,
As thou with pious pity aidest mine.

88 I was of Montefeltro, and am Buonconte;
Giovanna, nor none other cares for me;
Hence among these I go with downcast front."

91 And I to him: "What violence or what chance
Led thee astray so far from Campaldino,
That never has thy sepulture been known?"

94 "Oh," he replied, "at Casentino's foot
A river crosses named Archiano, born
Above the Hermitage in Apennine.

97 There where the name thereof becometh void
Did I arrive, pierced through and through the throat,
Fleeing on foot, and bloodying the plain;

100 There my sight lost I, and my utterance
Ceased in the name of Mary, and thereat
I fell, and tenantless my flesh remained.

103 Truth will I speak, repeat it to the living;
God's Angel took me up, and he of hell
Shouted: 'O thou from heaven, why dost thou rob me?

106 Thou bearest away the eternal part of him,
For one poor little tear, that takes him from me;
But with the rest I'll deal in other fashion!'

109 Well knowest thou how in the air is gathered
That humid vapour which to water turns,
Soon as it rises where the cold doth grasp it.

112 He joined that evil will, which aye seeks evil,
To intellect, and moved the mist and wind
By means of power, which his own nature gave;

115 Thereafter when the day was spent, the valley
From Pratomagno to the great yoke covered
With fog, and made the heaven above intent,

118 So that the pregnant air to water changed;
Down fell the rain, and to the gullies came
Whate'er of it earth tolerated not;

121 And as it mingled with the mighty torrents,
Towards the royal river with such speed
It headlong rushed, that nothing held it back.

124 My frozen body near unto its outlet
The robust Archian found, and into Arno
Thrust it, and loosened from my breast the cross

127 I made of me, when agony o'ercame me;

It rolled me on the banks and on the bottom,
Then with its booty covered and begirt me."

130 "Ah, when thou hast returned unto the world,
And rested thee from thy long journeying,"
After the second followed the third spirit,

133 "Do thou remember me who am the Pia;
Siena made me, unmade me Maremma;
He knoweth it, who had encircled first,

136 Espousing me, my finger with his gem."

Canto VI

WHENE'ER is broken up the game of Zara,
He who has lost remains behind despondent,
The throws repeating, and in sadness learns;

4 The people with the other all depart;
One goes in front, and one behind doth pluck
And at his side one brings himself to mind;

7 He pauses not, and this and that one hears;
They crowd no more to whom his hand he stretches,
And from the throng he thus defends himself.

10 Even such was I in that dense multitude,
Turning to them this way and that my face,
And, promising, I freed myself therefrom.

13 There was the Aretine, who from the arms
Untamed of Ghin di Tacco had his death,
And he who fleeing from pursuit was drowned.

16 There was imploring with his hands outstretched
Frederick Novello, and that one of Pisa
Who made the good Marzucco seem so strong.

19 I saw Count Orso; and the soul divided
By hatred and by envy from its body,
As it declared, and not for crime committed,

Pierre de la Brosse I say; and here provide
While still on earth the Lady of Brabant,
So that for this she be of no worse flock!

As soon as I was free from all those shades
Who only prayed that some one else may pray,
So as to hasten their becoming holy,

Began I: "It appears that thou deniest,
O light of mine, expressly in some text,
That orison can bend decree of Heaven;

And ne'ertheless these people pray for this.
Might then their expectation bootless be
Or is to me thy saying not quite clear?"

And he to me: "My writing is explicit,
And not fallacious is the hope of these,
If with sane intellect 'tis well regarded;

For top of judgment doth not vail itself,
Because the fire of love fulfils at once
What he must satisfy who here installs him.

And there, where I affirmed that proposition,
Defect was not amended by a prayer,
Because the prayer from God was separate.

Verily, in so deep a questioning
Do not decide, unless she tell it thee,
Who light 'twixt truth and intellect shall be.

I know not if thou understand; I speak
Of Beatrice; her shalt thou see above,
Smiling and happy, on this mountain's top."

And I: "Good Leader, let us make more haste,
For I no longer tire me as before;
And see, e'en now the hill a shadow casts."

"We will go forward with this day" he answered,
"As far as now is possible for us;
But otherwise the fact is than thou thinkest.

Ere thou art up there, thou shalt see return

Him, who now hides himself behind the hill,
So that thou dost not interrupt his rays.

58 But yonder there behold! a soul that stationed
All, all alone is looking hitherward;
It will point out to us the quickest way."

61 We came up unto it; O Lombard soul,
How lofty and disdainful thou didst bear thee,
And grand and slow in moving of thine eyes!

64 Nothing whatever did it say to us,
But let us go our way, eying us only
After the manner of a couchant lion;

67 Still near to it Virgilius drew, entreating
That it would point us out the best ascent;
And it replied not unto his demand,

70 But of our native land and of our life
It questioned us; and the sweet Guide began:
"Mantua,"—and the shade, all in itself recluse,

73 Rose tow'rds him from the place where first it was.
Saying: "O Mantuan, I am Sordello
Of thine own land!" and one embraced the other.

76 Ah! servile Italy, grief's hostelry!
A ship without a pilot in great tempest!
No Lady thou of Provinces, but brothel!

79 That noble soul was so impatient, only
At the sweet sound of his own native land,
To make its citizen glad welcome there;

82 And now within thee are not without war
Thy living ones, and one doth gnaw the other
Of those whom one wall and one fosse shut in!

85 Search, wretched one, all round about the shores
Thy seaboard, and then look within thy bosom,
If any part of thee enjoyeth peace!

88 What boots it, that for thee Justinian
The bridle mend, if empty be the saddle?

Withouten this the shame would be the less.

91 Ah! people, thou that oughtest to be devout,
And to let Caesar sit upon the saddle,
If well thou hearest what God teacheth thee,

94 Behold how fell this wild beast has become,
Being no longer by the spur corrected,
Since thou hast laid thy hand upon the bridle.

97 O German Albert! who abandonest
Her that has grown recalcitrant and savage,
And oughtest to bestride her saddle-bow,

100 May a just judgment from the stars down fall
Upon thy blood, and be it new and open,
That thy successor may have fear thereof;

103 Because thy father and thyself have suffered,
By greed of those transalpine lands distrained,
The garden of the empire to be waste.

106 Come and behold Montecchi and Cappelletti,
Monaldi and Fillippeschi, careless man!
Those sad already, and these doubt-depressed!

109 Come, cruel one! come and behold the oppression
Of thy nobility, and cure their wounds,
And thou shalt see how safe is Santafiore!

112 Come and behold thy Rome, that is lamenting,
Widowed, alone, and day and night exclaims,
"My Caesar, why hast thou forsaken me?"

115 Come and behold how loving are the people;
And if for us no pity moveth thee,
Come and be made ashamed of thy renown!

118 And if it lawful be, O Jove Supreme!
Who upon earth for us wast crucified,
Are thy just eyes averted otherwhere?

121 Or preparation is't, that, in the abyss
Of thine own counsel, for some good thou makest
From our perception utterly cut off?

124 For all the towns of Italy are full
Of tyrants, and becometh a Marcellus
Each peasant churl who plays the partisan!

127 My Florence! well mayst thou contented be
With this digression, which concerns thee not,
Thanks to thy people who such forethought take!

130 Many at heart have justice, but shoot slowly,
That unadvised they come not to the bow,
But on their very lips thy people have it!

133 Many refuse to bear the common burden;
But thy solicitous people answereth
Without being asked, and crieth: "I submit."

136 Now be thou joyful, for thou hast good reason;
Thou affluent, thou in peace, thou full of wisdom!
If I speak true, the event conceals it not.

139 Athens and Lacedaemon, they who made
The ancient laws, and were so civilized,
Made towards living well a little sign

142 Compared with thee, who makest such fine-spun
Provisions, that to middle of November
Reaches not what thou in October spinnest.

145 How oft, within the time of thy remembrance,
Laws, money, offices, and usages
Hast thou remodelled, and renewed thy members?

148 And if thou mind thee well, and see the light,
Thou shalt behold thyself like a sick woman,
Who cannot find repose upon her down,

151 But by her tossing wardeth off her pain.

Canto VII

AFTER the gracious and glad salutations
Had three and four times been reiterated,
Sordello backward drew and said, "Who are you?"

4 "Or ever to this mountain were directed
The souls deserving to ascend to God,
My bones were buried by Octavian.

7 I am Virgilius; and for no crime else
Did I lose heaven, than for not having faith;"
In this wise then my Leader made reply.

10 As one who suddenly before him sees
Something whereat he marvels, who believes
And yet does not, saying, "It is! it is not!"

13 So he appeared; and then bowed down his brow,
And with humility returned towards him,
And, where inferiors embrace, embraced him.

16 "O glory of the Latians, thou," he said,
"Through whom our language showed what it could do
O pride eternal of the place I came from,

19 What merit or what grace to me reveals thee?
If I to hear thy words be worthy, tell me
If thou dost come from Hell, and from what cloister."

22 "Through all the circles of the doleful realm,"
Responded he, "have I come hitherward;
Heaven's power impelled me, and with that I come.

25 I by not doing, not by doing, lost
The sight of that high sun which thou desirest,
And which too late by me was recognized.

28 A place there is below not sad with torments,
But darkness only, where the lamentations
Have not the sound of wailing, but are sighs.

31 There dwell I with the little innocents
Snatched by the teeth of Death, or ever they
Were from our human sinfulness exempt.

34 There dwell I among those who the three saintly
Virtues did not put on, and without vice
The others knew and followed all of them.

37 But if thou know and can, some indication
Give us by which we may the sooner come
Where Purgatory has its right beginning."

40 He answered: "No fixed place has been assigned us;
'Tis lawful for me to go up and round;
So far as I can go, as guide I join thee.

43 But see already how the day declines,
And to go up by night we are not able;
Therefore 'tis well to think of some fair sojourn.

46 Souls are there on the right hand here withdrawn;
If thou permit me I will lead thee to them,
And thou shalt know them not without delight."

49 "How is this?" was the answer; "should one wish
To mount by night would he prevented be
By others? or mayhap would not have power?"

52 And on the ground the good Sordello drew
His finger, saying, "See, this line alone
Thou couldst not pass after the sun is gone;

55 Not that aught else would hindrance give, however,
To going up, save the nocturnal darkness;
This with the want of power the will perplexes.

58 We might indeed therewith return below,
And, wandering, walk the hill-side round about,
While the horizon holds the day imprisoned."

61 Thereon my Lord, as if in wonder, said:
"Do thou conduct us thither, where thou sayest
That we can take delight in tarrying."

64 Little had we withdrawn us from that place,
When I perceived the mount was hollowed out
In fashion as the valleys here are hollowed.

67 "Thitherward," said that shade, "will we repair,
Where of itself the hill-side makes a lap

And there for the new day will we await."

70 'Twixt hill and plain there was a winding path
Which led us to the margin of that dell,
Where dies the border more than half away

73 Gold and fine silver, and scarlet and pearl-white,
The Indian wood resplendent and serene,
Fresh emerald the moment it is broken,

76 By herbage and by flowers within that hollow
Planted, each one in colour would be vanquished,
As by its greater vanquished is the less.

79 Nor in that place had nature painted only,
But of the sweetness of a thousand odours
Made there a mingled fragrance and unknown.

82 "Salve Regina," on the green and flowers
There seated, singing, spirits I beheld,
Which were not visible outside the valley.

85 "Before the scanty sun now seeks his nest,"
Began the Mantuan who had led us thither,
"Among them do not wish me to conduct you.

88 Better from off this ledge the acts and faces
Of all of them will you discriminate,
Than in the plain below received among them.

91 He who sits highest, and the semblance bears
Of having what he should have done neglected,
And to the others' song moves not his lips,

94 Rudolph the Emperor was, who had the power
To heal the wounds that Italy have slain,
So that through others slowly she revives.

97 The other, who in look doth comfort him,
Governed the region where the water springs,
The Moldau bears the Elbe, and Elbe the sea.

100 His name was Ottocar; and in swaddling-clothes
Far better he than bearded Winceslaus
His son, who feeds in luxury and ease.

And the small-nosed, who close in council seems
With him that has an aspect so benign,
Died fleeing and disflowering the lily;

Look there, how he is beating at his breast!
Behold the other one, who for his cheek
Sighing has made of his own palm a bed;

Father and father-in-law of France's Pest
Are they, and know his vicious life and lewd,
And hence proceeds the grief that so doth pierce them.

He who appears so stalwart, and chimes in,
Singing, with that one of the manly nose,
The cord of every valour wore begirt;

And if as King had after him remained
The stripling who in rear of him is sitting;
Well had the valour passed from vase to vase

Which cannot of the other heirs be said.
Frederick and Jacomo possess the realms,
But none the better heritage possesses.

Not oftentimes upriseth through the branches
The probity of man; and this He wills
Who gives it, so that we may ask of Him.

Eke to the large-nosed reach my words, no less
Than to the other, Pier, who with him sings;
Whence Provence and Apulia grieve already;

The plant is as inferior to its seed,
As more than Beatrice and Margaret
Costanza boasteth of her husband still.

Behold the monarch of the simple life,
Harry of England, sitting there alone;
He in his branches has a better issue.

He who the lowest on the ground among them
Sits looking upward, is the Marquis William,
For whose sake Alessandra and her war

Make Monferrat and Canavese weep."

Canto VIII

'TWAS now the hour that turneth back desire
In those who sail the sea, and melts the heart,
The day they've said to their sweet friends farewell,

4 And the new pilgrim penetrates with love,
If he doth hear from far away a bell
That seemeth to deplore the dying day,

7 When I began to make of no avail
My hearing, and to watch one of the souls
Uprisen, that begged attention with its hand.

10 It joined and lifted upward both its palms,
Fixing its eyes upon the orient,
As if it said to God, "Naught else I care for."

13 "Te lucis ante"[4] so devoutly issued
Forth from its mouth, and with such dulcet notes,
It made me issue forth from my own mind.

16 And then the others, sweetly and devoutly,
Accompanied it through all the hymn entire,
Having their eyes on the supernal wheels.

19 Here, Reader, fix thine eyes well on the truth,
For now indeed so subtile is the veil,
Surely to penetrate within is easy.

22 I saw that army of the gentle-born
Thereafterward in silence upward gaze,
As if in expectation, pale and humble;

25 And from on high come forth and down descend,
I saw two Angels with two flaming swords,
Truncated and deprived of their points.

28 Green as the little leaflets just now born
Their garments were, which, by their verdant pinions
Beaten and blown abroad, they trailed behind.

31 One just above us came to take his station,
And one descended to the opposite bank,

4 "You are the light before."

So that the people were contained between them.

34 Clearly in them discerned I the blond head;
But in their faces was the eye bewildered,
As faculty confounded by excess.

37 "From Mary's bosom both of them have come,"
Sordello said, "as guardians of the valley
Against the serpent, that will come anon."

40 Whereupon I, who knew not by what road,
Turned round about, and closely drew myself,
Utterly frozen, to the faithful shoulders.

43 And once again Sordello: "Now descend we
'Mid the grand shades, and we will speak to them;
Right pleasant will it be for them to see you."

46 Only three steps I think that I descended,
And was below, and saw one who was looking
Only at me, as if he fain would know me.

49 Already now the air was growing dark,
But not so that between his eyes and mine
It did not show what it before locked up.

52 Tow'rds me he moved, and I tow'rds him did move;
Noble Judge Nino! how it me delighted,
When I beheld thee not among the damned!

55 No greeting fair was left unsaid between us;
Then asked he: "How long is it since thou camest
O'er the far waters to the mountain's foot?"

58 "Oh!" said I to him, "through the dismal places
I came this morn; and am in the first life,
Albeit the other, going thus, I gain."

61 And on the instant my reply was heard,
He and Sordello both shrank back from me,
Like people who are suddenly bewildered.

64 One to Virgilius, and the other turned
To one who sat there, crying, "Up, Currado!
Come and behold what God in grace has willed!"

67 Then, turned to me: "By that especial grace
Thou owest unto Him, who so conceals

His own first wherefore, that it has no ford,

70 When thou shalt be beyond the waters wide,
Tell my Giovanna that she pray for me,
Where answer to the innocent is made.

73 I do not think her mother loves me more,
Since she has laid aside her wimple white,
Which she, unhappy, needs must wish again.

76 Through her full easily is comprehended
How long in woman lasts the fire of love,
If eye or touch do not relight it often.

79 So fair a hatchment will not make for her
The Viper marshalling the Milanese
A-field, as would have made Gallura's Cock."

82 In this wise spake he, with the stamp impressed
Upon his aspect of that righteous zeal
Which measurably burneth in the heart.

85 My greedy eyes still wandered up to heaven,
Still to that point where slowest are the stars
Even as a wheel the nearest to its axle.

88 And my Conductor: "Son, what dost thou gaze at
Up there?" And I to him: "At those three torches
With which this hither pole is all on fire."

91 And he to me: "The four resplendent stars
Thou sawest this morning are down yonder low,
And these have mounted up to where those were."

94 As he was speaking, to himself Sordello
Drew him, and said, "Lo there our Adversary!"
And pointed with his finger to look thither.

97 Upon the side on which the little valley
No barrier hath, a serpent was; perchance
The same which gave to Eve the bitter food.

100 'Twixt grass and flowers came on the evil streak,
Turning at times its head about, and licking
Its back like to a beast that smoothes itself.

103 I did not see, and therefore cannot say

How the celestial falcons 'gan to move,
But well I saw that they were both in motion.

106 Hearing the air cleft by their verdant wings,
The serpent fled, and round the Angels wheeled,
Up to their stations flying back alike.

109 The shade that to the Judge had near approached
When he had called, throughout that whole assault
Had not a moment loosed its gaze on me.

112 "So may the light that leadeth thee on high
Find in thine own free-will as much of wax
As needful is up to the highest azure,"

115 Began it, "if some true intelligence
Of Valdimagra or its neighbourhood
Thou knowest, tell it me, who once was great there.

118 Currado Malaspina was I called;
I'm not the elder, but from him descended;
To mine I bore the love which here refineth."

121 "O," said I unto him, "through your domains
I never passed, but where is there a dwelling
Throughout all Europe, where they are not known?

124 That fame, which doeth honour to your house,
Proclaims its Signors and proclaims its land,
So that he knows of them who ne'er was there.

127 And, as I hope for heaven, I swear to you
Your honoured family in naught abates
The glory of the purse and of the sword.

130 It is so privileged by use and nature,
That though a guilty head misguide the world,
Sole it goes right, and scorns the evil way."

133 And he: "Now go; for the sun shall not lie
Seven times upon the pillow which the Ram
With all his four feet covers and bestrides,

136 Before that such a courteous opinion
Shall in the middle of thy head be nailed
With greater nails than of another's speech,

139 Unless the course of justice standeth still."

Canto IX

THE concubine of old Tithonus now
Gleamed white upon the eastern balcony,
Forth from the arms of her sweet paramour;

With gems her forehead all relucent was,
Set in the shape of that cold animal
Which with its tail doth smite amain the nations,

And of the steps, with which she mounts, the Night
Had taken two in that place where we were,
And now the third was bending down its wings;

When I, who something had of Adam in me,
Vanquished by sleep, upon the grass reclined,
There were all five of us already sat.

Just at the hour when her sad lay begins
The little swallow, near unto the morning,
Perchance in memory of her former woes,

And when the mind of man, a wanderer
More from the flesh, and less by thought imprisoned,
Almost prophetic in its visions is,

In dreams it seemed to me I saw suspended
An eagle in the sky, with plumes of gold,
With wings wide open, and intent to stoop,

And this, it seemed to me, was where had been
By Ganymede his kith and kin abandoned,
When to the high consistory he was rapt.

I thought within myself, perchance he strikes
From habit only here, and from elsewhere
Disdains to bear up any in his feet.

Then wheeling somewhat more, it seemed to me,
Terrible as the lightning he descended,
And snatched me upward even to the fire.

Therein it seemed that he and I were burning,
And the imagined fire did scorch me so,
That of necessity my sleep was broken.

Terrible as the lightning he descended,
And snatched me upward even to the fire.

Gustave Doré

34 Not otherwise Achilles started up,
Around him turning his awakened eyes,
And knowing not the place in which he was,

37 What time from Chiron stealthily his mother
Carried him sleeping in her arms to Scyros,
Wherefrom the Greeks withdrew him afterwards,

40 Than I upstarted, when from off my face
Sleep fled away; and pallid I became,
As doth the man who freezes with affright.

43 Only my Comforter was at my side,
And now the sun was more than two hours high,
And turned towards the sea-shore was my face.

46 "Be not intimidated," said my Lord,
"Be reassured, for all is well with us;
Do not restrain, but put forth all thy strength.

49 Thou hast at length arrived at Purgatory;
See there the cliff that closes it around;
See there the entrance, where it seems disjoined.

52 Whilom at dawn, which doth precede the day,
When inwardly thy spirit was asleep
Upon the flowers that deck the land below,

55 There came a Lady and said: 'I am Lucia;
Let me take this one up, who is asleep;
So will I make his journey easier for him.'

58 Sordello and the other noble shapes
Remained; she took thee, and, as day grew bright,
Upward she came, and I upon her footsteps.

61 She laid thee here; and first her beauteous eyes
That open entrance pointed out to me;
Then she and sleep together went away."

64 In guise of one whose doubts are reassured,
And who to confidence his fear doth change,
After the truth has been discovered to him,

67 So did I change; and when without disquiet

My Leader saw me, up along the cliff
He moved, and I behind him, tow'rd the height.

70 Reader, thou seest well how I exalt
My theme, and therefore if with greater art
I fortify it, marvel not thereat.

73 Nearer approached we, and were in such place,
That there, where first appeared to me a rift
Like to a crevice that disparts a wall,

76 I saw a portal, and three stairs beneath,
Diverse in colour, to go up to it,
And a gate-keeper, who yet spake no word.

79 As I opened more and more mine eyes,
I saw him seated on the highest stair,
Such in the face that I endured it not.

82 And in his hand he had a naked sword,
Which so reflected back the sunbeams tow'rds us,
That oft in vain I lifted up mine eyes.

85 "Tell it from where you are, what is't you wish?"
Began he to exclaim; "where is the escort?
Take heed your coming hither harm you not!"

88 "A Lady of Heaven, with these things conversant,"
My Master answered him, "but even now
Said to us, 'Thither go; there is the portal.'"

91 "And may she speed your footsteps in all good,"
Again began the courteous janitor;
"Come forward then unto these stairs of ours."

94 Thither did we approach; and the first stair
Was marble white, so polished and so smooth,
I mirrored myself therein as I appear.

97 The second, tinct of deeper hue than perse,
Was of a calcined and uneven stone,
Cracked all asunder lengthwise and across.

100 The third, that uppermost rests massively,
Porphyry seemed to me, as flaming red

As blood that from a vein is spurting forth.

Both of his feet was holding upon this
The Angel of God, upon the threshold seated,
Which seemed to me a stone of diamond.

Along the three stairs upward with good will
Did my Conductor draw me, saying: "Ask
Humbly that he the fastening may undo."

Devoutly at the holy feet I cast me,
For mercy's sake besought that he would open,
But first upon my breast three times I smote.

Seven P's upon my forehead he described
With the sword's point, and, "Take heed that thou wash
These wounds, when thou shalt be within," he said.

Ashes, or earth that dry is excavated,
Of the same colour were with his attire,
And from beneath it he drew forth two keys.

One was of gold, and the other was of silver;
First with the white, and after with the yellow,
Plied he the door, so that I was content.

"Whenever faileth either of these keys
So that it turn not rightly in the lock,"
He said to us, "this entrance doth not open.

More precious one is, but the other needs
More art and intellect ere it unlock,
For it is that which doth the knot unloose.

From Peter I have them; and he bade me err
Rather in opening than in keeping shut,
If people but fall down before my feet."

Then pushed the portals of the sacred door,
Exclaiming: "Enter; but I give you warning
That forth returns whoever looks behind."

And when upon their hinges were turned round
The swivels of that consecrated gate,
Which are of metal, massive and sonorous,

136 Roared not so loud, nor so discordant seemed
Tarpeia, when was ta'en from it the good
Metellus, wherefore meagre it remained.

139 At the first thunder-peal I turned attentive,
And "Te Deum laudamus" seemed to hear
In voices mingled with sweet melody.

142 Exactly such an image rendered me
That which I heard, as we are wont to catch,
When people singing with the organ stand;

145 For now we hear, and now hear not, the words.

Canto X

WHEN we had crossed the threshhold of the door
Which the perverted love of souls disuses,
Because it makes the crooked way seem straight,

4 Re-echoing I heard it closed again;
And if I had turned back mine eyes upon it,
What for my failing had been fit excuse?

7 We mounted upward through a rifted rock,
Which undulated to this side and that,
Even as a wave receding and advancing.

10 "Here it behoves us use a little art,"
Began my Leader, "to adapt ourselves
Now here, now there, to the receding side."

13 And this our footsteps so infrequent made,
That sooner had the moon's decreasing disk
Regained its bed to sink again to rest,

16 Than we were forth from out that needle's eye;
But when we free and in the open were
There where the mountain backward piles itself,

19 I wearied out, and both of us uncertain
About our way, we stopped upon a plain

More desolate than roads across the deserts.

22 From where its margin borders on the void,
To foot of the high bank that ever rises,
A human body three times told would measure;

25 And far as eye of mine could wing its flight,
Now on the left, and on the right flank now,
The same this cornice did appear to me.

28 Thereon our feet had not been moved as yet,
When I perceived the embankment round about,
Which all right of ascent had interdicted,

31 To be of marble white, and so adorned
With sculptures, that not only Polycletus,
But Nature's self, had there been put to shame.

34 The Angel, who came down to earth with tidings
Of peace, that had been wept for many a year,
And opened Heaven from its long interdict,

37 In front of us appeared so truthfully
There sculptured in a gracious attitude,
He did not seem an image that is silent.

40 One would have sworn that he was saying, "Ave",
For she was there in effigy portrayed
Who turned the key to ope the exalted love,

43 And in her mien this language had impressed,
"Ecce ancilla Dei,"[5] as distinctly
As any figure stamps itself in wax.

46 "Keep not thy mind upon one place alone,"
The gentle Master said, who had me standing
Upon that side where people have their hearts;

49 Whereat I moved mine eyes, and I beheld
In rear of Mary, and upon that side
Where he was standing who conducted me,

52 Another story on the rock imposed;
Wherefore I passed Virgilius and drew near,
So that before mine eyes it might be set.

5 "Behold the handmaid of God!"

55 There sculptured in the self-same marble were
The cart and oxen, drawing the holy ark,
Wherefore one dreads an office not appointed.

58 People appeared in front, and all of them
In seven choirs divided, of two senses
Made one say "No," the other, "Yes, they sing."

61 Likewise unto the smoke of the frankincense,
Which there was imaged forth, the eyes and nose
Were in the yes and no discordant made.

64 Preceded there the vessel benedight,
Dancing with girded loins, the humble Psalmist,
And more and less than King was he in this.

67 Opposite, represented at the window
Of a great palace, Michal looked upon him,
Even as a woman scornful and afflicted.

70 I moved my feet from where I had been standing,
To examine near at hand another story
Which after Michal glimmered white upon me.

73 There the high glory of the Roman Prince
Was chronicled, whose great beneficence
Moved Gregory to his great victory;

76 'Tis of the Emperor Trajan I am speaking;
And a poor widow at his bridle stood,
In attitude of weeping and of grief.

79 Around about him seemed it thronged and full
Of cavaliers, and the eagles in the gold
Above them visibly in the wind were moving.

82 The wretched woman in the midst of these
Seemed to be saying: "Give me vengeance, Lord,
For my dead son, for whom my heart is breaking."

85 And he to answer her: "Now wait until
I shall return." And she: "My Lord," like one
In whom grief is impatient, "shouldst thou not

88 Return?" And he: "Who shall be where I am

Will give it thee." And she: "Good deed of others
What boots it thee, if thou neglect thine own?"

91 Whence he: "Now comfort thee, for it behoves me
That I discharge my duty ere I move;
Justice so wills, and pity doth retain me."

94 He who on no new thing has ever looked
Was the creator of this visible language,
Novel to us, for here it is not found.

97 While I delighted me in contemplating
The images of such humility,
And dear to look on for their Maker's sake,

100 "Behold, upon this side, but rare they make
Their steps," the Poet murmured, "many people,
These will direct us to the lofty stairs."

103 Mine eyes, that in beholding were intent
To see new things, of which they curious are,
In turning round towards him were not slow.

106 But still I wish not, Reader, thou shouldst swerve
From thy good purposes, because thou hearest
How God ordaineth that the debt be paid;

109 Attend not to the fashion of the torment,
Think of what follows; think that at the worst
It cannot reach beyond the mighty sentence.

112 "Master," began I, "that which I behold
Moving towards us seems to me not persons,
And what I know not, so in sight I waver."

115 And he to me: "The grievous quality
Of this their torment bows them so to earth,
That my own eyes at first contended with it;

118 But look there fixedly, and disentangle
By sight what cometh underneath those stones;
Already canst thou see how each is stricken."

121 O ye proud Christians! wretched, weary ones!
Who, in the vision of the mind infirm

Confidence have in your backsliding steps,

Do ye not comprehend that we are worms,
Born to bring forth the angelic butterfly
That flieth unto judgment without screen?

Why floats aloft your spirit high in air?
Like are ye unto insects undeveloped
Even as the worm in whom formation fails!

As to sustain a ceiling or a roof,
In place of corbel, oftentimes a figure
Is seen to join its knees unto its breast,

Which makes of the unreal real anguish
Arise in him who sees it, fashioned thus
Beheld I those, when I had ta'en good heed.

True is it, they were more or less bent down,
According as they more or less were laden;
And he who had most patience in his looks

Weeping did seem to say, "I can no more!"

Canto XI

"OUR Father, thou who dwellest in the heavens,
Not circumscribed, but from the greater love
Thou bearest to the first effects on high,

4 Praised be thy name and thine omnipotence
By every creature, as befitting is
To render thanks to thy sweet effluence.

7 Come unto us the peace of thy dominion,
For unto it we cannot of ourselves,
If it come not, with all our intellect.

10 Even as thine own Angels of their will
Make sacrifice to thee, Hosanna singing,
So may all men make sacrifice of theirs.

13 Give unto us this day our daily manna,
Withouten which in this rough wilderness
Backward goes he who toils most to advance.

16 And even as we the trespass we have suffered
Pardon in one another, pardon thou
Benignly, and regard not our desert.

19 Our virtue, which is easily o'ercome,
Put not to proof with the old Adversary,
But thou from him who spurs it so, deliver.

22 This last petition verily, dear Lord,
Not for ourselves is made, who need it not,
But for their sake who have remained behind us."

25 Thus for themselves and us good furtherance
Those shades imploring, went beneath a weight
Like unto that of which we sometimes dream,

28 Unequally in anguish round and round
And weary all, upon that foremost cornice,
Purging away the smoke-stains of the world

31 If there good words are always said for us,
What may not here be said and done for them,
By those who have a good root to their will?

34 Well may we help them wash away the marks
That hence they carried, so that clean and light
They may ascend unto the starry wheels!

37 "Ah! so may pity and justice you disburden
Soon, that ye may have power to move the wing,
That shall uplift you after your desire,

40 Show us on which hand tow'rd the stairs the way
Is shortest, and if more than one the passes,
Point us out that which least abruptly falls;

43 For he who cometh with me, through the burden
Of Adam's flesh wherewith he is invested,
Against his will is chary of his climbing."

46 The words of theirs which they returned to those
That he whom I was following had spoken,
It was not manifest from whom they came,

49 But it was said: "To the right hand come with us
Along the bank, and ye shall find a pass
Possible for living person to ascend.

52 And were I not impeded by the stone,
Which this proud neck of mine doth subjugate,
Whence I am forced to hold my visage down,

55 Him, who still lives and does not name himself,
Would I regard, to see if I may know him
And make him piteous unto this burden.

58 A Latian was I, and born of a great Tuscan;
Guglielmo Aldobrandeschi was my father;
I know not if his name were ever with you.

61 The ancient blood and deeds of gallantry
Of my progenitors so arrogant made me
That, thinking not upon the common mother,

64 All men I held in scorn to such extent
I died therefor, as know the Sienese,
And every child in Campagnatico.

67 I am Omberto; and not to me alone

Has pride done harm, but all my kith and kin
Has with it dragged into adversity.

70 And here must I this burden bear for it
Till God be satisfied, since I did not
Among the living, here among the dead."

73 Listening I downward bent my countenance;
And one of them, not this one who was speaking,
Twisted himself beneath the weight that cramps him,

76 And looked at me, and knew me, and called out,
Keeping his eyes laboriously fixed
On me, who all bowed down was going with them.

79 "O," asked I him, "art thou not Oderisi,
Agobbio's honour, and honour of that art
Which is in Paris called illuminating?"

82 "Brother," said he, "more laughing are the leaves
Touched by the brush of Franco Bolognese;
All his the honour now, and mine in part.

85 In sooth I had not been so courteous
While I was living, for the great desire
Of excellence, on which my heart was bent.

88 Here of such pride is paid the forfeiture;
And yet I should not be here, were it not
That, having power to sin, I turned to God.

91 O thou vain glory of the human powers,
How little green upon thy summit lingers,
If 't be not followed by an age of grossness!

94 In painting Cimabue thought that he
Should hold the field, now Giotto has the cry,
So that the other's fame is growing dim.

97 So has one Guido from the other taken
The glory of our tongue, and he perchance
Is born, who from the nest shall chase them both.

100 Naught is this mundane rumour but a breath
Of wind, that comes now this way and now that,
And changes name, because it changes side.

103 What fame shalt thou have more, if old peel off
From thee thy flesh, than if thou hadst been dead
Before thou left the 'pappo' and the 'dindi,'

106 Ere pass a thousand years? which is a shorter
Space to the eterne, than twinkling of an eye
Unto the circle that in heaven wheels slowest.

109 With him, who takes so little of the road
In front of me, all Tuscany resounded;
And now he scarce is lisped of in Siena,

112 Where he was lord, what time was overthrown
The Florentine delirium, that superb
Was at that day as now 'tis prostitute.

115 Your reputation is the colour of grass
Which comes and goes, and that discolours it
By which it issues green from out the earth."

118 And I: "Thy true speech fills my heart with good
Humility, and great tumour thou assuagest;
But who is he, of whom just now thou spakest?"

121 "That," he replied, "is Provenzan Salvani,
And he is here because he had presumed
To bring Siena all into his hands.

124 He has gone thus, and goeth without rest
E'er since he died; such money renders back
In payment he who is on earth too daring."

127 And I: "If every spirit who awaits
The verge of life before that he repent,
Remains below there and ascends not hither,

130 (Unless good orison shall him bestead,)
Until as much time as he lived be passed,
How was the coming granted him in largess?"

133 "When he in greatest splendour lived," said he,
"Freely upon the Campo of Siena,
All shame being laid aside, he placed himself;

136 And there to draw his friend from the duress
Which in the prison-house of Charles he suffered,

He brought himself to tremble in each vein.

139 I say no more, and know that I speak darkly;
Yet little time shall pass before thy neighbours
Will so demean themselves that thou canst gloss it.

142 This action has released him from those confines."

Canto XII

ABREAST, like oxen going in a yoke,
I with that heavy-laden soul went on,
As long as the sweet pedagogue permitted;

4 But when he said, "Leave him, and onward pass,
For here 'tis good that with the sail and oars,
As much as may be, each push on his barque;"

7 Upright, as walking wills it, I redressed
My person, notwithstanding that my thoughts
Remained within me downcast and abashed.

10 I had moved on, and followed willingly
The footsteps of my Master, and we both
Already showed how light of foot we were,

13 When unto me he said: "Cast down thine eyes;
'Twere well for thee, to alleviate the way,
To look upon the bed beneath thy feet."

16 As, that some memory may exist of them
Above the buried dead their tombs in earth
Bear sculptured on them what they were before;

19 Whence often there we weep for them afresh,
From pricking of remembrance, which alone
To the compassionate doth set its spur;

22 So saw I there, but of a better semblance
In point of artifice, with figures covered
Whate'er as pathway from the mount projects.

Abreast, like oxen going in a yoke,
I with that heavy-laden soul went on.

Gustave Doré

I saw that one who was created noble
More than all other creatures, down from heaven
Flaming with lightnings fall upon one side.

I saw Briareus smitten by the dart
Celestial, lying on the other side,
Heavy upon the earth by mortal frost.

I saw Thymbraeus, Pallas saw, and Mars,
Still clad in armour round about their father,
Gaze at the scattered members of the giants.

I saw, at foot of his great labour, Nimrod,
As if bewildered, looking at the people
Who had been proud with him in Sennaar.

O Niobe! with what afflicted eyes
Thee I beheld upon the pathway traced
Between thy seven and seven children slain!

O Saul! how fallen upon thy proper sword
Didst thou appear there lifeless in Gilboa,
That felt thereafter neither rain nor dew!

O mad Arachne! so I thee beheld
E'en then half spider, sad upon the shreds
Of fabric wrought in evil hour for thee!

O Rehoboam! no more seems to threaten
Thine image there; but full of consternation
A chariot bears it off, when none pursues!

Displayed moreo'er the adamantine pavement
How unto his own mother made Alcmaeon
Costly appear the luckless ornament;

Displayed how his own sons did throw themselves
Upon Sennacherib within the temple,
And how, he being dead, they left him there;

Displayed the ruin and the cruel carnage
That Tomyris wrought, when she to Cyrus said,
"Blood didst thou thirst for, and with blood I glut thee!"

Displayed how routed fled the Assyrians

After that Holofernes had been slain,
And likewise the remainder of that slaughter

61 I saw there Troy in ashes and in caverns;
O Ilion! thee, how abject and debased,
Displayed the image that is there discerned!

64 Whoe'er of pencil master was or stile,
That could portray the shades and traits which there
Would cause each subtile genius to admire?

67 Dead seemed the dead, the living seemed alive;
Better than I saw not who saw the truth,
All that I trod upon while bowed I went.

70 Now wax ye proud, and on with looks uplifted,
Ye sons of Eve, and bow not down your faces
So that ye may behold your evil ways!

73 More of the mount by us was now encompassed,
And far more spent the circuit of the sun,
Than had the mind preoccupied imagined,

76 When he, who ever watchful in advance
Was going on, began: "Lift up thy head,
'Tis no more time to go thus meditating.

79 Lo there an Angel who is making haste
To come towards us; lo, returning is
From service of the day the sixth handmaiden,

82 With reverence thine acts and looks adorn,
So that he may delight to speed us upward;
Think that this day will never dawn again."

85 I was familiar with his admonition
Ever to lose no time; so on this theme
He could not unto me speak covertly.

88 Towards us came the being beautiful
Vested in white, and in his countenance
Such as appears the tremulous morning star.

91 His arms he opened, and opened then his wings;
"Come," said he, "near at hand here are the steps,
And easy from henceforth is the ascent."

At this announcement few are they who come!
Oh human creatures, born to soar aloft,
Why fall ye thus before a little wind?

He led us on to where the rock was cleft;
There smote upon my forehead with his wings,
Then a safe passage promised unto me.

As on the right hand, to ascend the mount
Where seated is the church that lordeth it
O'er the well-guided, above Rubaconte,

The bold abruptness of the ascent is broken
By stairways that were made there in the age
When still were safe the ledger and the stave,

E'en thus attempered is the bank which falls
Sheer downward from the second circle there
But on this side and that the high rock graze

As we were turning thitherward our persons.
"Beati pauperes spiritu,"[6] voices
Sang in such wise that speech could tell it not.

Ah me! how different are these entrances
From the Infernal! for with anthems here
One enters, and below with wild laments.

We now were hunting up the sacred stairs,
And it appeared to me by far more easy
Than on the plain it had appeared before.

Whence I: "My Master, say, what heavy thing
Has been uplifted from me, so that hardly
Aught of fatigue is felt by me in walking?"

He answered: "When the Ps which have remained
Still on thy face almost obliterate
Shall wholly, as the first is, be erased

Thy feet will be so vanquished by good will,
That none alone they shall not feel fatigue,
But urging up will be to them delight."

6 "Blessed are the poor in spirit."

127 Then did I even as they do who are going
With something on the head to them unknown,
Unless the signs of others make them doubt,

130 Wherefore the hand to ascertain is helpful,
And seeks and finds, and doth fulfil the office
Which cannot be accomplished by the sight;

133 And with the fingers of the right hand spread
I found but six the letters, that had carved
Upon my temples he who bore the keys;

136 Upon beholding which my Leader smiled.

Canto XIII

WE were upon the summit of the stairs,
Where for the second time is cut away
The mountain, which ascending shriveth all

4 There in like manner doth a cornice bind
The hill all round about, as does the first,
Save that its arc more suddenly is curved.

7 Shade is there none, nor sculpture that appears;
So seems the bank, and so the road seems smooth
With but the livid colour of the stone.

10 "If to inquire we wait for people here,"
The Poet said, "I fear that peradventure
Too much delay will our election have."

13 Then steadfast on the sun his eyes he fixed.
Made his right side the centre of his motion,
And turned the left part of himself about.

16 "O thou sweet light! with trust in whom I enter
Upon this novel journey, do thou lead us,"
Said he, "as one within here should be led.

19 Thou warmest the world, thou shinest over it;
If other reason prompt not otherwise,

Thy rays should evermore our leaders be!"

22 As much as here is counted for a mile,
So much already there had we advanced
In little time, by dint of ready will;

25 And tow'rds us there were heard to fly, albeit
They were not visible, spirits uttering
Unto Love's table courteous invitations,

28 The first voice that passed onward in its flight,
"Vinum non habent,"[7] said in accents loud,
And went reiterating it behind us.

31 And ere it wholly grew inaudible
Because of distance, passed another, crying,
"I am Orestes!" and it also stayed not.

34 "O," said I, "Father, these, what voices are they?"
And even as I asked, behold the third,
Saying: "Love those from whom ye have had evil!"

37 And the good Master said: "This circle scourges
The sin of envy, and on that account
Are drawn from love the lashes of the scourge.

40 The bridle of another sound shall be;
I think that thou wilt hear it, as I judge,
Before thou comest to the Pass of Pardon.

43 But fix thine eyes athwart the air right steadfast,
And people thou wilt see before us sitting,
And each one close against the cliff is seated."

46 Then wider than at first mine eyes I opened;
I looked before me, and saw shades with mantles
Not from the colour of the stone diverse.

49 And when we were a little farther onward
I heard a cry of, "Mary, pray for us!"
A cry of, "Michael, Peter, and all Saints!"

52 I do not think there walketh still on earth
A man so hard, that he would not be pierced

---

7 "They have no wine."

With pity at what afterward I saw.

55 For when I had approached so near to them
That manifest to me their acts became,
Drained was I at the eyes by heavy grief.

58 Covered with sackcloth vile they seemed to me,
And one sustained the other with his shoulder,
And all of them were by the bank sustained.

61 Thus do the blind, in want of livelihood,
Stand at the doors of churches asking alms,
And one upon another leans his head

64 So that in others pity soon may rise,
Not only at the accent of their words,
But at their aspect, which no less implores.

67 And as unto the blind the sun comes not
So to the shades, of whom just now I spake,
Heaven's light will not be bounteous of itself;

70 For all their lids an iron wire transpierces,
And sews them up, as to a sparhawk wild
Is done, because it will not quiet stay.

73 To me it seemed, in passing, to do outrage,
Seeing the others without being seen;
Wherefore I turned me to my counsel sage.

76 Well knew he what the mute one wished to say,
And therefore waited not for my demand,
But said: "Speak, and be brief, and to the point."

79 I had Virgilius upon that side
Of the embankment from which one may fall,
Since by no border 'tis engarlanded;

82 Upon the other side of me I had
The shades devout, who through the horrible seam
Pressed out the tears so that they bathed their cheeks.

85 To them I turned me, and, "O people, certain,"
Began I, "of beholding the high light,
Which your desire has solely in its care,

So may grace speedily dissolve the scum
Upon your consciences, that limpidly
Through them descend the river of the mind,

Tell me, for dear 'twill be to me and gracious,
If any soul among you here is Latian,
And 'twill perchance be good for him I learn it."

"O brother mine, each one is citizen
Of one true city; but thy meaning is,
Who may have lived in Italy a pilgrim."

By way of answer this I seemed to hear
A little farther on than where I stood,
Whereat I made myself still nearer heard.

Among the rest I saw a shade that waited
In aspect, and should any one ask how,
Its chin it lifted upward like a blind man.

"Spirit," I said, "who stoopest to ascend,
If thou art he who did reply to me,
Make thyself known to me by place or name."

"Sienese was I," it replied, "and with
The others here recleanse my guilty life,
Weeping to Him to lend himself to us.

Sapient I was not, although I Sapia
Was called, and I was at another's harm
More happy far than at my own good fortune.

And that thou mayst not think that I deceive thee,
Hear if I was as foolish as I tell thee.
The arc already of my years descending,

My fellow-citizens near unto Colle
Were joined in battle with their adversaries,
And I was praying God for what he willed.

Routed were they, and turned into the bitter
Passes of flight; and I, the chase beholding,
A joy received unequalled by all others;

So that I lifted upward my bold face

Crying to God, 'Henceforth I fear thee not,'
As did the blackbird at the little sunshine.

124 Peace I desired with God at the extreme
Of my existence, and as yet would not
My debt have been by penitence discharged,

127 Had it not been that in remembrance held me
Pier Pettignano in his holy prayers,
Who out of charity was grieved for me.

130 But who art thou, that into our conditions
Questioning goest, and hast thine eyes unbound
As I believe, and breathing dost discourse?"

133 "Mine eyes," I said, "will yet be here ta'en from me,
But for short space; for small is the offence
Committed by their being turned with envy.

136 Far greater is the fear, wherein suspended
My soul is, of the torment underneath,
For even now the load down there weighs on me."

139 And she to me: "Who led thee, then, among us
Up here, if to return below thou thinkest?"
And I: "He who is with me, and speaks not;

142 And living am I; therefore ask of me,
Spirit elect, if thou wouldst have me move
O'er yonder yet my mortal feet for thee."

145 "O, this is such a novel thing to hear,"
She answered, "that great sign it is God loves thee;
Therefore with prayer of thine sometimes assist me

148 And I implore, by what thou most desirest,
If e'er thou treadest the soil of Tuscany,
Well with my kindred reinstate my fame.

151 Them wilt thou see among that people vain
Who hope in Talamone, and will lose there
More hope than in discovering the Diana;

154 But there still more the admirals will lose."

Canto XIV

"WHO is this one that goes about our mountain,
Or ever Death has given him power of flight,
And opes his eyes and shuts them at his will?"

4 "I know not who, but know he's not alone;
Ask him thyself, for thou art nearer to him,
And gently, so that he may speak, accost him."

7 Thus did two spirits, leaning tow'rds each other,
Discourse about me there on the right hand;
Then held supine their faces to address me.

10 And said the one: "O soul, that, fastened still
Within the body, tow'rds the heaven art going,
For charity console us, and declare

13 Whence comest and who art thou; for thou mak'st us
As much to marvel at this grace of thine
As must a thing that never yet has been."

16 And I: "Through midst of Tuscany there wanders
A streamlet that is born in Falterona,
And not a hundred miles of course suffice it;

19 From thereupon do I this body bring.
To tell you who I am were speech in vain,
Because my name as yet makes no great noise."

22 "If well thy meaning I can penetrate
With intellect of mine," then answered me
He who first spake, "thou speakest of the Arno."

25 And said the other to him: "Why concealed
This one the appellation of that river,
Even as a man doth of things horrible?"

28 And thus the shade that questioned was of this
Himself acquitted: "I know not; but truly
'Tis fit the name of such a valley perish:

31 For from its fountain-head (where is so pregnant
The Alpine mountain whence is cleft Peloro

That in few places it that mark surpasses)

34 To where it yields itself in restoration
Of what the heaven doth of the sea dry up.
Whence have the rivers that which goes with them,

37 Virtue is like an enemy avoided
By all, as is a serpent, through misfortune
Of place, or through bad habit that impels them;

40 On which account have so transformed their nature
The dwellers in that miserable valley,
It seems that Circe had them in her pasture.

43 'Mid ugly swine, of acorns worthier
Than other food for human use created,
It first directeth its impoverished way.

46 Curs findeth it thereafter, coming downward,
More snarling than their puissance demands,
And turns from them disdainfully its muzzle.

49 It goes on falling, and the more it grows,
The more it finds the dogs becoming wolves,
This maledict and misadventurous ditch.

52 Descended then through many a hollow gulf,
It finds the foxes so replete with fraud,
They fear no cunning that may master them.

55 Nor will I cease because another hears me;
And well 'twill be for him, if still he mind him
Of what a truthful spirit to me unravels.

58 Thy grandson I behold, who doth become
A hunter of those wolves upon the bank
Of the wild stream. and terrifies them all.

61 He sells their flesh, it being yet alive;
Thereafter slaughters them like ancient beeves;
Many of life, himself of praise, deprives.

64 Blood-stained he issues from the dismal forest;
He leaves it such, a thousand years from now
In its primeval state 'tis not re-wooded."

67 As at the announcement of impending ills
The face of him who listens is disturbed,
From whate'er side the peril seize upon him;

70 So I beheld that other soul, which stood
Turned round to listen, grow disturbed and sad,
When it had gathered to itself the word.

73 The speech of one and aspect of the other
Had me desirous made to know their names,
And question mixed with prayers I made thereof,

76 Whereat the spirit which first spake to me
Began again: "Thou wishest I should bring me
To do for thee what thou'lt not do for me;

79 But since God willeth that in thee shine forth
Such grace of his, I'll not be chary with thee;
Know, then, that I Guido del Duca am.

82 My blood was so with envy set on fire,
That if I had beheld a man make merry,
Thou wouldst have seen me sprinkled o'er with pallor.

85 From my own sowing such the straw I reap!
O human race! why dost thou set thy heart
Where interdict of partnership must be?

88 This is Renier; this is the boast and honour
Of the house of Calboli, where no one since
Has made himself the heir of his desert.

91 And not alone his blood is made devoid,
'Twixt Po and mount, and sea-shore and the Reno,
Of good required for truth and for diversion;

94 For all within these boundaries is full
Of venomous roots, so that too tardily
By cultivation now would they diminish.

97 Where is good Lizio, and Arrigo Manardi,
Pier Traversaro, and Guido di Carpigna,
O Romagnuoli into bastards turned?

100 When in Bologna will a Fabbro rise?

When in Faenza a Bernardin di Fosco,
The noble scion of ignoble seed?

103 Be not astonished, Tuscan, if I weep
When I remember, with Guido da Prata,
Ugolin d'Azzo, who was living with us,

106 Frederick Tignoso and his company
The house of Traversara, and th' Anastagi,
And one race and the other is extinct.

109 The dames and cavaliers, the toils and ease
That filled our souls with love and courtesy,
There where the hearts have so malicious grown!

112 O Brettinoro! why dost thou not flee,
Seeing that all thy family is gone,
And many people, not to be corrupted?

115 Bagnacaval does well in not begetting
And ill does Castrocaro, and Conio worse,
In taking trouble to beget such Counts.

118 Will do well the Pagani, when their Devil
Shall have departed; but not therefore pure
Will testimony of them e'er remain.

121 O Ugolin de' Fantoli, secure
Thy name is, since no longer is awaited
One who, degenerating, can obscure it!

124 But go now, Tuscan, for it now delights me
To weep far better than it does to speak,
So much has our discourse my mind distressed."

127 We were aware that those beloved souls
Heard us depart; therefore, by keeping silent,
They made us of our pathway confident.

130 When we became alone by going onward,
Thunder, when it doth cleave the air, appeared
A voice, that counter to us came, exclaiming:

133 "Shall slay me whosoever findeth me!"
And fled as the reverberation dies

If suddenly the cloud asunder bursts.

136 As soon as hearing had a truce from this,
Behold another, with so great a crash,
That it resembled thunderings following fast:

139 "I am Aglaurus, who became a stone!"
And then, to press myself close to the Poet,
I backward, and not forward, took a step.

142 Already on all sides the air was quiet;
And said he to me: "That was the hard curb
That ought to hold a man within his bounds;

145 But you take in the bait so that the hook
Of the old Adversary draws you to him,
And hence availeth little curb or call.

148 The heavens are calling you, and wheel around you,
Displaying to you their eternal beauties,
And still your eye is looking on the ground;

151 Whence He who all discerns, chastises you."

Canto XV

AS much as 'twixt the close of the third hour
And dawn of day appeareth of that sphere
Which aye in fashion of a child is playing,

4 So much it now appeared, towards the night,
Was of his course remaining to the sun;
There it was evening, and 'twas midnight here;

7 And the rays smote the middle of our faces,
Because by us the mount was so encircled,
That straight towards the west we now were going

10 When I perceived my forehead overpowered
Beneath the splendour far more than at first,
And stupor were to me the things unknown,

13 Whereat towards the summit of my brow
I raised my hands, and made myself the visor
Which the excessive glare diminishes.

16 As when from off the water, or a mirror,
The sunbeam leaps unto the opposite side,
Ascending upward in the selfsame measure

19 That it descends, and deviates as far
From falling of a stone in line direct,
(As demonstrate experiment and art,)

22 So it appeared to me that by a light
Refracted there before me I was smitten;
On which account my sight was swift to flee.

25 "What is that, Father sweet, from which I cannot
So fully screen my sight that it avail me,"
Said I, "and seems towards us to be moving?"

28 "Marvel thou not, if dazzle thee as yet
The family of heaven," he answered me;
"An angel 'tis, who comes to invite us upward.

31 Soon will it be, that to behold these things
Shall not be grievous, but delightful to thee
As much as nature fashioned thee to feel."

34 When we had reached the Angel benedight,
With joyful voice he said: "Here enter in
To stairway far less steep than are the others."

37 We mounting were, already thence departed,
And "Beati misericordes"[8] was
Behind us sung, "Rejoice, thou that o'ercomest!"

40 My Master and myself, we two alone
Were going upward, and I thought, in going,
Some profit to acquire from words of his;

43 And I to him directed me, thus asking:
"What did the spirit of Romagna mean,
Mentioning interdict and partnership?"

46 Whence he to me: "Of his own greatest failing
He knows the harm; and therefore wonder not
If he reprove us, that we less may rue it

49 Because are thither pointed your desires
Where by companionship each share is lessened,
Envy doth ply the bellows to your sighs.

52 But if the love of the supernal sphere
Should upwardly direct your aspiration,
There would not be that fear within your breast;

55 For there, as much the more as one says 'Our,'
So much the more of good each one possesses,
And more of charity in that cloister burns."

58 "I am more hungering to be satisfied,"
I said, "than if I had before been silent,
And more of doubt within my mind I gather.

61 How can it be, that boon distributed
The more possessors can more wealthy make
Therein, than if by few it be possessed?"

64 And he to me: "Because thou fixest still
Thy mind entirely upon earthly things,
Thou pluckest darkness from the very light.

8 "Blessed are the merciful."

67 That goodness infinite and ineffable
Which is above there, runneth unto love,
As to a lucid body comes the sunbeam.

70 So much it gives itself as it finds ardour,
So that as far as charity extends,
O'er it increases the eternal valour.

73 And the more people thitherward aspire,
More are there to love well, and more they love there,
And, as a mirror, one reflects the other.

76 And if my reasoning appease thee not,
Thou shalt see Beatrice; and she will fully
Take from thee this and every other longing.

79 Endeavour, then, that soon may be extinct,
As are the two already, the five wounds
That close themselves again by being painful."

82 Even as I wished to say, "Thou dost appease me,"
I saw that I had reached another circle,
So that my eager eyes made me keep silence.

85 There it appeared to me that in a vision
Ecstatic on a sudden I was rapt,
And in a temple many persons saw;

88 And at the door a woman, with the sweet
Behaviour of a mother, saying: "Son,
Why in this manner hast thou dealt with us?

91 Lo, sorrowing, thy father and myself
Were seeking for thee;"—and as here she ceased
That which appeared at first had disappeared.

94 Then I beheld another with those waters
Adown her cheeks which grief distils whenever
From great disdain of others it is born,

97 And saying: "If of that city thou art lord,
For whose name was such strife among the gods
And whence doth every science scintillate,

100 Avenge thyself on those audacious arms

That clasped our daughter, O Pisistratus;"
And the lord seemed to me benign and mild

103 To answer her with aspect temperate:
"What shall we do to those who wish us ill
If he who loves us be by us condemned?"

106 Then saw I people hot in fire of wrath,
With stones a young man slaying, clamorously
Still crying to each other, "Kill him! Kill him!"

109 And him I saw bow down, because of death
That weighed already on him, to the earth,
But of his eyes made ever gates to heaven,

112 Imploring the high Lord, in so great strife,
That he would pardon those his persecutors,
With such an aspect as unlocks compassion.

115 Soon as my soul had outwardly returned
To things external to it which are true,
Did I my not false errors recognize.

118 My Leader, who could see me bear myself
Like to a man that rouses him from sleep,
Exclaimed: "What ails thee, that thou canst not stand?

121 But hast been coming more than half a league
Veiling thine eyes, and with thy legs entangled
In guise of one whom wine or sleep subdues?"

124 "O my sweet Father, if thou listen to me,
I'll tell thee," said I, "what appeared to me,
When thus from me my legs were ta'en away."

127 And he: "If thou shouldst have a hundred masks
Upon thy face, from me would not be shut
Thy cogitations, howsoever small.

130 What thou hast seen was that thou mayst not fail
To ope thy heart unto the waters of peace
Which from the eternal fountain are diffused.

133 I did not ask, 'What ails thee?' as he does
Who only looketh with the eyes that see not
When of the soul bereft the body lies,

136 But asked it to give vigour to thy feet;
Thus must we needs urge on the sluggards, slow
To use their wakefulness when it returns."

139 We passed along, athwart the twilight peering
Forward as far as ever eye could stretch
Against the sunbeams serotine and lucent;

142 And lo! by slow degrees a smoke approached
In our direction, sombre as the night,
Nor was there place to hide one's self therefrom.

145 This of our eyes and the pure air bereft us.

Canto XVI

DARKNESS of hell and of a night deprived
Of every planet under a poor sky,
As much as may be tenebrous with cloud,

4 Ne'er made unto my sight so thick a veil,
As did that smoke which there enveloped us,
Nor to the feeling of so rough a texture;

7 For not an eye it suffered to stay open;
Whereat mine escort, faithful and sagacious,
Drew near to me and offered me his shoulder.

10 E'en as a blind man goes behind his guide,
Lest he should wander, or should strike against
Aught that may harm or peradventure kill him,

13 So went I through the bitter and foul air,
Listening unto my Leader, who said only,
"Look that from me thou be not separated."

16 Voices I heard, and every one appeared
To supplicate for peace and misericord
The Lamb of God who takes away our sins.

19 Still "Agnus Dei" their exordium was;

One word there was in all, and metre one,
So that all harmony appeared among them.

22 "Master," I said, "are spirits those I hear?"
And he to me: "Thou apprehendest truly,
And they the knot of anger go unloosing."

25 "Now who art thou, that cleavest through our smoke
And art discoursing of us even as though
Thou didst by calends still divide the time?"

28 After this manner by a voice was spoken;
Whereon my Master said: "Do thou reply,
And ask if on this side the way go upward,"

31 And I: "O creature that dost cleanse thyself
To return beautiful to Him who made thee,
Thou shalt hear marvels if thou follow me."

34 "Thee will I follow far as is allowed me,"
He answered; "and if smoke prevent our seeing,
Hearing shall keep us joined instead thereof."

37 Thereon began I: "With that swathing band
Which death unwindeth am I going upward,
And hither came I through the infernal anguish.

40 And if God in his grace has me infolded,
So that he wills that I behold his court
By method wholly out of modern usage,

43 Conceal not from me who ere death thou wast,
But tell it me, and tell me if I go
Right for the pass, and be thy words our escort."

46 "Lombard was I, and I was Marco called;
The world I knew, and loved that excellence,
At which has each one now unbent his bow.

49 For mounting upward, thou art going right."
Thus he made answer, and subjoined: "I pray thee
To pray for me when thou shalt be above."

52 And I to him: "My faith I pledge to thee
To do what thou dost ask me; but am bursting

Inly with doubt, unless I rid me of it.

55 First it was simple, and is now made double
By thy opinion, which makes certain to me,
Here and elsewhere, that which I couple with it.

58 The world forsooth is utterly deserted
By every virtue, as thou tellest me,
And with iniquity is big and covered;

61 But I beseech thee point me out the cause,
That I may see it, and to others show it;
For one in the heavens, and here below one puts it."

64 A sigh profound that grief forced into Ai!
He first sent forth, and then began he: "Brother,
The world is blind, and sooth thou comest from it!

67 Ye who are living every cause refer
Still upward to the heavens, as if all things
They of necessity moved with themselves.

70 If this were so, in you would be destroyed
Free will, nor any justice would there be
In having joy for good, or grief for evil.

73 The heavens your movements do initiate,
I say not all; but granting that I say it,
Light has been given you for good and evil,

76 And free volition; which, if some fatigue
In the first battles with the heavens it suffers,
Afterwards conquers all, if well 'tis nurtured.

79 To greater force and to a better nature,
Though free, ye subject are, and that creates
The mind in you the heavens have not in charge.

82 Hence, if the present world doth go astray,
In you the cause is, be it sought in you;
And I therein will now be thy true spy.

85 Forth from the hand of Him, who fondles it
Before it is, like to a little girl
Weeping and laughing in her childish sport,

88 Issues the simple soul, that nothing knows,
Save that, proceeding from a joyous Maker,
Gladly it turns to that which gives it pleasure.

91 Of trivial good at first it tastes the savour;
Is cheated by it, and runs after it,
If guide or rein turn not aside its love.

94 Hence it behoved laws for a rein to place,
Behoved a king to have, who at the least
Of the true city should discern the tower.

97 The laws exist, but who sets hand to them?
No one; because the shepherd who precedes
Can ruminate, but cleaveth not the hoof;

100 Wherefore the people that perceives its guide
Strike only at the good for which it hankers,
Feeds upon that, and farther seeketh not.

103 Clearly canst thou perceive that evil guidance
The cause is that has made the world depraved,
And not that nature is corrupt in you.

106 Rome, that reformed the world, accustomed was
Two suns to have, which one road and the other,
Of God and of the world, made manifest.

109 One has the other quenched, and to the crosier
The sword is joined, and ill beseemeth it
That by main force one with the other go,

112 Because, being joined, one feareth not the other;
If thou believe not, think upon the grain,
For by its seed each herb is recognized.

115 In the land laved by Po and Adige,
Valour and courtesy used to be found,
Before that Frederick had his controversy;

118 Now in security can pass that way
Whoever will abstain, through sense of shame,
From speaking with the good, or drawing near them.

121 True, three old men are left, in whom upbraids

The ancient age the new, and late they deem it
That God restore them to the better life:

124 Currado da Palazzo, and good Gherardo,
And Guido da Castel, who better named is,
In fashion of the French, the simple Lombard:

127 Say thou henceforward that the Church of Rome,
Confounding in itself two governments,
Falls in the mire, and soils itself and burden."

130 "O Marco mine," I said, "thou reasonest well;
And now discern I why the sons of Levi
Have been excluded from the heritage.

133 But what Gherardo is it, who, as sample
Of a lost race, thou sayest has remained
In reprobation of the barbarous age?"

136 "Either thy speech deceives me, or it tempts me,"
He answered me, "for speaking Tuscan to me,
It seems of good Gherardo naught thou knowest.

139 By other surname do I know him not,
Unless I take it from his daughter Gaia.
May God be with you, for I come no farther.

142 Behold the dawn, that through the smoke rays out,
Already whitening; and I must depart—
Yonder the Angel is—ere he appear."

145 Thus did he speak, and would no farther hear me.

Canto XVII

REMEMBER, Reader, if e'er in the Alps
A mist o'ertook thee, through which thou couldst see
Not otherwise than through its membrane

4 How, when the vapours humid and condensed
Begin to dissipate themselves, the sphere
Of the sun feebly enters in among them,

7 And thy imagination will be swift
In coming to perceive how I re-saw
The sun at first, that was already setting.

10 Thus, to the faithful footsteps of my Master
Mating mine own, I issued from that cloud
To rays already dead on the low shores.

13 O thou, Imagination, that dost steal us
So from without sometimes, that man perceives not,
Although around may sound a thousand trumpets,

16 Who moveth thee, if sense impel thee not?
Moves thee a light, which in the heaven takes form,
By self, or by a will that downward guides it.

19 Of her impiety, who changed her form
Into the bird that most delights in singing,
In my imagining appeared the trace;

22 And hereupon my mind was so withdrawn
Within itself, that from without there came
Nothing that then might be received by it.

25 Then reigned within my lofty fantasy
One crucified, disdainful and ferocious
In countenance, and even thus was dying.

28 Around him were the great Ahasuerus,
Esther his wife, and the just Mordecai,
Who was in word and action so entire.

31 And even as this image burst asunder
Of its own self, in fashion of a bubble

In which the water it was made of fails,

There rose up in my vision a young maiden
Bitterly weeping, and she said: "O queen,
Why hast thou wished in anger to be naught?

Thou'st slain thyself, Lavinia not to lose;
Now hast thou lost me; I am she who mourns,
Mother, at thine ere at another's ruin."

As sleep is broken, when upon a sudden
New light strikes in upon the eyelids closed,
And broken quivers ere it dieth wholly,

So this imagining of mine fell down
As soon as the effulgence smote my face,
Greater by far than what is in our wont.

I turned me round to see where I might be,
When said a voice, "Here is the passage up;"
Which from all other purposes removed me,

And made my wish so full of eagerness
To look and see who was it that was speaking,
It never rests till meeting face to face;

But as before the sun, which quells the sight,
And in its own excess its figure veils,
Even so my power was insufficient here.

"This is a spirit divine, who in the way
Of going up directs us without asking
And who with his own light himself conceals.

He does with us as man doth with himself;
For he who sees the need, and waits the asking,
Malignly leans already tow'rds denial.

Accord we now our feet to such inviting,
Let us make haste to mount ere it grow dark;
For then we could not till the day return."

Thus my Conductor said; and I and he
Together turned our footsteps to a stairway,
And I, as soon as the first step I reached

67 Near me perceived a motion as of wings
And fanning in the face, and saying, "Beati
Pacifi[9], who are without ill anger."

70 Already over us were so uplifted
The latest sunbeams, which the night pursues,
That upon many sides the stars appeared.

73 "O manhood mine, why dost thou vanish so?"
I said within myself; for I perceived
The vigour of my legs was put in truce.

76 We at the point were where no more ascends
The stairway upward, and were motionless,
Even as a ship, which at the shore arrives;

79 And I gave heed a little, if I might hear
Aught whatsoever in the circle new;
Then to my Master turned me round and said:

82 "Say, my sweet Father, what delinquency
Is purged here in the circle where we are?
Although our feet may pause, pause not thy speech."

85 And he to me: "The love of good, remiss
In what it should have done, is here restored;
Here plied again the ill-belated oar;

88 But still more openly to understand,
Turn unto me thy mind, and thou shalt gather
Some profitable fruit from our delay.

91 Neither Creator nor a creature ever,
Son," he began, "was destitute of love
Natural or spiritual; and thou knowest it.

94 The natural was ever without error;
But err the other may by evil object,
Or by too much, or by too little vigour.

97 While in the first it well directed is,
And in the second moderates itself,
It cannot be the cause of sinful pleasure;

9 "Blessed are the peacemakers."

100 But when to ill it turns, and, with more care
Or lesser than it ought, runs after good,
'Gainst the Creator works his own creation.

103 Hence thou mayst comprehend that love must be
The seed within yourselves of every virtue,
And every act that merits punishment.

106 Now inasmuch as never from the welfare
Of its own subject can love turn its sight,
From their own hatred all things are secure;

109 And since we cannot think of any being
Standing alone, nor from the First divided,
Of hating Him is all desire cut off.

112 Hence if, discriminating, I judge well,
The evil that one loves is of one's neighbour,
And this is born in three modes in your clay.

115 There are, who, by abasement of their neighbour,
Hope to excel, and therefore only long
That from his greatness he may be cast down;

118 There are, who power, grace, honour, and renown
Fear they may lose because another rises,
Thence are so sad that the reverse they love;

121 And there are those whom injury seems to chafe,
So that it makes them greedy for revenge,
And such must needs shape out another's harm.

124 This threefold love is wept for down below;
Now of the other will I have thee hear,
That runneth after good with measure faulty.

127 Each one confusedly a good conceives
Wherein the mind may rest, and longeth for it;
Therefore to overtake it each one strives.

130 If languid love to look on this attract you,
Or in attaining unto it, this cornice,
After just penitence, torments you for it.

133 There's other good that does not make man happy;

'Tis not felicity, 'tis not the good
Essence, of every good the fruit and root.

136 The love that yields itself too much to this
Above us is lamented in three circles;
But how tripartite it may be described,

139 I say not, that thou seek it for thyself."

Canto XVIII

AN end had put unto his reasoning
The lofty Teacher, and attent was looking
Into my face, if I appeared content;

4 And I, whom a new thirst still goaded on,
Without was mute, and said within: "Perchance
The too much questioning I make annoys him."

7 But that true Father, who had comprehended
The timid wish, that opened not itself,
By speaking gave me hardihood to speak.

10 Whence I: "My sight is, Master, vivified
So in thy light, that clearly I discern
Whate'er thy speech importeth or describe—

13 Therefore I thee entreat, sweet Father dear,
To teach me love, to which thou dost refer
Every good action and its contrary."

16 "Direct," he said, "towards me the keen eyes
Of intellect, and clear will be to thee
The error of the blind, who would be leaders.

19 The soul, which is created apt to love,
Is mobile unto everything that pleases,
Soon as by pleasure she is waked to action.

22 Your apprehension from some real thing
An image draws, and in yourselves displays it
So that it makes the soul turn unto it.

25 And if, when turned, towards it she incline,
Love is that inclination; it is nature,
Which is by pleasure bound in you anew

28 Then even as the fire doth upward move
By its own form, which to ascend is born,
Where longest in its matter it endures,

31 So comes the captive soul into desire,
Which is a motion spiritual, and ne'er rests
Until she doth enjoy the thing beloved.

34 Now may apparent be to thee how hidden
The truth is from those people, who aver
All love is in itself a laudable thing,

37 Because its matter may perchance appear
Aye to be good; but yet not each impression
Is good, albeit good may be the wax."

40 "Thy words, and my sequacious intellect,"
I answered him, "have love revealed to me;
But that has made me more impregned with doubt;

43 For if love from without be offered us,
And with another foot the soul go not,
If right or wrong she go, 'tis not her merit."

46 And he to me: "What reason seeth here,
Myself can tell thee; beyond that await
For Beatrice since 'tis a work of faith.

49 Every substantial form, that segregate
From matter is, and with it is united,
Specific power has in itself collected,

52 Which without act is not perceptible,
Nor shows itself except by its effect,
As life does in a plant by the green leaves.

55 But still, whence cometh the intelligence
Of the first notions, man is ignorant,
And the affection for the first allurements,

58 Which are in you as instinct in the bee

To make its honey; and this first desire
Merit of praise or blame containeth not.

61 Now, that to this all others may be gathered,
Innate within you is the power that counsels,
And it should keep the threshold of assent.

64 This is the principle, from which is taken
Occasion of desert in you, according
As good and guilty loves it takes and winnows.

67 Those who, in reasoning, to the bottom went,
Were of this innate liberty aware,
Therefore bequeathed they Ethics to the world.

70 Supposing, then, that from necessity
Springs every love that is within you kindled,
Within yourselves the power is to restrain it.

73 The noble virtue Beatrice understands
By the free will; and therefore see that thou
Bear it in mind, if she should speak of it."

76 The moon, belated almost unto midnight,
Now made the stars appear to us more rare,
Formed like a bucket, that is all ablaze,

79 And counter to the heavens ran through those paths
Which the sun sets aflame, when he of Rome
Sees it 'twixt Sardes and Corsicans go down;

82 And that patrician shade, for whom is named
Pietola more than any Mantuan town,
Had laid aside the burden of my lading;

85 Whence I, who reason manifest and plain
In answer to my questions had received,
Stood like a man in drowsy reverie.

88 But taken from me was this drowsiness
Suddenly by a people, that behind
Our backs already had come round to us.

91 And as, of old, Ismenus and Asopus
Beside them saw at night the rush and throng,

If but the Thebans were in need of Bacchus,

So they along that circle curve their step,
From what I saw of those approaching us,
Who by good-will and righteous love are ridden.

Full soon they were upon us, because running
Moved onward all that mighty multitude,
And two in the advance cried out, lamenting,

"Mary in haste unto the mountain ran,
And Caesar, that he might subdue Ilerda,
Thrust at Marseilles, and then ran into Spain."

"Quick! quick! so that the time may not be lost
By little love!" forthwith the others cried,
"For ardour in well-doing freshens grace!"

"O folk, in whom an eager fervour now
Supplies perhaps delay and negligence,
Put by you in well-doing, through lukewarmness,

This one who lives, and truly I lie not,
Would fain go up, if but the sun relight us;
So tell us where the passage nearest is."

These were the words of him who was my Guide;
And some one of those spirits said: "Come on
Behind us, and the opening shalt thou find;

So full of longing are we to move onward,
That stay we cannot; therefore pardon us,
If thou for churlishness our justice take.

I was San Zeno's Abbot at Verona,
Under the empire of good Barbarossa,
Of whom still sorrowing Milan holds discourse

And he has one foot in the grave already,
Who shall ere long lament that monastery,
And sorry be of having there had power,

Because his son, in his whole body sick,
And worse in mind, and who was evil-born,
He put into the place of its true pastor."

127 If more he said, or silent was, I know not
He had already passed so far beyond us;
But this I heard, and to retain it pleased me.

130 And he who was in every need my succour
Said: "Turn thee hitherward; see two of them
Come fastening upon slothfulness their teeth."

133 In rear of all they shouted: "Sooner were
The people dead to whom the Sea was opened,
Than their inheritors the Jordan saw;

136 And those who the fatigue did not endure
Unto the issue, with Anchises' son,
Themselves to life withouten glory offered."

139 Then when from us so separated were
Those shades, that they no longer could be seen,
Within me a new thought did entrance find,

142 Whence others many and diverse were born
And so I lapsed from one into another
That in a reverie mine eyes I closed,

145 And meditation into dream transmuted.

Canto XIX

IT was the hour when the diurnal heat
No more can warm the coldness of the moon,
Vanquished by earth, or peradventure Saturn

4 When geomancers their Fortuna Major
See in the orient before the dawn
Rise by a path that long remains not dim,

7 There came to me in dreams a stammering woman
Squint in her eyes, and in her feet distorted,
With hands dissevered and of sallow hue.

10 I looked at her; and as the sun restores
The frigid members which the night benumbs,
Even thus my gaze did render voluble

13 Her tongue, and made her all erect thereafter
In little while, and the lost countenance
As love desires it so in her did colour.

16 When in this wise she had her speech unloosed,
She 'gan to sing so, that with difficulty
Could I have turned my thoughts away from her

19 "I am," she sang, "I am the Siren sweet
Who mariners amid the main unman.
So full am I of pleasantness to hear

22 I drew Ulysses from his wandering way
Unto my song, and he who dwells with me
Seldom departs so wholly I content him."

25 Her mouth was not yet closed again, before
Appeared a Lady saintly and alert
Close at my side to put her to confusion.

28 "Virgilius, O Virgilius! who is this?"
Sternly she said; and he was drawing near
With eyes still fixed upon that modest one.

31 She seized the other and in front laid open,
Rending her garments, and her belly showed me;
This waked me with the stench that issued from it.

34 I turned mine eyes, and good Virgilius said:
"At least thrice have I called thee; rise and come;
Find we the opening by which thou mayst enter."

37 I rose; and full already of high day
Were all the circles of the Sacred Mountain,
And with the new sun at our back we went.

40 Following behind him, I my forehead bore
Like unto one who has it laden with thought,
Who makes himself the half arch of a bridge,

43 When I heard say, "Come, here the passage is,"
Spoken in a manner gentle and benign,
Such as we hear not in this mortal region.

46 With open wings, which of a swan appeared,
Upward he turned us who thus spake to us
Between the two walls of the solid granite.

49 He moved his pinions afterwards and fanned us,
Affirming those 'qui lugent'[10] to be blessed,
For they shall have their souls with comfort filled.

52 "What aileth thee, that aye to earth thou gazest?"
To me my Guide began to say, we both
Somewhat beyond the Angel having mounted.

55 And I: "With such misgiving makes me go
A vision new, which bends me to itself,
So that I cannot from the thought withdraw me."

58 "Didst thou behold," he said, "that old enchantress,
Who sole above us henceforth is lamented?
Didst thou behold how man is freed from her?

61 Suffice it thee, and smite earth with thy heels,
Thine eyes lift upward to the lure, that whirls
The Eternal King with revolutions vast."

64 Even as the hawk, that first his feet surveys,
Then turns him to the call and stretches forward,
Through the desire of food that draws him thither,

10 "those who mourn"

67 Such I became, and such, as far as cleaves
The rock to give a way to him who mounts,
Went on to where the circling doth begin.

70 On the fifth circle when I had come forth,
People I saw upon it who were weeping,
Stretched prone upon the ground, all downward turned.

73 "Adhaesit pavemento anima mea,"[11]
I heard them say with sighings so profound,
That hardly could the words be understood.

76 "O ye elect of God, whose sufferings
Justice and Hope both render less severe,
Direct ye us towards the high ascents."

79 "If ye are come secure from this prostration,
And wish to find the way most speedily,
Let your right hands be evermore outside."

82 Thus did the Poet ask, and thus was answered
By them somewhat in front of us; whence I
In what was spoken divined the rest concealed,

85 And unto my Lord's eyes mine eyes I turned;
Whence he assented with a cheerful sign
To what the sight of my desire implored.

88 When of myself I could dispose at will,
Above that creature did I draw myself,
Whose words before had caused me to take note,

91 Saying: "O Spirit, in whom weeping ripens
That without which to God we cannot turn,
Suspend awhile for me thy greater care.

94 Who wast thou, and why are your backs turned upwards,
Tell me, and if thou wouldst that I procure thee
Anything there whence living I departed."

97 And he to me: "Wherefore our backs the heaven
Turns to itself, know shalt thou; but beforehand
'Scias quod ego fui successor Petri.'[12]

11 "My soul cleaved to the floor."

12 "You may know that I was the successor of Peter."

Between Siestri and Chiaveri descends
A river beautiful, and of its name
The title of my blood its summit makes.

A month and little more essayed I how
Weighs the great cloak on him from mire who keeps it,
For all the other burdens seem a feather.

Tardy, ah woe is me! was my conversion;
But when the Roman Shepherd I was made,
Then I discovered life to be a lie.

I saw that there the heart was not at rest,
Nor farther in that life could one ascend;
Whereby the love of this was kindled in me.

Until that time a wretched soul and parted
From God was I, and wholly avaricious;
Now, as thou seest, I here am punished for it.

What avarice does is here made manifest
In the purgation of these souls converted,
And no more bitter pain the Mountain has.

Even as our eye did not uplift itself
Aloft, being fastened upon earthly things,
So justice here has merged it in the earth.

As avarice had extinguished our affection
For every good, whereby was action lost,
So justice here doth hold us in restraint,

Bound and imprisoned by the feet and hands;
And so long as it pleases the just Lord
Shall we remain immovable and prostrate."

I on my knees had fallen, and wished to speak;
But even as I began, and he was 'ware,
Only by listening, of my reverence,

"What cause," he said, "has downward bent thee thus?"
And I to him: "For your own dignity,
Standing, my conscience stung me with remorse."

What cause, he said, has downward bent thee thus?

Gustave Doré

133 "Straighten thy legs, and upward raise thee, brother,"
He answered: "Err not, fellow-servant am I
With thee and with the others to one power.

136 If e'er that holy, evangelic sound,
Which sayeth 'neque nubent,'[13] thou hast heard,
Well canst thou see why in this wise I speak.

139 Now go; no longer will I have thee linger,
Because thy stay doth incommode my weeping,
With which I ripen that which thou hast said.

142 On earth I have a grandchild named Alagia,
Good in herself, unless indeed our house
Malevolent may make her by example,

145 And she alone remains to me on earth."

Canto XX

ILL strives the will against a better will;
Therefore, to pleasure him, against my pleasure
I drew the sponge not saturate from the water.

4 Onward I moved, and onward moved my Leader,
Through vacant places, skirting still the rock,
As on a wall close to the battlements;

7 For they that through their eyes pour drop by drop
The malady which all the world pervades,
On the other side too near the verge approach.

10 Accursed mayst thou be, thou old she-wolf,
That more than all the other beasts hast prey,
Because of hunger infinitely hollow!

13 O heaven, in whose gyrations some appear
To think conditions here below are changed,
When will he come through whom she shall depart?

16 Onward we went with footsteps slow and scarce,

13 "nor do they marry"

And I attentive to the shades I heard
Piteously weeping and bemoaning them;

19 And I by peradventure heard "Sweet Mary!"
Uttered in front of us amid the weeping
Even as a woman does who is in child-birth;

22 And in continuance: "How poor thou wast
Is manifested by that hostelry
Where thou didst lay thy sacred burden down."

25 Thereafterward I heard: "O good Fabricius,
Virtue with poverty didst thou prefer
To the possession of great wealth with vice."

28 So pleasurable were these words to me
That I drew farther onward to have knowledge
Touching that spirit whence they seemed to come.

31 He furthermore was speaking of the largess
Which Nicholas unto the maidens gave,
In order to conduct their youth to honour.

34 "O soul that dost so excellently speak,
Tell me who wast thou," said I, "and why only
Thou dost renew these praises well deserved?

37 Not without recompense shall be thy word,
If I return to finish the short journey
Of that life which is flying to its end."

40 And he: "I'll tell thee, not for any comfort
I may expect from earth, but that so much
Grace shines in thee or ever thou art dead.

43 I was the root of that malignant plant
Which overshadows all the Christian world,
So that good fruit is seldom gathered from it;

46 But if Douay and Ghent, and Lille and Bruges
Had Power, soon vengeance would be taken on it;
And this I pray of Him who judges all.

49 Hugh Capet was I called upon the earth;
From me were born the Louises and Philips,
By whom in later days has France been governed.

I was the son of a Parisian butcher,
What time the ancient kings had perished all,
Excepting one, contrite in cloth of gray.

I found me grasping in my hands the rein
Of the realm's government, and so great power
Of new acquest, and so with friends abounding,

That to the widowed diadem promoted
The head of mine own offspring was, from whom
The consecrated bones of these began.

So long as the great dowry of Provence
Out of my blood took not the sense of shame,
'Twas little worth, but still it did no harm.

Then it began with falsehood and with force
Its rapine; and thereafter, for amends,
Took Ponthieu, Normandy, and Gascony.

Charles came to Italy, and for amends
A victim made of Conradin, and then
Thrust Thomas back to heaven, for amends.

A time I see, not very distant now,
Which draweth forth another Charles from France,
The better to make known both him and his.

Unarmed he goes, and only with the lance
That Judas jousted with; and that he thrusts
So that he makes the paunch of Florence burst.

He thence not land, but sin and infamy,
Shall gain, so much more grievous to himself
As the more light such damage he accounts.

The other, now gone forth, ta'en in his ship,
See I his daughter sell, and chaffer for her
As corsairs do with other female slaves.

What more, O Avarice, canst thou do to us,
Since thou my blood so to thyself hast drawn,
It careth not for its own proper flesh?

That less may seem the future ill and past,

I see the flower-de-luce Alagna enter,
And Christ in his own Vicar captive made.

88 I see him yet another time derided;
I see renewed the vinegar and gall,
And between living thieves I see him slain.

91 I see the modern Pilate so relentless,
This does not sate him, but without decretal
He to the temple bears his sordid sails!

94 When, O my Lord, shall I be joyful made
By looking on the vengeance which, concealed,
Makes sweet thine anger in thy secrecy?

97 What I was saying of that only bride
Of the Holy Ghost, and which occasioned thee
To turn towards me for some commentary,

100 So long has been ordained to all our prayers
As the day lasts; but when the night comes on,
Contrary sound we take instead thereof.

103 At that time we repeat Pygmalion,
Of whom a traitor, thief, and parricide
Made his insatiable desire of gold;

106 And the misery of avaricious Midas,
That followed his inordinate demand,
At which forevermore one needs but laugh.

109 The foolish Achan each one then records,
And how he stole the spoils; so that the wrath
Of Joshua still appears to sting him here.

112 Then we accuse Sapphira with her husband,
We laud the hoof-beats Heliodorus had,
And the whole mount in infamy encircles

115 Polymnestor who murdered Polydorus.
Here finally is cried: 'O Crassus, tell us,
For thou dost know, what is the taste of gold?'

118 Sometimes we speak, one loud, another low,
According to desire of speech, that spurs us

To greater now and now to lesser pace.

121 But in the good that here by day is talked of,
Erewhile alone I was not; yet near by
No other person lifted up his voice."

124 From him already we departed were,
And made endeavour to o'ercome the road
As much as was permitted to our power,

127 When I perceived, like something that is falling,
The mountain tremble, whence a chill seized on me,
As seizes him who to his death is going.

130 Certes so violently shook not Delos,
Before Latona made her nest therein
To give birth to the two eyes of the heaven.

133 Then upon all sides there began a cry,
Such that the Master drew himself towards me,
Saying, "Fear not, while I am guiding thee."

136 "Gloria in excelsis Deo," all
Were saying, from what near I comprehended,
Where it was possible to hear the cry.

139 We paused immovable and in suspense;
Even as the shepherds who first heard that song,
Until the trembling ceased, and it was finished.

142 No ignorance ever with so great a strife
Had rendered me importunate to know,
If erreth not in this my memory,

145 As meditating then I seemed to have;
Nor out of haste to question did I dare,
Nor of myself I there could aught perceive;

148 So I went onward timorous and thoughtful.

Canto XXI

THE natural thirst, that ne'er is satisfied
Excepting with the water for whose grace
The woman of Samaria besought,

4 Put me in travail, and haste goaded me
Along the encumbered path behind my Leader
And I was pitying that righteous vengeance;

7 And lo! in the same manner as Luke writeth
That Christ appeared to two upon the way
From the sepulchral cave already risen,

10 A shade appeared to us, and came behind us,
Down gazing on the prostrate multitude,
Nor were we ware of it, until it spake,

13 Saying, "My brothers, may God give you peace!"
We turned us suddenly, and Virgilius rendered
To him the countersign thereto conforming.

16 Thereon began he: "In the blessed council,
Thee may the court veracious place in peace,
That me doth banish in eternal exile!"

19 "How," said he, and the while we went with speed,
"If ye are shades whom God deigns not on high,
Who up his stairs so far has guided you?"

22 And said my Teacher: "If thou note the marks
Which this one bears and which the Angel traces,
Well shalt thou see he with the good must reign.

25 But because she who spinneth day and night
For him had not yet drawn the distaff off,
Which Clotho lays for each one and compacts,

28 His soul, which is thy sister and my own,
In coming upwards could not come alone,
By reason that it sees not in our fashion.

31 Whence I was drawn from out the ample throat
Of Hell to be his guide, and I shall guide him
As far on as my school has power to lead.

34 But tell us, if thou knowest, why such a shudder
Erewhile the mountain gave, and why together
All seemed to cry, as far as its moist feet?"

37 In asking he so hit the very eye
Of my desire, that merely with the hope
My thirst became the less unsatisfied.

40 "Naught is there," he began, "that without order
May the religion of the mountain feel,
Nor aught that may be foreign to its custom.

43 Free is it here from every permutation;
What from itself heaven in itself receiveth
Can be of this the cause, and naught beside;

46 Because that neither rain, nor hail, nor snow,
Nor dew, nor hoar-frost any higher falls
Than the short, little stairway of three steps.

49 Dense clouds do not appear, nor rarefied,
Nor coruscation, nor the daughter of Thaumas,
That often upon earth her region shifts;

52 No arid vapour any farther rises
Than to the top of the three steps I spake of,
Whereon the Vicar of Peter has his feet.

55 Lower down perchance it trembles less or more,
But, for the wind that in the earth is hidden
I know not how, up here it never trembled.

58 It trembles here, whenever any soul
Feels itself pure, so that it soars, or moves
To mount aloft, and such a cry attends it.

61 Of purity the will alone gives proof,
Which, being wholly free to change its convent,
Takes by surprise the soul, and helps it fly.

64 First it wills well; but the desire permits not,
Which divine justice with the self-same will
There was to sin, upon the torment sets.

67 And I, who have been lying in this pain

Five hundred years and more, but just now felt
A free volition for a better seat.

70 Therefore thou heardst the earthquake, and the pious
Spirits along the mountain rendering praise
Unto the Lord, that soon he speed them upwards."

73 So said he to him; and since we enjoy
As much in drinking as the thirst is great,
I could not say how much it did me good.

76 And the wise Leader: "Now I see the net
That snares you here, and how ye are set free,
Why the earth quakes, and wherefore ye rejoice.

79 Now who thou wast be pleased that I may know;
And why so many centuries thou hast here
Been lying, let me gather from thy words."

82 "In days when the good Titus, with the aid
Of the supremest King, avenged the wounds
Whence issued forth the blood by Judas sold,

85 Under the name that most endures and honours,
Was I on earth," that spirit made reply,
"Greatly renowned, but not with faith as yet.

88 My vocal spirit was so sweet, that Rome
Me, a Thoulousian, drew unto herself,
Where I deserved to deck my brows with myrtle.

91 Statius the people name me still on earth;
I sang of Thebes, and then of great Achilles;
But on the way fell with my second burden.

94 The seeds unto my ardour were the sparks
Of that celestial flame which heated me,
Whereby more than a thousand have been fired;

97 Of the Aeneid speak I, which to me
A mother was, and was my nurse in song;
Without this weighed I not a drachma's weight.

100 And to have lived upon the earth what time
Virgilius lived, I would accept one sun
More than I must ere issuing from my ban."

These words towards me made Virgilius turn
With looks that in their silence said, "Be silent!"
But yet the power that wills cannot do all things;

For tears and laughter are such pursuivants
Unto the passion from which each springs forth,
In the most truthful least the will they follow.

I only smiled, as one who gives the wink;
Whereat the shade was silent, and it gazed
Into mine eyes, where most expression dwells;

And, "As thou well mayst consummate a labour
So great," it said, "why did thy face just now
Display to me the lightning of a smile?"

Now am I caught on this side and on that;
One keeps me silent, one to speak conjures me,
Wherefore I sigh, and I am understood.

"Speak," said my Master, "and be not afraid
Of speaking, but speak out, and say to him
What he demands with such solicitude."

Whence I: "Thou peradventure marvellest,
O antique spirit, at the smile I gave;
But I will have more wonder seize upon thee.

This one, who guides on high these eyes of mine,
Is that Virgilius, from whom thou didst learn
To sing aloud of men and of the Gods.

If other cause thou to my smile imputedst,
Abandon it as false, and trust it was
Those words which thou hast spoken concerning him."

Already he was stooping to embrace
My Teacher's feet; but he said to him: "Brother,
Do not; for shade thou art, and shade beholdest."

And he uprising: "Now canst thou the sum
Of love which warms me to thee comprehend,
When this our vanity I disremember,

Treating a shadow as substantial thing."

Canto XXII

ALREADY was the Angel left behind us,
The Angel who to the sixth round had turned us,
Having erased one mark from off my face;

4 And those who have in justice their desire
Had said to us, "Beati," in their voices,
With "sitio,"[14] and without more ended it,

7 And I, more light than through the other passes,
Went onward so, that without any labour
I followed upward the swift-footed spirits;

10 When thus Virgilius began: "The love
Kindled by virtue aye another kindles,
Provided outwardly its flame appear.

13 Hence from the hour that Juvenal descended
Among us into the infernal Limbo,
Who made apparent to me thy affection,

16 My kindliness towards thee was as great
As ever bound one to an unseen person,
So that these stairs will now seem short to me.

19 But tell me, and forgive me as a friend,
If too great confidence let loose the rein,
And as a friend now hold discourse with me;

22 How was it possible within thy breast
For avarice to find place, 'mid so much wisdom
As thou wast filled with by thy diligence?"

25 These words excited Statius at first
Somewhat to laughter; afterward he answered:
"Each word of thine is love's dear sign to me.

28 Verily oftentimes do things appear
Which give fallacious matter to our doubts,
Instead of the true causes which are hidden!

31 Thy question shows me thy belief to be

14 "Blessed are the thirsty."

That I was niggard in the other life,
It may be from the circle where I was;

34 Therefore know thou, that avarice was removed
Too far from me; and this extravagance
Thousands of lunar periods have punished.

37 And were it not that I my thoughts uplifted,
When I the passage heard where thou exclaimest,
As if indignant, unto human nature,

40 'To what impellest thou not, O cursed hunger
Of gold, the appetite of mortal men?'
Revolving I should feel the dismal joustings.

43 Then I perceived the hands could spread too wide
Their wings in spending, and repented me
As well of that as of my other sins;

46 How many with shorn hair shall rise again
Because of ignorance, which from this sin
Cuts off repentance living and in death!

49 And know that the transgression which rebuts
By direct opposition any sin
Together with it here its verdure dries.

52 Therefore if I have been among that folk
Which mourns its avarice, to purify me,
For its opposite has this befallen me."

55 "Now when thou sangest the relentless weapons
Of the twofold affliction of Jocasta,"
The singer of the Songs Bucolic said,

58 "From that which Clio there with thee preludes,
It does not seem that yet had made thee faithful
That faith without which no good works suffice.

61 If this be so, what candles or what sun
Scattered thy darkness so that thou didst trim
Thy sails behind the Fisherman thereafter?"

64 And he to him: "Thou first directedst me
Towards Parnassus, in its grots to drink,
And first concerning God didst me enlighten.

Thou didst as he who walketh in the night,
Who bears his light behind, which helps him not,
But wary makes the persons after him,

When thou didst say: 'The age renews itself,
Justice returns, and man's primeval time,
And a new progeny descends from heaven.'

Through thee I Poet was, through thee a Christian;
But that thou better see what I design,
To colour it will I extend my hand.

Already was the world in every part
Pregnant with the true creed, disseminated
By messengers of the eternal kingdom;

And thy assertion, spoken of above,
With the new preachers was in unison;
Whence I to visit them the custom took.

Then they became so holy in my sight,
That, when Domitian persecuted them,
Not without tears of mine were their laments;

And all the while that I on earth remained,
Them I befriended, and their upright customs
Made me disparage all the other sects.

And ere I led the Greeks unto the rivers
Of Thebes, in poetry, I was baptized,
But out of fear was covertly a Christian,

For a long time professing paganism;
And this lukewarmness caused me the fourth circle
To circuit round more than four centuries.

Thou, therefore, who hast raised the covering
That hid from me whatever good I speak of,
While in ascending we have time to spare,

Tell me, in what place is our friend Terentius,
Caecilius, Plautus, Varro, if thou knowest;
Tell me if they are damned, and in what alley."

"These, Persius and myself, and others many,"

Replied my Leader, "with that Grecian are
Whom more than all the rest the Muses suckled,

103 In the first circle of the prison blind;
Ofttimes we of the mountain hold discourse
Which has our nurses ever with itself.

106 Euripides is with us, Antiphon,
Simonides, Agatho, and many other
Greeks who of old their brows with laurel decked.

109 There some of thine own people may be seen,
Antigone, Deiphile and Argìa,
And there Ismene mournful as of old.

112 There she is seen who pointed out Langia;
There is Tiresias' daughter, and there Thetis,
And there Deidamia with her sisters."

115 Silent already were the poets both,
Attent once more in looking round about,
From the ascent and from the walls released;

118 And four handmaidens of the day already
Were left behind, and at the pole the fifth
Was pointing upward still its burning horn,

121 What time my Guide: "I think that tow'rds thee
Our dexter shoulders it behoves us turn,
Circling the mount as we are wont to do."

124 Thus in that region custom was our ensign;
And we resumed our way with less suspicion
For the assenting of that worthy soul.

127 They in advance went on, and I alone
Behind them, and I listened to their speech,
Which gave me lessons in the art of song

130 But soon their sweet discourses interrupted
A tree which midway in the road we found,
With apples sweet and grateful to the smell.

133 And even as a fir-tree tapers upward
From bough to bough, so downwardly did that;

I think in order that no one might climb it.

136 On that side where our pathway was enclosed
Fell from the lofty rock a limpid water,
And spread itself abroad upon the leaves.

139 The Poets twain unto the tree drew near,
And from among the foliage a voice
Cried: "Of this food ye shall have scarcity."

142 Then said: "More thoughtful Mary was of making
The marriage feast complete and honourable,
Than of her mouth which now for you responds;

145 And for their drink the ancient Roman women
With water were content; and Daniel
Disparaged food, and understanding won.

148 The primal age was beautiful as gold;
Acorns it made with hunger savorous,
And nectar every rivulet with thirst.

151 Honey and locusts were the aliments
That fed the Baptist in the wilderness;
Whence he is glorious, and so magnified

154 As by the Evangel is revealed to you."

Canto XXIII

THE while among the verdant leaves mine eyes
I riveted, as he is wont to do
Who wastes his lifc pursuing little birds,

My more than Father said unto me: "Son
Come now; because the time that is ordained us
More usefully should be apportioned out."

I turned my face and no less soon my steps
Unto the Sages, who were speaking so
They made the going of no cost to me;

And lo! were heard a song and a lament,
"Labia mea, Domine,"[15] in fashion
Such that delight and dolence it brought forth.

"O my sweet Father, what is this I hear?"
Began I; and he answered: "Shades that go
Perhaps the knot unloosing of their debt."

In the same way that thoughtful pilgrims do,
Who, unknown people on the road o'ertaking,
Turn themselves round to them, and do not stop,

Even thus, behind us with a swifter motion
Coming and passing onward, gazed upon us
A crowd of spirits silent and devout.

Each in his eyes was dark and cavernous,
Pallid in face, and so emaciate
That from the bones the skin did shape itself.

I do not think that so to merest rind
Could Erisichthon have been withered up
By famine, when most fear he had of it.

Thinking within myself I said: "Behold,
This is the folk who lost Jerusalem,
When Mary made a prey of her own son."

15 "My lips, Lord."

31 Their sockets were like rings without the gems;
Whoever in the face of men reads 'omo'
Might well in these have recognised the 'm.'

34 Who would believe the odour of an apple,
Begetting longing, could consume them so,
And that of water, without knowing how?

37 I still was wondering what so famished them,
For the occasion not yet manifest
Of their emaciation and sad squalor;

40 And lo! from out the hollow of his head
His eyes a shade turned on me, and looked keenly;
Then cried aloud: "What grace to me is this?"

43 Never should I have known him by his look;
But in his voice was evident to me
That which his aspect had suppressed within it.

46 This spark within me wholly re-enkindled
My recognition of his altered face,
And I recalled the features of Forese.

49 "Ah, do not look at this dry leprosy,"
Entreated he, "which doth my skin discolour,
Nor at default of flesh that I may have;

52 But tell me truth of thee, and who are those
Two souls, that yonder make for thee an escort;
Do not delay in speaking unto me."

55 "That face of thine, which dead I once bewept,
Gives me for weeping now no lesser grief,"
I answered him, "beholding it so changed!

58 But tell me, for God's sake, what thus denudes you?
Make me not speak while I am marvelling,
For ill speaks he who's full of other longings."

61 And he to me: "From the eternal council
Falls power into the water and the tree
Behind us left, whereby I grow so thin.

64 All of this people who lamenting sing,

For following beyond measure appetite
In hunger and thirst are here re-sanctified.

67 Desire to eat and drink enkindles in us
The scent that issues from the apple-tree,
And from the spray that sprinkles o'er the verdure;

70 And not a single time alone, this ground
Encompassing, is refreshed our pain,—
I say our pain, and ought to say our solace,—

73 For the same wish doth lead us to the tree
Which led the Christ rejoicing to say 'Eli,'
When with his veins he liberated us."

76 And I to him: "Forese, from that day
When for a better life thou changedst worlds,
Up to this time five years have not rolled round.

79 If sooner were the power exhausted in thee
Of sinning more, than thee the hour surprised
Of that good sorrow which to God reweds us,

82 How hast thou come up hitherward already?
I thought to find thee down there underneath,
Where time for time doth restitution make."

85 And he to me: "Thus speedily has led me
To drink of the sweet wormwood of these torrnents,
My Nella with her overflowing tears;

88 She with her prayers devout and with her sighs
Has drawn me from the coast where one awaits,
And from the other circles set me free.

91 So much more dear and pleasing is to God
My little widow, whom so much I loved,
As in good works she is the more alone;

94 For the Barbagia of Sardinia
By far more modest in its women is
Than the Barbagia I have left her in.

97 O brother sweet, what wilt thou have me say?
A future time is in my sight already,
To which this hour will not be very old,

100 When from the pulpit shall be interdicted
To the unblushing womankind of Florence
To go about displaying breast and paps.

103 What savages were e'er, what Saracens,
Who stood in need, to make them covered go,
Of spiritual or other discipline?

106 But if the shameless women were assured
Of what swift Heaven prepares for them, already
Wide open would they have their mouths to howl;

109 For if my foresight here deceive me not,
They shall be sad ere he has bearded cheeks
Who now is hushed to sleep with lullaby.

112 O brother, now no longer hide thee from me;
See that not only I, but all these people
Are gazing there, where thou dost veil the sun."

115 Whence I to him: "If thou bring back to mind
What thou with me hast been and I with thee,
The present memory will be grievous still.

118 Out of that life he turned me back who goes
In front of me, two days agone when round
The sister of him yonder showed herself,"

121 And to the sun I pointed. "Through the deep
Night of the truly dead has this one led me,
With this true flesh, that follows after him.

124 Thence his encouragements have led me up,
Ascending and still circling round the mount
That you doth straighten, whom the world made crooked.

127 He says that he will bear me company,
Till I shall be where Beatrice will be;
There it behoves me to remain without him.

130 This is Virgilius, who thus says to me,"
And him I pointed at; "the other is
That shade for whom just now shook every slope

133 Your realm, that from itself discharges him."

Canto XXIV

NOR speech the going, nor the going that
Slackened; but talking we went bravely on,
Even as a vessel urged by a good wind.

4 And shadows, that appeared things doubly dead,
From out the sepulchres of their eyes betrayed
Wonder at me, aware that I was living.

7 And I, continuing my colloquy,
Said: "Peradventure he goes up more slowly
Than he would do, for other people's sake.

10 But tell me, if thou knowest, where is Piccarda;
Tell me if any one of note I see
Among this folk that gazes at me so."

13 "My sister, who, 'twixt beautiful and good,
I know not which was more, triumphs rejoicing
Already in her crown on high Olympus."

16 So said he first, and then: "'Tis not forbidden
To name each other here, so milked away
Is our resemblance by our dieting.

19 This," pointing with his finger, "is Buonagiunta,
Buonagiunta, of Lucca; and that face
Beyond him there, more peaked than the others,

22 Has held the holy Church within his arms;
From Tours was he, and purges by his fasting
Bolsena's eels and the Vernaccia wine."

25 He named me many others one by one;
And all contented seemed at being named,
So that for this I saw not one dark look.

28 I saw for hunger bite the empty air
Ubaldin dalla Pila, and Boniface,
Who with his crook had pastured many people.

31 I saw Messer Marchese, who had leisure
Once at Forli for drinking with less dryness,

And he was one who ne'er felt satisfied.

34 But as he does who scans, and then doth prize
One more than others, did I him of Lucca,
Who seemed to take most cognizance of me.

37 He murmured, and I know not what "Gentucca"
From that place heard I, where he felt the wound
Of justice, that doth macerate them so.

40 "O soul," I said, "that seemest so desirous
To speak with me, do so that I may hear thee,
And with thy speech appease thyself and me."

43 "A maid is born, and wears not yet the veil,"
Began he, "who to thee shall pleasant make
My city, howsoever men may blame it.

46 Thou shalt go on thy way with this prevision;
If by my murmuring thou hast been deceived,
True things hereafter will declare it to thee.

49 But say if him I here behold, who forth
Evoked the new-invented rhymes, beginning,
'Ladies, that have intelligence of love?'"

52 And I to him: "One am I, who, whenever
Love doth inspire me, note, and in that measure
Which he within me dictates, singing go."

55 "O brother, now I see," he said, "the knot
Which me, the Notary, and Guittone held
Short of the sweet new style that now I hear.

58 I do perceive full clearly how your pens
Go closely following after him who dictates,
Which with our own forsooth came not to pass;

61 And he who sets himself to go beyond,
No difference sees from one style to another;"
And as if satisfied, he held his peace.

64 Even as the birds, that winter tow'rds the Nile,
Sometimes into a phalanx form themselves,
Then fly in greater haste, and go in file;

67 In such wise all the people who were there,
Turning their faces, hurried on their steps,
Both by their leanness and their wishes light.

70 And as a man, who weary is with trotting,
Lets his companions onward go, and walks,
Until he vents the panting of his chest;

73 So did Forese let the holy flock
Pass by, and came with me behind it, saying,
"When will it be that I again shall see thee?"

76 "How long," I answered, "I may live, I know not;
Yet my return will not so speedy be,
But I shall sooner in desire arrive;

79 Because the place where I was set to live
From day to day of good is more depleted,
And unto dismal ruin seems ordained."

82 "Now go," he said, "for him most guilty of it
At a beast's tail behold I dragged along
Towards the valley where is no repentance.

85 Faster at every step the beast is going,
Increasing evermore until it smites him,
And leaves the body vilely mutilated.

88 Not long those wheels shall turn," and he uplifted
His eyes to heaven, "ere shall be clear to thee
That which my speech no farther can declare.

91 Now stay behind; because the time so precious
Is in this kingdom, that I lose too much
By coming onward thus abreast with thee."

94 As sometimes issues forth upon a gallop
A cavalier from out a troop that ride,
And seeks the honour of the first encounter,

97 So he with greater strides departed from us;
And on the road remained I with those two,
Who were such mighty marshals of the world.

100 And when before us he had gone so far
Mine eyes became to him such pursuivants

As was my understanding to his words,

103 Appeared to me with laden and living boughs
Another apple-tree, and not far distant,
From having but just then turned thitherward.

106 People I saw beneath it lift their hands,
And cry I know not what towards the leaves,
Like little children eager and deluded,

109 Who pray, and he they pray to doth not answer,
But, to make very keen their appetite,
Holds their desire aloft, and hides it not

112 Then they departed as if undeceived;
And now we came unto the mighty tree
Which prayers and tears so manifold refuses.

115 "Pass farther onward without drawing near;
The tree of which Eve ate is higher up,
And out of that one has this tree been raised."

118 Thus said I know not who among the branches;
Whereat Virgilius, Statius, and myself
Went crowding forward on the side that rises.

121 "Be mindful," said he, "of the accursed ones
Formed of the cloud-rack, who inebriate
Combated Theseus with their double breasts;

124 And of the Jews who showed them soft in drinking,
Whence Gideon would not have them for companions
When he tow'rds Midian the hills descended."

127 Thus, closely pressed to one of the two borders,
On passed we, hearing sins of gluttony,
Followed forsooth by miserable gains;

130 Then set at large upon the lonely road,
A thousand steps and more we onward went,
In contemplation, each without a word.

133 "What go ye thinking thus, ye three alone?"
Said suddenly a voice, whereat I started
As terrified and timid beasts are wont.

I raised my head to see who this might be,
And never in a furnace was there seen
Metals or glass so lucent and so red

As one I saw who said: "If it may please you
To mount aloft, here it behoves you turn;
This way goes he who goeth after peace."

His aspect had bereft me of my sight,
So that I turned me back unto my Teachers,
Like one who goeth as his hearing guides him.

And as, the harbinger of early dawn,
The air of May doth move and breathe out fragrance,
Impregnate all with herbage and with flowers,

So did I feel a breeze strike in the midst
My front, and felt the moving of the plumes
That breathed around an odour of ambrosia,

And heard it said: "Blessed are they whom grace,
So much illumines, that the love of taste
Excites not in their breasts too great desire,

Hungering at all times so far as is just."

Canto XXV

NOW was it the ascent no hindrance brooked,
Because the sun had his meridian circle
To Taurus left, and night to Scorpio;

4 Wherefore as doth a man who tarries not,
But goes his way, whate'er to him appear,
If of necessity the sting transfix him,

7 In this wise did we enter through the gap,
Taking the stairway, one before the other,
Which by its narrowness divides the climbers.

10 And as the little stork that lifts its wing
With a desire to fly, and does not venture
To leave the nest, and lets it downward droop,

13 Even such was I, with the desire of asking
Kindled and quenched, unto the motion coming
He makes who doth address himself to speak.

16 Not for our pace, though rapid it might be,
My father sweet forbore, but said: "Let fly
The bow of speech thou to the barb hast drawn."

19 With confidence I opened then my mouth,
And I began: "How can one meagre grow
There where the need of nutriment applies not?"

22 "If thou wouldst call to mind how Meleager
Was wasted by the wasting of a brand,
This would not," said he, "be to thee so sour;

25 And wouldst thou think how at each tremulous motion
Trembles within a mirror your own image:
That which seems hard would mellow seem to thee.

28 But that thou mayst content thee in thy wish
Lo Statius here; and him I call and pray
He now will be the healer of thy wounds."

31 "If I unfold to him the eternal vengeance,"
Responded Statius, "where thou present art,

Be my excuse that I can naught deny thee."

Then he began: "Son, if these words of mine
Thy mind doth contemplate and doth receive,
They'll be thy light unto the How thou sayest.

The perfect blood, which never is drunk up
Into the thirsty veins, and which remaineth
Like food that from the table thou removest,

Takes in the heart for all the human members
Virtue informative, as being that
Which to be changed to them goes through the veins

Again digest, descends it where 'tis better
Silent to be than say; and then drops thence
Upon another's blood in natural vase.

There one together with the other mingles,
One to be passive meant, the other active
By reason of the perfect place it springs from;

And being conjoined, begins to operate,
Coagulating first, then vivifying
What for its matter it had made consistent.

The active virtue, being made a soul
As of a plant, (in so far different,
This on the way is, that arrived already,)

Then works so much, that now it moves and feels
Like a sea-fungus, and then undertakes
To organize the powers whose seed it is.

Now, Son, dilates and now distends itself
The virtue from the generator's heart,
Where nature is intent on all the members.

But how from animal it man becomes
Thou dost not see as yet; this is a point
Which made a wiser man than thou once err

So far, that in his doctrine separate
He made the soul from possible intellect,
For he no organ saw by this assumed.

67 Open thy breast unto the truth that's coming,
And know that, just as soon as in the foetus
The articulation of the brain is perfect,

70 The primal Motor turns to it well pleased
At so great art of nature, and inspires
A spirit new with virtue all replete,

73 Which what it finds there active doth attract
Into its substance, and becomes one soul,
Which lives, and feels, and on itself revolves.

76 And that thou less may wonder at my word,
Behold the sun's heat, which becometh wine,
Joined to the juice that from the vine distils.

79 Whenever Lachesis has no more thread,
It separates from the flesh, and virtually
Bears with itself the human and divine;

82 The other faculties are voiceless all;
The memory, the intelligence, and the will
In action far more vigorous than before.

85 Without a pause it falleth of itself
In marvellous way on one shore or the other;
There of its roads it first is cognizant.

88 Soon as the place there circumscribeth it,
The virtue informative rays round about,
As, and as much as, in the living members.

91 And even as the air, when full of rain,
By alien rays that are therein reflected,
With divers colours shows itself adorned,

94 So there the neighbouring air doth shape itself
Into that form which doth impress upon it
Virtually the soul that has stood still.

97 And then in manner of the little flame,
Which followeth the fire where'er it shifts,
After the spirit followeth its new form.

100 Since afterwards it takes from this its semblance,

It is called shade; and thence it organizes
Thereafter every sense, even to the sight.

103 Thence is it that we speak, and thence we laugh;
Thence is it that we form the tears and sighs,
That on the mountain thou mayhap hast heard.

106 According as impress us our desires
And other affections, so the shade is shaped,
And this is cause of what thou wonderest at."

109 And now unto the last of all the circles
Had we arrived, and to the right hand turned,
And were attentive to another care.

112 There the embankment shoots forth flames of fire,
And upward doth the cornice breathe a blast
That drives them back, and from itself sequesters.

115 Hence we must needs go on the open side,
And one by one; and I did fear the fire
On this side, and on that the falling down.

118 My Leader said: "Along this place one ought
To keep upon the eyes a tightened rein,
Seeing that one so easily might err."

121 "Summae Deus clementiae,"[16] in the bosom
Of the great burning chanted then I heard,
Which made me no less eager to turn round;

124 And spirits saw I walking through the flame;
Wherefore I looked, to my own steps and theirs
Apportioning my sight from time to time.

127 After the close which to that hymn is made,
Aloud they shouted, "Virum non cognosco;"[17]
Then recommenced the hymn with voices low.

130 This also ended, cried they: "To the wood
Diana ran, and drove forth Helice
Therefrom, who had of Venus felt the poison."

---

16 "God of supreme clemency."

17 "I know no man."

133 Then to their song returned they; then the wives
They shouted, and the husbands who were chaste.
As virtue and the marriage vow imposes.

136 And I believe that them this mode suffices,
For all the time the fire is burning them;
With such care is it needful, and such food,

139 That the last wound of all should be closed up.

Canto XXVI

WHILE on the brink thus one before the other
We went upon our way, oft the good Master
Said: "Take thou heed! suffice it that I warn thee."

4 On the right shoulder smote me now the sun,
That, raying out, already the whole west
Changed from its azure aspect into white.

7 And with my shadow did I make the flame
Appear more red; and even to such a sign
Shades saw I many, as they went, give heed.

10 This was the cause that gave them a beginning
To speak of me; and to themselves began they
To say: "That seems not a factitious body!"

13 Then towards me, as far as they could come,
Came certain of them, always with regard
Not to step forth where they would not be burned.

16 "O thou who goest, not from being slower
But reverent perhaps, behind the others,
Answer me, who in thirst and fire am burning.

19 Nor to me only is thine answer needful;
For all of these have greater thirst for it
Than for cold water Ethiop or Indian.

22 Tell us how is it that thou makest thyself
A wall unto the sun, as if thou hadst not

Entered as yet into the net of death."

25 Thus one of them addressed me, and I straight
Should have revealed myself, were I not bent
On other novelty that then appeared.

28 For through the middle of the burning road
There came a people face to face with these,
Which held me in suspense with gazing at them.

31 There see I hastening upon either side
Each of the shades, and kissing one another.
Without a pause, content with brief salute.

34 Thus in the middle of their brown battalions
Muzzle to muzzle one ant meets another
Perchance to spy their journey or their fortune.

37 No sooner is the friendly greeting ended,
Or ever the first footstep passes onward,
Each one endeavours to outcry the other;

40 The new-come people: "Sodom and Gomorrah!"
The rest: "Into the cow Pasiphae enters,
So that the bull unto her lust may run!"

43 Then as the cranes, that to Riphaen mountains
Might fly in part, and part towards the sands,
These of the frost, those of the sun avoidant,

46 One folk is going, and the other coming,
And weeping they return to their first songs,
And to the cry that most befitteth them;

49 And close to me approached, even as before,
The very same who had entreated me,
Attent to listen in their countenance.

52 I, who their inclination twice had seen
Began: "O souls secure in the possession,
Whene'er it may be, of a state of peace,

55 Neither unripe nor ripened have remained
My members upon earth, but here are with me
With their own blood and their articulations.

58 I go up here to be no longer blind;
A Lady is above, who wins this grace,
Whereby the mortal through your world I bring.

61 But as your greatest longing satisfied
May soon become, so that the Heaven may house you
Which full of love is, and most amply spreads,

64 Tell me, that I again in books may write it,
Who are you, and what is that multitude
Which goes upon its way behind your backs?"

67 Not otherwise with wonder is bewildered
The mountaineer, and staring round is dumb,
When rough and rustic to the town he goes,

70 Than every shade became in its appearance;
But when they of their stupor were disburdened,
Which in high hearts is quickly quieted,

73 "Blessed be thou, who of our border-lands,"
He recommenced who first had questioned us,
"Experience freightest for a better life.

76 The folk that comes not with us have offended
In that for which once Caesar, triumphing,
Heard himself called in contumely, 'Queen.'

79 Therefore they separate, exclaiming, 'Sodom!'
Themselves reproving, even as thou hast heard,
And add unto their burning by their shame.

82 Our own transgression was hermaphrodite;
But because we observed not human law,
Following like unto beasts our appetite,

85 In our opprobrium by us is read,
When we part company, the name of her
Who bestialized herself in bestial wood.

88 Now knowest thou our acts, and what our crime was;
Wouldst thou perchance by name know who we are,
There is not time to tell, nor could I do it.

91 Thy wish to know me shall in sooth be granted;

I'm Guido Guinicelli, and now purge me,
Having repented ere the hour extreme."

94 The same that in the sadness of Lycurgus
Two sons became, their mother re-beholding,
Such I became, but rise not to such height,

97 The moment I heard name himself the father
Of me and of my betters, who had ever
Practised the sweet and gracious rhymes of love;

100 And without speech and hearing thoughtfully
For a long time I went, beholding him,
Nor for the fire did I approach him nearer.

103 When I was fed with looking, utterly
Myself I offered ready for his service,
With affirmation that compels belief

106 And he to me: "Thou leavest footprints such
In me, from what I hear, and so distinct,
Lethe cannot efface them, nor make dim.

109 But if thy words just now the truth have sworn,
Tell me what is the cause why thou displayest
In word and look that dear thou holdest me?"

112 And I to him: "Those dulcet lays of yours
Which, long as shall endure our modern fashion,
Shall make for ever dear their very ink!"

115 "O brother," said he, "he whom I point out,"
And here he pointed at a spirit in front,
"Was of the mother tongue a better smith.

118 Verses of love and proses of romance,
He mastered all; and let the idiots talk,
Who think the Lemosin surpasses him.

121 To clamour more than truth they turn their faces,
And in this way establish their opinion,
Ere art or reason has by them been heard.

124 Thus many ancients with Guittone did,
From cry to cry still giving him applause,
Until the truth has conquered with most persons.

127 Now, if thou hast such ample privilege
'Tis granted thee to go unto the cloister
Wherein is Christ the abbot of the college,

130 To him repeat for me a Paternoster,
So far as needful to us of this world,
Where power of sinning is no longer ours."

133 Then, to give place perchance to one behind,
Whom he had near, he vanished in the fire
As fish in water going to the bottom.

136 I moved a little tow'rds him pointed out,
And said that to his name my own desire
An honourable place was making ready.

139 He of his own free will began to say:
'Tan m' abellis vostre cortes deman,
Que jeu nom' puesc ni vueill a vos cobrire;

142 Jeu sui Arnaut, que plor e vai chantan;
Consiros vei a passada folor,
E vei jauzen lo jorn qu' esper denan.

145 Ara vus prec per aquella valor,
Que vus condus al som de la scalina,
Sovenga vus a temprar ma dolor.'[18]

148 Then hid him in the fire that purifies them.

18 So pleases me your courteous demand,
I cannot and I will not hide me from you.

I am Arnaut, who weep and singing go;
Contrite I see the folly of the past,
And joyous see the hoped-for day before me.

Therefore do I implore you, by that power
Which guides you to the summit of the stairs,
Be mindful to assuage my suffering!

Canto XXVII

AS when he vibrates forth his earliest rays,
In regions where his Maker shed his blood,
(The Ebro falling under lofty Libra,

4 And waters in the Ganges burnt with noon,)
So stood the Sun; hence was the day departing,
When the glad Angel of God appeared to us.

7 Outside the flame he stood upon the verge,
And chanted forth, "Beati mundo corde,"[19]
In voice by far more living than our own.

10 Then: "No one farther goes, souls sanctified,
If first the fire bite not; within it enter,
And be not deaf unto the song beyond."

13 When we were close behind him thus he said;
Wherefore e'en such became I, when I heard him,
As he is who is put into the grave.

16 Upon my clasped hands I straightened me,
Scanning the fire, and vividly recalling
The human bodies I had once seen burned.

19 Towards me turned themselves my good Conductors,
And unto me Virgilius said: "My son,
Here may indeed be torment, but not death.

22 Remember thee, remember! and if I
On Geryon have safely guided thee,
What shall I do now I am nearer God?

25 Believe for certain, shouldst thou stand a full
Millenniunn in the bosom of this flame,
It could not make thee bald a single hair.

28 And if perchance thou think that I deceive thee,
Draw near to it, and put it to the proof
With thine own hands upon thy garment's hem.

31 Now lay aside, now lay aside all fear,

---

19 "Blessed are the pure in heart."

Turn hithenward, and onward come securely;"
And I still motionless, and 'gainst my conscience!

34 Seeing me stand still motionless and stubborn,
Somewhat disturbed he said: "Now look thou, Son,
'Twixt Beatrice and thee there is this wall."

37 As at the name of Thisbe oped his lids
The dying Pyramus, and gazed upon her,
What time the mulberry became vermilion,

40 Even thus, my obduracy being softened,
I turned to my wise Guide, hearing the name
That in my memory evermore is welling.

43 Whereat he wagged his head, and said: "How now?
Shall we stay on this side?" then smiled as one
Does at a child who's vanquished by an apple.

46 Then into the fire in front of me he entered,
Beseeching Statius to come after me,
Who a long way before divided us.

49 When I was in it, into molten glass
I would have cast me to refresh myself,
So without measure was the burning there!

52 And my sweet Father, to encourage me,
Discoursing still of Beatrice went on,
Saying: "Her eyes I seem to see already!"

55 A voice, that on the other side was singing,
Directed us, and we, attent alone
On that, came forth where the ascent began.

58 "Venite, bendicti Patri mei,"[20]
Sounded within a splendour, which was there
Such it o'ercame me, and I could not look.

61 "The sun departs," it added, "and night cometh;
Tarry ye not, but onward urge your steps,
So long as yet the west becomes not dark."

64 Straight forward through the rock the path ascended

20 "Come, you blessed of my Father."

In such a way that I cut off the rays
Before me of the sun, that now was low.

67 And of few stairs we yet had made assay,
Ere by the vanished shadow the sun's setting
Behind us we perceived, I and my Sages.

70 And ere in all its parts immeasurable
The horizon of one aspect had become,
And Night her boundless dispensation held,

73 Each of us of a stair had made his bed;
Because the nature of the mount took from us
The power of climbing, more than the delight.

76 Even as in ruminating passive grow
The goats, who have been swift and venturesome
Upon the mountain-tops ere they were fed,

79 Hushed in the shadow, while the sun is hot,
Watched by the herdsman, who upon his staff
Is leaning, and in leaning tendeth them;

82 And as the shepherd, lodging out of doors,
Passes the night beside his quiet flock,
Watching that no wild beast may scatter it,

85 Such at that hour were we, all three of us,
I like the goat, and like the herdsmen they,
Begirt on this side and on that by rocks.

88 Little could there be seen of things without;
But through that little I beheld the stars
More luminous and larger than their wont.

91 Thus ruminating, and beholding these,
Sleep seized upon me,—sleep, that oftentimes
Before a deed is done has tidings of it.

94 It was the hour, I think, when from the East
First on the mountain Citherea beamed,
Who with the fire of love seems always burning;

97 Youthful and beautiful in dreams methought
I saw a lady walking in a meadow,

Gathering flowers; and singing she was saying:

100 "Know whosoever may my name demand
That I am Leah, and go moving round
My beauteous hands to make myself a garland.

103 To please me at the mirror, here I deck me,
But never does my sister Rachel leave
Her looking-glass, and sitteth all day long.

106 To see her beauteous eyes as eager is she,
As I am to adorn me with my hands;
Her, seeing, and me, doing satisfies."

109 And now before the antelucan splendours
That unto pilgrims the more grateful rise,
As, home-returning, less remote they lodge,

112 The darkness fled away on every side,
And slumber with it; whereupon I rose,
Seeing already the great Masters risen.

115 "That apple sweet, which through so many branches
The care of mortals goeth in pursuit of,
To-day shall put in peace thy hungerings."

118 Speaking to me, Virgilius of such words
As these made use; and never were there guerdons
That could in pleasantness compare with these.

121 Such longing upon longing came upon me
To be above, that at each step thereafter
For flight I felt in me the pinions growing

124 When underneath us was the stairway all
Run o'er, and we were on the highest step,
Virgilius fastened upon me his eyes,

127 And said: "The temporal fire and the eternal,
Son, thou hast seen, and to a place art come
Where of myself no farther I discern.

130 By intellect and art I here have brought thee;
Take thine own pleasure for thy guide henceforth;
Beyond the steep ways and the narrow art thou.

133 Behold the sun, that shines upon thy forehead,
Behold the grass, the flowerets, and the shrubs
Which of itself alone this land produces.

136 Until rejoicing come the beauteous eyes
Which weeping caused me to come unto thee,
Thou canst sit down, and thou canst walk among them.

139 Expect no more or word or sign from me;
Free and upright and sound is thy free-will,
And error were it not to do its bidding;

142 Thee o'er thyself I therefore crown and mitre!"

Canto XXVIII

EAGER already to search in and round
The heavenly forest, dense and living-green,
Which tempered to the eyes the new-born day,

4 Withouten more delay I left the bank,
Taking the level country slowly, slowly
Over the soil that everywhere breathes fragrance.

7 A softly-breathing air, that no mutation
Had in itself, upon the forehead smote me
No heavier blow than of a gentle wind,

10 Whereat the branches, lightly tremulous,
Did all of them bow downward toward that side
Where its first shadow casts the Holy Mountain;

13 Yet not from their upright direction swayed,
So that the little birds upon their tops
Should leave the practice of each art of theirs;

16 But with full ravishment the hours of prime,
Singing, received they in the midst of leaves,
That ever bore a burden to their rhymes,

19 Such as from branch to branch goes gathering on
Through the pine forest on the shore of Chiassi,

When Eolus unlooses the Sirocco.

22 Already my slow steps had carried me
Into the ancient wood so far, that I
Could not perceive where I had entered it

25 And lo! my further course a stream cut off,
Which tow'rd the left hand with its little waves
Bent down the grass that on its margin sprang.

28 All waters that on earth most limpid are
Would seem to have within themselves some mixture
Compared with that which nothing doth conceal,

31 Although it moves on with a brown, brown current
Under the shade perpetual, that never
Ray of the sun lets in, nor of the moon.

34 With feet I stayed, and with mine eyes I passed
Beyond the rivulet, to look upon
The great variety of the fresh may.

37 And there appeared to me (even as appears
Suddenly something that doth turn aside
Through very wonder every other thought)

40 A lady all alone, who went along
Singing and culling floweret after floweret,
With which her pathway was all painted over.

43 "Ah, beauteous lady, who in rays of love
Dost warm thyself, if I may trust to looks,
Which the heart's witnesses are wont to be,

46 May the desire come unto thee to draw
Near to this river's bank," I said to her,
"So much that I might hear what thou art singing.

49 Thou makest me remember where and what
Proserpina that moment was when lost
Her mother her, and she herself the Spring."

52 As turns herself, with feet together pressed
And to the ground, a lady who is dancing,
And hardly puts one foot before the other,

On the vermilion and the yellow flowerets
She turned towards me, not in other wise
Than maiden who her modest eyes casts down;

And my entreaties made to be content,
So near approaching, that the dulcet sound
Came unto me together with its meaning

As soon as she was where the grasses are
Bathed by the waters of the beauteous river,
To lift her eyes she granted me the boon.

I do not think there shone so great a light
Under the lids of Venus, when transfixed
By her own son, beyond his usual custom!

Erect upon the other bank she smiled,
Bearing full many colours in her hands
Which that high land produces without seed.

Apart three paces did the river make us;
But Hellespont, where Xerxes passed across,
(A curb still to all human arrogance,)

More hatred from Leander did not suffer
For rolling between Sestos and Abydos,
Than that from me, because it oped not then.

"Ye are new-comers; and because I smile,"
Began she, "peradventure, in this place
Elect to human nature for its nest,

Some apprehension keeps you marvelling;
But the psalm 'Delectasti' giveth light
Which has the power to uncloud your intellect.

And thou who foremost art, and didst entreat me,
Speak, if thou wouldst hear more; for I came ready
To all thy questionings, as far as needful."

"The water," said I, "and the forest's sound,
Are combating within me my new faith
In something which I heard opposed to this."

Whence she: "I will relate how from its cause

Proceedeth that which maketh thee to wonder,
And purge away the cloud that smites upon thee.

91 The Good Supreme, sole in itself delighting,
Created man good, and this goodly place
Gave him as hansel of eternal peace.

94 By his default short while he sojourned here;
By his default to weeping and to toil
He changed his innocent laughter and sweet play.

97 That the disturbance which below is made
By exhalations of the land and water,
(Which far as may be follow after heat,)

100 Might not upon mankind wage any war,
This mount ascended tow'rds the heaven so high,
And is exempt, from there where it is locked.

103 Now since the universal atmosphere
Turns in a circuit with the primal motion
Unless the circle is broken on some side,

106 Upon this height, that all is disengaged
In living ether, doth this motion strike
And make the forest sound, for it is dense;

109 And so much power the stricken plant possesses
That with its virtue it impregns the air,
And this, revolving, scatters it around;

112 And yonder earth, according as 'tis worthy
In self or in its clime, conceives and bears
Of divers qualities the divers trees;

115 It should not seem a marvel then on earth,
This being heard, whenever any plant
Without seed manifest there taketh root.

118 And thou must know, this holy table-land
In which thou art is full of every seed,
And fruit has in it never gathered there.

121 The water which thou seest springs not from vein
Restored by vapour that the cold condenses,

Like to a stream that gains or loses breath

But issues from a fountain safe and certain,
Which by the will of God as much regains
As it discharges, open on two sides.

Upon this side with virtue it descends,
Which takes away all memory of sin;
On that, of every good deed done restores it.

Here Lethe, as upon the other side
Eunoe, it is called; and worketh not
If first on either side it be not tasted.

This every other savour doth transcend;
And notwithstanding slaked so far may be
Thy thirst, that I reveal to thee no more,

I'll give thee a corollary still in grace,
Nor think my speech will be to thee less dear
If it spread out beyond my promise to thee.

Those who in ancient times have feigned in song
The Age of Gold and its felicity,
Dreamed of this place perhaps upon Parnassus.

Here was the human race in innocence;
Here evermore was Spring, and every fruit;
This is the nectar of which each one speaks."

Then backward did I turn me wholly round
Unto my Poets, and saw that with a smile
They had been listening to these closing words;

Then to the beautiful lady turned mine eyes.

Canto XXIX

SINGING like unto an enamoured lady
She, with the ending of her words, continued:
"Beati quorum tecta sunt peccata."[21]

4 And even as Nymphs, that wandered all alone
Among the sylvan shadows, sedulous
One to avoid and one to see the sun,

7 She then against the stream moved onward, going
Along the bank, and I abreast of her,
Her little steps with little steps attending

10 Between her steps and mine were not a hundred,
When equally the margins gave a turn,
In such a way, that to the East I faced.

13 Nor even thus our way continued far
Before the lady wholly turned herself
Unto me, saying, "Brother, look and listen!"

16 And lo! a sudden lustre ran across
On every side athwart the spacious forest,
Such that it made me doubt if it were lightning.

19 But since the lightning ceases as it comes,
And that continuing brightened more and more,
Within my thought I said, "What thing is this?"

22 And a delicious melody there ran
Along the luminous air, whence holy zeal
Made me rebuke the hardihood of Eve;

25 For there where earth and heaven obedient were,
The woman only, and but just created,
Could not endure to stay 'neath any veil;

28 Underneath which had she devoutly stayed,
I sooner should have tasted those delights
Ineffable, and for a longer time.

31 While 'mid such manifold first-fruits I walked

21 "Blessed are they whose sins are covered."

Of the eternal pleasure all enrapt,
And still solicitous of more delights,

34 In front of us like an enkindled fire
Became the air beneath the verdant boughs,
And the sweet sound as singing now was heard.

37 O Virgins sacrosanct! if ever hunger,
Vigils, or cold for you I have endured,
The occasion spurs me their reward to claim!

40 Now Helicon must needs pour forth for me,
And with her choir Urania must assist me,
To put in verse things difficult to think.

43 A little farther on, seven trees of gold
In semblance the long space still intervening
Between ourselves and them did counterfeit;

46 But when I had approached so near to them
The common object, which the sense deceives,
Lost not by distance any of its marks,

49 The faculty that lends discourse to reason
Did apprehend that they were candlesticks,
And in the voices of the song "Hosanna!"

52 Above them flamed the harness beautiful,
Far brighter than the moon in the serene
Of midnight, at the middle of her month.

55 I turned me round, with admiration filled,
To good Virgilius, and he answered me
With visage no less full of wonderment.

58 Then back I turned my face to those high things,
Which moved themselves towards us so sedately,
They had been distanced by new-wedded brides.

61 The lady chid me: "Why dost thou burn only
So with affection for the living lights,
And dost not look at what comes after them?"

64 Then saw I people, as behind their leaders,
Coming behind them, garmented in white,

And such a whiteness never was on earth.

67 The water on my left flank was resplendent,
And back to me reflected my left side,
E'en as a mirror, if I looked therein.

70 When I upon my margin had such post
That nothing but the stream divided us,
Better to see I gave my steps repose;

73 And I beheld the flamelets onward go,
Leaving behind themselves the air depicted,
And they of trailing pennons had the semblance,

76 So that it overhead remained distinct
With sevenfold lists, all of them of the colours
Whence the sun's bow is made, and Delia's girdle.

79 These standards to the rearward longer were
Than was my sight; and, as it seemed to
Ten paces were the outermost apart.

82 Under so fair a heaven as I describe
The four and twenty Elders, two by two,
Came on incoronate with flower-de-luce.

85 They all of them were singing: "Blessed thou
Among the daughters of Adam art, and blessed
For evermore shall be thy loveliness."

88 After the flowers and other tender grasses
In front of me upon the other margin
Were disencumbered of that race elect,

91 Even as in heaven star followeth after star,
There came close after them four animals,
Incoronate each one with verdant leaf.

94 Plumed with six wings was every one of them,
The plumage full of eyes; the eyes of Argus
If they were living would be such as these.

97 Reader! to trace their forms no more I waste
My rhymes; for other spendings press me so,
That I in this cannot be prodigal.

Under so fair a heaven as I describe
The four and twenty Elders, two by two,
Came on incoronate with flower-de-luce.

Gustave Doré

But read Ezekiel, who depicteth them
As he beheld them from the region cold
Coming with cloud, with whirlwind, and with fire;

And such as thou shalt find them in his pages,
Such were they here; saving that in their plumage
John is with me, and differeth from him.

The interval between these four contained
A chariot triumphal on two wheels,
Which by a Griffin's neck came drawn along;

And upward he extended both his wings
Between the middle list and three and three,
So that he injured none by cleaving it.

So high they rose that they were lost to sight;
His limbs were gold, so far as he was bird,
And white the others with vermilion mingled.

Not only Rome with no such splendid car
E'er gladdened Africanus, or Augustus,
But poor to it that of the Sun would be,—

That of the Sun, which swerving was burnt up
At the importunate orison of Earth,
When Jove was so mysteriously just.

Three maidens at the right wheel in a circle
Came onward dancing; one so very red
That in the fire she hardly had been noted.

The second was as if her flesh and bones
Had all been fashioned out of emerald;
The third appeared as snow but newly fallen.

And now they seemed conducted by the white,
Now by the red, and from the song of her
The others took their step, or slow or swift.

Upon the left hand four made holiday
Vested in purple, following the measure
Of one of them with three eyes in her head.

In rear of all the group here treated of

Two old men I beheld, unlike in habit,
But like in gait, each dignified and grave.

136 One showed himself as one of the disciples
Of that supreme Hippocrates, whom nature
Made for the animals she holds most dear;

139 Contrary care the other manifested,
With sword so shining and so sharp, it caused
Terror to me on this side of the river.

142 Thereafter four I saw of humble aspect,
And behind all an aged man alone
Walking in sleep with countenance acute.

145 And like the foremost company these seven
Were habited; yet of the flower-de-luce
No garland round about the head they wore,

148 But of the rose and other flowers vermilion;
At little distance would the sight have sworn
That all were in a flame above their brows.

151 And when the car was opposite to me
Thunder was heard; and all that folk august
Seemed to have further progress interdicted,

154 There with the vanward ensigns standing still.

Canto XXX

WHEN the Septentrion of the highest heaven
(Which never either setting knew or rising,
Nor veil of other cloud than that of sin,

4 And which made every one therein aware
Of his own duty, as the lower makes
Whoever turns the helm to come to port)

7 Motionless halted, the veracious people,
That came at first between it and the Griffin,
Turned themselves to the car, as to their peace.

10 And one of them, as if by Heaven commissioned,
Singing, "Veni, sponsa, de Libano"[22]
Shouted three times, and all the others after.

13 Even as the Blessed at the final summons
Shall rise up quickened each one from his cavern,
Uplifting light the reinvested flesh,

16 So upon that celestial chariot
A hundred rose 'ad vocem tanti senis,'[23]
Ministers and messengers of life eternal.

19 They all were saying, "Benedictus qui venis,"[24]
And, scattering flowers above and round about,
"Manibus o date lilia plenis."[25]

22 Ere now have I beheld, as day began,
The eastern hemisphere all tinged with rose,
And the other heaven with fair serene adorned;

25 And the sun's face, uprising, overshadowed
So that by tempering influence of vapours
For a long interval the eye sustained it;

28 Thus in the bosom of a cloud of flowers
Which from those hands angelical ascended,

---

22 "Come, my spouse, from Lebanon."

23 "At the voice of so great an elder."

24 "Blessed are you who come."

25 "O give lilies with full hands."

And downward fell again inside and out,

31 Over her snow-white veil with olive cinct
Appeared a lady under a green mantle,
Vested in colour of the living flame.

34 And my own spirit, that already now
So long a time had been, that in her presence
Trembling with awe it had not stood abashed,

37 Without more knowledge having by mine eyes,
Through occult virtue that from her proceeded
Of ancient love the mighty influence felt.

40 As soon as on my vision smote the power
Sublime, that had already pierced me through
Ere from my boyhood I had yet come forth,

43 To the left hand I turned with that reliance
With which the little child runs to his mother,
When he has fear, or when he is afflicted,

46 To say unto Virgilius: "Not a drachm
Of blood remains in me, that does not tremble;
I know the traces of the ancient flame."

49 But us Virgilius of himself deprived
Had left, Virgilius, sweetest of all fathers,
Virgilius, to whom I for safety gave me:

52 Nor whatsoever lost the ancient mother
Availed my cheeks now purified from dew,
That weeping they should not again be darkened.

55 "Dante, because Virgilius has departed
Do not weep yet, do not weep yet awhile;
For by another sword thou need'st must weep."

58 E'en as an admiral, who on poop and prow
Comes to behold the people that are working
In other ships. and cheers them to well-doing,

61 Upon the left hand border of the car,
When at the sound I turned of my own name,
Which of necessity is here recorded,

Over her snow-white veil with olive cinct
Appeared a lady under a green mantle,
Vested in colour of the living flame.

Gustave Doré

64 I saw the Lady, who erewhile appeared
Veiled underneath the angelic festival,
Direct her eyes to me across the river.

67 Although the veil, that from her head descended,
Encircled with the foliage of Minerva,
Did not permit her to appear distinctly,

70 In attitude still royally majestic
Continued she, like unto one who speaks,
And keeps his warmest utterance in reserve:

73 "Look at me well; in sooth I'm Beatrice!
How didst thou deign to come unto the Mountain?
Didst thou not know that man is happy here?"

76 Mine eyes fell downward into the clear fountain,
But, seeing myself therein, I sought the grass,
So great a shame did weigh my forehead down.

79 As to the son the mother seems superb,
So she appeared to me; for somewhat bitter
Tasteth the savour of severe compassion.

82 Silent became she, and the Angels sang
Suddenly, "In te, Domine, speravi":[26]
But beyond 'pedes meos'[27] did not pass.

85 Even as the snow among the living rafters
Upon the back of Italy congeals,
Blown on and drifted by Sclavonian winds,

88 And then, dissolving, trickles through itself
Whene'er the land that loses shadow breathes,
So that it seems a fire that melts a taper;

91 E'en thus was I without a tear or sigh,
Before the song of those who sing for ever
After the music of the eternal spheres.

94 But when I heard in their sweet melodies
Compassion for me, more than had they said,

26 "I put my trust in You, Lord."

27 "my feet"

"O wherefore, lady, dost thou thus upbraid him?"

The ice, that was about my heart congealed,
To air and water changed, and in my anguish
Through mouth and eyes came gushing from my breast.

She, on the right-hand border of the car
Still firmly standing, to those holy beings
Thus her discourse directed afterwards:

"Ye keep your watch in the eternal day,
So that nor night nor sleep can steal from you
One step the ages make upon their path;

Therefore my answer is with greater care,
That he may hear me who is weeping yonder,
So that the sin and dole be of one measure.

Not only by the work of those great wheels,
That destine every seed unto some end,
According as the stars are in conjunction,

But by the largess of celestial graces,
Which have such lofty vapours for their rain
That near to them our sight approaches not,

Such had this man become in his new life
Potentially, that every righteous habit
Would have made admirable proof in him;

But so much more malignant and more savage
Becomes the land untilled and with bad seed,
The more good earthly vigour it possesses.

Some time did I sustain him with my look;
Revealing unto him my youthful eyes,
I led him with me turned in the right way.

As soon as ever of my second age
I was upon the threshold and changed life,
Himself from me he took and gave to others.

When from the flesh to spirit I ascended,
And beauty and virtue were in me increased,
I was to him less dear and less delightful;

130 And into ways untrue he turned his steps,
Pursuing the false images of good,
That never any promises fulfil;

133 Nor prayer for inspiration me availed,
By means of which in dreams and otherwise
I called him back, so little did he heed them.

136 So low he fell, that all appliances
For his salvation were already short,
Save showing him the people of perdition.

139 For this I visited the gates of death,
And unto him, who so far up has led him,
My intercessions were with weeping borne.

142 God's lofty fiat would be violated,
If Lethe should be passed, and if such viands
Should tasted be, withouten any scot

145 Of penitence that gushes forth in tears."

Canto XXXI

"O THOU who art beyond the sacred river,"
Turning to me the point of her discourse,
That edgewise even had seemed to me so keen,

4 She recommenced, continuing without pause,
"Say, say if this be true; to such a charge,
Thy own confession needs must be conjoined."

7 My faculties were in so great confusion,
That the voice moved, but sooner was extinct
Than by its organs it was set at large.

10 Awhile she waited; then she said: "What thinkest?
Answer me; for the mournful memories
In thee not yet are by the waters injured."

13 Confusion and dismay together mingled
Forced such a Yes! from out my mouth, that sight

Was needful to the understanding of it.

16 Even as a cross-bow breaks, when 'tis discharged
Too tensely drawn the bowstring and the bow,
And with less force the arrow hits the mark,

19 So I gave way beneath that heavy burden,
Outpouring in a torrent tears and sighs,
And the voice flagged upon its passage forth.

22 Whence she to me: "In those desires of mine
Which led thee to the loving of that good,
Beyond which there is nothing to aspire to,

25 What trenches lying traverse or what chains
Didst thou discover, that of passing onward
Thou shouldst have thus despoiled thee of the hope?

28 And what allurements or what vantages
Upon the forehead of the others showed,
That thou shouldst turn thy footsteps unto them?"

31 After the heaving of a bitter sigh,
Hardly had I the voice to make response,
And with fatigue my lips did fashion it.

34 Weeping I said: "The things that present were
With their false pleasure turned aside my steps,
Soon as your countenance concealed itself."

37 And she: "Shouldst thou be silent, or deny
What thou confessest, not less manifest
Would be thy fault, by such a Judge 'tis known

40 But when from one's own cheeks comes bursting forth
The accusal of the sin, in our tribunal
Against the edge the wheel doth turn itself

43 But still, that thou mayst feel a greater shame
For thy transgression, and another time
Hearing the Sirens thou mayst be more strong,

46 Cast down the seed of weeping and attend;
So shalt thou hear, how in an opposite way
My buried flesh should have directed thee.

49 Never to thee presented art or nature
Pleasure so great as the fair limbs wherein
I was enclosed, which scattered are in earth.

52 And if the highest pleasure thus did fail thee
By reason of my death. What mortal thing
Should then have drawn thee into its desire?

55 Thou oughtest verily at the first shaft
Of things fallacious to have risen up
To follow me, who was no longer such.

58 Thou oughtest not to have stooped thy pinions downward
To wait for further blows, or little girl,
Or other vanity of such brief use.

61 The callow birdlet waits for two or three,
But to the eyes of those already fledged,
In vain the net is spread or shaft is shot."

64 Even as children silent in their shame
Stand listening with their eyes upon the ground,
And conscious of their fault, and penitent;

67 So was I standing; and she said: "If thou
In hearing sufferest pain, lift up thy beard
And thou shalt feel a greater pain in seeing."

70 With less resistance is a robust holm
Uprooted, either by a native wind
Or else by that from regions of Iarbas,

73 Than I upraised at her command my chin;
And when she by the beard the face demanded,
Well I perceived the venom of her meaning.

76 And as my countenance was lifted up,
Mine eye perceived those creatures beautiful
Had rested from the strewing of the flowers;

79 And, still but little reassured, mine eyes
Saw Beatrice turned round towards the monster,
That is one person only in two natures.

82 Beneath her veil, beyond the margent green,

She seemed to me far more her ancient self
To excel, than others here, when she was here.

85 So pricked me then the thorn of penitence,
That of all other things the one which turned me
Most to its love became the most my foe.

88 Such self-conviction stung me at the heart
O'erpowered I fell, and what I then became
She knoweth who had furnished me the cause.

91 Then, when the heart restored my outward sense,
The lady I had found alone, above me
I saw, and she was saying, "Hold me, hold me."

94 Up to my throat she in the stream had drawn me,
And, dragging me behind her, she was moving
Upon the water lightly as a shuttle.

97 When I was near unto the blessed shore,
"Asperges me," I heard so sweetly sung,
Remember it I cannot, much less write it

100 The beautiful lady opened wide her arms,
Embraced my head, and plunged me underneath,
Where I was forced to swallow of the water.

103 Then forth she drew me, and all dripping brought
Into the dance of the four beautiful,
And each one with her arm did cover me.

106 "We here are Nymphs, and in the Heaven are stars;
Ere Beatrice descended to the world,
We as her handmaids were appointed her.

109 We'll lead thee to her eyes; but for the pleasant
Light that within them is, shall sharpen thine
The three beyond, who more profoundly look."

112 Thus singing they began; and afterwards
Unto the Griffin's breast they led me with them,
Where Beatrice was standing, turned towards us.

115 "See that thou dost not spare thine eyes," they said;
"Before the emeralds have we stationed thee,

Whence Love aforetime drew for thee his weapons."

118 A thousand longings, hotter than the flame,
Fastened mine eyes upon those eyes relucent,
That still upon the Griffin steadfast stayed.

121 As in a glass the sun, not otherwise
Within them was the twofold monster shining,
Now with the one, now with the other nature.

124 Think, Reader, if within myself I marvelled,
When I beheld the thing itself stand still,
And in its image it transformed itself.

127 While with amazement filled and jubilant,
My soul was tasting of the food, that while
It satisfies us makes us hunger for it,

130 Themselves revealing of the highest rank
In bearing, did the other three advance,
Singing to their angelic saraband.

133 "Turn, Beatrice, O turn thy holy eyes,"
Such was their song, "unto thy faithful one,
Who has to see thee ta'en so many steps.

136 In grace do us the grace that thou unveil
Thy face to him, so that he may discern
The second beauty which thou dost conceal."

139 O splendour of the living light eternal!
Who underneath the shadow of Parnassus
Has grown so pale, or drunk so at its cistern,

142 He would not seem to have his mind encumbered
Striving to paint thee as thou didst appear,
Where the harmonious heaven o'ershadowed thee,

145 When in the open air thou didst unveil?

Canto XXXII

SO steadfast and attentive were mine eyes
In satisfying their decennial thirst,
That all my other senses were extinct,

4 And upon this side and on that they had
Walls of indifference, so the holy smile
Drew them unto itself with the old net

7 When forcibly my sight was turned away
Towards my left hand by those goddesses,
Because I heard from them a "Too intently!"

10 And that condition of the sight which is
In eyes but lately smitten by the sun
Bereft me of my vision some short while;

13 But to the less when sight re-shaped itself,
I say the less in reference to the greater
Splendour from which perforce I had withdrawn,

16 I saw upon its right wing wheeled about
The glorious host returning with the sun
And with the sevenfold flames upon their faces.

19 As underneath its shields, to save itself,
A squadron turns, and with its banner wheels,
Before the whole thereof can change its front,

22 That soldiery of the celestial kingdom
Which marched in the advance had wholly passed us
Before the chariot had turned its pole.

25 Then to the wheels the maidens turned themselves,
And the Griffin moved his burden benedight,
But so that not a feather of him fluttered.

28 The lady fair who drew me through the ford
Followed with Statius and myself the wheel
Which made its orbit with the lesser arc.

31 So passing through the lofty forest, vacant
By fault of her who in the serpent trusted,

Angelic music made our steps keep time.

34 Perchance as great a space had in three flights
An arrow loosened from the string o'erpassed,
As we had moved when Beatrice descended.

37 I heard them murmur altogether, "Adam!"
Then circled they about a tree despoiled
Of blooms and other leafage on each bough.

40 Its tresses, which so much the more dilate
As higher they ascend, had been by Indians
Among their forests marvelled at for height.

43 "Blessed art thou, O Griffin, who dost not
Pluck with thy beak these branches sweet to taste,
Since appetite by this was turned to evil."

46 After this fashion round the tree robust
The others shouted; and the twofold creature:
"Thus is preserved the seed of all the just."

49 And turning to the pole which he had dragged,
He drew it close beneath the widowed bough,
And what was of it unto it left bound.

52 In the same manner as our trees (when downward
Falls the great light, with that together mingled
Which after the celestial Lasca shines)

55 Begin to swell, and then renew themselves,
Each one with its own colour, ere the Sun
Harness his steeds beneath another star:

58 Less than of rose and more than violet
A hue disclosing, was renewed the tree
That had erewhile its boughs so desolate.

61 I never heard, nor here below is sung,
The hymn which afterward that people sang,
Nor did I bear the melody throughout.

64 Had I the power to paint how fell asleep
Those eyes compassionless, of Syrinx hearing,
Those eyes to which more watching cost so dear,

67 Even as a painter who from model paints
I would portray how I was lulled asleep;
He may, who well can picture drowsihood.

70 Therefore I pass to what time I awoke,
And say a splendour rent from me the veil
Of slumber, and a calling: "Rise, what dost thou?"

73 As to behold the apple-tree in blossom
Which makes the Angels greedy for its fruit,
And keeps perpetual bridals in the Heaven,

76 Peter and John and James conducted were,
And, overcome, recovered at the word
By which still greater slumbers have been broken,

79 And saw their school diminished by the loss
Not only of Elias, but of Moses,
And the apparel of their Master changed;

82 So I revived, and saw that piteous one
Above me standing, who had been conductress
Aforetime of my steps beside the river,

85 And all in doubt I said, "Where's Beatrice?"
And she: "Behold her seated underneath
The leafage new, upon the root of it.

88 Behold the company that circles her;
The rest behind the Griffin are ascending
With more melodious song, and more profound."

91 And if her speech were more diffuse I know not,
Because already in my sight was she
Who from the hearing of aught else had shut me.

94 Alone she sat upon the very earth,
Left there as guardian of the chariot
Which I had seen the biform monster fasten.

97 Encircling her, a cloister made themselves
The seven Nymphs, with those lights in their hands
Which are secure from Aquilon and Auster.

100 "Short while shalt thou be here a forester,

And thou shalt be with me for evermore
A citizen of that Rome where Christ is Roman.

103 Therefore, for that world's good which liveth ill,
Fix on the car thine eyes, and what thou seest.
Having returned to earth, take heed thou write."

106 Thus Beatrice; and I, who at the feet
Of her commandments all devoted was,
My mind and eyes directed where she willed.

109 Never descended with so swift a motion
Fire from a heavy cloud, when it is raining
From out the region which is most remote,

112 As I beheld the bird of Jove descend
Down through the tree, rending away the bark,
As well as blossoms and the foliage new,

115 And he with all his might the chariot smote,
Whereat it reeled, like vessel in a tempest
Tossed by the waves, now starboard and now larboard.

118 Thereafter saw I leap into the body
Of the triumphal vehicle a Fox,
That seemed unfed with any wholesome food.

121 But for his hideous sins upbraiding him,
My Lady put him to as swift a flight
As such a fleshless skeleton could bear.

124 Then by the way that it before had come,
Into the chariot's chest I saw the Eagle
Descend, and leave it feathered with his plumes.

127 And such as issues from a heart that mourns,
A voice from Heaven there issued, and it said:
"My little bark, how badly art thou freighted!"

130 Methought, then, that the earth did yawn between
Both wheels, and I saw rise from it a Dragon,
Who through the chariot upward fixed his tail,

133 And as a wasp that draweth back its sting,
Drawing unto himself his tail malign,

Drew out the floor, and went his way rejoicing

136 That which remained behind, even as with grass
A fertile region, with the feathers, offered
Perhaps with pure intention and benign,

139 Reclothed itself, and with them were reclothed
The pole and both the wheels so speedily,
A sigh doth longer keep the lips apart.

142 Transfigured thus the holy edifice
Thrust forward heads upon the parts of it,
Three on the pole and one at either corner.

145 The first were horned like oxen; but the four
Had but a single horn upon the forehead;
A monster such had never yet been seen!

148 Firm as a rock upon a mountain high,
Seated upon it, there appeared to me
A shameless whore, with eyes swift glancing round,

151 And, as if not to have her taken from him,
Upright beside her I beheld a giant;
And ever and anon they kissed each other.

154 But because she her wanton, roving eye
Turned upon me, her angry paramour
Did scourge her from her head unto her feet.

157 Then full of jealousy, and fierce with wrath,
He loosed the monster, and across the forest
Dragged it so far, he made of that alone

160 A shield unto the whore and the strange beast.

Canto XXXIII

"DEUS venerunt gentes,"[28] alternating
Now three, now four, melodious psalmody
The maidens in the midst of tears began;

4 And Beatrice, compassionate and sighing,
Listened to them with such a countenance,
That scarce more changed was Mary at the cross.

7 But when the other virgins place had given
For her to speak, uprisen to her feet
With colour as of fire, she made response:

10 "'Modicum, et non videbitis me;
Et iterum,' my sisters predilect,
'Modicum, et vos videbitis me.'"[29]

13 Then all the seven in front of her she placed;
And after her, by beckoning only, moved
Me and the lady and the sage who stayed.

16 So she moved onward; and I do not think
That her tenth step was placed upon the ground,
When with her eyes upon mine eyes she smote,

19 And with a tranquil aspect, "Come more quickly,"
To me she said, "that, if I speak with thee,
To listen to me thou mayst be well placed."

22 As soon as I was with her as I should be,
She said to me: "Why, brother, dost thou not
Venture to question now, in coming with me?"

25 As unto those who are too reverential,
Speaking in presence of superiors,
Who drag no living utterance to their teeth,

28 It me befell, that without perfect sound
Began I: "My necessity, Madonna,
You know, and that which thereunto is good."

---

28 "God came to the nations."

29 "A little while, and you will not see me; and again a little while, and you will see me."

And she to me: "Of fear and bashfulness
Henceforward I will have thee strip thyself,
So that thou speak no more as one who dreams.

Know that the vessel which the serpent broke
Was, and is not; but let him who is guilty
Think that God's vengeance does not fear a sop.

Without an heir shall not for ever be
The Eagle that left his plumes upon the car,
Whence it became a monster, then a prey;

For verily I see, and hence narrate it,
The stars already near to bring the time,
From every hindrance safe, and every bar,

Within which a Five-hundred, Ten, and Five,
One sent from God, shall slay the thievish woman
And that same giant who is sinning with her.

And peradventure my dark utterance,
Like Themis and the Sphinx, may less persuade thee,
Since, in their mode, it clouds the intellect;

But soon the facts shall be the Naiades
Who shall this difficult enigma solve,
Without destruction of the flocks and harvests.

Note thou; and even as by me are uttered
These words, so teach them unto those who live
That life which is a running unto death;

And bear in mind, whene'er thou writest them,
Not to conceal what thou hast seen the plant,
That twice already has been pillaged here.

Whoever pillages or shatters it,
With blasphemy of deed offendeth God,
Who made it holy for his use alone.

For biting that, in pain and in desire
Five thousand years and more the first-born soul
Craved Him, who punished in himself the bite.

Thy genius slumbers, if it deem it not

For special reason so pre-eminent
In height, and so inverted in its summit

67 And if thy vain imaginings had not been
Water of Elsa round about thy mind,
And Pyramus to the mulberry, their pleasure,

70 Thou by so many circumstances only
The justice of the interdict of God
Morally in the tree wouldst recognize.

73 But since I see thee in thine intellect
Converted into stone and stained with sin,
So that the light of my discourse doth daze thee,

76 I will too, if not written, at least painted,
Thou bear it back within thee, for the reason
That cinct with palm the pilgrim's staff is borne."

79 And I: "As by a signet is the wax
Which does not change the figure stamped upon it,
My brain is now imprinted by yourself;

82 But wherefore so beyond my power of sight
Soars your desirable discourse, that aye
The more I strive, so much the more I lose it?"

85 "That thou mayst recognize," she said, "the school
Which thou hast followed, and mayst see how far
Its doctrine follows after my discourse,

88 And mayst behold your path from the divine
Distant as far as separated is
From earth the heaven that highest hastens on."

91 Whence her I answered: "I do not remember
That ever I estranged myself from you,
Nor have I conscience of it that reproves me."

94 "And if thou art not able to remember,"
Smiling she answered, "recollect thee now
That thou this very day hast drunk of Lethe;

97 And if from smoke a fire may be inferred,
Such an oblivion clearly demonstrates

Some error in thy will elsewhere intent.

Truly from this time forward shall my words
Be naked, so far as it is befitting
To lay them open unto thy rude gaze."

And more coruscant and with slower steps
The sun was holding the meridian circle,
Which, with the point of view, shifts here and there

When halted (as he cometh to a halt,
Who goes before a squadron as its escort,
If something new he find upon his way)

The ladies seven at a dark shadow's edge,
Such as, beneath green leaves and branches black,
The Alp upon its frigid border wears.

In front of them the Tigris and Euphrates
Methought I saw forth issue from one fountain,
And slowly part, like friends, from one another.

"O light, O glory of the human race!
What stream is this which here unfolds itself
From out one source, and from itself withdraws?"

For such a prayer, 'twas said unto me, "Pray
Matilda that she tell thee;" and here answered,
As one does who doth free himself from blame,

The beautiful lady: "This and other things
Were told to him by me; and sure I am
The water of Lethe has not hid them from him."

And Beatrice: "Perhaps a greater care,
Which oftentimes our memory takes away,
Has made the vision of his mind obscure.

But Eunoe behold, that yonder rises;
Lead him to it, and, as thou art accustomed,
Revive again the half-dead virtue in him."

Like gentle soul, that maketh no excuse,
But makes its own will of another's will
As soon as by a sign it is disclosed,

133 Even so, when she had taken hold of me,
The beautiful lady moved, and unto Statius
Said, in her womanly manner, "Come with him."

136 If, Reader, I possessed a longer space
For writing it, I yet would sing in part
Of the sweet draught that ne'er would satiate me;

139 But inasmuch as full are all the leaves
Made ready for this second canticle,
The curb of art no farther lets me go.

142 From the most holy water I returned
Regenerate, in the manner of new trees
That are renewed with a new foliage,

145 Pure and disposed to mount unto the stars.

Paradiso

Canto I

THE glory of Him who moveth everything
Doth penetrate the universe, and shine
In one part more and in another less.

4 Within that heaven which most his light receives
Was I, and things beheld which to repeat
Nor knows, nor can, who from above descends;

7 Because in drawing near to its desire
Our intellect ingulphs itself so far,
That after it the memory cannot go.

10 Truly whatever of the holy realm
I had the power to treasure in my mind
Shall now become the subject of my song.

13 O good Apollo, for this last emprise
Make of me such a vessel of thy power
As giving the beloved laurel asks!

16 One summit of Parnassus hitherto
Has been enough for me, but now with both
I needs must enter the arena left.

19 Enter into my bosom, thou, and breathe
As at the time when Marsyas thou didst draw
Out of the scabbard of those limbs of his.

22 O power divine, lend'st thou thyself to me
So that the shadow of the blessed realm
Stamped in my brain I can make manifest,

25 Thou'lt see me come unto thy darling tree,

And crown myself thereafter with those leaves
Of which the theme and thou shall make me worthy.

28 So seldom, Father, do we gather them
For triumph or of Caesar or of Poet,
(The fault and shame of human inclinations,)

31 That the Peneian foliage should bring forth
Joy to the joyous Delphic deity,
When any one it makes to thirst for it.

34 A little spark is followed by great flame;
Perchance with better voices after me
Shall prayer be made that Cyrrha may respond!

37 To mortal men by passages diverse
Uprises the world's lamp; but by that one
Which circles four uniteth with three crosses,

40 With better course and with a better star
Conjoined it issues, and the mundane wax
Tempers and stamps more after its own fashion.

43 Almost that passage had made morning there
And evening here, and there was wholly white
That hemisphere, and black the other part,

46 When Beatrice towards the left-hand side
I saw turned round, and gazing at the sun;
Never did eagle fasten so upon it!

49 And even as a second ray is wont
To issue from the first and reascend,
Like to a pilgrim who would fain return,

52 Thus of her action, through the eyes infused
In my imagination, mine I made,
And sunward fixed mine eyes beyond our wont.

55 There much is lawful which is here unlawful
Unto our powers, by virtue of the place
Made for the human species as its own.

58 Not long I bore it, nor so little while
But I beheld it sparkle round about

Like iron that comes molten from the fire;

61 And suddenly it seemed that day to day
Was added, as if He who has the power
Had with another sun the heaven adorned.

64 With eyes upon the everlasting wheels
Stood Beatrice all intent, and I, on her
Fixing my vision from above removed,

67 Such at her aspect inwardly became
As Glaucus, tasting of the herb that made him
Peer of the other gods beneath the sea.

70 To represent transhumanise in words
Impossible were; the example, then, suffice
Him for whom Grace the experience reserves.

73 If I was merely what of me thou newly
Createdst, Love who governest the heaven,
Thou knowest, who didst lift me with thy light!

76 When now the wheel, which thou dost make eternal
Desiring thee, made me attentive to it
By harmony thou dost modulate and measure,

79 Then seemed to me so much of heaven enkindled
By the sun's flame, that neither rain nor river
E'er made a lake so widely spread abroad.

82 The newness of the sound and the great light
Kindled in me a longing for their cause,
Never before with such acuteness felt;

85 Whence she, who saw me as I saw myself,
To quiet in me my perturbed mind,
Opened her mouth, ere I did mine to ask,

88 And she began: "Thou makest thyself so dull
With false imagining, that thou seest not
What thou wouldst see if thou hadst shaken it.

91 Thou art not upon earth, as thou believest;
But lightning, fleeing its appropriate site,
Ne'er ran as thou, who thitherward returnest."

94 If of my former doubt I was divested
By these brief little words more smiled than spoken,
I in a new one was the more ensnared;

97 And said: "Already did I rest content
From great amazement; but am now amazed
In what way I transcend these bodies light."

100 Whereupon she, after a pitying sigh,
Her eyes directed tow'rds me with that look
A mother casts on a delirious child;

103 And she began: "All things whate'er they be
Have order among themselves, and this is form,
That makes the universe resemble God.

106 Here do the higher creatures see the footprints
Of the Eternal Power, which is the end
Whereto is made the law already mentioned.

109 In the order that I speak of are inclined
All natures, by their destinies diverse,
More or less near unto their origin;

112 Hence they move onward unto ports diverse
O'er the great sea of being; and each one
With instinct given it which bears it on.

115 This bears away the fire towards the moon;
This is in mortal hearts the motive power;
This binds together and unites the earth.

118 Nor only the created things that are
Without intelligence this bow shoots forth,
But those that have both intellect and love.

121 The Providence that regulates all this
Makes with its light the heaven forever quiet,
Wherein that turns which has the greatest haste.

124 And thither now, as to a site decreed,
Bears us away the virtue of that cord
Which aims its arrows at a joyous mark.

127 True is it, that as oftentimes the form

Accords not with the intention of the art,
Because in answering is matter deaf,

130 So likewise from this course doth deviate
Sometimes the creature, who the power possesses,
Though thus impelled, to swerve some other way,

133 (In the same wise as one may see the fire
Fall from a cloud,) if the first impetus
Earthward is wrested by some false delight.

136 Thou shouldst not wonder more, if well I judge,
At thine ascent, than at a rivulet
From some high mount descending to the lowland.

139 Marvel it would be in thee, if deprived
Of hindrance, thou wert seated down below,
As if on earth the living fire were quiet."

142 Thereat she heavenward turned again her face.

Canto II

O YE, who in some pretty little boat,
Eager to listen, have been following
Behind my ship, that singing sails along,

4 Turn back to look again upon your shores;
Do not put out to sea, lest peradventure,
In losing me, you might yourselves be lost.

7 The sea I sail has never yet been passed;
Minerva breathes, and pilots me Apollo,
And Muses nine point out to me the Bears.

10 Ye other few who have the neck uplifted
Betimes to th' bread of Angels upon which
One liveth here and grows not sated by it,

13 Well may you launch upon the deep salt-sea
Your vessel, keeping still my wake before you
Upon the water that grows smooth again.

16 Those glorious ones who unto Colchos passed
Were not so wonder-struck as you shall be,
When Jason they beheld a ploughman made!

19 The con-created and perpetual thirst
For the realm deiform did bear us on,
As swift almost as ye the heavens behold.

22 Upward gazed Beatrice, and I at her;
And in such space perchance as strikes a bolt
And flies, and from the notch unlocks itself,

25 Arrived I saw me where a wondrous thing
Drew to itself my sight; and therefore she
From whom no care of mine could be concealed,

28 Towards me turning, blithe as beautiful,
Said unto me: "Fix gratefully thy mind
On God, who unto the first star has brought us."

31 It seemed to me a cloud encompassed us,
Luminous, dense, consolidate and bright
As adamant on which the sun is striking.

34 Into itself did the eternal pearl
Receive us, even as water doth receive
A ray of light, remaining still unbroken.

37 If I was body, (and we here conceive not
How one dimension tolerates another,
Which needs must be if body enter body,)

40 More the desire should be enkindled in us
That essence to behold, wherein is seen
How God and our own nature were united.

43 There will be seen what we receive by faith,
Not demonstrated, but self-evident
In guise of the first truth that man believes.

46 I made reply: "Madonna, as devoutly
As most I can do I give thanks to Him
Who has removed me from the mortal world.

49 But tell me what the dusky spots may be

Upon this body, which below on earth
Make people tell that fabulous tale of Cain?"

52 Somewhat she smiled; and then, "If the opinion
Of mortals be erroneous," she said,
"Where'er the key of sense doth not unlock,

55 Certes, the shafts of wonder should not pierce thee
Now, forasmuch as, following the senses,
Thou seest that the reason has short wings.

58 But tell me what thou think'st of it thyself."
And I: "What seems to us up here diverse,
Is caused, I think, by bodies rare and dense."

61 And she: "Right truly shalt thou see immersed
In error thy belief, if well thou hearest
The argument that I shall make against it.

64 Lights many the eighth sphere displays to you
Which in their quality and quantity
May noted be of aspects different.

67 If this were caused by rare and dense alone,
One only virtue would there be in all
Or more or less diffused, or equally.

70 Virtues diverse must be perforce the fruits
Of formal principles; and these, save one,
Of course would by thy reasoning be destroyed.

73 Besides, if rarity were of this dimness
The cause thou askest, either through and through
This planet thus attenuate were of matter,

76 Or else, as in a body is apportioned
The fat and lean, so in like manner this
Would in its volume interchange the leaves.

79 Were it the former, in the sun's eclipse
It would be manifest by the shining through,
Of light, as through aught tenuous interfused.

82 This is not so; hence we must scan the other,
And if it chance the other I demolish,

Then falsified will thy opinion be.

But if this rarity go not through and through,
There needs must be a limit, beyond which
Its contrary prevents the further passing,

And thence the foreign radiance is reflected,
Even as a colour cometh back from glass,
The which behind itself concealeth lead.

Now thou wilt say the sunbeam shows itself
More dimly there than in the other parts,
By being there reflected farther back.

From this reply experiment will free thee
If e'er thou try it, which is wont to be
The fountain to the rivers of your arts.

Three mirrors shalt thou take, and two remove
Alike from thee, the other more remote
Between the former two shall meet thine eyes.

Turned towards these, cause that behind thy back
Be placed a light, illuming the three mirrors
And coming back to thee by all reflected.

Though in its quantity be not so ample
The image most remote, there shalt thou see
How it perforce is equally resplendent.

Now, as beneath the touches of warm rays
Naked the subject of the snow remains
Both of its former colour and its cold,

Thee thus remaining in thy intellect,
Will I inform with such a living light,
That it shall tremble in its aspect to thee.

Within the heaven of the divine repose
Revolves a body, in whose virtue lies
The being of whatever it contains.

The following heaven, that has so many eyes,
Divides this being by essences diverse,
Distinguished from it, and by it contained.

118 The other spheres, by various differences,
All the distinctions which they have within them
Dispose unto their ends and their effects.

121 Thus do these organs of the world proceed,
As thou perceivest now, from grade to grade
Since from above they take, and act beneath.

124 Observe me well, how through this place I come
Unto the truth thou wishest, that hereafter
Thou mayst alone know how to keep the ford.

127 The power and motion of the holy spheres,
As from the artisan the hammer's craft,
Forth from the blessed motors must proceed.

130 The heaven, which lights so manifold make fair,
From the Intelligence profound, which turns it,
The image takes, and makes of it a seal.

133 And even as the soul within your dust
Through members different and accommodated
To faculties diverse expands itself,

136 So likewise this Intelligence diffuses
Its virtue multiplied among the stars.
Itself revolving on its unity.

139 Virtue diverse doth a diverse alloyage
Make with the precious body that it quickens,
In which, as life in you, it is combined.

142 From the glad nature whence it is derived,
The mingled virtue through the body shines,
Even as gladness through the living pupil.

145 From this proceeds whate'er from light to light
Appeareth different, not from dense and rare:
This is the formal principle that produces,

148 According to its goodness, dark and bright."

Canto III

THAT Sun, which erst with love my bosom warmed,
Of beauteous truth had unto me discovered,
By proving and reproving, the sweet aspect.

4 And, that I might confess myself convinced
And confident, so far as was befitting,
I lifted more erect my head to speak.

7 But there appeared a vision, which withdrew me
So close to it, in order to be seen,
That my confession I remembered not.

10 Such as through polished and transparent glass,
Or waters crystalline and undisturbed,
But not so deep as that their bed be lost,

13 Come back again the outlines of our faces
So feeble, that a pearl on forehead white
Comes not less speedily unto our eyes;

16 Such saw I many faces prompt to speak,
So that I ran in error opposite
To that which kindled love 'twixt man and fountain.

19 As soon as I became aware of them,
Esteeming them as mirrored semblances,
To see of whom they were, mine eyes I turned,

22 And nothing saw, and once more turned them forward
Direct into the light of my sweet Guide,
Who smiling kindled in her holy eyes.

25 "Marvel thou not," she said to me, "because
I smile at this thy puerile[1] conceit,
Since on the truth it trusts not yet its foot,

28 But turns thee, as 'tis wont, on emptiness.
True substances are these which thou beholdest,
Here relegate for breaking of some vow.

31 Therefore speak with them, listen and believe;

1 Childishly silly and trivial.

For the true light, which giveth peace to them,
Permits them not to turn from it their feet."

And I unto the shade that seemed most wishful
To speak directed me, and I began,
As one whom too great eagerness bewilders:

"O well-created spirit, who in the rays
Of life eternal dost the sweetness taste
Which being untasted ne'er is comprehended.

Grateful 'twill be to me, if thou content me
Both with thy name and with your destiny."
Whereat she promptly and with laughing eyes:

"Our charity doth never shut the doors
Against a just desire, except as one
Who wills that all her court be like herself.

I was a virgin sister in the world;
And if thy mind doth contemplate me well,
The being more fair will not conceal me from thee,

But thou shalt recognise I am Piccarda,
Who, stationed here among these other blessed,
Myself am blessed in the slowest sphere.

All our affections, that alone inflamed
Are in the pleasure of the Holy Ghost,
Rejoice at being of his order formed;

And this allotment, which appears so low,
Therefore is given us, because our vows
Have been neglected and in some part void."

Whence I to her: "In your miraculous aspects
There shines I know not what of the divine,
Which doth transform you from our first conceptions.

Therefore I was not swift in my remembrance;
But what thou tellest me now aids me so,
That the refiguring is easier to me.

But tell me, ye who in this place are happy,
Are you desirous of a higher place,

To see more or to make yourselves more friends?"

First with those other shades she smiled a little;
Thereafter answered me so full of gladness,
She seemed to burn in the first fire of love:

"Brother, our will is quieted by virtue
Of charity, that makes us wish alone
For what we have, nor gives us thirst for more.

If to be more exalted we aspired,
Discordant would our aspirations be
Unto the will of Him who here secludes us;

Which thou shalt see finds no place in these circles,
If being in charity is needful here,
And if thou lookest well into its nature;

Nay, 'tis essential to this blest existence
To keep itself within the will divine,
Whereby our very wishes are made one;

So that, as we are station above station
Throughout this realm, to all the realm 'tis pleasing,
As to the King, who makes his will our will.

And his will is our peace; this is the sea
To which is moving onward whatsoever
It doth create, and all that nature makes."

Then it was clear to me how everywhere
In heaven is Paradise, although the grace
Of good supreme there rain not in one measure

But as it comes to pass, if one food sates,
And for another still remains the longing,
We ask for this, and that decline with thanks.

E'en thus did I, with gesture and with word,
To learn from her what was the web wherein
She did not ply the shuttle to the end.

"A perfect life and merit high in-heaven
A lady o'er us," said she, "by whose rule
Down in your world they vest and veil themselves,

100 That until death they may both watch and sleep
Beside that Spouse who every vow accepts
Which charity conformeth to his pleasure.

103 To follow her, in girlhood from the world
I fled, and in her habit shut myself,
And pledged me to the pathway of her sect.

106 Then men accustomed unto evil more
Than unto good, from the sweet cloister tore me;
God knows what afterward my life became.

109 This other splendour, which to thee reveals
Itself on my right side, and is enkindled
With all the illumination of our sphere,

112 What of myself I say applies to her;
A nun was she, and likewise from her head
Was ta'en the shadow of the sacred wimple.

115 But when she too was to the world returned
Against her wishes and against good usage,
Of the heart's veil she never was divested.

118 Of great Costanza this is the effulgence,
Who from the second wind of Suabia
Brought forth the third and latest puissance."

121 Thus unto me she spake, and then began
"Ave Maria" singing, and in singing
Vanished, as through deep water something heavy.

124 My sight, that followed her as long a time
As it was possible, when it had lost her
Turned round unto the mark of more desire,

127 And wholly unto Beatrice reverted;
But she such lightnings flashed into mine eyes,
That at the first my sight endured it not;

130 And this in questioning more backward made me.

Canto IV

BETWEEN two viands, equally removed
And tempting, a free man would die of hunger
Ere either he could bring unto his teeth.

4 So would a lamb between the ravenings
Of two fierce wolves stand fearing both alike;
And so would stand a dog between two does.

7 Hence, if I held my peace, myself I blame not,
Impelled in equal measure by my doubts,
Since it must be so, nor do I commend.

10 I held my peace; but my desire was painted
Upon my face, and questioning with that
More fervent far than by articulate speech.

13 Beatrice did as Daniel had done
Relieving Nebuchadnezzar from the wrath
Which rendered him unjustly merciless,

16 And said: "Well see I how attracteth thee
One and the other wish, so that thy care
Binds itself so that forth it does not breathe.

19 Thou arguest, if good will be permanent,
The violence of others, for what reason
Doth it decrease the measure of my merit?

22 Again for doubting furnish thee occasion
Souls seeming to return unto the stars,
According to the sentiment of Plato.

25 These are the questions which upon thy wish
Are thrusting equally; and therefore first
Will I treat that which hath the most of gall.

28 He of the Seraphim most absorbed in God,
Moses, and Samuel, and whichever John
Thou mayst select, I say, and even Mary,

31 Have not in any other heaven their seats,
Than have those spirits that just appeared to thee,

Nor of existence more or fewer years;

34 But all make beautiful the primal circle,
And have sweet life in different degrees,
By feeling more or less the eternal breath.

37 They showed themselves here, not because allotted
This sphere has been to them, but to give sign
Of the celestial which is least exalted.

40 To speak thus is adapted to your mind,
Since only through the sense it apprehendeth
What then it worthy makes of intellect.

43 On this account the Scripture condescends
Unto your faculties, and feet and hands
To God attributes, and means something else;

46 And Holy Church under an aspect human
Gabriel and Michael represent to you,
And him who made Tobias whole again.

49 That which Timceus argues of the soul
Doth not resemble that which here is seen,
Because it seems that as he speaks he thinks.

52 He says the soul unto its star returns,
Believing it to have been severed thence
Whenever nature gave it as a form.

55 Perhaps his doctrine is of other guise
Than the words sound, and possibly may be
With meaning that is not to be derided.

58 If he doth mean that to these wheels return
The honour of their influence and the blame,
Perhaps his bow doth hit upon some truth.

61 This principle ill understood once warped
The whole world nearly, till it went astray
Invoking Jove and Mercury and Mars.

64 The other doubt which doth disquiet thee
Less venom has, for its malevolence
Could never lead thee otherwhere from me.

That as unjust our justice should appear
In eyes of mortals, is an argument
Of faith, and not of sin heretical.

But still, that your perception may be able
To thoroughly penetrate this verity,
As thou desirest, I will satisfy thee.

If it be violence when he who suffers
Co-operates not with him who uses force,
These souls were not on that account excused;

For will is never quenched unless it will,
But operates as nature doth in fire
If violence a thousand times distort it.

Hence, if it yieldeth more or less, it seconds
The force; and these have done so, having power
Of turning back unto the holy place.

If their will had been perfect, like to that
Which Lawrence fast upon his gridiron held,
And Mutius made severe to his own hand,

It would have urged them back along the road
Whence they were dragged, as soon as they were free;
But such a solid will is all too rare.

And by these words, if thou hast gathered them
As thou shouldst do, the argument is refuted
That would have still annoyed thee many times.

But now another passage runs accross
Before thine eyes, and such that by thyself
Thou couldst not thread it ere thou wouldst be weary.

I have for certain put into thy mind
That soul beatified could never lie.
For it is near the primal Truth,

And then thou from Piccarda might'st have heard
Costanza kept affection for the veil,
So that she seemeth here to contradict me.

Many times, brother, has it come to pass,

That, to escape from peril, with reluctance
That has been done it was not right to do,

103 E'en as Alcaemon (who, being by his father
Thereto entreated, his own mother slew)
Not to lose pity pitiless became.

106 At this point I desire thee to remember
That force with will commingles, and they cause
That the offences cannot be excused.

109 Will absolute consenteth not to evil;
But in so far consenteth as it fears,
If it refrain, to fall into more harm.

112 Hence when Piccarda uses this expression,
She meaneth the will absolute, and I
The other, so that both of us speak truth."

115 Such was the flowing of the holy river
That issued from the fount whence springs all truth;
This put to rest my wishes one and all.

118 "O love of the first lover, O divine,"
Said I forthwith, "whose speech inundates me
And warms me so, it more and more revives me,

121 My own affection is not so profound
As to suffice in rendering grace for grace;
Let Him, who sees and can, thereto respond.

124 Well I perceive that never sated is
Our intellect unless the Truth illume it,
Beyond which nothing true expands itself.

127 It rests therein, as wild beast in his lair,
When it attains it; and it can attain it;
If not, then each desire would frustrate be.

130 Therefore springs up, in fashion of a shoot,
Doubt at the foot of truth; and this is nature,
Which to the top from height to height impels us.

133 This doth invite me, this assurance give me
With reverence, Lady, to inquire of you

Another true, which is obscure to me.

136 I wish to know if man can satisfy you
For broken vows with other good deeds, so
That in your balance they will not be light."

139 Beatrice gazed upon me with her eyes
Full of the sparks of love, and so divine,
That, overcome my power, I turned my back

142 And almost lost myself with eyes downcast.

Canto V

"IF in the heat of love I flame upon thee
Beyond the measure that on earth is seen,
So that the valour of thine eyes I vanquish,

4 Marvel thou not thereat; for this proceeds
From perfect sight, which as it apprehends
To the good apprehended moves its feet.

7 Well I perceive how is already shining
Into thine intellect the eternal light,
That only seen enkindles always love;

10 And if some other thing your love seduce,
'Tis nothing but a vestige of the same,
Ill understood, which there is shining through.

13 Thou fain wouldst know if with another service
For broken vow can such return be made
As to secure the soul from further claim."

16 This canto thus did Beatrice begin;
And as a man who breaks not off his speech,
Continued thus her holy argument:

19 "The greatest gift that in his largess God
Creating made, and unto his own goodness
Nearest conformed, and that which he doth prize

22 Most highly, is the freedom of the will,
Wherewith the creatures of intelligence
Both all and only were and are endowed.

25 Now wilt thou see, if thence thou reasonest,
The high worth of a vow, if it he made
O that when thou consentest God consents:

28 For, closing between God and man the compact,
A sacrifice is of this treasure made,
Such as I say, and made by its own act.

31 What can be rendered then as compensation?
Think'st thou to make good use of what thou'st offered,
With gains ill gotten thou wouldst do good deed.

34 Now art thou certain of the greater point;
But because Holy Church in this dispenses,
Which seems against the truth which I have shown thee,

37 Behoves thee still to sit awhile at table,
Because the solid food which thou hast taken
Requireth further aid for thy digestion.

40 Open thy mind to that which I reveal,
And fix it there within; for 'tis not knowledge,
The having heard without retaining it.

43 In the essence of this sacrifice two things
Convene together; and the one is that
Of which 'tis made, the other is the agreement.

46 This last for evermore is cancelled not
Unless complied with, and concerning this
With such precision has above been spoken.

49 Therefore it was enjoined upon the Hebrews
To offer still, though sometimes what was offered
Might be commuted, as thou ought'st to know.

52 The other, which is known to thee as matter,
May well indeed be such that one errs not
If it for other matter be exchanged.

55 But let none shift the burden on his shoulder

At his arbitrament, without the turning
Both of the white and of the yellow key;

58 And every permutation deem as foolish,
If in the substitute the thing relinquished,
As the four is in six, be not contained.

61 Therefore whatever thing has so great weight
In value that it drags down every balance,
Cannot be satisfied with other spending.

64 Let mortals never take a vow in jest;
Be faithful and not blind in doing that,
As Jephthah was in his first offering,

67 Whom more beseemed to say, 'I have done wrong,
Than to do worse by keeping; and as foolish
Thou the great leader of the Greeks wilt find,

70 Whence wept Iphigenia her fair face,
And made for her both wise and simple weep,
Who heard such kind of worship spoken of.'

73 Christians, be ye more serious in your movements;
Be ye not like a feather at each wind,
And think not every water washes you.

76 Ye have the Old and the New Testament,
And the Pastor of the Church who guideth you;
Let this suffice you unto your salvation.

79 If evil appetite cry aught else to you,
Be ye as men, and not as silly sheep,
So that the Jew among you may not mock you.

82 Be ye not as the lamb that doth abandon
Its mother's milk, and frolicsome and simple
Combats at its own pleasure with itself."

85 Thus Beatrice to me even as I write it;
Then all desireful turned herself again
To that part where the world is most alive.

88 Her silence and her change of countenance
Silence imposed upon my eager mind,

That had already in advance new questions;

91 And as an arrow that upon the mark
Strikes ere the bowstring quiet hath become,
So did we speed into the second realm.

94 My Lady there so joyful I beheld,
As into the brightness of that heaven she entered,
More luminous thereat the planet grew;

97 And if the star itself was changed and smiled,
What became I, who by my nature am
Exceeding mutable in every guise!

100 As, in a fish-pond which is pure and tranquil,
The fishes draw to that which from without
Comes in such fashion that their food they deem it;

103 So I beheld more than a thousand splendours
Drawing towards us, and in each was heard.
"Lo, this is she who shall increase our love."

106 And as each one was coming unto us,
Full of beatitude the shade was seen,
By the effulgence clear that issued from it.

109 Think, Reader, if what here is just beginning
No farther should proceed, how thou wouldst have
An agonizing need of knowing more;

112 And of thyself thou'lt see how I from these
Was in desire of hearing their conditions,
As they unto mine eyes were manifest.

115 "O thou well-born, unto whom Grace concedes
To see the thrones of the eternal triumph,
Or ever yet the warfare be abandoned

118 With light that through the whole of heaven is spread;
Kindled are we, and hence if thou desirest
To know of us, at thine own pleasure sate thee."

121 Thus by some one among those holy spirits
Was spoken, and by Beatrice: "Speak, speak
Securely, and believe them even as Gods."

124 "Well I perceive how thou dost nest thyself
In thine own light, and drawest it from thine eyes,
Because they coruscate when thou dost smile,

127 But know not who thou art, nor why thou hast,
Spirit august, thy station in the sphere
That veils itself to men in alien rays."

130 This said I in direction of the light
Which first had spoken to me; whence it became
By far more lucent than it was before.

133 Even as the sun, that doth conceal himself
By too much light, when heat has worn away
The tempering influence of the vapours dense,

136 By greater rapture thus concealed itself
In its own radiance the figure saintly,
And thus close, close enfolded answered me

139 In fashion as the following canto sings.

Canto VI

"AFTER that Constantine the eagle turned
Against the course of heaven, which it had followed
Behind the ancient who Lavinia took,

4 Two hundred years and more the bird of God
In the extreme of Europe held itself,
Near to the mountains whence it issued first;

7 And under shadow of the sacred plumes
It governed there the world from hand to hand,
And, changing thus, upon mine own alighted.

10 Caesar I was, and am Justinian,
Who, by the will of primal Love I feel,
Took from the laws the useless and redundant;

13 And ere unto the work I was attent,
One nature to exist in Christ, not more,

Believed, and with such faith was I contented.

16 But blessed Agapetus, he who was
The supreme pastor, to the faith sincere
Pointed me out the way by words of his.

19 Him I believed, and what was his assertion
I now see clearly, even as thou seest
Each contradiction to be false and true.

22 As soon as with the Church I moved my feet,
God in his grace it pleased with this high task
To inspire me, and I gave me wholly to it,

25 And to my Belisarius I commended
The arms, to which was heaven's right hand so joined
It was a signal that I should repose.

28 Now here to the first question terminates
My answer; but the character thereof
Constrains me to continue with a sequel,

31 In order that thou see with how great reason
Men move against the standard sacrosanct,
Both who appropriate and who oppose it.

34 Behold how great a power has made it worthy
Of reverence, beginning from the hour
When Pallas died to give it sovereignty.

37 Thou knowest it made in Alba its abode
Three hundred years and upward, till at last
The three to three fought for it yet again.

40 Thou knowest what it achieved from Sabine wrong
Down to Lucretia's sorrow, in seven kings
O'ercoming round about the neighboring nations;

43 Thou knowest what it achieved, borne by the Romans
Illustrious against Brennus, against Pyrrhus,
Against the other princes and confederates.

46 Torquatus thence and Quinctius, who from locks
Unkempt was named, Decii and Fabii,
Received the fame I willingly embalm;

It struck to earth the pride of the Arabians,
Who, following Hannibal, had passed across
The Alpine ridges, Po, from which thou glidest;

Beneath it triumphed while they yet were young
Pompey and Scipio, and to the hill
Beneath which thou wast born it bitter seemed;

Then, near unto the time when heaven had willed
To bring the whole world to its mood serene,
Did Caesar by the will of Rome assume it.

What it achieved from Var unto the Rhine,
Isere beheld and Saone, beheld the Seine,
And every valley whence the Rhone is filled;

What it achieved when it had left Ravenna,
And leaped the Rubicon, was such a flight
That neither tongue nor pen could follow it.

Round towards Spain it wheeled its legions;
Towards Durazzo, and Pharsalia smote
That to the calid Nile was felt the pain.

Antandros and the Simois, whence it started,
It saw again, and there where Hector lies,
And ill for Ptolemy then roused itself.

From thence it came like lightning upon Juba;
Then wheeled itself again into your West,
Where the Pompeian clarion it heard.

From what it wrought with the next standard-bearer
Brutus and Cassius howl in Hell together,
And Modena and Perugia dolent were;

Still doth the mournful Cleopatra weep
Because thereof, who, fleeing from before it,
Took from the adder sudden and black death.

With him it ran even to the Red Sea shore;
With him it placed the world in so great peace,
That unto Janus was his temple closed.

But what the standard that has made me speak

Achieved before, and after should achieve
Throughout the mortal realm that lies beneath it,

85 Becometh in appearance mean and dim,
If in the hand of the third Caesar seen
With eye unclouded and affection pure,

88 Because the living Justice that inspires me
Granted it, in the hand of him I speak of,
The glory of doing vengeance for its wrath.

91 Now here attend to what I answer thee;
Later it ran with Titus to do vengeance
Upon the vengeance of the ancient sin.

94 And when the tooth of Lombardy had bitten
The Holy Church, then underneath its wings
Did Charlemagne victorious succor her.

97 Now hast thou power to judge of such as those
Whom I accused above, and of their crimes,
Which are the cause of all your miseries.

100 To the public standard one the yellow lilies
Opposes, the other claims it for a party,
So that 'tis hard to see which sins the most.

103 Let, let the Ghibellines ply their handicraft
Beneath some other standard; for this ever
Ill follows he who it and justice parts.

106 And let not this new Charles e'er strike it down,
He and his Guelfs, but let him fear the talons
That from a nobler lion stripped the fell.

109 Already oftentimes the sons have wept
The father's crime; and let him not believe
That God will change His scutcheon for the lilies.

112 This little planet doth adorn itself
With the good spirits that have active been,
That fame and honour might come after them;

115 And whensoever the desires mount thither,
Thus deviating, must perforce the rays

Of the true love less vividly mount upward.

118 But in commensuration of our wages
With our desert is portion of our joy,
Because we see them neither less nor greater.

121 Herein doth living Justice sweeten so
Affection in us, that for evermore
It cannot warp to any iniquity.

124 Voices diverse make up sweet melodies
So in this life of ours the seats diverse
Render sweet harmony among these spheres;

127 And in the compass of this present pearl
Shineth the sheen of Romeo, of whom
The grand and beauteous work was ill rewarded.

130 But the Provencals who against him wrought,
They have not laughed, and therefore ill goes he
Who makes his hurt of the good deeds of others.

133 Four daughters, and each one of them a queen,
Had Raymond Berenger, and this for him
Did Romeo, a poor man and a pilgrim;

136 And then malicious words incited him
To summon to a reckoning this just man,
Who rendered to him seven and five for ten.

139 Then he departed poor and stricken in years,
And if the world could know the heart he had,
In begging bit by bit his livelihood,

142 Though much it laud him, it would laud him more."

Canto VII

"OSANNA sanctus Deus Sabaoth,
Superillustrans claritate tua
Felices ignes horum malahoth!"[2]

4 In this wise, to his melody returning,
This substance, upon which a double light
Doubles itself, was seen by me to sing,

7 And to their dance this and the others moved,
And in the manner of swift-hurrying sparks
Veiled themselves from me with a sudden distance.

10 Doubting was I, and saying, "Tell her, tell her,"
Within me, "tell her," saying, "tell my Lady,"
Who slakes my thirst with her sweet effluences;

13 And yet that reverence which doth lord it over
The whole of me only by B and ICE,
Bowed me again like unto one who drowses.

16 Short while did Beatrice endure me thus;
And she began, lighting me with a smile
Such as would make one happy in the fire:

19 "According to infallible advisement,
After what manner a just vengeance justly
Could be avenged has put thee upon thinking,

22 But I will speedily thy mind unloose;
And do thou listen, for these words of mine
Of a great doctrine will a present make thee.

25 By not enduring on the power that wills
Curb for his good, that man who ne'er was born,
Damning himself damned all his progeny;

28 Whereby the human species down below
Lay sick for many centuries in great error,
Till to descend it pleased the Word of God

31 To where the nature, which from its own Maker

2 "Hosanna to the Holy God of Hosts, illuminating by your brilliance the happy fires of these realms."

Estranged itself, he joined to him in person
By the sole act of his eternal love.

34 Now unto what is said direct thy sight;
This nature when united to its Maker,
Such as created, was sincere and good;

37 But by itself alone was banished forth
From Paradise, because it turned aside
Out of the way of truth and of its life.

40 Therefore the penalty the cross held out,
If measured by the nature thus assumed,
None ever yet with so great justice stung,

43 And none was ever of so great injustice,
Considering who the Person was that suffered,
Within whom such a nature was contracted.

46 From one act therefore issued things diverse;
To God and to the Jews one death was pleasing;
Earth trembled at it and the Heaven was opened.

49 It should no longer now seem difficult
To thee, when it is said that a just vengeance
By a just court was afterward avenged.

52 But now do I behold thy mind entangled
From thought to thought within a knot, from which
With great desire it waits to free itself

55 Thou sayest, 'Well discern I what I hear;
But it is hidden from me why God willed
For our redemption only this one mode.'

58 Buried remaineth, brother, this decree
Unto the eyes of every one whose nature
Is in the flame of love not yet adult.

61 Verily, inasmuch as at this mark
One gazes long and little is discerned,
Wherefore this mode was worthiest will I say.

64 Goodness Divine, which from itself doth spurn
All envy, burning in itself so sparkles
That the eternal beauties it unfolds.

67 Whate'er from this immediately distils
Has afterwards no end, for ne'er removed
Is its impression when it sets its seal.

70 Whate'er from this immediately rains down
Is wholly free, because it is not subject
Unto the influences of novel things.

73 The more conformed thereto, the more it pleases;
For the blest ardour that irradiates all things
In that most like itself is most vivacious.

76 With all of these things has advantaged been
The human creature; and if one be wanting,
From his nobility he needs must fall.

79 'Tis sin alone which doth disfranchise him,
And render him unlike the Good Supreme,
So that he little with its light is blanched,

82 And to his dignity no more returns,
Unless he fill up where transgression empties
With righteous pains for criminal delights.

85 Your nature when it sinned so utterly
In its own seed. out of these dignities
Even as out of Paradise was driven,

88 Nor could itself recover, if thou notest
With nicest subtilty, by any way,
Except by passing one of these two fords:

91 Either that God through clemency alone
Had pardon granted, or that man himself
Had satisfaction for his folly made.

94 Fix now thine eye deep into the abyss
Of the eternal counsel, to my speech
As far as may be fastened steadfastly!

97 Man in his limitations had not power
To satisfy, not having power to sink
In his humility obeying then,

100 Far as he disobeying thought to rise;

And for this reason man has been from power
Of satisfying by himself excluded.

103 Therefore it God behoved in his own ways
Man to restore unto his perfect life
I say in one, or else in both of them.

106 But since the action of the doer is
So much more grateful, as it more presents
The goodness of the heart from which it issues,

109 Goodness Divine, that doth imprint the world,
Has been contented to proceed by each
And all its ways to lift you up again;

112 Nor 'twixt the first day and the final night
Such high and such magnificent proceeding
By one or by the other was or shall be;

115 For God more bounteous was himself to give
To make man able to uplift himself,
Than if he only of himself had pardoned;

118 And all the other modes were insufficient
For justice, were it not the Son of God
Himself had humbled to become incarnate.

121 Now, to fill fully each desire of thine,
Return I to elucidate one place,
In order that thou there mayst see as I do.

124 Thou sayst: 'I see the air, I see the fire,
The water, and the earth, and all their mixtures
Come to corruption, and short while endure;

127 And these things notwithstanding were created;'
Therefore if that which I have said were true,
They should have been secure against corruption.

130 The Angels, brother, and the land sincere
In which thou art, created may be called
Just as they are in their entire existence;

133 But all the elements which thou hast named,
And all those things which out of them are made,

By a created virtue are informed.

136 Created was the matter which they have;
Created was the informing influence
Within these stars that round about them go.

139 The soul of every brute and of the plants
By its potential temperament attracts
The ray and motion of the holy lights;

142 But your own life immediately inspires
Supreme Beneficence, and enamours it
So with herself, it evermore desires her.

145 And thou from this mayst argue furthermore
Your resurrection, if thou think again
How human flesh was fashioned at that time

148 When the first parents both of them were made."

Canto VIII

THE world used in its peril to believe
That the fair Cypria delirious love
Rayed out, in the third epicycle turning;

4 Wherefore not only unto her paid honour
Of sacrifices and of votive cry
The ancient nations in the ancient error,

7 But both Dione honoured they and Cupid,
That as her mother, this one as her son,
And said that he had sat in Dido's lap;

10 And they from her, whence I beginning take,
Took the denomination of the star
That woos the sun, now following, now in front.

13 I was not ware of our ascending to it;
But of our being in it gave full faith
My Lady whom I saw more beauteous grow.

16 And as within a flame a spark is seen,
And as within a voice a voice discerned,
When one is steadfast, and one comes and goes,

19 Within that light beheld I other lamps
Move in a circle, speeding more and less,
Methinks in measure of their inward vision.

22 From a cold cloud descended never winds,
Or visible or not, so rapidly
They would not laggard and impeded seem

25 To any one who had those lights divine
Seen come towards us, leaving the gyration
Begun at first in the high Seraphim.

28 And behind those that most in front appeared
Sounded "Osanna!" so that never since
To hear again was I without desire.

31 Then unto us more nearly one approached,
And it alone began: "We all are ready
Unto thy pleasure, that thou joy in us.

34 We turn around with the celestial Princes,
One gyre and one gyration and one thirst,
To whom thou in the world of old didst say,

37 'Ye who, intelligent, the third heaven are moving;'
And are so full of love, to pleasure thee
A little quiet will not be less sweet."

40 After these eyes of mine themselves had offered
Unto my Lady reverently, and she
Content and certain of herself had made them,

43 Back to the light they turned, which so great promise
Made of itself, and "Say, who art thou?" was
My voice, imprinted with a great affection.

46 O how and how much I beheld it grow
With the new joy that superadded was
Unto its joys, as soon as I had spoken!

49 Thus changed, it said to me: "The world possessed me

Short time below; and, if it had been more,
Much evil will be which would not have been.

52 My gladness keepeth me concealed from thee,
Which rayeth round about me, and doth hide me
Like as a creature swathed in its own silk.

55 Much didst thou love me, and thou hadst good reason;
For had I been below, I should have known thee
Somewhat beyond the foliage of my love.

58 That left-hand margin, which doth bathe itself
In Rhone, when it is mingled with the Sorgue,
Me for its lord awaited in due time,

61 And that horn of Ausonia, which is towned
With Bari, with Gaeta and Catona,
Whence Tronto and Verde in the sea disgorge.

64 Already flashed upon my brow the crown
Of that dominion which the Danube waters
After the German borders it abandons;

67 And beautiful Trinacria, that is murky
'Twixt Pachino and Peloro, (on the gulf
Which greatest scath from Eurus doth receive,)

70 Not through Typhoeus, but through nascent sulphur,
Would have awaited her own monarchs still,
Through me from Charles descended and from Rudolph,

73 If evil lordship, that exasperates ever
The subject populations, had not moved
Palermo to the outcry of 'Death! death!'

76 And if my brother could but this foresee,
The greedy poverty of Catalonia
Straight would he flee, that it might not molest him;

79 For verily 'tis needful to provide,
Through him or other, so that on his bark
Already freighted no more freight be placed.

82 His nature, which from liberal covetous
Descended, such a soldiery would need

As should not care for hoarding in a chest."

85 "Because I do believe the lofty joy
Thy speech infuses into me, my Lord,
Where every good thing doth begin and end

88 Thou seest as I see it, the more grateful
Is it to me; and this too hold I dear,
That gazing upon God thou dost discern it.

91 Glad hast thou made me; so make clear to me,
Since speaking thou hast stirred me up to doubt,
How from sweet seed can bitter issue forth."

94 This I to him; and he to me: "If I
Can show to thee a truth, to what thou askest
Thy face thou'lt hold as thou dost hold thy back.

97 The Good which all the realm thou art ascending
Turns and contents, maketh its providence
To be a power within these bodies vast

100 And not alone the natures are foreseen
Within the mind that in itself is perfect,
But they together with their preservation.

103 For whatsoever thing this bow shoots forth
Falls foreordained unto an end foreseen,
Even as a shaft directed to its mark.

106 If that were not, the heaven which thou dost walk
Would in such manner its effects produce,
That they no longer would be arts, but ruins.

109 This cannot be, if the Intelligences
That keep these stars in motion are not maimed,
And maimed the First that has not made them perfect.

112 Wilt thou this truth have clearer made to thee?"
And I: "Not so; for 'tis impossible
That nature tire, I see, in what is needful."

115 Whence he again: "Now say, would it be worse
For men on earth were they not citizens?"
"Yes," I replied; "and here I ask no reason."

"And can they be so, if below they live not
Diversely unto offices diverse?
No, if your master writeth well for you."

So came he with deductions to this point;
Then he concluded: "Therefore it behoves
The roots of your effects to be diverse.

Hence one is Solon born, another Xerxes,
Another Melchisedec, and another he
Who, flying through the air, his son did lose.

Revolving Nature, which a signet is
To mortal wax, doth practise well her art,
But not one inn distinguish from another;

Thence happens it that Esau differeth
In seed from Jacob; and Quirinus comes
From sire so vile that he is given to Mars.

A generated nature its own way
Would always make like its progenitors,
If Providence divine were not triumphant.

Now that which was behind thee is before thee;
But that thou know that I with thee am pleased,
With a corollary will I mantle thee.

Evermore nature, if it fortune find
Discordant to it, like each other seed
Out of its region, maketh evil thrift;

And if the world below would fix its mind
On the foundation which is laid by nature,
Pursuing that, 'twould have the people good.

But you unto religion wrench aside
Him who was born to gird him with the sword,
And make a king of him who is for sermons;

Therefore your footsteps wander from the road."

Canto IX

BEAUTIFUL Clemence, after that thy Charles
Had me enlightened, he narrated to me
The treacheries his seed should undergo;

4 But said: "Be still and let the years roll round;"
So I can only say, that lamentation
Legitimate shall follow on your wrongs.

7 And of that holy light the life already
Had to the Sun which fills it turned again,
As to that good which for each thing sufficeth.

10 Ah, souls deceived, and creatures impious,
Who from such good do turn away your hearts,
Directing upon vanity your foreheads!

13 And now, behold, another of those splendours
Approached me, and its will to pleasure me
It signified by brightening outwardly.

16 The eyes of Beatrice, that fastened were
Upon me, as before, of dear assent
To my desire assurance gave to me.

19 "Ah, bring swift compensation to my wish,
Thou blessed spirit," I said, "and give me proof
That what I think in thee I can reflect!"

22 Whereat the light, that still was new to me,
Out of its depths, whence it before was singing,
As one delighted to do good, continued:

25 "Within that region of the land depraved
Of Italy, that lies between Rialto
And fountain heads of Brenta and of Piava,

28 Rises a hill, and mounts not very high,
Wherefrom descended formerly a torch
That made upon that region great assault.

31 Out of one root were born both I and it;
Cunizza was I called, and here I shine

Because the splendour of this star o'ercame me.

34 But gladly to myself the cause I pardon
Of my allotment, and it does not grieve me,
Which would perhaps seem strong unto your vulgar.

37 Of this so luculent and precious jewel,
Which of our heaven is nearest unto me,
Great fame remained; and ere it die away

40 This hundredth year shall yet quintupled be.
See if man ought to make him excellent,
So that another life the first may leave!

43 And thus thinks not the present multitude
Shut in by Adige and Tagliamento,
Nor yet for being scourged is penitent.

46 But soon 'twill be that Padua in the marsh
Will change the water that Vicenza bathes,
Because the folk are stubborn against duty;

49 And where the Sile and Cagnano join
One lordeth it, and goes with lofty head,
For catching whom e'en now the net is making.

52 Feltro moreover of her impious pastor
Shall weep the crime, which shall so monstrous be
That for the like none ever entered Malta.

55 Ample exceedingly would be the vat
That of the Ferrarese could hold the blood,
And weary who should weigh it ounce by ounce,

58 Of which this courteous priest shall make a gift
To show himself a partisan; and such gifts
Will to the living of the land conform.

61 Above us there are mirrors, thrones you call them,
From which shines out on us God Judicant,
So that this utterance seems good to us."

64 Here it was silent, and it had the semblance
Of being turned elsewhither, by the wheel
On which it entered as it was before.

67 The other joy, already known to me,
Became a thing transplendent in my sight,
As a fine ruby smitten by the sun.

70 Through joy effulgence is acquired above,
As here a smile; but down below, the shade
Outwardly darkens, as the mind is sad.

73 "God seeth all things, and in Him, blest spirit,
Thy sight is," said I, "so that never will
Of his can possibly from thee be hidden;

76 Thy voice, then, that for ever makes the heavens
Glad, with the singing of those holy fires
Which of their six wings make themselves a cowl,

79 Wherefore does it not satisfy my longings?
Indeed, I would not wait thy questioning
If I in thee were as thou art in me."

82 "The greatest of the valleys where the water
Expands itself," forthwith its words began,
"That sea excepted which the earth engarlands,

85 Between discordant shores against the sun
Extends so far, that it meridian makes
Where it was wont before to make the horizon.

88 I was a dweller on that valley's shore
'Twixt Ebro and Magra that with journey short
Doth from the Tuscan part the Genoese.

91 With the same sunset and same sunrise nearly
Sit Buggia and the city whence I was,
That with its blood once made the harbour hot.

94 Folco that people called me unto whom
My name was known; and now with me this heaven
Imprints itself, as I did once with it;

97 For more the daughter of Belus never burned,
Offending both Sichaeus and Creusa,
Than I, so long as it became my locks,

100 Nor yet that Rodophean, who deluded

Was by Demophoon, nor yet Alcides,
When Iole he in his heart had locked.

103 Yet here is no repenting, but we smile,
Not at the fault, which comes not back to mind,
But at the power which ordered and foresaw.

106 Here we behold the art that doth adorn
With such affection, and the good discover
Whereby the world above turns that below.

109 But that thou wholly satisfied mayst bear
Thy wishes hence which in this sphere are born,
Still farther to proceed behoveth me.

112 Thou fain wouldst know who is within this light
That here beside me thus is scintillating,
Even as a sunbeam in the limpid water.

115 Then know thou, that within there is at rest
Rahab, and being to our order joined,
With her in its supremest grade 'tis sealed.

118 Into this heaven, where ends the shadowy cone
Cast by your world, before all other souls
First of Christ's triumph was she taken up.

121 Full meet it was to leave her in some heaven,
Even as a palm of the high victory
Which he acquired with one palm and the other,

124 Because she favoured the first glorious deed
Of Joshua upon the Holy Land,
That little stirs the memory of the Pope.

127 Thy city, which an offshoot is of him
Who first upon his Maker turned his back,
And whose ambition is so sorely wept,

130 Brings forth and scatters the accursed flower
Which both the sheep and lambs hath led astray
Since it has turned the shepherd to a wolf.

133 For this the Evangel and the mighty Doctors
Are derelict, and only the Decretals

So studied that it shows upon their margins.

136 On this are Pope and Cardinals intent;
Their meditations reach not Nazareth,
There where his pinions Gabriel unfolded

139 But Vatican and the other parts elect
Of Rome, which have a cemetery been
Unto the soldiery that followed Peter

142 Shall soon be free from this adultery."

Canto X

LOOKING into his Son with all the Love
Which each of them eternally breathes forth
The Primal and unutterable Power

4 Whate'er before the mind or eye revolves
With so much order made, there can be none
Who this beholds without enjoying Him.

7 Lift up then, Reader, to the lofty wheels
With me thy vision straight unto that part
Where the one motion on the other strikes,

10 And there begin to contemplate with joy
That Master's art, who in himself so loves it
That never doth his eye depart therefrom.

13 Behold how from that point goes branching off
The oblique circle, which conveys the planets,
To satisfy the world that calls upon them

16 And if their pathway were not thus inflected,
Much virtue in the heavens would be in vain,
And almost every power below here dead.

19 If from the straight line distant more or less
Were the departure, much would wanting be
Above and underneath of mundane order.

22 Remain now, Reader, still upon thy bench,
In thought pursuing that which is foretasted,
If thou wouldst jocund be instead of weary.

25 I've set before thee; henceforth feed thyself,
For to itself diverteth all my care
That theme whereof I have been made the scribe.

28 The greatest of the ministers of nature,
Who with the power of heaven the world imprints
And measures with his light the time for us,

31 With that part which above is called to mind
Conjoined, along the spirals was revolving,
Where each time earlier he presents himself

34 And I was with him; but of the ascending
I was not conscious, saving as a man
Of a first thought is conscious ere it come;

37 And Beatrice, she who is seen to pass
From good to better, and so suddenly
That not by time her action is expressed,

40 How lucent in herself must she have been!
And what was in the sun, wherein I entered,
Apparent not by colour but by light,

43 I, though I call on genius, art, and practice,
Cannot so tell that it could be imagined;
Believe one can, and let him long to see it.

46 And if our fantasies too lowly are
For altitude so great, it is no marvel,
Since o'er the sun was never eye could go.

49 Such in this place was the fourth family
Of the high Father, who forever sates it,
Showing how he breathes forth and how begets.

52 And Beatrice began: "Give thanks, give thanks
Unto the Sun of Angels, who to this
Sensible one has raised thee by his grace!"

55 Never was heart of mortal so disposed

To worship, nor to give itself to God
With all its gratitude was it so ready,

58 As at those words did I myself become;
And all my love was so absorbed in Him,
That in oblivion Beatrice was eclipsed.

61 Nor this displeased her; but she smiled at it
So that the splendour of her laughing eyes
My single mind on many things divided.

64 Lights many saw I, vivid and triumphant,
Make us a centre and themselves a circle,
More sweet in voice than luminous in aspect.

67 Thus girt about the daughter of Latona
We sometimes see, when pregnant is the air,
So that it holds the thread which makes her zone.

70 Within the court of Heaven, whence I return,
Are many jewels found, so fair and precious
They cannot be transported from the realm;

73 And of them was the singing of those lights.
Who takes not wings that he may fly up thither,
The tidings thence may from the dumb await!

76 As soon as singing thus those burning suns
Had round about us whirled themselves three times,
Like unto stars neighbouring the steadfast poles,

79 Ladies they seemed, not from the dance released,
But who stop short, in silence listening
Till they have gathered the new melody.

82 And within one I heard beginning: "When
The radiance of grace, by which is kindled
True love, and which thereafter grows by loving,

85 Within thee multiplied is so resplendent
That it conducts thee upward by that stair,
Where without reascending none descends,

88 Who should deny the wine out of his vial
Unto thy thirst, in liberty were not

Except as water which descends not seaward.

91 Fain wouldst thou know with what plants is enflowered
This garland that encircles with delight
The Lady fair who makes thee strong for heaven.

94 Of the lambs was I of the holy flock
Which Dominic conducteth by a road
Where well one fattens if he strayeth not.

97 He who is nearest to me on the right
My brother and master was; and he Albertus
Is of Cologne, I Thomas of Aquinum.

100 If thou of all the others wouldst be certain,
Follow behind my speaking with thy sight
Upward along the blessed garland turning.

103 That next effulgence issues from the smile
Of Gratian, who assisted both the courts
In such wise that it pleased in Paradise.

106 The other which near by adorns our choir
That Peter was who, e'en as the poor widow,
Offered his treasure unto Holy Church.

109 The fifth light, that among us is the fairest,
Breathes forth from such a love, that all the world
Below is greedy to learn tidings of it.

112 Within it is the lofty mind, where knowledge
So deep was put, that, if the true be true,
To see so much there never rose a second.

115 Thou seest next the lustre of that taper,
Which in the flesh below looked most within
The angelic nature and its ministry.

118 Within that other little light is smiling
The advocate of the Christian centuries,
Out of whose rhetoric Augustine was furnished.

121 Now if thou trainest thy mind's eye along
From light to light pursuant of my praise,
With thirst already of the eighth thou waitest.

By seeing every good therein exults
The sainted soul, which the fallacious world
Makes manifest to him who listeneth well;

The body whence 'twas hunted forth is lying
Down in Cieldauro, and from martyrdom
And banishment it came unto this peace.

See farther onward flame the burning breath
Of Isidore, of Beda, and of Richard
Who was in contemplation more than man.

This, whence to me returneth thy regard,
The light is of a spirit unto whom
In his grave meditations death seemed slow.

It is the light eternal of Sigier,
Who, reading lectures in the Street of Straw,
Did syllogize invidious verities."

Then, as a horologe[3] that calleth us
What time the Bride of God is rising up
With matins to her Spouse that he may love her,

Wherein one part the other draws and urges,
Ting! ting! resounding with so sweet a note,
That swells with love the spirit well disposed,

Thus I beheld the glorious wheel move round,
And render voice to voice, in modulation
And sweetness that can not be comprehended,

Excepting there where joy is made eternal.

---

3 A timepiece.

Canto XI

O THOU insensate care of mortal men,
How inconclusive are the syllogisms
That make thee beat thy wings in downward flight!

One after laws and one to aphorisms
Was going, and one following the priesthood,
And one to reign by force or sophistry,

And one in theft, and one in state affairs,
One in the pleasures of the flesh involved
Wearied himself, one gave himself to ease;

When I, from all these things emancipate,
With Beatrice above there in the Heavens
With such exceeding glory was received!

When each one had returned unto that point
Within the circle where it was before,
It stood as in a candlestick a candle;

And from within the effulgence which at first
Had spoken unto me, I heard begin
Smiling while it more luminous became:

“Even as I am kindled in its ray,
So, looking into the Eternal Light,
The occasion of thy thoughts I apprehend.

Thou doubtest, and wouldst have me to resift
In language so extended and so open
My speech, that to thy sense it may be plain,

Where just before I said, ‘where well one fattens,’
And where I said, ‘there never rose a second’;
And here ’tis needful we distinguish well.

The Providence, which governeth the world
With counsel, wherein all created vision
Is vanquished ere it reach unto the bottom,

(So that towards her own Beloved might go
The bride of Him who, uttering a loud cry,

Espoused her with his consecrated blood,

34 Self-confident and unto Him more faithful,)
Two Princes did ordain in her behoof,
Which on this side and that might be her guide.

37 The one was all seraphical in ardour;
The other by his wisdom upon earth
A splendour was of light cherubical.

40 One will I speak of, for of both is spoken
In praising one, whichever may be taken,
Because unto one end their labours were.

43 Between Tupino and the stream that falls
Down from the hill elect of blessed Ubald,
A fertile slope of lofty mountain hangs,

46 From which Perugia feels the cold and heat
Through Porta Sole, and behind it weep
Gualdo and Nocera their grievous yoke.

49 From out that slope, there where it breaketh most
Its steepness, rose upon the world a sun
As this one does sometimes from out the Ganges;

52 Therefore let him who speaketh of that place,
Say not Ascesi, for he would say little,
But Orient, if he properly would speak.

55 He was not yet far distant from his rising
Before he had begun to make the earth
Some comfort from his mighty virtue feel.

58 For he in youth his father's wrath incurred
For certain Dame, to whom, as unto death,
The gate of pleasure no one doth unlock;

61 And was before his spiritual court
'Et coram patre'[4] unto her united;
Then day by day more fervently he loved her.

64 She, reft of her first husband, scorned, obscure,
One thousand and one hundred years and more,

4 "In the presence of his father."

Waited without a suitor till he came.

67 Naught it availed to hear, that with Amyclas
Found her unmoved at sounding of his voice
He who struck terror into all the world;

70 Naught it availed being constant and undaunted,
So that, when Mary still remained below,
She mounted up with Christ upon the cross?

73 But that too darkly I may not proceed,
Francis and Poverty for these two lovers
Take thou henceforward in my speech diffuse.

76 Their concord and their joyous semblances,
The love, the wonder, and the sweet regard,
They made to be the cause of holy thoughts;

79 So much so that the venerable Bernard
First bared his feet, and after so great peace
Ran, and, in running, thought himself too slow.

82 O wealth unknown! O veritable good!
Giles bares his feet, and bares his feet Sylvester
Behind the bridegroom, so doth please the bride!

85 Then goes his way that father and that master,
He and his Lady and that family
Which now was girding on the humble cord;

88 Nor cowardice of heart weighed down his brow
At being son of Peter Bernardone,
Nor for appearing marvellously scorned;

91 But regally his hard determination
To Innocent he opened, and from him
Received the primal seal upon his Order.

94 After the people mendicant increased
Behind this man, whose admirable life
Better in glory of the heavens were sung,

97 Incoronated with a second crown
Was through Honorius by the Eternal Spirit
The holy purpose of this Archimandrite.

100 And when he had, through thirst of martyrdom,
In the proud presence of the Sultan preached
Christ and the others who came after him,

103 And, finding for conversion too unripe
The folk, and not to tarry there in vain,
Returned to fruit of the Italic grass,

106 On the rude rock 'twixt Tiber and the Arno
From Christ did he receive the final seal,
Which during two whole years his members bore.

109 When He, who chose him unto so much good,
Was pleased to draw him up to the reward
That he had merited by being lowly,

112 Unto his friars, as to the rightful heirs,
His most dear Lady did he recommend,
And bade that they should love her faithfully;

115 And from her bosom the illustrious soul
Wished to depart, returning to its realm,
And for its body wished no other bier.

118 Think now what man was he, who was a fit
Companion over the high seas to keep
The bark of Peter to its proper bearings.

121 And this man was our Patriarch; hence whoever
Doth follow him as he commands can see
That he is laden with good merchandise.

124 But for new pasturage his flock has grown
So greedy, that it is impossible
They be not scattered over fields diverse;

127 And in proportion as his sheep remote
And vagabond go farther off from him,
More void of milk return they to the fold.

130 Verily some there are that fear a hurt,
And keep close to the shepherd; but so few,
That little cloth doth furnish forth their hoods.

133 Now if my utterance be not indistinct,

If thine own hearing hath attentive been,
If thou recall to mind what I have said,

136 In part contented shall thy wishes be;
For thou shalt see the plant that's chipped away,
And the rebuke that lieth in the words,

139 'Where well one fattens, if he strayeth not.'"

Canto XII

SOON as the blessed flame had taken up
The final word to give it utterance,
Began the holy millstone to revolve,

4 And in its gyre had not turned wholly round,
Before another in a ring enclosed it,
And motion joined to motion, song to song;

7 Song that as greatly doth transcend our Muses,
Our Sirens, in those dulcet clarions,
As primal splendour that which is reflected.

10 And as are spanned athwart a tender cloud
Two rainbows parallel and like in colour,
When Juno to her handmaid gives command,

13 (The one without born of the one within,
Like to the speaking of that vagrant one
Whom love consumed as doth the sun the vapours,)

16 And make the people here, through covenant
God set with Noah, presageful of the world
That shall no more be covered with a flood,

19 In such wise of those sempiternal roses
The garlands twain encompassed us about,
And thus the outer to the inner answered.

22 After the dance, and other grand rejoicings,
Both of the singing, and the flaming forth
Effulgence with effulgence blithe and tender,

In such wise of those sempiternal roses
The garlands twain encompassed us about,
And thus the outer to the inner answered.

Gustave Doré

25 Together, at once, with one accord had stopped,
(Even as the eyes, that, as volition moves them,
Must needs together shut and lift themselves,)

28 Out of the heart of one of the new lights
There came a voice, that needle to the star
Made me appear in turning thitherward.

31 And it began: "The love that makes me fair
Draws me to speak about the other leader,
By whom so well is spoken here of mine.

34 'Tis right, where one is, to bring in the other,
That, as they were united in their warfare,
Together likewise may their glory shine.

37 The soldiery of Christ, which it had cost
So dear to arm again, behind the standard
Moved slow and doubtful and in numbers few,

40 When the Emperor who reigneth evermore
Provided for the host that was in peril,
Through grace alone and not that it was worthy;

43 And, as was said, he to his Bride brought succour
With champions twain, at whose deed, at whose word
The straggling people were together drawn.

46 Within that region where the sweet west wind
Rises to open the new leaves, wherewith
Europe is seen to clothe herself afresh,

49 Not far off from the beating of the waves,
Behind which in his long career the sun
Sometimes conceals himself from every man,

52 Is situate the fortunate Calahorra,
Under protection of the mighty shield
In which the Lion subject is and sovereign.

55 Therein was born the amorous paramour
Of Christian Faith, the athlete consecrate,
Kind to his own and cruel to his foes;

58 And when it was created was his mind

Replete with such a living energy,
That in his mother her it made prophetic.

As soon as the espousals were complete
Between him and the Faith at holy font,
Where they with mutual safety dowered each

The woman, who for him had given assent,
Saw in a dream the admirable fruit
That issue would from him and from his heirs;

And that he might be construed as he was,
A spirit from this place went forth to name him
With His possessive whose he wholly was.

Dominic was he called; and him I speak of
Even as of the husbandman whom Christ
Elected to his garden to assist him.

Envoy and servant sooth he seemed of Christ,
For the first love made manifest in him
Was the first counsel that was given by Christ.

Silent and wakeful many a time was he
Discovered by his nurse upon the ground,
As if he would have said, 'For this I came.'

O thou his father, Felix verily!
O thou his mother, verily Joanna,
If this, interpreted, means as is said!

Not for the world which people toil for now
In following Ostiense and Taddeo,
But through his longing after the true manna,

He in short time became so great a teacher,
That he began to go about the vineyard,
Which fadeth soon, if faithless be the dresser;

And of the See, (that once was more benignant
Unto the righteous poor, not through itself,
But him who sits there and degenerates,)

Not to dispense or two or three for six,
Not any fortune of first vacancy,

'Non decimas quae sunt pauperum Dei,'[5]

94 He asked for, but against the errant world
Permission to do battle for the seed,
Of which these four and twenty plants surround.

97 Then with the doctrine and the will together,
With office apostolical he moved,
Like torrent which some lofty vein out-presses;

100 And in among the shoots heretical
His impetus with greater fury smote,
Wherever the resistance was the greatest.

103 Of him were made thereafter divers runnels,
Whereby the garden catholic is watered,
So that more living its plantations stand.

106 If such the one wheel of the Biga was,
In which the Holy Church itself defended
And in the field its civic battle won,

109 Truly full manifest should be to thee
The excellence of the other, unto whom
Thomas so courteous was before my coming.

112 But still the orbit, which the highest part
Of its circumference made, is derelict,
So that the mould is where was once the crust.

115 His family, that had straight forward moved
With feet upon his footprints, are turned round
So that they set the point upon the heel.

118 And soon aware they will be of the harvest
Of this bad husbandry, when shall the tares
Complain the granary is taken from them.

121 Yet say I, he who searcheth leaf by leaf
Our volume through, would still some page discover
Where he could read, 'I am as I am wont.'

124 'Twill not be from Casal nor Acquasparta,
From whence come such unto the written word

5 "Do not tithe the things of the poor of God."

That one avoids it, and the other narrows.

Bonaventura of Bagnoregio's life
Am I, who always in great offices
Postponed considerations sinister.

Here are Illuminato and Agostino,
Who of the first barefooted beggars were
That with the cord the friends of God became.

Hugh of Saint Victor is among them here,
And Peter Mangiador, and Peter of Spain,
Who down below in volumes twelve is shining;

Nathan the seer, and metropolitan
Chrysostom, and Anselmus, and Donatus
Who deigned to lay his hand to the first art;

Here is Rabanus, and beside me here
Shines the Calabrian Abbot Joachim,
He with the spirit of prophecy endowed.

To celebrate so great a paladin
Have moved me the impassioned courtesy
And the discreet discourses of Friar Thomas,

And with me they have moved this company."

Canto XIII

LET him imagine, who would well conceive
What now I saw, and let him while I speak
Retain the image as a steadfast rock,

4 The fifteen stars, that in their divers regions
The sky enliven with a light so great
That it transcends all clusters of the air;

7 Let him the Wain imagine unto which
Our vault of heaven sufficeth night and day,
So that in turning of its pole it fails not;

10 Let him the mouth imagine of the horn
That in the point beginneth of the axis
Round about which the primal wheel revolves,—

13 To have fashioned of themselves two signs in heaven,
Like unto that which Minos' daughter made,
The moment when she felt the frost of death;

16 And one to have its rays within the other,
And both to whirl themselves in such a manner
That one should forward go, the other backward;

19 And he will have some shadowing forth of that
True constellation and the double dance
That circled round the point at which I was;

22 Because it is as much beyond our wont,
As swifter than the motion of the Chiana
Moveth the heaven that all the rest outspeeds.

25 There sang they neither Bacchus, nor Apollo,
But in the divine nature Persons three,
And in one person the divine and human.

28 The singing and the dance fulfilled their measure,
And unto us those holy lights gave need,
Growing in happiness from care to care.

31 Then broke the silence of those saints concordant
The light in which the admirable life

Of God's own mendicant was told to me,

And said: "Now that one straw is trodden out
Now that its seed is garnered up already,
Sweet love invites me to thresh out the other.

Into that bosom, thou believest, whence
Was drawn the rib to form the beauteous cheek
Whose taste to all the world is costing dear,

And into that which, by the lance transfixed,
Before and since, such satisfaction made
That it weighs down the balance of all sin,

Whate'er of light it has to human nature
Been lawful to possess was all infused
By the same power that both of them created;

And hence at what I said above dost wonder,
When I narrated that no second had
The good which in the fifth light is enclosed.

Now ope thine eyes to what I answer thee,
And thou shalt see thy creed and my discourse
Fit in the truth as centre in a circle.

That which can die, and that which dieth not,
Are nothing but the splendour of the idea
Which by his love our Lord brings into being

Because that living Light, which from its fount
Effulgent flows, so that it disunites not
From Him nor from the Love in them intrined,

Through its own goodness reunites its rays
In nine subsistences, as in a mirror,
Itself eternally remaining One.

Thence it descends to the last potencies,
Downward from act to act becoming such
That only brief contingencies it makes;

And these contingencies I hold to be
Things generated, which the heaven produces
By its own motion, with seed and without.

Neither their wax, nor that which tempers it,
Remains immutable, and hence beneath
The ideal signet more and less shines through;

Therefore it happens, that the selfsame tree
After its kind bears worse and better fruit,
And ye are born with characters diverse.

If in perfection tempered were the wax,
And were the heaven in its supremest virtue,
The brilliance of the seal would all appear;

But nature gives it evermore deficient,
In the like manner working as the artist,
Who has the skill of art and hand that trembles.

If then the fervent Love, the Vision clear,
Of primal Virtue do dispose and seal,
Perfection absolute is there acquired.

Thus was of old the earth created worthy
Of all and every animal perfection;
And thus the Virgin was impregnate made;

So that thine own opinion I commend,
That human nature never yet has been,
Nor will be, what it was in those two persons.

Now if no farther forth I should proceed,
'Then in what way was he without a peer?'
Would be the first beginning of thy words.

But, that may well appear what now appears not,
Think who he was, and what occasion moved him
To make request, when it was told him, 'Ask.'

I've not so spoken that thou canst not see
Clearly he was a king who asked for wisdom,
That he might be sufficiently a king;

'Twas not to know the number in which are
The motors here above, or if 'necesse'
With a contingent e'er 'necesse' make,

'Non si est dare primum motum esse,'[6]

6 "If there is no first movement."

Or if in semicircle can be made
Triangle so that it have no right angle.

103 Whence, if thou notest this and what I said,
A regal prudence is that peerless seeing
In which the shaft of my intention strikes

106 And if on 'rose' thou turnest thy clear eyes,
Thou'lt see that it has reference alone
To kings who're many, and the good are rare.

109 With this distinction take thou what I said,
And thus it can consist with thy belief
Of the first father and of our Delight.

112 And lead shall this be always to thy feet,
To make thee, like a weary man, move slowly
Both to the Yes and No thou seest not;

115 For very low among the fools is he
Who affirms without distinction, or denies,
As well in one as in the other case;

118 Because it happens that full often bends
Current opinion in the false direction,
And then the feelings bind the intellect.

121 Far more than uselessly he leaves the shore,
(Since he returneth not the same he went,)
Who fishes for the truth, and has no skill;

124 And in the world proofs manifest thereof
Parmenides, Melissus, Brissus are,
And many who went on and knew not whither;

127 Thus did Sabellius, Arius, and those fools
Who have been even as swords unto the Scriptures
In rendering distorted their straight faces.

130 Nor yet shall people be too confident
In judging, even as he is who doth count
The corn in field or ever it be ripe.

133 For I have seen all winter long the thorn
First show itself intractable and fierce,

And after bear the rose upon its top;

136 And I have seen a ship direct and swift
Run o'er the sea throughout its course entire,
To perish at the harbour's mouth at last.

139 Let not Dame Bertha nor Ser Martin think,
Seeing one steal, another offering make,
To see them in the arbitrament divine;

142 For one may rise, and fall the other may."

Canto XIV

FROM centre unto rim, from rim to centre,
In a round vase the water moves itself,
As from without 'tis struck or from within.

4 Into my mind upon a sudden dropped
What I am saying, at the moment when
Silent became the glorious life of Thomas,

7 Because of the resemblance that was born
Of his discourse and that of Beatrice,
Whom, after him, it pleased thus to begin:

10 "This man has need (and does not tell you so,
Nor with the voice, nor even in his thought)
Of going to the root of one truth more.

13 Declare unto him if the light wherewith
Blossoms your substance shall remain with you
Eternally the same that it is now;

16 And if it do remain, say in what manner,
After ye are again made visible,
It can be that it injure not your sight."

19 As by a greater gladness urged and drawn
They who are dancing in a ring sometimes
Uplift their voices and their motions quicken;

22 So, at that orison devout and prompt,
The holy circles a new joy displayed
In their revolving and their wondrous song.

25 Whoso lamenteth him that here we die
That we may live above, has never there
Seen the refreshment of the eternal rain.

28 The One and Two and Three who ever liveth,
And reigneth ever in Three and Two and One,
Not circumscribed and all things circumscribing,

31 Three several times was chanted by each one
Among those spirits, with such melody
That for all merit it were just reward;

34 And, in the lustre most divine of all
The lesser ring, I heard a modest voice,
Such as perhaps the Angel's was to Mary,

37 Answer: "As long as the festivity
Of Paradise shall be, so long our love
Shall radiate round about us such a vesture.

40 Its brightness is proportioned to the ardour,
The ardour to the vision; and the vision
Equals what grace it has above its worth.

43 When, glorious and sanctified, our flesh
Is reassumed, then shall our persons be
More pleasing by their being all complete;

46 For will increase whate'er bestows on us
Of light gratuitous the Good Supreme,
Light which enables us to look on Him;

49 Therefore the vision must perforce increase,
Increase the ardour which from that is kindled,
Increase the radiance which from this proceeds.

52 But even as a coal that sends forth flame,
And by its vivid whiteness overpowers it
So that its own appearance it maintains,

55 Thus the effulgence that surrounds us now

Shall be o'erpowered in aspect by the flesh,
Which still to-day the earth doth cover up;

58 Nor can so great a splendour weary us,
For strong will be the organs of the body
To everything which hath the power to please us."

61 So sudden and alert appeared to me
Both one and the other choir to say Amen,
That well they showed desire for their dead bodies;

64 Nor sole for them perhaps, but for the mothers,
The fathers, and the rest who had been dear
Or ever they became eternal flames.

67 And lo! all round about of equal brightness
Arose a lustre over what was there,
Like an horizon that is clearing up.

70 And as at rise of early eve begin
Along the welkin new appearances,
So that the sight seems real and unreal,

73 It seemed to me that new subsistences
Began there to be seen, and make a circle
Outside the other two circumferences.

76 O very sparkling of the Holy Spirit,
How sudden and incandescent it became
Unto mine eyes, that vanquished bore it not!

79 But Beatrice so beautiful and smiling
Appeared to me, that with the other sights
That followed not my memory I must leave her.

82 Then to uplift themselves mine eyes resumed
The power, and I beheld myself translated
To higher salvation with my Lady only.

85 Well was I ware that I was more uplifted
By the enkindled smiling of the star,
That seemed to me more ruddy than its wont.

88 With all my heart, and in that dialect
Which is the same in all, such holocaust

To God I made as the new grace beseemed;

91 And not yet from my bosom was exhausted
The ardour of sacrifice, before I knew
This offering was accepted and auspicious;

94 For with so great a lustre and so red
Splendours appeared to me in twofold rays,
I said: "O Helios who dost so adorn them!"

97 Even as distinct with less and greater lights
Glimmers between the two poles of the world
The Galaxy that maketh wise men doubt,

100 Thus constellated in the depths of Mars,
Those rays described the venerable sign
That quadrants joining in a circle make.

103 Here doth my memory overcome my genius;
For on that cross as levin gleamed forth Christ,
So that I cannot find ensample worthy;

106 But he who takes his cross and follows Christ
Again will pardon me what I omit,
Seeing in that aurora lighten Christ.

109 From horn to horn, and 'twixt the top and base,
Lights were in motion, brightly scintillating
As they together met and passed each other;

112 Thus level and aslant and swift and slow
We here behold, renewing still the sight,
The particles of bodies long and short,

115 Across the sunbeam move, wherewith is listed
Sometimes the shade, which for their own defence
People with cunning and with art contrive.

118 And as a lute and harp, accordant strung
With many strings, a dulcet tinkling make
To him by whom the notes are not distinguished,

121 So from the lights that there to me appeared
Upgathered through the cross a melody,
Which rapt me, not distinguishing the hymn.

124 Well was I ware it was of lofty laud,
Because there came to me, "Arise and conquer!"
As unto him who hears and comprehends not.

127 So much enamoured I became therewith,
That until then there was not anything
That e'er had fettered me with such sweet bonds.

130 Perhaps my word appears somewhat too bold,
Postponing the delight of those fair eyes,
Into which gazing my desire has rest;

133 But who bethinks him that the living seals
Of every beauty grow in power ascending,
And that I there had not turned round to those,

136 Can me excuse, if I myself accuse
To excuse myself, and see that I speak truly:
For here the holy joy is not disclosed,

139 Because ascending it becomes more pure.

Canto XV

A WILL benign, in which reveals itself
Ever the love that righteously inspires,
As in the iniquitous, cupidity,

4 Silence imposed upon that dulcet lyre,
And quieted the consecrated chords,
That Heaven's right hand doth tighten and relax.

7 How unto just entreaties shall be deaf
Those substances, which, to give me desire
Of praying them, with one accord grew silent?

10 'Tis well that without end he should lament,
Who for the love of thing that doth not last
Eternally despoils him of that love!

13 As through the pure and tranquil evening air
There shoots from time to time a sudden fire,

Moving the eyes that steadfast were before,

16 And seems to be a star that changeth place,
Except that in the part where it is kindled
Nothing is missed, and this endureth little;

19 So from the horn that to the right extends
Unto that cross's foot there ran a star
Out of the constellation shining there;

22 Nor was the gem dissevered from its ribbon,
But down the radiant fillet ran along,
So that fire seemed it behind alabaster.

25 Thus piteous did Anchises' shade reach forward,
If any faith our greatest Muse deserve,
When in Elysium he his son perceived.

28 "O sanguis meus, O super infusa
Gratia Dei, sicut tibi, cui
Bis unquam Coeli janua reclusa?"[7]

31 Thus that effulgence; whence I gave it heed;
Then round unto my Lady turned my sight,
And on this side and that was stupefied;

34 For in her eyes was burning such a smile
That with mine own methought I touched the bottom
Both of my grace and of my Paradise!

37 Then, pleasant to the hearing and the sight,
The spirit joined to its beginning things
I understood not, so profound it spake;

40 Nor did it hide itself from me by choice,
But by necessity; for its conception
Above the mark of mortals set itself

43 And when the bow of burning sympathy
Was so far slackened, that its speech descended
Towards the mark of our intelligence,

46 The first thing that was understood by me

7 "Oh blood of mine, O grace of God poured down from above, to whom, as to you, shall the gates of heaven have ever been opened twice?"

Was "Benedight be Thou, O Trine and One,
Who hast unto my seed so courteous been!"

49 And it continued: "Hunger long and grateful,
Drawn from the reading of the mighty volume
Wherein is never changed the white nor dark,

52 Thou hast appeased, my son, within this light
In which I speak to thee, by grace of her
Who to this lofty flight with plumage clothed thee.

55 Thou thinkest that to me thy thought doth pass
From Him who is the first, as from the unit,
If that be known, ray out the five and six;

58 And therefore who I am thou askest not,
And why I seem more joyous unto thee
Than any other of this gladsome crowd.

61 Thou think'st the truth; because the small and great
Of this existence look into the mirror
Wherein, before thou think'st, thy thought thou showest.

64 But that the sacred love, in which I watch
With sight perpetual, and which makes me thirst
With sweet desire, may better be fulfilled,

67 Now let thy voice secure and frank and glad
Proclaim the wishes, the desire proclaim,
To which my answer is decreed already."

70 To Beatrice I turned me, and she heard
Before I spake, and smiled to me a sign,
That made the wings of my desire increase;

73 Then in this wise began I: "Love and knowledge,
When on you dawned the first Equality,
Of the same weight for each of you became;

76 For in the Sun, which lighted you and burned
With heat and radiance, they so equal are,
That all similitudes are insufficient.

79 But among mortals will and argument,
For reason that to you is manifest,

Diversely feathered in their pinions are.

82 Whence I, who mortal am, feel in myself
This inequality; so give not thanks
Save in my heart, for this paternal welcome.

85 Truly do I entreat thee, living topaz!
Set in this precious jewel as a gem,
That thou wilt satisfy me with thy name."

88 "O leaf of mine, in whom I pleasure took
E'en while awaiting, I was thine own root!"
Such a beginning he in answer made me,

91 Then said to me: "That one from whom is named
Thy race, and who a hundred years and more
Has circled round the mount on the first cornice,

94 A son of mine and thy great-grandsire was;
Well it behoves thee that the long fatigue
Thou shouldst for him make shorter with thy works.

97 Florence, within the ancient boundary
From which she taketh still her tierce and nones,
Abode in quiet, temperate and chaste.

100 No golden chain she had, nor coronal,
Nor ladies shod with sandal shoon, nor girdle
That caught the eye more than the person did.

103 Not yet the daughter at her birth struck fear
Into the father, for the time and dower
Did not o'errun this side or that the measure.

106 No houses had she void of families,
Not yet had thither come Sardanapalus
To show what in a chamber can be done;

109 Not yet surpassed had Montemalo been
By your Uccellatojo, which surpassed
Shall in its downfall be as in its rise.

112 Bellincion Berti saw I go begirt
With leather and with bone, and from the mirror
His dame depart without a painted face;

And him of Nerli saw, and him of Vecchio,
Contented with their simple suits of buff
And with the spindle and the flax their dames.

O fortunate women! and each one was certain
Of her own burial-place, and none as yet
For sake of France was in her bed deserted.

One o'er the cradle kept her studious watch,
And in her lullaby the language used
That first delights the fathers and the mothers;

Another, drawing tresses from her distaff,
Told o'er among her family the tales
Of Trojans and of Fesole and Rome.

As great a marvel then would have been held,
A Lapo Salterello, a Cianghella,
As Cincinnatus or Cornelia now.

To such a quiet, such a beautiful
Life of the citizen, to such a safe
Community, and to so sweet an inn,

Did Mary give me, with loud cries invoked,
And in your ancient Baptistery at once
Christian and Cacciaguida I became.

Moronto was my brother, and Eliseo;
From Val di Pado came to me my wife,
And from that place thy surname was derived.

I followed afterward the Emperor Conrad,
And he begirt me of his chivalry,
So much I pleased him with my noble deeds.

I followed in his train against that law's
Iniquity, whose people doth usurp
Your just possession, through your Pastor's fault.

There by that execrable race was I
Released from bonds of the fallacious world,
The love of which defileth many souls,

And came from martyrdom unto this peace."

Canto XVI

O THOU our poor nobility of blood,
If thou dost make the people glory in thee
Down here where our affection languishes,

4 A marvellous thing it ne'er will be to me;
For there where appetite is not perverted,
I say in Heaven, of thee I made a boast!

7 Truly thou art a cloak that quickly shortens,
So that unless we piece thee day by day
Time goeth round about thee with his shears!

10 With 'You,' which Rome was first to tolerate,
(Wherein her family less perseveres,)
Yet once again my words beginning made;

13 Whence Beatrice, who stood somewhat apart,
Smiling, appeared like unto her who coughed
At the first failing writ of Guenever.

16 And I began: "You are my ancestor,
You give to me all hardihood to speak,
You lift me so that I am more than I.

19 So many rivulets with gladness fill
My mind, that of itself it makes a joy
Because it can endure this and not burst.

22 Then tell me, my beloved root ancestral,
Who were your ancestors, and what the years
That in your boyhood chronicled themselves?

25 Tell me about the sheepfold of Saint John,
How large it was, and who the people were
Within it worthy of the highest seats."

28 As at the blowing of the winds a coal
Quickens to flame, so I beheld that light
Become resplendent at my blandishments.

31 And as unto mine eyes it grew more fair,
With voice more sweet and tender, but not in

This modern dialect, it said to me:

34 "From uttering of the 'Ave,' till the birth
In which my mother, who is now a saint,
Of me was lightened who had been her burden,

37 Unto its Lion had this fire returned
Five hundred fifty times and thirty more,
To reinflame itself beneath his paw.

40 My ancestors and I our birthplace had
Where first is found the last ward of the city
By him who runneth in your annual game.

43 Suffice it of my elders to hear this;
But who they were, and whence they thither came,
Silence is more considerate than speech.

46 All those who at that time were there between
Mars and the Baptist, fit for bearing arms,
Were a fifth part of those who now are living;

49 But the community, that now is mixed
With Campi and Certaldo and Figghine,
Pure in the lowest artisan was seen.

52 O how much better 'twere to have as neighbours
The folk of whom I speak, and at Galluzzo
And at Trespiano have your boundary,

55 Than have them in the town, and bear the stench
Of Aguglione's churl, and him of Signa
Who has sharp eyes for trickery already.

58 Had not the folk, which most of all the world
Degenerates, been a step-dame unto Caesar,
But as a mother to her son benignant,

61 Some who turn Florentines, and trade and discount,
Would have gone back again to Simifonte
There where their grandsires went about as beggars.

64 At Montemurlo still would be the Counts,
The Cerchi in the parish of Acone,
Perhaps in Valdigrieve the Buondelmonti.

67 Ever the intermingling of the people
Has been the source of malady in cities,
As in the body food it surfeits on;

70 And a blind bull more headlong plunges down
Than a blind lamb; and very often cuts
Better and more a single sword than five.

73 If Luni thou regard, and Urbisaglia,
How they have passed away, and how are passing
Chiusi and Sinigaglia after them,

76 To hear how races waste themselves away
Will seem to thee no novel thing nor hard
Seeing that even cities have an end.

79 All things of yours have their mortality,
Even as yourselves; but it is hidden in some
That a long while endure, and lives are short;

82 And as the turning of the lunar heaven
Covers and bares the shores without a pause,
In the like manner fortune does with Florence.

85 Therefore should not appear a marvellous thing
What I shall say of the great Florentines
Of whom the fame is hidden in the Past.

88 I saw the Ughi, saw the Catellini,
Filippi, Greci, Ormanni, and Alberichi,
Even in their fall illustrious citizens;

91 And saw, as mighty as they ancient were,
With him of La Sannella him of Arca,
And Soldanier, Ardinghi, and Bostichi.

94 Near to the gate that is at present laden
With a new felony of so much weight
That soon it shall be jetsam from the bark,

97 The Ravignani were, from whom descended
The County Guido, and whoe'er the name
Of the great Bellincione since hath taken.

100 He of La Pressa knew the art of ruling

Already, and already Galigajo
Had hilt and pommel gilded in his house.

103 Mighty already was the Column Vair,
Sacchetti, Giuochi, Fifant, and Barucci,
And Galli, and they who for the bushel blush.

106 The stock from which were the Calfucci born
Was great already, and already chosen
To curule chairs the Sizii and Arrigucci.

109 O how beheld I those who are undone
By their own pride! and how the Balls of Gold
Florence enflowered in all their mighty deeds!

112 So likewise did the ancestors of those
Who evermore, when vacant is your church,
Fatten by staying in consistory.

115 The insolent race, that like a dragon follows
Whoever flees, and unto him that shows
His teeth or purse is gentle as a lamb,

118 Already rising was, but from low people;
So that it pleased not Ubertin Donato
That his wife's father should make him their kin.

121 Already had Caponsacco to the Market
From Fesole descended, and already
Giuda and Infangato were good burghers.

124 I'll tell a thing incredible, but true;
One entered the small circuit by a gate
Which from the Della Pera took its name!

127 Each one that bears the beautiful escutcheon
Of the great baron whose renown and name
The festival of Thomas keepeth fresh,

130 Knighthood and privilege from him received;
Though with the populace unites himself
To-day the man who binds it with a border.

133 Already were Gualterotti and Importuni;
And still more quiet would the Borgo be

If with new neighbours it remained unfed.

136 The house from which is born your lamentation,
Through just disdain that death among you brought
And put an end unto your joyous life,

139 Was honoured in itself and its companions.
O Buondelmonte, how in evil hour
Thou fled'st the bridal at another's promptings!

142 Many would be rejoicing who are sad,
If God had thee surrendered to the Ema
The first time that thou camest to the city.

145 But it behoved the mutilated stone
Which guards the bridge, that Florence should provide
A victim in her latest hour of peace.

148 With all these families, and others with them,
Florence beheld I in so great repose,
That no occasion had she whence to weep;

151 With all these families beheld so just
And glorious her people, that the lily
Never upon the spear was placed reversed,

154 Nor by division was vermilion made."

Canto XVII

AS came to Clymene, to be made certain
Of that which he had heard against himself,
He who makes fathers chary still to children,

4 Even such was I, and such was I perceived
By Beatrice and by the holy light
That first on my account had changed its place.

7 Therefore my Lady said to me: "Send forth
The flame of thy desire, so that it issue
Imprinted well with the internal stamp;

10 Not that our knowledge may be greater made
By speech of thine, but to accustom thee
To tell thy thirst, that we may give thee drink."

13 "O my beloved tree, (that so dost lift thee,
That even as minds terrestrial perceive
No triangle containeth two obtuse,

16 So thou beholdest the contingent things
Ere in themselves they are, fixing thine eyes
Upon the point in which all times are present,)

19 While I was with Virgilius conjoined
Upon the mountain that the souls doth heal,
And when descending into the dead world,

22 Were spoken to me of my future life
Some grievous words; although I feel myself
In sooth foursquare against the blows of chance.

25 On this account my wish would be content
To hear what fortune is approaching me,
Because foreseen an arrow comes more slowly."

28 Thus did I say unto that selfsame light
That unto me had spoken before, and even
As Beatrice willed was my own will confessed.

31 Not in vague phrase, in which the foolish folk
Ensnared themselves of old, ere yet was slain

The Lamb of God who taketh sins away,

34 But with clear words and unambiguous
Language responded that paternal love,
Hid and revealed by its own proper smile:

37 "Contingency, that outside of the volume
Of your materiality extends not,
Is all depicted in the eternal aspect.

40 Necessity however thence it takes not,
Except as from the eye, in which 'tis mirrored,
A ship that with the current down descends.

43 From thence, e'en as there cometh to the ear
Sweet harmony from an organ, comes in sight
To me the time that is preparing for thee.

46 As forth from Athens went Hippolytus,
By reason of his step-dame false and cruel,
So thou from Florence must perforce depart.

49 Already this is willed, and this is sought for;
And soon it shall be done by him who thinks it,
Where every day the Christ is bought and sold.

52 The blame shall follow the offended party
In outcry as is usual; but the vengeance
Shall witness to the truth that doth dispense it.

55 Thou shalt abandon everything beloved
Most tenderly, and this the arrow is
Which first the bow of banishment shoots forth.

58 Thou shalt have proof how savoureth of salt
The bread of others, and how hard a road
The going down and up another's stairs.

61 And that which most shall weigh upon thy shoulders
Will be the bad and foolish company
With which into this valley thou shalt fall;

64 For all ingrate, all mad and impious
Will they become against thee; but soon after
They, and not thou, shall have the forehead scarlet

67 Of their bestiality their own proceedings
Shall furnish proof; so 'twill be well for thee
A party to have made thee by thyself.

70 Thine earliest refuge and thine earliest inn
Shall be the mighty Lombard's courtesy,
Who on the Ladder bears the holy bird,

73 Who such benign regard shall have for thee
That 'twixt you twain, in doing and in asking,
That shall be first which is with others last.

76 With him shalt thou see one who at his birth
Has by this star of strength been so impressed,
That notable shall his achievements be.

79 Not yet the people are aware of him
Through his young age, since only nine years yet
Around about him have these wheels revolved

82 But ere the Gascon cheat the noble Henry,
Some sparkles of his virtue shall appear
In caring not for silver nor for toil.

85 So recognized shall his magnificence
Become hereafter, that his enemies
Will not have power to keep mute tongues about it.

88 On him rely, and on his benefits;
By him shall many people be transformed,
Changing condition rich and mendicant;

91 And written in thy mind thou hence shalt bear
Of him, but shalt not say it"—and things said he
Incredible to those who shall be present.

94 Then added: "Son, these are the commentaries
On what was said to thee; behold the snares
That are concealed behind few revolutions;

97 Yet would I not thy neighbours thou shouldst envy,
Because thy life into the future reaches
Beyond the punishment of their perfidies."

100 When by its silence showed that sainted soul

That it had finished putting in the woof
Into that web which I had given it warped,

103 Began I, even as he who yearneth after,
Being in doubt, some counsel from a person
Who seeth, and uprightly wills, and loves:

106 "Well see I, father mine, how spurreth on
The time towards me such a blow to deal me
As heaviest is to him who most gives way.

109 Therefore with foresight it is well I arm me,
That, if the dearest place be taken from me,
I may not lose the others by my songs.

112 Down through the world of infinite bitterness,
And o'er the mountain, from whose beauteous summit
The eyes of my own Lady lifted me,

115 And afterward through heaven from light to light,
I have learned that which, if I tell again,
Will be a savour of strong herbs to many.

118 And if I am a timid friend to truth,
I fear lest I may lose my life with those
Who will hereafter call this time the olden."

121 The light in which was smiling my own treasure
Which there I had discovered, flashed at first
As in the sunshine doth a golden mirror;

124 Then made reply: "A conscience overcast
Or with its own or with another's shame,
Will taste forsooth the tartness of thy word;

127 But ne'ertheless, all falsehood laid aside,
Make manifest thy vision utterly,
And let them scratch wherever is the itch;

130 For if thine utterance shall offensive be
At the first taste, a vital nutriment
'Twill leave thereafter, when it is digested.

133 This cry of thine shall do as doth the wind,
Which smiteth most the most exalted summits,

And that is no slight argument of honour.

136 Therefore are shown to thee within these wheels,
Upon the mount and in the dolorous valley,
Only the souls that unto fame are known;

139 Because the spirit of the hearer rests not,
Nor doth confirm its faith by an example
Which has the root of it unknown and hidden,

142 Or other reason that is not apparent."

Canto XVIII

NOW was alone rejoicing in its word
That soul beatified, and I was tasting
My own, the bitter tempering with the sweet,

4 And the Lady who to God was leading me
Said: "Change thy thought; consider that I am
Near unto Him who every wrong disburdens."

7 Unto the loving accents of my comfort
I turned me round, and then what love I saw
Within those holy eyes I here relinquish;

10 Not only that my language I distrust,
But that my mind cannot return so far
Above itself, unless another guide it.

13 Thus much upon that point can I repeat,
That, her again beholding, my affection
From every other longing was released.

16 While the eternal pleasure, which direct
Rayed upon Beatrice, from her fair face
Contented me with its reflected aspect,

19 Conquering me with the radiance of a smile,
She said to me, "Turn thee about and listen;
Not in mine eyes alone is Paradise."

22 Even as sometimes here do we behold
The affection in the look, if it be such
That all the soul is wrapt away by it,

25 So, by the flaming of the effulgence holy
To which I turned, I recognized therein
The wish of speaking to me somewhat farther.

28 And it began: "In this fifth resting-place
Upon the tree that liveth by its summit,
And aye bears fruit, and never loses leaf,

31 Are blessed spirits that below, ere yet
They came to Heaven, were of such great renown
That every Muse therewith would affluent be.

34 Therefore look thou upon the cross's horns;
He whom I now shall name will there enact
What doth within a cloud its own swift fire."

37 I saw athwart the Cross a splendour drawn
By naming Joshua, (even as he did it,)
Nor noted I the word before the deed;

40 And at the name of the great Maccabee
I saw another move itself revolving,
And gladness was the whip unto that top.

43 Likewise for Charlemagne and for Orlando,
Two of them my regard attentive followed
As followeth the eye its falcon flying.

46 William thereafterward, and Renouard,
And the Duke Godfrey, did attract my sight
Along upon that Cross, and Robert Guiscard.

49 Then, moved and mingled with the other lights
The soul that had addressed me showed how great
An artist 'twas among the heavenly singers.

52 To my right side I turned myself around,
My duty to behold in Beatrice
Either by words or gesture signified;

55 And so translucent I beheld her eyes,

So full of pleasure, that her countenance
Surpassed its other and its latest wont.

58 And as, by feeling greater delectation,
A man in doing good from day to day
Becomes aware his virtue is increasing,

61 So I became aware that my gyration
With heaven together had increased its arc,
That miracle beholding more adorned.

64 And such as is the change, in little lapse
Of time, in a pale woman, when her face
Is from the load of bashfulness unladen.

67 Such was it in mine eyes, when I had turned,
Caused by the whiteness of the temperate star,
The sixth, which to itself had gathered me.

70 Within that Jovial torch did I behold
The sparkling of the love which was therein
Delineate our language to mine eyes.

73 And even as birds uprisen from the shore,
As in congratulation o'er their food,
Make squadrons of themselves, now round, now long,

76 So from within those lights the holy creatures
Sang flying to and fro, and in their figures
Made of themselves now D, now I, now L.

79 First singing they to their own music moved;
Then one becoming of these characters,
A little while they rested and were silent.

82 O divine Pegasea, thou who genius
Dost glorious make, and render it long-lived,
And this through thee the cities and the kingdoms,

85 Illume me with thyself, that I may bring
Their figures out as have them conceived!
Apparent be thy power in these brief verses!

88 Themselves then they displayed in five times seven
Vowels and consonants; and I observed
The parts as they seemed spoken unto me.

So from within those lights the holy creatures
Sang flying to and fro.

Gustave Doré

91 'Diligite justitiam,' these were
First verb and noun of all that was depicted;
'Qui judicatis terram'[8] were the last.

94 Thereafter in the M of the fifth word
Remained they so arranged, that Jupiter
Seemed to be silver there with gold inlaid.

97 And other lights I saw descend where was
The summit of the M, and pause there singing
The good, I think, that draws them to itself.

100 Then, as in striking upon burning logs
Upward there fly innumerable sparks,
Whence fools are wont to look for auguries,

103 More than a thousand lights seemed thence to rise,
And to ascend, some more, and others less,
Even as the Sun that lights them had allotted;

106 And, each one being quiet in its place,
The head and neck beheld I of an eagle
Delineated by that inlaid fire.

109 He who there paints has none to be his guide;
But Himself guides; and is from Him remembered
That virtue which is form unto the nest.

112 The other beatitude, that contented seemed
At first to bloom a lily on the M,
By a slight motion followed out the imprint.

115 O gentle star! what and how many gems
Did demonstrate to me, that all our justice
Effect is of that heaven which thou ingemmest!

118 Wherefore I pray the Mind, in which begin
Thy motion and thy virtue, to regard
Whence comes the smoke that vitiates thy rays;

121 So that a second time it now be wroth
With buying and with selling in the temple
Whose walls were built with signs and martyrdoms!

8 "Love justice, you who judge the earth."

124 O soldiery of heaven, whom I contemplate,
Implore for those who are upon the earth
All gone astray after the bad example!

127 Once 'twas the custom to make war with swords;
But now 'tis made by taking here and there
The bread the pitying Father shuts from none.

130 Yet thou, who writest but to cancel, think
That Peter and that Paul, who for this vineyard
Which thou art spoiling died, are still alive!

133 Well canst thou say: "So steadfast my desire
Is unto him who willed to live alone,
And for a dance was led to martyrdom,

136 That I know not the Fisherman nor Paul."

Canto XIX

APPEARED before me with its wings outspread
The beautiful image that in sweet fruition
Made jubilant the interwoven souls;

4 Appeared a little ruby each, wherein
Ray of the sun was burning so enkindled
That each into mine eyes refracted it.

7 And what it now behoves me to retrace
Nor voice has e'er reported, nor ink written,
Nor was by fantasy e'er comprehended;

10 For speak I saw, and likewise heard, the beak,
And utter with its voice both 'I' and 'My,'
When in conception it was 'We' and 'Our.'

13 And it began: "Being just and merciful
Am I exalted here unto that glory
Which cannot be exceeded by desire;

16 And upon earth I left my memory
Such, that the evil-minded people there
Commend it, but continue not the story."

19 So doth a single heat from many embers
Make itself felt, even as from many loves
Issued a single sound from out that image.

22 Whence I thereafter: "O perpetual flowers
Of the eternal joy, that only one
Make me perceive your odours manifold,

25 Exhaling, break within me the great fast
Which a long season has in hunger held me,
Not finding for it any food on earth.

28 Well do I know, that if in heaven its mirror
Justice Divine another realm doth make,
Yours apprehends it not through any veil.

31 You know how I attentively address me
To listen; and you know what is the doubt
That is in me so very old a fast."

34 Even as a falcon issuing from his hood,
Doth move his head, and with his wings applaud him
Showing desire, and making himself fine,

37 Saw I become that standard, which of lauds
Was interwoven of the grace divine,
With such songs as he knows who there rejoices.

40 Then it began: "He who a compass turned
On the world's outer verge, and who within it
Devised so much occult and manifest,

43 Could not the impress of his power so make
On all the universe, as that his Word
Should not remain in infinite excess.

46 And this makes certain that the first proud being,
Who was the paragon of every creature,
By not awaiting light fell immature.

49 And hence appears it, that each minor nature
Is scant receptacle unto that good
Which has no end, and by itself is measured.

52 In consequence our vision, which perforce

Must be some ray of that intelligence
With which all things whatever are replete,

55 Cannot in its own nature be so potent,
That it shall not its origin discern
Far beyond that which is apparent to it.

58 Therefore into the justice sempiternal
The power of vision that your world receives,
As eye into the ocean, penetrates;

61 Which, though it see the bottom near the shore,
Upon the deep perceives it not, and yet
'Tis there, but it is hidden by the depth.

64 There is no light but comes from the serene
That never is o'ercast, nay, it is darkness
Or shadow of the flesh, or else its poison.

67 Amply to thee is opened now the cavern
Which has concealed from thee the living justice
Of which thou mad'st such frequent questioning.

70 For saidst thou: 'Born a man is on the shore
Of Indus, and is none who there can speak
Of Christ, nor who can read, nor who can write;

73 And all his inclinations and his actions
Are good, so far as human reason sees,
Without a sin in life or in discourse:

76 He dieth unbaptised and without faith;
Where is this justice that condemneth him?
Where is his fault, if he do not believe?'

79 Now who art thou, that on the bench wouldst sit
In judgment at a thousand miles away,
With the short vision of a single span?

82 Truly to him who with me subtilizes,
If so the Scripture were not over you,
For doubting there were marvellous occasion.

85 O animals terrene, O stolid minds,
The primal will, that in itself is good,

Ne'er from itself, the Good Supreme, has moved.

88 So much is just as is accordant with it;
No good created draws it to itself,
But it, by raying forth, occasions that."

91 Even as above her nest goes circling round
The stork when she has fed her little ones,
And he who has been fed looks up at her,

94 So lifted I my brows, and even such
Became the blessed image, which its wings
Was moving, by so many counsels urged.

97 Circling around it sang, and said: "As are
My notes to thee, who dost not comprehend them,
Such is the eternal judgment to you mortals."

100 Those lucent splendours of the Holy Spirit
Grew quiet then, but still within the standard
That made the Romans reverend to the world

103 It recommenced: "Unto this kingdom never
Ascended one who had not faith in Christ,
Before or since he to the tree was nailed.

106 But look thou, many crying are, 'Christ, Christ!'
Who at the judgment shall be far less near
To him than some shall be who knew not Christ.

109 Such Christians shall the Ethiop condemn
When the two companies shall be divided,
The one for ever rich, the other poor.

112 What to your kings may not the Persians say,
When they that volume opened shall behold
In which are written down all their dispraises?

115 There shall be seen, among the deeds of Albert,
That which ere long shall set the pen in motion,
For which the realm of Prague shall be deserted.

118 There shall be seen the woe that on the Seine
He brings by falsifying of the coin,
Who by the blow of a wild boar shall die.

There shall be seen the pride that causes thirst,
Which makes the Scot and Englishman so mad
That they within their boundaries cannot rest;

Be seen the luxury and effeminate life
Of him of Spain, and the Bohemian,
Who valour never knew and never wished;

Be seen the Cripple of Jerusalem,
His goodness represented by an I,
While the reverse an M shall represent;

Be seen the avarice and poltroonery
Of him who guards the Island of the Fire,
Wherein Anchises finished his long life;

And to declare how pitiful he is
Shall be his record in contracted letters
Which shall make note of much in little space.

And shall appear to each one the foul deeds
Of uncle and of brother who a nation
So famous have dishonoured, and two crowns.

And he of Portugal and he of Norway
Shall there be known, and he of Rascia too,
Who saw in evil hour the coin of Venice.

O happy Hungary, if she let herself
Be wronged no farther! and Navarre the happy,
If with the hills that gird her she be armed!

And each one may believe that now, as hansel
Thereof, do Nicosia and Famagosta
Lament and rage because of their own beast,

Who from the others' flank departeth not."

Canto XX

WHEN he who all the world illuminates
Out of our hemisphere so far descends
That on all sides the daylight is consumed,

4 The heaven, that erst by him alone was kindled,
Doth suddenly reveal itself again
By many lights, wherein is one resplendent;

7 And came into my mind this act of heaven,
When the ensign of the world and of its leaders
Had silent in the blessed beak become;

10 Because those living luminaries all,
By far more luminous, did songs begin
Lapsing and falling from my memory.

13 O gentle Love, that with a smile dost cloak thee,
How ardent in those sparks didst thou appear,
That had the breath alone of holy thoughts!

16 After the precious and pellucid crystals,
With which begemmed the sixth light I beheld,
Silence imposed on the angelic bells,

19 I seemed to hear the murmuring of a river
That clear descendeth down from rock to rock,
Showing the affluence of its mountain-top.

22 And as the sound upon the cithern's neck
Taketh its form, and as upon the vent
Of rustic pipe the wind that enters it,

25 Even thus, relieved from the delay of waiting,
That murmuring of the eagle mounted up
Along its neck, as if it had been hollow.

28 There it became a voice, and issued thence
From out its beak, in such a form of words
As the heart waited for wherein I wrote them.

31 "The part in me which sees and bears the sun
In mortal eagles," it began to me,

"Now fixedly must needs be looked upon;

34 For of the fires of which I make my figure,
Those whence the eye doth sparkle in my head
Of all their orders the supremest are.

37 He who is shining in the midst as pupil
Was once the singer of the Holy Spirit,
Who bore the ark from city unto city;

40 Now knoweth he the merit of his song,
In so far as effect of his own counsel,
By the reward which is commensurate.

43 Of five, that make a circle for my brow,
He that approacheth nearest to my beak
Did the poor widow for her son console;

46 Now knoweth he how dearly it doth cost
Not following Christ, by the experience
Of this sweet life and of its opposite.

49 He who comes next in the circumference
Of which I speak, upon its highest arc,
Did death postpone by penitence sincere;

52 Now knoweth he that the eternal judgment
Suffers no change, albeit worthy prayer
Maketh below to-morrow of to-day.

55 The next who follows, with the laws and me,
Under the good intent that bore bad fruit
Became a Greek by ceding to the pastor;

58 Now knoweth he how all the ill deduced
From his good action is not harmful to him,
Although the world thereby may be destroyed.

61 And he, whom in the downward arc thou seest,
Guglielmo was, whom the same land deplores
That weepeth Charles and Frederick yet alive;

64 Now knoweth he how heaven enamoured is
With a just king; and in the outward show
Of his effulgence he reveals it still.

67 Who would believe, down in the errant world,
That e'er the Trojan Ripheus in this round
Could be the fifth one of the holy lights?

70 Now knoweth he enough of what the world
Has not the power to see of grace divine,
Although his sight may not discern the bottom."

73 Like as a lark that in the air expatiates,
First singing and then silent with content
Of the last sweetness that doth satisfy her,

76 Such seemed to me the image of the imprint
Of the eternal pleasure, by whose will
Doth everything become the thing it is.

79 And notwithstanding to my doubt I was
As glass is to the colour that invests it,
To wait the time in silence it endured not,

82 But forth from out my mouth, "What things are these?"
Extorted with the force of its own weight;
Whereat I saw great joy of coruscation.

85 Thereafterward with eye still more enkindled
The blessed standard made to me reply,
To keep me not in wonderment suspended:

88 "I see that thou believest in these things
Because I say them, but thou seest not how;
So that, although believed in, they are hidden.

91 Thou doest as he doth who a thing by name
Well apprehendeth, but its quiddity
Cannot perceive, unless another show it.

94 Regnum coelorum[9] suffereth violence
From fervent love, and from that living hope
That overcometh the Divine volition;

97 Not in the guise that man o'ercometh man,
But conquers it because it will be conquered,
And conquered conquers by benignity.

9 "The kingdom of heaven"

The first life of the eyebrow and the fifth
Cause thee astonishment, because with them
Thou seest the region of the angels painted.

They passed not from their bodies, as thou thinkest,
Gentiles, but Christians in the steadfast faith
Of feet that were to suffer and had suffered.

For one from Hell, where no one e'er turns back
Unto good will, returned unto his bones,
And that of living hope was the reward,—

Of living hope, that placed its efficacy
In prayers to God made to resuscitate him,
So that 'twere possible to move his will.

The glorious soul concerning which I speak,
Returning to the flesh, where brief its stay,
Believed in Him who had the power to aid it;

And, in believing, kindled to such fire
Of genuine love, that at the second death
Worthy it was to come unto this joy.

The other one, through grace, that from so deep
A fountain wells that never hath the eye
Of any creature reached its primal wave,

Set all his love below on righteousness;
Wherefore from grace to grace did God unclose
His eye to our redemption yet to be,

Whence he believed therein, and suffered not
From that day forth the stench of paganism,
And he reproved therefor the folk perverse.

Those Maidens three, whom at the right-hand wheel
Thou didst behold, were unto him for baptism
More than a thousand years before baptizing.

O thou predestination, how remote
Thy root is from the aspect of all those
Who the First Cause do not behold entire!

And you, O mortals! hold yourselves restrained

In judging; for ourselves, who look on God,
We do not know as yet all the elect;

136 And sweet to us is such a deprivation,
Because our good in this good is made perfect,
That whatsoe'er God wills, we also will."

139 After this manner by that shape divine,
To make clear in me my short-sightedness,
Was given to me a pleasant medicine;

142 And as good singer a good lutanist
Accompanies with vibrations of the chords,
Whereby more pleasantness the song acquires,

145 So, while it spake, do I remember me
That I beheld both of those blessed lights,
Even as the winking of the eyes concords,

148 Moving unto the words their little flames.

Canto XXI

ALREADY on my Lady's face mine eyes
Again were fastened, and with these my mind,
And from all other purpose was withdrawn;

4 And she smiled not; but "If I were to smile,"
She unto me began, "thou wouldst become
Like Semele, when she was turned to ashes.

7 Because my beauty, that along the stairs
Of the eternal palace more enkindles,
As thou hast seen, the farther we ascend,

10 If it were tempered not, is so resplendent
That all thy mortal power in its effulgence
Would seem a leaflet that the thunder crushes.

13 We are uplifted to the seventh splendour,
That underneath the burning Lion's breast
Now radiates downward mingled with his power.

16 Fix in direction of thine eyes the mind,
And make of them a mirror for the figure
That in this mirror shall appear to thee."

19 He who could know what was the pasturage
My sight had in that blessed countenance,
When I transferred me to another care,

22 Would recognize how grateful was to me
Obedience unto my celestial escort,
By counterpoising one side with the other.

25 Within the crystal which, around the world
Revolving, bears the name of its dear leader,
Under whom every wickedness lay dead,

28 Coloured like gold, on which the sunshine gleams,
A stairway I beheld to such a height
Uplifted, that mine eye pursued it not.

31 Likewise beheld I down the steps descending
So many splendours, that I thought each light
That in the heaven appears was there diffused.

34 And as accordant with their natural custom
The rooks together at the break of day
Bestir themselves to warm their feathers cold;

37 Then some of them fly off without return,
Others come back to where they started from,
And others, wheeling round, still keep at home;

40 Such fashion it appeared to me was there
Within the sparkling that together came,
As soon as on a certain step it struck,

43 And that which nearest unto us remained
Became so clear, that in my thought I said,
"Well I perceive the love thou showest me;

46 But she, from whom I wait the how and when
Of speech and silence, standeth still; whence I
Against desire do well if I ask not."

Coloured like gold, on which the sunshine gleams,
A stairway I beheld to such a height
Uplifted, that mine eye pursued it not.

Gustave Doré

49 She thereupon, who saw my silentness
In the sight of Him who seeth everything,
Said unto me, "Let loose thy warm desire."

52 And I began: "No merit of my own
Renders me worthy of response from thee;
But for her sake who granteth me the asking,

55 Thou blessed life that dost remain concealed
In thy beatitude, make known to me
The cause which draweth thee so near my side;

58 And tell me why is silent in this wheel
The dulcet symphony of Paradise,
That through the rest below sounds so devoutly."

61 "Thou hast thy hearing mortal as thy sight,"
It answer made to me; "they sing not here,
For the same cause that Beatrice has not smiled.

64 Thus far adown the holy stairway's steps
Have I descended but to give thee welcome
With words, and with the light that mantles me;

67 Nor did more love cause me to be more ready,
For love as much and more up there is burning,
As doth the flaming manifest to thee.

70 But the high charity, that makes us servants
Prompt to the counsel which controls the world,
Allotteth here, even as thou dost observe."

73 "I see full well," said I, "O sacred lamp!
How love unfettered in this court sufficeth
To follow the eternal Providence;

76 But this is what seems hard for me to see,
Wherefore predestinate wast thou alone
Unto this office from among thy consorts."

79 No sooner had I come to the last word,
Than of its middle made the light a centre,
Whirling itself about like a swift millstone.

82 When answer made the love that was therein:

"On me directed is a light divine,
Piercing through this in which I am embosomed,

85 Of which the virtue with my sight conjoined
Lifts me above myself so far, I see
The supreme essence from which this is drawn.

88 Hence comes the joyfulness with which I flame,
For to my sight, as far as it is clear,
The clearness of the flame I equal make.

91 But that soul in the heaven which is most pure,
That seraph which his eye on God most fixes,
Could this demand of thine not satisfy;

94 Because so deeply sinks in the abyss
Of the eternal statute what thou askest,
From all created sight it is cut off.

97 And to the mortal world, when thou returnest,
This carry back, that it may not presume
Longer tow'rd such a goal to move its feet.

100 The mind, that shineth here, on earth doth smoke;
From this observe how can it do below
That which it cannot though the heaven assume it?"

103 Such limit did its words prescribe to me,
The question I relinquished, and restricted
Myself to ask it humbly who it was.

106 "Between two shores of Italy rise cliffs,
And not far distant from thy native place,
So high, the thunders far below them sound,

109 And form a ridge that Catria is called,
'Neath which is consecrate a hermitage
Wont to be dedicate to worship only."

112 Thus unto me the third speech recommenced,
And then, continuing, it said: "Therein
Unto God's service I became so steadfast,

115 That feeding only on the juice of olives
Lightly I passed away the heats and frosts,

Contented in my thoughts contemplative.

118 That cloister used to render to these heavens
Abundantly, and now is empty grown,
So that perforce it soon must be revealed.

121 I in that place was Peter Damiano;
And Peter the Sinner was I in the house
Of Our Lady on the Adriatic shore.

124 Little of mortal life remained to me,
When I was called and dragged forth to the hat
Which shifteth evermore from bad to worse.

127 Came Cephas, and the mighty Vessel came
Of the Holy Spirit, meagre and barefooted,
Taking the food of any hostelry.

130 Now some one to support them on each side
The modern shepherds need, and some to lead them,
So heavy are they, and to hold their trains.

133 They cover up their palfreys with their cloaks,
So that two beasts go underneath one skin;
O Patience, that dost tolerate so much!"

136 At this voice saw I many little flames
From step to step descending and revolving,
And every revolution made them fairer.

139 Round about this one came they and stood still,
And a cry uttered of so loud a sound,
It here could find no parallel, nor I

142 Distinguished it, the thunder so o'ercame me.

Canto XXII

OPPRESSED with stupor, I unto my guide
Turned like a little child who always runs
For refuge there where he confideth most;

4 And she, even as a mother who straightway
Gives comfort to her pale and breathless boy
With voice whose wont it is to reassure him,

7 Said to me: "Knowest thou not thou art in heaven,
And knowest thou not that heaven is holy all
And what is alone here cometh from good zeal?

10 After what wise the singing would have changed thee
And I by smiling, thou canst now imagine,
Since that the cry has startled thee so much,

13 In which if thou hadst understood its prayers
Already would be known to thee the vengeance
Which thou shalt look upon before thou diest.

16 The sword above here smiteth not in haste
Nor tardily, howe'er it seem to him
Who fearing or desiring waits for it.

19 But turn thee round towards the others now,
For very illustrious spirits shalt thou see,
If thou thy sight directest as I say."

22 As it seemed good to her mine eyes I turned,
And saw a hundred spherules that together
With mutual rays each other more embellished.

25 I stood as one who in himself represses
The point of his desire, and ventures not
To question, he so feareth the too much.

28 And now the largest and most luculent
Among those pearls came forward, that it might
Make my desire concerning it content.

31 Within it then I heard: "If thou couldst see
Even as myself the charity that burns

Among us, thy conceits would be expressed;

34 But, that by waiting thou mayst not come late
To the high end, I will make answer even
Unto the thought of which thou art so chary.

37 That mountain on whose slope Cassino stands
Was frequented of old upon its summit
By a deluded folk and ill-disposed;

40 And I am he who first up thither bore
The name of Him who brought upon the earth
The truth that so much sublimateth us.

43 And such abundant grace upon me shone
That all the neighbouring towns I drew away
From the impious worship that seduced the world.

46 These other fires, each one of them, were men
Contemplative, enkindled by that heat
Which maketh holy flowers and fruits spring up.

49 Here is Macarius, here is Romualdus,
Here are my brethren, who within the cloisters
Their footsteps stayed and kept a steadfast heart."

52 And I to him: "The affection which thou showest
Speaking with me, and the good countenance
Which I behold and note in all your ardours,

55 In me have so my confidence dilated
As the sun doth the rose, when it becomes
As far unfolded as it hath the power.

58 Therefore I pray, and thou assure me, father,
If I may so much grace receive, that I
May thee behold with countenance unveiled."

61 He thereupon: "Brother, thy high desire
In the remotest sphere shall be fulfilled,
Where are fulfilled all others and my own.

64 There perfect is, and ripened, and complete,
Every desire; within that one alone
Is every part where it has always been;

For it is not in space, nor turns on poles,
And unto it our stairway reaches up,
Whence thus from out thy sight it steals away.

Up to that height the Patriarch Jacob saw it
Extending its supernal part, what time
So thronged with angels it appeared to him.

But to ascend it now no one uplifts
His feet from off the earth, and now my Rule
Below remaineth for mere waste of paper.

The walls that used of old to be an Abbey
Are changed to dens of robbers, and the cowls
Are sacks filled full of miserable flour.

But heavy usury is not taken up
So much against God's pleasure as that fruit
Which maketh so insane the heart of monks;

For whatsoever hath the Church in keeping
Is for the folk that ask it in God's name,
Not for one's kindred or for something worse.

The flesh of mortals is so very soft,
That good beginnings down below suffice not
From springing of the oak to bearing acorns.

Peter began with neither gold nor silver,
And I with orison and abstinence,
And Francis with humility his convent.

And if thou lookest at each one's beginning,
And then regardest whither he has run,
Thou shalt behold the white changed into brown.

In verity the Jordan backward turned,
And the sea's fleeing, when God willed were more
A wonder to behold, than succour here."

Thus unto me he said; and then withdrew
To his own band, and the band closed together
Then like a whirlwind all was upward rapt.

The gentle Lady urged me on behind them

Up o'er that stairway by a single sign,
So did her virtue overcome my nature;

Nor here below, where one goes up and down
By natural law, was motion e'er so swift
That it could be compared unto my wing.

Reader, as I may unto that devout
Triumph return, on whose account I often
For my transgressions weep and beat my breast,—

Thou hadst not thrust thy finger in the fire
And drawn it out again, before I saw
The sign that follows Taurus, and was in it.

O glorious stars, O light impregnated
With mighty virtue, from which I acknowledge
All of my genius, whatsoe'er it be,

With you was born, and hid himself with you,
He who is father of all mortal life,
When first I tasted of the Tuscan air;

And then when grace was freely given to me
To enter the high wheel which turns you round,
Your region was allotted unto me.

To you devoutly at this hour my soul
Is sighing, that it virtue may acquire
For the stern pass that draws it to itself.

"Thou art so near unto the last salvation,"
Thus Beatrice began, "thou oughtest now
To have thine eyes unclouded and acute

And therefore, ere thou enter farther in,
Look down once more, and see how vast a world
Thou hast already put beneath thy feet;

So that thy heart, as jocund as it may,
Present itself to the triumphant throng
That comes rejoicing through this rounded ether."

With my sight returned through one and all
The sevenfold spheres, and I beheld this globe

Such that I smiled at its ignoble semblance.

136 And that opinion I approve as best
Which doth account it least; and he who thinks
Of something else may truly be called just.

139 I saw the daughter of Latona shining
Without that shadow, which to me was cause
That once I had believed her rare and dense.

142 The aspect of thy son, Hyperion,
Here I sustained, and saw how move themselves
Around and near him Maia and Dione.

145 Thence there appeared the temperateness of Jove
'Twixt son and father, and to me was clear
The change that of their whereabout they make

148 And all the seven made manifest to me
How great they are, and eke how swift they are,
And how they are in distant habitations.

151 The threshing-floor that maketh us so proud,
To me revolving with the eternal Twins,
Was all apparent made from hill to harbour!

154 Then to the beauteous eyes mine eyes I turned.

Canto XXIII

EVEN as a bird, 'mid the beloved leaves,
Quiet upon the nest of her sweet brood
Throughout the night, that hideth all things from us,

4 Who, that she may behold their longed-for looks
And find the food wherewith to nourish them,
In which, to her, grave labours grateful are,

7 Anticipates the time on open spray
And with an ardent longing waits the sun,
Gazing intent as soon as breaks the dawn:

10 Even thus my Lady standing was, erect
And vigilant, turned round towards the zone
Underneath which the sun displays less haste;

13 So that beholding her distraught and wistful,
Such I became as he is who desiring
For something yearns, and hoping is appeased.

16 But brief the space from one when to the other;
Of my awaiting, say I, and the seeing
The welkin grow resplendent more and more.

19 And Beatrice exclaimed: "Behold the hosts
Of Christ's triumphal march, and all the fruit
Harvested by the rolling of these spheres!"

22 It seemed to me her face was all aflame;
And eyes she had so full of ecstasy
That I must needs pass on without describing.

25 As when in nights serene of the full moon
Smiles Trivia among the nymphs eternal
Who paint the firmament through all its gulfs,

28 Saw I, above the myriads of lamps,
A Sun that one and all of them enkindled,
E'en as our own doth the supernal sights,

31 And through the living light transparent shone
The lucent substance so intensely clear
Into my sight, that I sustained it not.

34 O Beatrice, thou gentle guide and dear!
To me she said: "What overmasters thee
A virtue is from which naught shields itself.

37 There are the wisdom and the omnipotence
That oped the thoroughfares 'twixt heaven and earth,
For which there erst had been so long a yearning."

40 As fire from out a cloud unlocks itself,
Dilating so it finds not room therein,
And down, against its nature, falls to earth,

43 So did my mind, among those aliments
Becoming larger, issue from itself,
And that which it became cannot remember.

46 "Open thine eyes, and look at what I am:
Thou hast beheld such things, that strong enough
Hast thou become to tolerate my smile."

49 I was as one who still retains the feeling
Of a forgotten vision, and endeavours
In vain to bring it back into his mind.

52 Then I this invitation heard, deserving
Of so much gratitude, it never fades
out of the book that chronicles the past.

55 If at this moment sounded all the tongues
That Polyhymnia and her sisters made
Most lubrical with their delicious milk,

58 To aid me, to a thousandth of the truth
It would not reach, singing the holy smile
And how the holy aspect it illumed.

61 And therefore, representing Paradise,
The sacred poem must perforce leap over,
Even as a man who finds his way cut off;

64 But whoso thinketh of the ponderous theme,
And of the mortal shoulder laden with it
Should blame it not, if under this it tremble.

67 It is no passage for a little boat

This which goes cleaving the audacious prow,
Nor for a pilot who would spare himself.

70 "Why doth my face so much enamour thee,
That to the garden fair thou turnest not,
Which under the rays of Christ is blossoming?

73 There is the Rose in which the Word Divine
Became incarnate; there the lilies are
By whose perfume the good way was discovered."

76 Thus Beatrice; and I, who to her counsels
Was wholly ready, once again betook me
Unto the battle of the feeble brows.

79 As in the sunshine, that unsullied streams
Through fractured cloud, ere now a meadow of flowers
Mine eyes with shadow covered o'er have seen,

82 So troops of splendours manifold I saw
Illumined from above with burning rays,
Beholding not the source of the effulgence.

85 O power benignant that dost so imprint them!
Thou didst exalt thyself to give more scope
There to mine eyes, that were not strong enough.

88 The name of that fair flower I e'er invoke
Morning and evening utterly enthralled
My soul to gaze upon the greater fire.

91 And when in both mine eyes depicted were
The glory and greatness of the living star
Which there excelleth, as it here excelled,

94 Athwart the heavens a little torch descended
Formed in a circle like a coronal,
And cinctured it, and whirled itself about it.

97 Whatever melody most sweetly soundeth
On earth, and to itself most draws the soul,
Would seem a cloud that, rent asunder, thunders,

100 Compared unto the sounding of that lyre
Wherewith was crowned the sapphire beautiful,

Which gives the clearest heaven its sapphire hue.

103 “I am Angelic Love, that circle round
The joy sublime which breathes from out the womb
That was the hostelry of our Desire;

106 And I shall circle, Lady of Heaven, while
Thou followest thy Son, and mak’st diviner
The sphere supreme, because thou enterest there.”

109 Thus did the circulated melody
Seal itself up; and all the other lights
Were making to resound the name of Mary.

112 The regal mantle of the volumes all
Of that world, which most fervid is and living
With breath of God and with his works and ways,

115 Extended over us its inner border,
So very distant, that the semblance of it
There where I was not yet appeared to me.

118 Therefore mine eyes did not possess the power
Of following the incoronated flame.
Which mounted upward near to its own seed.

121 And as a little child, that towards its mother
Stretches its arms, when it the milk has taken,
Through impulse kindled into outward flame,

124 Each of those gleams of whiteness upward reached
So with its summit, that the deep affection
They had for Mary was revealed to me.

127 Thereafter they remained there in my sight,
‘Regina coeli’[10] singing with such sweetness,
That ne’er from me has the delight departed.

130 O, what exuberance is garnered up
Within those richest coffers, which had been
Good husbandmen for sowing here below!

133 There they enjoy and live upon the treasure
Which was acquired while weeping in the exile

10 “Queen of Heaven”

Of Babylon, wherein the gold was left.

136 There triumpheth, beneath the exalted Son
Of God and Mary, in his victory,
Both with the ancient council and the new,

139 He who doth keep the keys of such a glory.

Canto XXIV

"O COMPANY elect to the great supper
Of the Lamb benedight, who feedeth you
So that for ever full is your desire,

4 If by the grace of God this man foretaste
Something of that which falleth from your table,
Or ever death prescribe to him the time,

7 Direct your mind to his immense desire,
And him somewhat bedew; ye drinking are
For ever at the fount whence comes his thought."

10 Thus Beatrice; and those souls beatified
Transformed themselves to spheres on steadfast poles,
Flaming intensely in the guise of comets.

13 And as the wheels in works of horologes
Revolve so that the first to the beholder
Motionless seems, and the last one to fly,

16 So in like manner did those carols, dancing
In different measure, of their affluence
Give me the gauge, as they were swift or slow.

19 From that one which I noted of most beauty
Beheld I issue forth a fire so happy
That none it left there of a greater brightness;

22 And around Beatrice three several times
It whirled itself with so divine a song,
My fantasy repeats it not to me;

25 Therefore the pen skips, and I write it not,
Since our imagination for such folds,
Much more our speech, is of a tint too glaring.

28 "O holy sister mine, who us implorest
With such devotion, by thine ardent love
Thou dost unbind me from that beautiful sphere!"

31 Thereafter, having stopped, the blessed fire
Unto my Lady did direct its breath,
Which spake in fashion as I here have said.

34 And she: "O light eterne of the great man
To whom our Lord delivered up the keys
He carried down of this miraculous joy,

37 This one examine on points light and grave,
As good beseemeth thee, about the Faith
By means of which thou on the sea didst walk.

40 If he love well, and hope well, and believe
From thee 'tis hid not; for thou hast thy sight
There where depicted everything is seen.

43 But since this kingdom has made citizens
By means of the true Faith, to glorify it
'Tis well he have the chance to speak thereof."

46 As baccalaureate arms himself, and speaks not
Until the master doth propose the question,
To argue it, and not to terminate it,

49 So did I arm myself with every reason,
While she was speaking, that I might be ready
For such a questioner and such profession.

52 "Say, thou good Christian; manifest thyself;
What is the Faith?" Whereat I raised my brow
Unto that light wherefrom was this breathed forth.

55 Then turned I round to Beatrice, and she
Prompt signals made to me that I should pour
The water forth from my internal fountain.

58 "May grace, that suffers me to make confession,"

Began I, "to the great centurion,
Cause my conceptions all to be explicit!"

61 And I continued: "As the truthful pen,
Father, of thy dear brother wrote of it,
Who put with thee Rome into the good way,

64 Faith is the substance of the things we hope for,
And evidence of those that are not seen;
And this appears to me its quiddity."

67 Then heard I: "Very rightly thou perceivest,
If well thou understandest why he placed it
With substances and then with evidences."

70 And I thereafterward: "The things profound,
That here vouchsafe to me their apparition,
Unto all eyes below are so concealed,

73 That they exist there only in belief,
Upon the which is founded the high hope,
And hence it takes the nature of a substance.

76 And it behoveth us from this belief
To reason without having other sight,
And hence it has the nature of evidence."

79 Then heard I: "If whatever is acquired
Below by doctrine were thus understood,
No sophist's subtlety would there find place."

82 Thus was breathed forth from that enkindled love;
Then added: "Very well has been gone over
Already of this coin the alloy and weight;

85 But tell me if thou hast it in thy purse?"
And I: "Yes, both so shining and so round
That in its stamp there is no peradventure."

88 Thereafter issued from the light profound
That there resplendent was: "This precious jewel,
Upon the which is every virtue founded,

91 Whence hadst thou it?" And I: "The large outpouring
Of Holy Spirit, which has been diffused

Upon the ancient parchments and the new,

94 A syllogism is, which proved it to me
With such acuteness, that, compared therewith,
All demonstration seems to me obtuse."

97 And then I heard: "The ancient and the new
Postulates, that to thee are so conclusive,
Why dost thou take them for the word divine?"

100 And I: "The proofs, which show the truth to me,
Are the works subsequent, whereunto Nature
Ne'er heated iron yet, nor anvil beat."

103 'Twas answered me: "Say, who assureth thee
That those works ever were? The thing itself
That must be proved, nought else to thee affirms it."

106 "Were the world to Christianity converted,"
I said, "withouten miracles, this one
Is such, the rest are not its hundredth part;

109 Because that poor and fasting thou didst enter
Into the field to sow there the good plant,
Which was a vine and has become a thorn!"

112 This being finished, the high, holy Court
Resounded through the spheres, "One God we praise!"
In melody that there above is chanted.

115 And then that Baron, who from branch to branch,
Examining, had thus conducted me,
Till the extremest leaves we were approaching,

118 Again began: "The Grace that dallying
Plays with thine intellect thy mouth has opened,
Up to this point, as it should opened be,

121 So that I do approve what forth emerged;
But now thou must express what thou believest,
And whence to thy belief it was presented."

124 "O holy father, spirit who beholdest
What thou believedst so that thou o'ercamest,
Towards the sepulchre, more youthful feet,"

Began I, "thou dost wish me in this place
The form to manifest of my prompt belief,
And likewise thou the cause thereof demandest.

And I respond: In one God I believe,
Sole and eterne, who moveth all the heavens
With love and with desire, himself unmoved;

And of such faith not only have I proofs
Physical and metaphysical, but gives them
Likewise the truth that from this place rains down

Through Moses, through the Prophets and the Psalms,
Through the Evangel, and through you, who wrote
After the fiery Spirit sanctified you;

In Persons three eterne believe, and these
One essence I believe, so one and trine
They bear conjunction both with 'sunt' and 'est.'

With the profound condition and divine
Which now I touch upon, doth stamp my mind
Ofttimes the doctrine evangelical.

This the beginning is, this is the spark
Which afterwards dilates to vivid flame,
And, like a star in heaven, is sparkling in me."

Even as a lord who hears what pleaseth him
His servant straight embraces, gratulating
For the good news as soon as he is silent;

So, giving me its benediction, singing,
Three times encircled me, when I was silent,
The apostolic light, at whose command

I spoken had, in speaking I so pleased him.

Canto XXV

IF e'er it happen that the Poem Sacred,
To which both heaven and earth have set their hand,
So that it many a year hath made me lean,

4 O'ercome the cruelty that bars me out
From the fair sheepfold, where a lamb I slumbered
An enemy to the wolves that war upon it,

7 With other voice forthwith, with other fleece
Poet will I return, and at my font
Baptismal will I take the laurel crown;

10 Because into the Faith that maketh known
All souls to God there entered I, and then
Peter for her sake thus my brow encircled.

13 Thereafterward towards us moved a light
Out of that band whence issued the first-fruits
Which of his vicars Christ behind him left,

16 And then my Lady, full of ecstasy,
Said unto me: "Look, look! behold the Baron
For whom below Galicia is frequented."

19 In the same way as, when a dove alights
Near his companion, both of them pour forth,
Circling about and murmuring, their affection,

22 So one beheld I by the other grand
Prince glorified to be with welcome greeted,
Lauding the food that there above is eaten.

25 But when their gratulations were complete,
Silently 'coram me'[11] each one stood still,
So incandescent it o'ercame my sight.

28 Smiling thereafterwards, said Beatrice:
"Illustrious life, by whom the benefactions
Of our Basilica have been described,

31 Make Hope resound within this altitude;

11 "before me"

Thou knowest as oft thou dost personify it
As Jesus to the three gave greater clearness."

34 "Lift up thy head, and make thyself assured;
For what comes hither from the mortal world
Must needs be ripened in our radiance."

37 This comfort came to me from the second fire;
Wherefore mine eyes I lifted to the hills,
Which bent them down before with too great weight.

40 "Since, through his grace, our Emperor wills that thou
Shouldst find thee face to face, before thy death,
In the most secret chamber, with his Counts,

43 So that, the truth beholden of this court,
Hope, which below there rightfully enamours,
Thereby thou strengthen in thyself and others,

46 Say what it is, and how is flowering with it
Thy mind, and say from whence it came to thee."
Thus did the second light again continue.

49 And the Compassionate, who piloted
The plumage of my wings in such high flight,
Did in reply anticipate me thus:

52 "No child whatever the Church Militant
Of greater hope possesses, as is written
In that Sun which irradiates all our band;

55 Therefore it is conceded him from Egypt
To come into Jerusalem to see,
Or ever yet his warfare be completed.

58 The two remaining points, that not for knowledge
Have been demanded, but that he report
How much this virtue unto thee is pleasing,

61 To him I leave; for hard he will not find them,
Nor of self-praise; and let him answer them;
And may the grace of God in this assist him!"

64 As a disciple, who his teacher follows,
Ready and willing, where he is expert,

That his proficiency may be displayed,

67 "Hope," said I, "is the certain expectation
Of future glory, which is the effect
Of grace divine and merit precedent.

70 From many stars this light comes unto me;
But he instilled it first into my heart
Who was chief singer unto the chief captain.

73 'Sperent in te,'[12] in the high Theody
He sayeth, 'those who know thy name;'and who
Knoweth it not, if he my faith possess?

76 Thou didst instil me, then, with his instilling
In the Epistle, so that I am full,
And upon others rain again your rain."

79 While I was speaking, in the living bosom
Of that combustion quivered an effulgence,
Sudden and frequent, in the guise of lightning;

82 Then breathed: "The love wherewith I am inflamed
Towards the virtue still which followed me
Unto the palm and issue of the field,

85 Wills that I breathe to thee that thou delight
In her; and grateful to me is thy telling
Whatever things Hope promises to thee."

88 And I: "The ancient Scriptures and the new
The mark establish, and this shows it me,
Of all the souls whom God hath made his friends.

91 Isaiah saith, that each one garmented
In his own land shall be with twofold garments
And his own land is this delightful life.

94 Thy brother, too, far more explicitly,
There where he treateth of the robes of white,
This revelation manifests to us."

97 And first, and near the ending of these words,
"Sperent in te" from over us was heard,

12 "They trust in you."

To which responsive answered all the carols.

100 Thereafterward a light among them brightened,
So that, if Cancer one such crystal had,
Winter would have a month of one sole day.

103 And as uprises, goes, and enters the dance
A winsome maiden, only to do honour
To the new bride, and not from any failing,

106 Even thus did I behold the brightened splendour
Approach the two, who in a wheel revolved
As was beseeming to their ardent love.

109 Into the song and music there it entered;
And fixed on them my Lady kept her look,
Even as a bride silent and motionless.

112 "This is the one who lay upon the breast
Of him our Pelican; and this is he
To the great office from the cross elected."

115 My Lady thus; but therefore none the more
Did move her sight from its attentive gaze
Before or afterward these words of hers.

118 Even as a man who gazes, and endeavours
To see the eclipsing of the sun a little,
And who, by seeing, sightless doth become,

121 So I became before that latest fire,
While it was said, "Why dost thou daze thyself
To see a thing which here hath no existence?

124 Earth in the earth my body is, and shall be
With all the others there, until our number
With the eternal proposition tallies.

127 With the two garments in the blessed cloister
Are the two lights alone that have ascended:
And this shalt thou take back into your world."

130 And at this utterance the flaming circle
Grew quiet, with the dulcet intermingling
Of sound that by the trinal breath was made,

133 As to escape from danger or fatigue
The oars that erst were in the water beaten
Are all suspended at a whistle's sound.

136 Ah, how much in my mind was I disturbed,
When I turned round to look on Beatrice,
That her I could not see, although I was

139 Close at her side and in the Happy World!

Canto XXVI

WHILE I was doubting for my vision quenched,
Out of the flame refulgent that had quenched it
Issued a breathing, that attentive made me,

4 Saying: "While thou recoverest the sense
Of seeing which in me thou hast consumed,
'Tis well that speaking thou shouldst compensate it.

7 Begin then, and declare to what thy soul
Is aimed, and count it for a certainty,
Sight is in thee bewildered and not dead;

10 Because the Lady, who through this divine
Region conducteth thee, has in her look
The power the hand of Ananias had."

13 I said: "As pleaseth her, or soon or late
Let the cure come to eyes that portals were
When she with fire I ever burn with entered.

16 The Good, that gives contentment to this Court,
The Alpha and Omega is of all
The writing that love reads me low or loud."

19 The selfsame voice, that taken had from me
The terror of the sudden dazzlement,
To speak still farther put it in my thought;

22 And said: "In verity with finer sieve
Behoveth thee to sift; thee it behoveth

To say who aimed thy bow at such a target."

And I: "By philosophic arguments,
And by authority that hence descends,
Such love must needs imprint itself in me;

For Good, so far as good, when comprehended
Doth straight enkindle love, and so much greater
As more of goodness in itself it holds;

Then to that Essence (whose is such advantage
That every good which out of it is found
Is nothing but a ray of its own light)

More than elsewhither must the mind be moved
Of every one, in loving, who discerns
The truth in which this evidence is founded.

Such truth he to my intellect reveals
Who demonstrates to me the primal love
Of all the sempiternal substances.

The voice reveals it of the truthful Author,
Who says to Moses, speaking of Himself,
'I will make all my goodness pass before thee.'

Thou too revealest it to me, beginning
The loud Evangel, that proclaims the secret
Of heaven to earth above all other edict."

And I heard say: "By human intellect
And by authority concordant with it,
Of all thy loves reserve for God the highest.

But say again if other cords thou feelest,
Draw thee towards Him, that thou mayst proclaim
With how many teeth this love is biting thee."

The holy purpose of the Eagle of Christ
Not latent was nay, rather I perceived
Whither he fain would my profession lead.

Therefore I recommenced: "All of those bites
Which have the power to turn the heart to God
Unto my charity have been concurrent.

58 The being of the world, and my own being,
The death which He endured that I may live,
And that which all the faithful hope, as I do,

61 With the forementioned vivid consciousness
Have drawn me from the sea of love perverse,
And of the right have placed me on the shore.

64 The leaves, wherewith embowered is all the garden
Of the Eternal Gardener, do I love
As much as he has granted them of good."

67 As soon as I had ceased, a song most sweet
Throughout the heaven resounded, and my Lady
Said with the others, "Holy, holy, holy!"

70 And as at some keen light one wakes from sleep
By reason of the visual spirit that runs
Unto the splendour passed from coat to coat,

73 And he who wakes abhorreth what he sees,
So all unconscious is his sudden waking,
Until the judgment cometh to his aid,

76 So from before mine eyes did Beatrice
Chase every mote with radiance of her own,
That cast its light a thousand miles and more.

79 Whence better after than before I saw,
And in a kind of wonderment I asked
About a fourth light that I saw with us.

82 And said my Lady: "There within those rays
Gazes upon its Maker the first soul
That ever the first virtue did create."

85 Even as the bough that downward bends its top
At transit of the wind, and then is lifted
By its own virtue, which inclines it upward,

88 Likewise did I, the while that she was speaking,
Being amazed, and then I was made bold
By a desire to speak wherewith I burned.

91 And I began: "O apple, that mature
Alone hast been produced, O ancient father,

To whom each wife is daughter and daughter-in-law,

94 Devoutly as I can I supplicate thee
That thou wouldst speak to me; thou seest my wish;
And I, to hear thee quickly, speak it not."

97 Sometimes an animal, when covered, struggles
So that his impulse needs must be apparent,
By reason of the wrappage following it;

100 And in like manner the primeval soul
Made clear to me athwart its covering
How jubilant it was to give me pleasure.

103 Then breathed: "Without thy uttering it to me,
Thine inclination better I discern
Than thou whatever thing is surest to thee;

106 For I behold it in the truthful mirror,
That of Himself all things parhelion makes,
And none makes Him parhelion of itself

109 Thou fain wouldst hear how long ago God placed me
Within the lofty garden, where this Lady
Unto so long a stairway thee disposed.

112 And how long to mine eyes it was a pleasure,
And of the great disdain the proper cause,
And the language that I used and that I made.

115 Now, son of mine, the tasting of the tree
Not in itself was cause of so great exile,
But solely the o'erstepping of the bounds.

118 There, whence thy Lady moved Virgilius,
Four thousand and three hundred and two circuits
Made by the sun, this Council I desired;

121 And him I saw return to all the lights
Of his highway nine hundred times and thirty,
Whilst I upon the earth was tarrying.

124 The language that I spake was quite extinct
Before that in the work interminable
The people under Nimrod were employed;

127 For nevermore result of reasoning
(Because of human pleasure that doth change,
Obedient to the heavens) was durable.

130 A natural action is it that man speaks;
But whether thus or thus, doth nature leave
To your own art, as seemeth best to you.

133 Ere I descended to the infernal anguish,
'El' was on earth the name of the Chief Good,
From whom comes all the joy that wraps me round

136 'Eli' he then was called, and that is proper,
Because the use of men is like a leaf
On bough, which goeth and another cometh.

139 Upon the mount that highest o'er the wave
Rises was I, in life or pure or sinful,
From the first hour to that which is the second,

142 As the sun changes quadrant, to the sixth."

Canto XXVII

"GLORY be to the Father, to the Son,
And Holy Ghost!" all Paradise began,
So that the melody inebriate made me.

4 What I beheld seemed unto me a smile
Of the universe; for my inebriation
Found entrance through the hearing and the sight.

7 O joy! O gladness inexpressible!
O perfect life of love and peacefulness!
O riches without hankering secure!

10 Before mine eyes were standing the four torches
Enkindled, and the one that first had come
Began to make itself more luminous;

13 And even such in semblance it became
As Jupiter would become, if he and Mars

Were birds, and they should interchange their feathers.

16 That Providence, which here distributeth
Season and service, in the blessed choir
Had silence upon every side imposed

19 When I heard say: "If I my colour change,
Marvel not at it; for while I am speaking
Thou shalt behold all these their colour change.

22 He who usurps upon the earth my place,
My place, my place, which vacant has become
Before the presence of the Son of God,

25 Has of my cemetery made a sewer
Of blood and stench, whereby the Perverse One
Who fell from here, below there is appeased!"

28 With the same colour which, through sun adverse,
Painteth the clouds at evening or at morn,
Beheld I then the whole of heaven suffused.

31 And as a modest woman, who abides
Sure of herself, and at another's failing,
From listening only, timorous becomes,

34 Even thus did Beatrice change countenance;
And I believe in heaven was such eclipse,
When suffered the supreme Omnipotence;

37 Thereafterward proceeded forth his words
With voice so much transmuted from itself,
The very countenance was not more changed.

40 "The spouse of Christ has never nurtured been
On blood of mine, of Linus and of Cletus,
To be made use of in acquest of gold;

43 But in acquest of this delightful life
Sixtus and Pius, Urban and Calixtus,
After much lamentation, shed their blood.

46 Our purpose was not, that on the right hand
Of our successors should in part be seated
The Christian folk, in part upon the other;

49 Nor that the keys which were to me confided
Should e'er become the escutcheon on a banner,
That should wage war on those who are baptized;

52 Nor I be made the figure of a seal
To privileges venal and mendacious,
Whereat I often redden and flash with fire.

55 In garb of shepherds the rapacious wolves
Are seen from here above o'er all the pastures!
O wrath of God, why dost thou slumber still?

58 To drink our blood the Caorsines and Gascons
Are making ready. O thou good beginning,
Unto how vile an end must thou needs fall!

61 But the high Providence, that with Scipio
At Rome the glory of the world defended,
Will speedily bring aid, as I conceive;

64 And thou, my son, who by thy mortal weight
Shalt down return again, open thy mouth;
What I conceal not, do not thou conceal."

67 As with its frozen vapours downward falls
In flakes our atmosphere, what time the horn
Of the celestial Goat doth touch the sun,

70 Upward in such array saw I the ether
Become, and flaked with the triumphant vapours,
Which there together with us had remained.

73 My sight was following up their semblances,
And followed till the medium, by excess,
The passing farther onward took from it;

76 Whereat the Lady, who beheld me freed
From gazing upward, said to me: "Cast down
Thy sight, and see how far thou art turned round."

79 Since the first time that I had downward looked,
I saw that I had moved through the whole arc
Which the first climate makes from midst to end;

82 So that I saw the mad track of Ulysses

Past Gades, and this side, well nigh the shore
Whereon became Europa a sweet burden.

85 And of this threshing-floor the site to me
Were more unveiled, but the sun was proceeding
Under my feet, a sign and more removed.

88 My mind enamoured, which is dallying
At all times with my Lady, to bring back
To her mine eyes was more than ever ardent.

91 And if or Art or Nature has made bait
To catch the eyes and so possess the mind,
In human flesh or in its portraiture,

94 All joined together would appear as nought
To the divine delight which shone upon me
When to her smiling face I turned me round.

97 The virtue that her look endowed me with
From the fair nest of Leda tore me forth,
And up into the swiftest heaven impelled me.

100 Its parts exceeding full of life and lofty
Are all so uniform, I cannot say
Which Beatrice selected for my place.

103 But she, who was aware of my desire,
Began, the while she smiled so joyously
That God seemed in her countenance to rejoice:

106 "The nature of that motion, which keeps quiet
The centre and all the rest about it moves,
From hence begins as from its starting point.

109 And in this heaven there is no other where
Than in the Mind Divine, wherein is kindled
The love that turns it, and the power it rains.

112 Within a circle light and love embrace it
Even as this doth the others, and that precinct
He who encircles it alone controls.

115 Its motion is not by another meted,
But all the others measured are by this,

As ten is by the half and by the fifth.

118 And in what manner time in such a pot
May have its roots, and in the rest its leaves,
Now unto thee can manifest be made.

121 O Covetousness, that mortals dost ingulf
Beneath thee so, that no one hath the power
Of drawing back his eyes from out thy waves!

124 Full fairly blossoms in mankind the will;
But the uninterrupted rain converts
Into abortive wildings the true plums.

127 Fidelity and innocence are found
Only in children; afterwards they both
Take flight or e'er the cheeks with down are covered.

130 One, while he prattles still, observes the fasts,
Who, when his tongue is loosed, forthwith devours
Whatever food under whatever moon;

133 Another, while he prattles, loves and listens
Unto his mother, who when speech is perfect
Forthwith desires to see her in her grave.

136 Even thus is swarthy made the skin so white
In its first aspect of the daughter fair
Of him who brings the morn, and leaves the night.

139 Thou, that it may not be a marvel to thee,
Think that on earth there is no one who governs;
Whence goes astray the human family.

142 Ere January be unwintered wholly
By the centesimal on earth neglected,
Shall these supernal circles roar so loud;

145 The tempest that has been so long awaited
Shall whirl the poops about where are the prows;
So that the fleet shall run its course direct,

148 And the true fruit shall follow on the flower."

Canto XXVIII

AFTER the truth against the present life
Of miserable mortals was unfolded
By her who doth imparadise my mind,

4 As in a looking-glass a taper's flame
He sees who from behind is lighted by it,
Before he has it in his sight or thought,

7 And turns him round to see if so the glass
Tell him the truth, and sees that it accords
Therewith as doth a music with its metre,

10 In similar wise my memory recollecteth
That I did, looking into those fair eyes,
Of which Love made the springes to ensnare me.

13 And as I turned me round, and mine were touched
By that which is apparent in that volume,
Whenever on its gyre we gaze intent,

16 A point beheld I, that was raying out
Light so acute, the sight which it enkindles
Must close perforce before such great acuteness.

19 And whatsoever star seems smallest here
Would seem to be a moon, if placed beside it,
As one star with another star is placed.

22 Perhaps at such a distance as appears
A halo cincturing the light that paints it,
When densest is the vapour that sustains it,

25 Thus distant round the point a circle of fire
So swiftly whirled, that it would have surpassed
Whatever motion soonest girds the world;

28 And this was by another circumcinct,
That by a third, the third then by a fourth,
By a fifth the fourth, and then by a sixth the fifth;

31 The seventh followed thereupon in width
So ample now, that Juno's messenger
Entire would be too narrow to contain it.

34 Even so the eighth and ninth; and every one
More slowly moved, according as it was
In number distant farther from the first.

37 And that one had its flame most crystalline
From which less distant was the stainless spark,
I think because more with its truth imbued.

40 My Lady, who in my anxiety
Beheld me much perplexed, said: "From that point
Dependent is the heaven and nature all.

43 Behold that circle most conjoined to it,
And know thou, that its motion is so swift
Through burning love whereby it is spurred on."

46 And I to her: "If the world were arranged
In the order which I see in yonder wheels,
What's set before me would have satisfied me;

49 But in the world of sense we can perceive
That evermore the circles are diviner
As they are from the centre more remote;

52 Wherefore if my desire is to be ended
In this miraculous and angelic temple,
That has for confines only love and light,

55 To hear behoves me still how the example
And the exemplar go not in one fashion,
Since for myself in vain I contemplate it."

58 "If thine own fingers unto such a knot
Be insufficient, it is no great wonder,
So hard hath it become for want of trying."

61 My Lady thus; then said she: "Do thou take
What I shall tell thee, if thou wouldst be sated,
And exercise on that thy subtlety.

64 The circles corporal are wide and narrow
According to the more or less of virtue
Which is distributed through all their parts.

67 The greater goodness works the greater weal,

The greater weal the greater body holds,
If perfect equally are all its parts.

70 Therefore this one which sweeps along with it
The universe sublime, doth correspond
Unto the circle which most loves and knows.

73 On which account, if thou unto the virtue
Apply thy measure, not to the appearance
Of substances that unto thee seem round,

76 Thou wilt behold a marvellous agreement,
Of more to greater, and of less to smaller,
In every heaven, with its Intelligence."

79 Even as remaineth splendid and serene
The hemisphere of air, when Boreas
Is blowing from that cheek where he is mildest,

82 Because is purified and resolved the rack
That erst disturbed it, till the welkin laughs
With all the beauties of its pageantry;

85 Thus did I likewise, after that my Lady
Had me provided with her clear response,
And like a star in heaven the truth was seen.

88 And soon as to a stop her words had come,
Not otherwise does iron scintillate
When molten, than those circles scintillated.

91 Their coruscation all the sparks repeated,
And they so many were, their number makes
More millions than the doubling of the chess.

94 I heard them sing "Hosanna" choir by choir
To the fixed point which holds them at the 'Ubi,'
And ever will, where they have ever been.

97 And she, who saw the dubious meditations
Within my mind, "The primal circles," said,
"Have shown thee Seraphim and Cherubim.

100 Thus rapidly they follow their own bonds,
To be as like the point as most they can,
And can as far as they are high in vision.

And soon as to a stop her words had come,
Not otherwise does iron scintillate
When molten, than those circles scintillated.

Gustave Doré

Those other Loves, that round about them go,
Thrones of the countenance divine are called,
Because they terminate the primal Triad.

And thou shouldst know that they all have delight
As much as their own vision penetrates
The Truth, in which all intellect finds rest.

From this it may be seen how blessedness
Is founded in the faculty which sees,
And not in that which loves, and follows next;

And of this seeing merit is the measure,
Which is brought forth by grace, and by good will;
Thus on from grade to grade doth it proceed.

The second Triad, which is germinating
In such wise in this sempiternal spring,
That no nocturnal Aries despoils,

Perpetually 'Hosanna' warbles forth
With threefold melody, that sounds in three
Orders of joy, with which it is intrined.

The three Divine are in this hierarchy,
First the Dominions, and the Virtues next;
And the third order is that of the Powers.

Then in the dances twain penultimate
The Principalities and Archangels wheel;
The last is wholly of angelic sports.

These orders upward all of them are gazing,
And downward so prevail, that unto God
They all attracted are and all attract.

And Dionysius with so great desire
To contemplate these Orders set himself;
He named them and distinguished them as I do.

But Gregory afterwards dissented from him;
Wherefore, as soon as he unclosed his eyes
Within this heaven, he at himself did smile.

And if so much of secret truth a mortal

Proffered on earth, I would not have thee marvel,
For he who saw it here revealed it to him,

139 With much more of the truth about these circles."

Canto XXIX

AT what time both the children of Latona,
Surmounted by the Ram and by the Scales,
Together make a zone of the horizon,

4 As long as from the time the zenith holds them
In equipoise, till from that girdle both
Changing their hemisphere disturb the balance,

7 So long, her face depicted with a smile,
Did Beatrice keep silence while she gazed
Fixedly at the point which had o'ercome me.

10 Then she began: "I say, and I ask not
What thou dost wish to hear, for I have seen it
Where centres every When and every 'Ubi.'

13 Not to acquire some good unto himself,
Which is impossible, but that his splendour
In its resplendency may say, 'Subsisto,'[13]

16 In his eternity outside of time,
Outside all other limits, as it pleased him,
Into new Loves the Eternal Love unfolded.

19 Nor as if torpid did he lie before;
For neither after nor before proceeded
The going forth of God upon these waters.

22 Matter and Form unmingled and conjoined
Came into being that had no defect,
E'en as three arrows from a three-stringed bow.

25 And as in glass, in amber, or in crystal
A sunbeam flashes so, that from its coming

13 "I submit."

To its full being is no interval,

28 So from its Lord did the triform effect
Ray forth into its being all together,
Without discrimination of beginning.

31 Order was con-created and constructed
In substances, and summit of the world
Were those wherein the pure act was produced.

34 Pure potentiality held the lowest part;
Midway bound potentiality with act
Such bond that it shall never be unbound.

37 Jerome has written unto you of angels
Created a long lapse of centuries
Or ever yet the other world was made;

40 But written is this truth in many places
By writers of the Holy Ghost, and thou
Shalt see it if thou lookest well thereat,

43 And even reason seeth it somewhat,
For it would not concede that for so long
Could be the motors without their perfection.

46 Now dost thou know both where and when these Loves
Created were, and how; so that extinct
In thy desire already are three fires.

49 Nor could one reach, in counting, unto twenty
So swiftly, as a portion of these angels
Disturbed the subject of your elements.

52 The rest remained, and they began this art
Which thou discernest, with so great delight
That never from their circling do they cease.

55 The occasion of the fall was the accursed
Presumption of that One, whom thou hast seen
By all the burden of the world constrained.

58 Those whom thou here beholdest modest were
To recognise themselves as of that goodness
Which made them apt for so much understanding;

61 On which account their vision was exalted
By the enlightening grace and their own merit,
So that they have a full and steadfast will.

64 I would not have thee doubt, but certain be,
'Tis meritorious to receive this grace,
According as the affection opens to it.

67 Now round about in this consistory
Much mayst thou contemplate, if these my words
Be gathered up, without all further aid.

70 But since upon the earth, throughout your schools,
They teach that such is the angelic nature
That it doth hear, and recollect, and will,

73 More will I say, that thou mayst see unmixed
The truth that is confounded there below,
Equivocating in such like prelections.

76 These substances, since in God's countenance
They jocund were, turned not away their sight
From that wherefrom not anything is hidden;

79 Hence they have not their vision intercepted
By object new, and hence they do not need
To recollect, through interrupted thought.

82 So that below, not sleeping, people dream,
Believing they speak truth, and not believing;
And in the last is greater sin and shame.

85 Below you do not journey by one path
Philosophising; so transporteth you
Love of appearance and the thought thereof.

88 And even this above here is endured
With less disdain, than when is set aside
The Holy Writ, or when it is distorted.

91 They think not there how much of blood it costs
To sow it in the world, and how he pleases
Who in humility keeps close to it.

94 Each striveth for appearance, and doth make

His own inventions; and these treated are
By preachers, and the Evangel holds its peace.

97 One sayeth that the moon did backward turn,
In the Passion of Christ, and interpose herself
So that the sunlight reached not down below;

100 And lies; for of its own accord the light
Hid itself; whence to Spaniards and to Indians,
As to the Jews, did such eclipse respond.

103 Florence has not so many Lapi and Bindi
As fables such as these, that every year
Are shouted from the pulpit back and forth,

106 In such wise that the lambs, who do not know,
Come back from pasture fed upon the wind,
And not to see the harm doth not excuse them.

109 Christ did not to his first disciples say,
'Go forth, and to the world preach idle tales,'
But unto them a true foundation gave;

112 And this so loudly sounded from their lips,
That, in the warfare to enkindle Faith,
They made of the Evangel shields and lances.

115 Now men go forth with jests and drolleries
To preach, and if but well the people laugh,
The hood puffs out, and nothing more is asked.

118 But in the cowl there nestles such a bird,
That, if the common people were to see it,
They would perceive what pardons they confide in.

121 For which so great on earth has grown the folly,
That, without proof of any testimony,
To each indulgence they would flock together.

124 By this Saint Anthony his pig doth fatten,
And many others, who are worse than pigs,
Paying in money without mark of coinage.

127 But since we have digressed abundantly,
Turn back thine eyes forthwith to the right path,
So that the way be shortened with the time.

130 This nature doth so multiply itself
In numbers, that there never yet was speech
Nor mortal fancy that can go so far.

133 And if thou notest that which is revealed
By Daniel, thou wilt see that in his thousands,
Number determinate is kept concealed.

136 The primal light, that all irradiates it,
By modes as many is received therein
As are the splendours wherewith it is mated.

139 Hence, inasmuch as on the act conceptive
The affection followeth, of love the sweetness
Therein diversely fervid is or tepid.

142 The height behold now and the amplitude
Of the eternal power, since it hath made
Itself so many mirrors, where 'tis broken,

145 One in itself remaining as before."

Canto XXX

PERCHANCE six thousand miles remote from us
Is glowing the sixth hour, and now this world
Inclines its shadow almost to a level,

4 When the mid-heaven begins to make itself
So deep to us, that here and there a star
Ceases to shine so far down as this depth,

7 And as advances bright exceedingly
The handmaid of the sun, the heaven is closed
Light after light to the most beautiful;

10 Not otherwise the Triumph, which for ever
Plays round about the point that vanquished me,
Seeming enclosed by what itself encloses,

13 Little by little from my vision faded;
Whereat to turn mine eyes on Beatrice

My seeing nothing and my love constrained me.

16 If what has hitherto been said of her
Were all concluded in a single praise,
Scant would it be to serve the present turn.

19 Not only does the beauty I beheld
Transcend ourselves, but truly I believe
Its Maker only may enjoy it all.

22 Vanquished do I confess me by this passage
More than by problem of his theme was ever
O'ercome the comic or the tragic poet;

25 For as the sun the sight that trembles most,
Even so the memory of that sweet smile
My mind depriveth of its very self.

28 From the first day that I beheld her face
In this life, to the moment of this look,
The sequence of my song has ne'er been severed;

31 But now perforce this sequence must desist
From following her beauty with my verse,
As every artist at his uttermost.

34 Such as I leave her to a greater fame
Than any of my trumpet, which is bringing
Its arduous matter to a final close,

37 With voice and gesture of a perfect leader
She recommenced: "We from the greatest body
Have issued to the heaven that is pure light;

40 Light intellectual replete with love,
Love of true good replete with ecstasy,
Ecstasy that transcendeth every sweetness.

43 Here shalt thou see the one host and the other
Of Paradise, and one in the same aspects
Which at the final judgment thou shalt see."

46 Even as a sudden lightning that disperses
The visual spirits, so that it deprives
The eye of impress from the strongest objects,

49 Thus round about me flashed a living light,
And left me swathed around with such a veil
Of its effulgence, that I nothing saw.

52 "Ever the Love which quieteth this heaven
Welcomes into itself with such salute,
To make the candle ready for its flame."

55 No sooner had within me these brief words
An entrance found, than I perceived myself
To be uplifted over my own power,

58 And I with vision new rekindled me,
Such that no light whatever is so pure
But that mine eyes were fortified against it.

61 And light I saw in fashion of a river
Fulvid with its effulgence, 'twixt two banks
Depicted with an admirable Spring.

64 Out of this river issued living sparks,
And on all sides sank down into the flowers,
Like unto rubies that are set in gold;

67 And then, as if inebriate with the odours,
They plunged again into the wondrous torrent,
And as one entered issued forth another.

70 "The high desire, that now inflames and moves thee
To have intelligence of what thou seest,
Pleaseth me all the more, the more it swells.

73 But of this water it behoves thee drink
Before so great a thirst in thee be slaked."
Thus said to me the sunshine of mine eyes;

76 And added: "The river and the topazes
Going in and out, and the laughing of the herbage,
Are of their truth foreshadowing prefaces;

79 Not that these things are difficult in themselves,
But the deficiency is on thy side,
For yet thou hast not vision so exalted."

82 There is no babe that leaps so suddenly

With face towards the milk, if he awake
Much later than his usual custom is,

85 As I did, that I might make better mirrors
Still of mine eyes, down stooping to the wave
Which flows that we therein be better made.

88 And even as the penthouse of mine eyelids
Drank of it, it forthwith appeared to me
Out of its length to be transformed to round.

91 Then as a folk who have been under masks
Seem other than before, if they divest
The semblance not their own they disappeared in,

94 Thus into greater pomp were changed for me
The flowerets and the sparks, so that I saw
Both of the Courts of Heaven made manifest.

97 O splendour of God! by means of which I saw
The lofty triumph of the realm veracious,
Give me the power to say how it I saw!

100 There is a light above, which visible
Makes the Creator unto every creature,
Who only in beholding Him has peace,

103 And it expands itself in circular form
To such extent, that its circumference
Would be too large a girdle for the sun.

106 The semblance of it is all made of rays
Reflected from the top of Primal Motion,
Which takes therefrom vitality and power;

109 And as a hill in water at its base
Mirrors itself, as if to see its beauty
When affluent most in verdure and in flowers,

112 So, ranged aloft all round about the light,
Mirrored I saw in more ranks than a thousand
All who above there have from us returned.

115 And if the lowest row collect within it
So great a light, how vast the amplitude

Is of this Rose in its extremest leaves!

My vision in the vastness and the height
Lost not itself, but comprehended all
The quantity and quality of that gladness.

There near and far nor add nor take away;
For there where God immediately doth govern,
The natural law in naught is relevant.

Into the yellow of the Rose Eternal
That spreads, and multiplies, and breathes an odour
Of praise unto the ever-vernal Sun

As one who silent is and fain would speak,
Me Beatrice drew on, and said: "Behold
Of the white stoles how vast the convent is!

Behold how vast the circuit of our city!
Behold our seats so filled to overflowing,
That here henceforward are few people wanting!

On that great throne whereon thine eyes are fixed
For the crown's sake already placed upon it,
Before thou suppest at this wedding feast

Shall sit the soul (that is to be Augustus
On earth) of noble Henry, who shall come
To redress Italy ere she be ready.

Blind covetousness, that casts its spell upon you,
Has made you like unto the little child,
Who dies of hunger and drives off the nurse.

And in the sacred forum then shall be
A Prefect such, that openly or covert
On the same road he will not walk with him.

But long of God he will not be endured
In holy office; he shall be thrust down
Where Simon Magus is for his deserts,

And make him of Alagna lower go!"

Canto XXXI

IN fashion then as of a snow-white rose
Displayed itself to me the saintly host,
Whom Christ in his own blood had made his bride,

4 But the other host, that flying sees and sings
The glory of Him who doth enamour it,
And the goodness that created it so noble,

7 Even as a swarm of bees, that sinks in flowers
One moment, and the next returns again
To where its labour is to sweetness turned,

10 Sank into the great flower, that is adorned
With leaves so many, and thence reascended
To where its love abideth evermore.

13 Their faces had they all of living flame,
And wings of gold, and all the rest so white
No snow unto that limit doth attain.

16 From bench to bench, into the flower descending,
They carried something of the peace and ardour
Which by the fanning of their flanks they won.

19 Nor did the interposing 'twixt the flower
And what was o'er it of such plenitude
Of flying shapes impede the sight and splendour;

22 Because the light divine so penetrates
The universe, according to its merit,
That naught can be an obstacle against it.

25 This realm secure and full of gladsomeness,
Crowded with ancient people and with modern,
Unto one mark had all its look and love.

28 O Trinal Light, that in a single star
Sparkling upon their sight so satisfies them,
Look down upon our tempest here below!

31 If the barbarians, coming from some region
That every day by Helice is covered,
Revolving with her son whom she delights in,

In fashion then as of a snow-white rose
Displayed itself to me the saintly host,
Whom Christ in his own blood had made his bride.

Gustave Doré

34 Beholding Rome and all her noble works,
Were wonder-struck, what time the Lateran
Above all mortal things was eminent,

37 I who to the divine had from the human,
From time unto eternity, had come,
From Florence to a people just and sane,

40 With what amazement must I have been filled!
Truly between this and the joy, it was
My pleasure not to hear, and to be mute.

43 And as a pilgrim who delighteth him
In gazing round the temple of his vow,
And hopes some day to retell how it was,

46 So through the living light my way pursuing
Directed I mine eyes o'er all the ranks,
Now up, now down, and now all round about.

49 Faces I saw of charity persuasive,
Embellished by His light and their own smile,
And attitudes adorned with every grace.

52 The general form of Paradise already
My glance had comprehended as a whole,
In no part hitherto remaining fixed,

55 And round I turned me with rekindled wish
My Lady to interrogate of things
Concerning which my mind was in suspense.

58 One thing I meant, another answered me;
I thought I should see Beatrice, and saw
An Old Man habited like the glorious people.

61 O'erflowing was he in his eyes and cheeks
With joy benign, in attitude of pity
As to a tender father is becoming.

64 And "She, where is she?" Instantly I said;
Whence he: "To put an end to thy desire,
Me Beatrice hath sent from mine own place.

67 And if thou lookest up to the third round
Of the first rank, again shalt thou behold her

Upon the throne her merits have assigned her."

Without reply I lifted up mine eyes,
And saw her, as she made herself a crown
Reflecting from herself the eternal rays.

Not from that region which the highest thunders
Is any mortal eye so far removed,
In whatsoever sea it deepest sinks,

As there from Beatrice my sight; but this
Was nothing unto me; because her image
Descended not to me by medium blurred.

"O Lady, thou in whom my hope is strong,
And who for my salvation didst endure
In Hell to leave the imprint of thy feet,

Of whatsoever things I have beheld,
As coming from thy power and from thy goodness
I recognise the virtue and the grace.

Thou from a slave hast brought me unto freedom,
By all those ways, by all the expedients,
Whereby thou hadst the power of doing it.

Preserve towards me thy magnificence,
So that this soul of mine, which thou hast healed,
Pleasing to thee be loosened from the body."

Thus I implored; and she, so far away,
Smiled, as it seemed, and looked once more at me
Then unto the eternal fountain turned.

And said the Old Man holy: "That thou mayst
Accomplish perfectly thy journeying,
Whereunto prayer and holy love have sent me,

Fly with thine eyes all round about this garden
For seeing it will discipline thy sight
Farther to mount along the ray divine.

And she, the Queen of Heaven, for whom I burn
Wholly with love, will grant us every grace,
Because that I her faithful Bernard am."

103 As he who peradventure from Croatia
Cometh to gaze at our Veronica,
Who through its ancient fame is never sated,

106 But says in thought, the while it is displayed,
"My Lord, Christ Jesus, God of very God,
Now was your semblance made like unto this?"

109 Even such was I while gazing at the living
Charity of the man, who in this world
By contemplation tasted of that peace.

112 "Thou son of grace, this jocund life," began he,
"Will not be known to thee by keeping ever
Thine eyes below here on the lowest place,

115 But mark the circles to the most remote,
Until thou shalt behold enthroned the Queen
To whom this realm is subject and devoted."

118 I lifted up mine eyes, and as at morn
The oriental part of the horizon
Surpasses that wherein the sun goes down,

121 Thus, as if going with mine eyes from vale
To mount, I saw a part in the remoteness
Surpass in splendour all the other front.

124 And even as there where we await the pole
That Phaeton drove badly, blazes more
The light, and is on either side diminished,

127 So likewise that pacific oriflamme[14]
Gleamed brightest in the centre, and each side
In equal measure did the flame abate.

130 And at that centre, with their wings expanded,
More than a thousand jubilant Angels saw I,
Each differing in effulgence and in kind.

133 I saw there at their sports and at their songs
A beauty smiling, which the gladness was
Within the eyes of all the other saints

14 "battle flag of peace"

136 And if I had in speaking as much wealth
As in imagining, I should not dare
To attempt the smallest part of its delight.

139 Bernard, as soon as he beheld mine eyes
Fixed and intent upon its fervid fervour,
His own with such affection turned to her

142 That it made mine more ardent to behold.

Canto XXXII

ABSORBED in his delight, that contemplator
Assumed the willing office of a teacher
And gave beginning to these holy words:

4 "The wound that Mary closed up and anointed,
She at her feet who is so beautiful,
She is the one who opened it and pierced it.

7 Within that order which the third seats make
Is seated Rachel, lower than the other,
With Beatrice, in manner as thou seest.

10 Sarah, Rebecca, Judith, and her who was
Ancestress of the Singei, who for dole
Of the misdeed said, 'Miserere mei,'

13 Canst thou behold from seat to seat descending
Down in gradation, as with each one's name
I through the nose go down from leaf to leaf.

16 And downward from the seventh row, even as
Above the same, succeed the Hebrew women,
Dividing all the tresses of the flower

19 Because, according to the view which Faith
In Christ had taken, these are the partition
By which the sacred stairways are divided.

22 Upon this side, where perfect is the flower
With each one of its petals, seated are
Those who believed in Christ who was to come.

Upon the other side, where intersected
With vacant spaces are the semicircles,
Are those who looked to Christ already come.

And as, upon this side, the glorious seat
Of the Lady of Heaven, and the other seats
Below it, such a great division make,

So opposite doth that of the great John,
Who, ever holy, desert and martyrdom
Endured, and afterwards two years in Hell.

And under him thus to divide were chosen
Francis, and Belledict, and Augustine,
And down to us the rest from round to round;

Behold now the high providence divine;
For one and other aspect of the Faith
In equal measure shall this garden fill.

And know that downward from that rank which cleaves
Midway the sequence of the two divisions,
Not by their proper merit are they seated

But by another's under fixed conditions;
For these are spirits one and all assoiled
Before they any true election had.

Well canst thou recognise it in their faces,
And also in their voices puerile,
If thou regard them well and hearken to them.

Now doubtest thou, and doubting thou art silent;
But I will loosen for thee the strong bond
In which thy subtile fancies hold thee fast.

Within the amplitude of this domain
No casual point can possibly find place,
No more than sadness can, or thirst, or hunger;

For by eternal law has been established
Whatever thou beholdest, so that closely
The ring is fitted to the finger here.

And therefore are these people, festinate[15]

15 Hasty.

Unto true life, not 'sine causa'[16] here
More and less excellent among themselves.

61 The King, by means of whom this realm reposes
In so great love and in so great delight
That no will ventureth to ask for more,

64 In his own joyous aspect every mind
Creating, at his pleasure dowers with grace
Diversely; and let here the effect suffice.

67 And this is clearly and expressly noted
For you in Holy Scripture, in those twins
Who in their mother had their anger roused.

70 According to the colour of the hair,
Therefore, with such a grace the light supreme
Consenteth that they worthily be crowned.

73 Without, then, any merit of their deeds,
Stationed are they in different gradations,
Differing only in their first acuteness.

76 'Tis true that in the early centuries,
With innocence, to work out their salvation
Sufficient was the faith of parents only.

79 After the earlier ages were completed,
Behoved it that the males by circumcision
Unto their innocent wings should virtue add;

82 But after that the time of grace had come
Without the baptism absolute of Christ,
Such innocence below there was retained.

85 Look now into the face that unto Christ
Hath most resemblance; for its brightness only
Is able to prepare thee to see Christ."

88 On her did I behold so great a gladness
Rain down, borne onward in the holy minds
Created through that altitude to fly,

91 That whatsoever I had seen before

16 "without cause"

Did not suspend me in such admiration,
Nor show me such similitude of God.

94 And the same Love that first descended there,
"Ave Maria, gratia plena,"[17] singing,
In front of her his wings expanded wide.

97 Unto the canticle divine responded
From every part the court beatified,
So that each sight became serener for it.

100 "O holy father, who for me endurest
To be below here, leaving the sweet place
In which thou sittest by eternal lot,

103 Who is the Angel that with so much joy
Into the eyes is looking of our Queen,
Enamoured so that he seems made of fire?"

106 Thus I again recourse had to the teaching
Of that one who delighted him in Mary
As doth the star of morning in the sun.

109 And he to me: "Such gallantry and grace
As there can be in Angel and in soul,
All is in him; and thus we fain would have it;

112 Because he is the one who bore the palm
Down unto Mary, when the Son of God
To take our burden on himself decreed.

115 But now come onward with thine eyes, as I
Speaking shall go, and note the great patricians
Of this most just and merciful of empires.

118 Those two that sit above there most enrapture
As being very near unto Augusta,
Are as it were the two roots of this Rose.

121 He who upon the left is near her placed
The father is, by whose audacious taste
The human species so much bitter tastes.

124 Upon the right thou seest that ancient father

17 "Hail Mary, full of grace."

Of Holy Church, into whose keeping Christ
The keys committed of this lovely flower.

And he who all the evil days beheld,
Before his death, of her the beauteous bride
Who with the spear and with the nails was won,

Beside him sits, and by the other rests
That leader under whom on manna lived
The people ingrate, fickle, and stiff-necked.

Opposite Peter seest thou Anna seated,
So well content to look upon her daughter,
Her eyes she moves not while she sings 'Hosanna.'

And opposite the eldest household father
Luma sits, she who thy Lady moved
When to rush downward thou didst bend thy brows.

But since the moments of thy vision fly,
Here will we make full stop, as a good tailor
Who makes the gown according to his cloth,

And unto the first Love will turn our eyes,
That looking upon Him thou penetrate
As far as possible through his effulgence.

Truly, lest peradventure thou recede,
Moving thy wings believing to advance,
By prayer behoves it that grace be obtained;

Grace from that one who has the power to aid thee;
And thou shalt follow me with thy affection
That from my words thy heart turn not aside."

And he began this holy orison.

Canto XXXIII

"THOU Virgin Mother, daughter of thy Son
Humble and high beyond all other creature,
The limit fixed of the eternal counsel,

4 Thou art the one who such nobility
To human nature gave, that its Creator
Did not disdain to make himself its creature.

7 Within thy womb rekindled was the love,
By heat of which in the eternal peace
After such wise this flower has germinated.

10 Here unto us thou art a noonday torch
Of charity, and below there among mortals
Thou art the living fountain-head of hope.

13 Lady thou art so great, and so prevailing,
That he who wishes grace, nor runs to thee
His aspirations without wings would fly.

16 Not only thy benignity gives succour
To him who asketh it, but oftentimes
Forerunneth of its own accord the asking.

19 In thee compassion is, in thee is pity,
In thee magnificence, in thee unites
Whate'er of goodness is in any creature.

22 Now doth this man, who from the lowest depth
Of the universe as far as here has seen
One after one the spiritual lives,

25 Supplicate thee through grace for so much power
That with his eyes he may uplift himself
Higher towards the uttermost salvation.

28 And I, who never burned for my own seeing
More than I do for his, all of my prayers
Proffer to thee, and pray they come not short,

31 That thou wouldst scatter from him every cloud
Of his mortality so with thy prayers,

That the Chief Pleasure be to him displayed.

34 Still farther do I pray thee, Queen, who canst
Whate'er thou wilt, that sound thou mayst preserve
After so great a vision his affections.

37 Let thy protection conquer human movements;
See Beatrice and all the blessed ones
My prayers to second clasp their hands to thee!"

40 The eyes beloved and revered of God,
Fastened upon the speaker, showed to us
How grateful unto her are prayers devout;

43 Then unto the Eternal Light they turned,
On which it is not credible could be
By any creature bent an eye so clear.

46 And I, who to the end of all desires
Was now approaching, even as I ought
The ardour of desire within me ended.

49 Bernard was beckoning unto me, and smiling,
That I should upward look; but I already
Was of my own accord such as he wished

52 Because my sight, becoming purified,
Was entering more and more into the ray
Of the High Light which of itself is true.

55 From that time forward what I saw was greater
Than our discourse, that to such vision yields,
And yields the memory unto such excess.

58 Even as he is who seeth in a dream,
And after dreaming the imprinted passion
Remains, and to his mind the rest returns not,

61 Even such am I, for almost utterly
Ceases my vision, and distilleth yet
Within my heart the sweetness born of it;

64 Even thus the snow is in the sun unsealed,
Even thus upon the wind in the light leaves
Were the soothsayings of the Sibyl lost.

67 O Light Supreme, that dost so far uplift thee
From the conceits of mortals, to my mind
Of what thou didst appear re-lend a little,

70 And make my tongue of so great puissance,
That but a single sparkle of thy glory
It may bequeath unto the future people;

73 For by returning to my memory somewhat,
And by a little sounding in these verses,
More of thy victory shall be conceived!

76 I think the keenness of the living ray
Which I endured would have bewildered me,
If but mine eyes had been averted from it;

79 And I remember that I was more bold
On this account to bear, so that I joined
My aspect with the Glory Infinite.

82 O grace abundant, by which I presumed
To fix my sight upon the Light Eternal,
So that the seeing I consumed therein!

85 I saw that in its depth far down is lying
Bound up with love together in one volume,
What through the universe in leaves is scattered;

88 Substance, and accident, and their operations,
All interfused together in such wise
That what I speak of is one simple light.

91 The universal fashion of this knot
Methinks I saw, since more abundantly
In saying this I feel that I rejoice.

94 One moment is more lethargy to me,
Than five and twenty centuries to the emprise
That startled Neptune with the shade of Argo!

97 My mind in this wise wholly in suspense,
Steadfast, immovable, attentive gazed,
And evermore with gazing grew enkindled.

100 In presence of that light one such becomes,

That to withdraw therefrom for other prospect
It is impossible he e'er consent;

103 Because the good, which object is of will,
Is gathered all in this, and out of it
That is defective which is perfect there.

106 Shorter henceforward will my language fall
Of what I yet remember, than an infant's
Who still his tongue doth moisten at the breast,

109 Not because more than one unmingled semblance
Was in the living light on which I looked,
For it is always what it was before;

112 But through the sight, that fortified itself
In me by looking, one appearance only
To me was ever changing as I changed.

115 Within the deep and luminous subsistence
Of the High Light appeared to me three circles,
Of threefold colour and of one dimension

118 And by the second seemed the first reflected
As Iris is by Iris, and the third
Seemed fire that equally from both is breathed.

121 O how all speech is feeble and falls short
Of my conceit, and this to what I saw
Is such, 'tis not enough to call it little!

124 O Light Eterne, sole in thyself that dwellest,
Sole knowest thyself, and, known unto thyself
And knowing, lovest and smilest on thyself!

127 That circulation, which being thus conceived
Appeared in thee as a reflected light,
When somewhat contemplated by mine eyes,

130 Within itself, of its own very colour
Seemed to me painted with our effigy,
Wherefore my sight was all absorbed therein.

133 As the geometrician, who endeavours
To square the circle, and discovers not

By taking thought, the principle he wants,

136 Even such was I at that new apparitlon;
I wished to see how the image to the circle
Conformed itself, and how it there finds place;

139 But my own wings were not enough for this,
Had it not been that then my mind there smote
A flash of lightning, wherein came its wish.

142 Here vigour failed the lofty fantasy:
But now was turning my desire and will,
Even as a wheel that equally is moved,

145 The Love which moves the sun and the other stars.

Commonplaces

Commonplaces

Commonplaces

Commonplaces